STEPHEN BREYER

The Court and the World

Stephen Breyer is an associate justice of the United States Supreme Court. He is a resident of Cambridge, Massachusetts, and Washington, D.C.

The Court and the World

The Court and the World

American Law and the New Global Realities

STEPHEN BREYER

VINTAGE BOOKS
A Division of Penguin Random House LLC
New York

FIRST VINTAGE BOOKS EDITION, AUGUST 2016

Copyright © 2015 by Stephen Breyer

All rights reserved. Published in the United States by Vintage Books, a division of Penguin Random House LLC, New York, and distributed in Canada by Random House of Canada, a division of Penguin Random House Canada Limited, Toronto. Originally published in hardcover in the United States by Alfred A. Knopf, a division of Penguin Random House LLC, New York, in 2015.

Vintage and colophon are registered trademarks of Penguin Random House LLC.

The Library of Congress has cataloged the Knopf edition as follows:
Breyer, Stephen G.
The court and the world: American law and the new global realities / Stephen Breyer.
pages cm
1. International courts.   2. National security—International cooperation.
3. International trade.   I. Title.
KZ6250.B74 2015   347.73'26—dc23   2015013258

Vintage Books Trade Paperback ISBN: 978-1-101-91207-2
eBook ISBN: 978-1-101-94620-6

Author photograph © Steve Petteway

www.vintagebooks.com

Printed in the United States of America
10   9   8   7   6   5   4   3   2

To Joanna

Contents

The Court and the World

Introduction

During a recent October hearing week, I took my seat on the Supreme Court bench, ready to listen to oral argument in two cases. The first involved a student from Thailand, studying in the United States, where he found the cost of textbooks too high. So he bought the same English-language textbooks in Thailand at lower prices, had them shipped to him in the States, and resold them to American students. Did he have the legal right to do so?[1]

The second case involved a group of lawyers challenging the constitutionality of a part of the Foreign Intelligence Surveillance Act (FISA). That section allows the government to listen electronically to certain conversations of foreigners abroad, conversations that might affect American foreign policy or national security. The petitioning American lawyers routinely represent Middle Easterners, some of whom may have ties to extremist organizations. Suspecting (though not knowing conclusively) that their clients were FISA targets, the lawyers claimed that the statute violated the confidentiality of their attorney-client communications. The question before the Court was whether, based on their suspicions, the lawyers had standing to challenge the constitutionality of the statute.[2]

These two cases have something in common: they call on the Court to consider foreign persons and activities, foreign commerce in the first instance and foreign threats to national security in the second. The fact of two such "foreign" cases out of the six cases argued that week would have been surprising when I first joined the Court nearly twenty years ago. But it is no longer unusual. More and more, cases before the

Court involve foreign activity. That is my professional reality, which I share with counterparts abroad, represented in our courtroom that same October day by the chief justice of Japan, who witnessed the hearing from public seating.

This book focuses upon the "foreign" aspect of the Court's docket. It seeks to make known the new challenges imposed by an ever more interdependent world—a world of instant communications and commerce, and shared problems of (for example) security, the environment, health, and trade, all of which ever more pervasively link individuals without regard to national boundaries. Indeed, at a moment when ordinary citizens may engage in direct transactions internationally for services available only locally before (online bed-and-breakfast rentals, for example), it has become clear that, even in ordinary matters, judicial awareness can no longer stop at the border.

This book assumes that the United States will remain a preeminent world power, due to its military and economic strength and the prestige of certain features of American life, including our long experience in creating, maintaining, and developing a fairly stable constitutional system of government. That system has allowed a large multiracial, multiethnic, and multireligious population to govern itself democratically while protecting basic human rights and resolving disputes under a rule of law. When, therefore, I use the frequently heard term *interdependence*, it is with these assumptions firmly in mind. Indeed, I want this book to explain just what that abstract term means concretely for the work of one American institution, the Supreme Court.

In order to illustrate the Court's changing perspective and evolving role in the world and the attendant challenges, I have divided this book into four basic parts. Each focuses on a different context in which we consider the world abroad, but together they also comprise a loose chronological progression, from a time when such considerations were still quite exceptional; to the present moment, when they have become rather routine; to a fast-emerging future, in which a measure of coordination with other jurisdictions will become increasingly necessary for the smooth functioning of our economy and our various institutions.

Part I focuses upon an important, long-standing constitutional question that typically arises out of our relations with the outside world: How can the Court effectively protect basic liberties in the face of security threats? That problem has taken on a particular urgency as those threats, notably terrorism, have grown amorphous and heedless of borders. I trace the evolution of constitutional doctrine concerning the Court's efforts to review presidential, or congressional, actions related to the preservation of national security. To understand that evolution is to understand why, in today's world, the judiciary's need to take account of foreign circumstances, both legal and nonlegal, has grown as it has.

Parts II and III focus upon areas of the law where consideration of foreign circumstances is a newer development but one well under way.

Part II concerns statutory interpretation. Should American statutes be understood to open the doors of American courts to foreign victims of human rights abuses? What is the geographical reach of commercial statutes, governing, say, antitrust violations or securities fraud? And can the Court interpret those statutes so that they work in harmony with similar laws of other nations?

Part III deals with the interpretation of treaties and the Constitution's related grant to Congress and the President of law-making and treaty-making powers. How is the Court to interpret treaties that concern unfamiliar subjects, such as the domestic relations law of foreign countries, or competing international dispute-resolution systems, such as international arbitration tribunals, or international administrative regimes regulating, say, health, safety, or the environment?

I end Part III with a brief discussion of the current political debate about the particular question of whether or to what extent the Court in its own decisions should refer to the decisions or conclusions of foreign courts. This has been a contentious subject, but as I suggest, Parts I, II, and III should make clear that the objections to this practice are not particularly relevant to the questions of foreign law and practice that the Court is likely to face, now and in the future.

Part IV concerns direct interactions that take place among judges and lawyers of different nations. To what extent do these exchanges help judges reach better decisions? How can American judges learn from others? Can members of our legal community act effectively as "constitutional diplomats"? Can American judges help their foreign counterparts further the rule of law itself? Though they figure importantly in our interdependent world, these interactions are typically invisible to the general public. I focus on them here because they may affect the way a justice of our Court understands part of his role. And that understanding may have more important consequences for the law than many matters that receive more attention, such as the debate over referring to the decisions of foreign courts.

In surveying the gamut of ways—some obvious, some less so—that the Court is called upon to consider foreign realities, I wish to make plain the institutional challenges we face. How, for example, is the Court to obtain the information about foreign law, legal practices, and circumstances that will allow it to reach sound legal decisions? How can it interpret our national laws and treaties with an eye toward permitting the kind of cooperation necessary to further the resolution of concrete problems (say, of the environment, commerce, and security) that transcend national borders? Can our American judicial system, by seeing itself as one part of a transnational or multinational judicial enterprise, help to advance acceptance of the rule of law itself? These questions are highly general. This book can do no more than to raise them while encouraging others to find better and more specific responses. By describing the scope of challenges facing the Court, it seeks to present an agenda for thought, analysis, consideration, and response by judges, lawyers, law teachers, and the interested public alike.

The different parts of this book emphasize and reemphasize two general themes. The first concerns the rule of law generally. Though problems of security, environment, health, trade, and the like increasingly cross borders, they still often call for legal solutions. The Internet, as I have mentioned, more and more permits ordinary citizens to do business internationally—for example, to reserve local transportation or to buy films or books from abroad. Those transactions will give rise to disputes, and we must have ways to resolve those disputes based on a rule of law. But there is no Supreme Court of the World with power to harmonize differences among the approaches of different nations. Thus such problems will require the judiciaries of different nations to address them separately but collaboratively. If they are to do so, they cannot automatically abdicate their authority at the water's edge.

To the contrary, if we can properly determine just when, where, and how our own Court's authority extends beyond our shores, we can better contribute to the solution of these problems through law. Moreover, if we can do so successfully, we will have reinforced the view that law can offer effective solutions to the problems of our times. We will thereby have helped to discourage resort to extralegal methods, which are often arbitrary or autocratic. In so doing, we will have helped to advance acceptance of the rule of law itself.

The second recurring theme is the need for courts to listen to what I might call "many voices." These include representatives of foreign governments, who can explain relevant policies; foreign lawyers, who can describe relevant foreign laws and practices; and ordinary citizens, whom our decisions may well affect though they live and work abroad. This approach is particularly important when we interpret, say, a treaty designed to help nations work together, or a securities or antitrust statute that foresees the possibility of harmonized multinational enforcement efforts. In calling attention to the need for harmonization (which sometimes goes by the name of *comity*), I do not ignore the basic fact that the American people can and must democratically determine their own laws. But listening to those who understand the content of relevant foreign law is perfectly consistent with the democratic formulation and interpretation of our own law. That is because, often, the best way to further the basic goals of, for instance, an American statute with foreign implications, or to properly enforce a treaty, or to determine how far beyond our shores our Constitution's protection may extend, is to take account of a foreign as well as the domestic legal landscape.

This book is based upon my experience as a judge. It does not survey the whole of international law or even of foreign law as it affects Americans. Nor does it comprehensively describe the instances in which courts must deal with questions involving that law. It illustrates and explains what I have seen and why I believe there is an ever-growing need for American courts to develop an understanding of, and working relationships with, foreign courts and legal institutions. It puts forth why I believe it important for Americans to understand and to appropriately apply international and foreign law. And it helps clarify, through example, why our federal courts may eventually have to take account of their relationships with foreign institutions just as they now take account of their relationships with state courts and other American federal and state legal institutions.

At the outset I raise two caveats. First, I want to discuss trends, tendencies, and general judicial responses. I cannot do so without discussing legal cases, often including their history in detail. Legal detail is often technical. I have tried to make the case law accessible and engaging to a lay reader, but I hope that, if confounded by detail, he or she may still profit from attention to the larger points, which I try to develop plainly.

Second, I discuss some cases that the Court has decided while I have been a member. In any such discussion, I rely entirely upon publicly available materials, normally the judicial opinions in the case itself. Should there seem to be any conflict between what I say and what an opinion says, I remind the reader that the opinion, not my view of it, is authoritative.

Finally, I hope that an understanding of the nature of our current engagement with foreign matters will persuade the reader that the best way to preserve American constitutional values (a major objective that I hold in common with those who fear the influence of foreign law) is to meet the challenges that the world, as reflected in concrete cases on our docket, actually presents. Doing so necessarily requires greater, not less, awareness of what is happening around us.

PART I

The Past Is Prologue

The Constitution, National Security, and Individual Rights

W e begin with a set of constitutional issues arising from foreign threats to our national security. To what extent does the Constitution permit the President and Congress to limit our civil liberties for the sake of national security? And how much power does it give the Court to review the balancing of the two concerns—or put another way, to second-guess Congress and the President in their efforts to do so? Until recently, the Court could, and often did, avoid deciding such questions. Over time, however, its willingness to grapple with them has grown.

The evolution of any legal doctrine takes place slowly. Law normally changes that way. The Court only rarely overturns an earlier decision. Otherwise the law would lack the stability necessary for ordinary citizens to rely upon it in planning their lives. But the Court does gradually change its approach. This is inevitable, as the nation changes over time, and as different presidents appoint different judges with different philosophical views about how the law—especially as embodied in abstractions like "liberty"—relates to individual Americans.

To protect the safety and security of the nation's citizens, the President, perhaps with the support of Congress, may believe it necessary to take an action that might otherwise seem beyond his constitutional authority. This might involve press censorship, detention of individuals without trial, searches conducted without warrants, or eavesdropping or wiretapping. The Constitution limits such actions—sometimes implicitly, sometimes explicitly—through provisions protecting free expression, a free press, freedom from unreasonable searches, freedom from imprisonment without trial, and so forth. But "the Constitution is not a suicide pact," as the saying goes.[1] Thus there arises the basic substantive question of whether it authorizes the President to curtail ordinary civil liberties for the sake of national security.

When obliged to face such a question, the Court may also have to answer a related one, likewise of critical importance: *Who* (i.e., what institution) is to decide whether a particular measure taken by the President (or Congress) imposes a restraint that is only temporary and necessary and therefore tolerable (i.e, within constitutional limits), or whether it goes too far? The *who* question normally amounts to deciding whether the courts or the elected branches of government are to have the last word. The Constitution does not directly answer either the *who* question or the "limits" question. But it does delegate to Congress and to the President the power to protect Americans from foreign attack. It explicitly gives Congress the authority to "declare War," to "raise and support Armies," to "provide and maintain a Navy," and to "regulat[e]" the armed forces (including the states' "militia").[2] It says that the "President" shall be "Commander in Chief" of the armed forces and that he can (with the Senate's "advice and consent") make "treaties."[3] It vests the executive power in the President, which includes the war power and the foreign affairs power. In a word, it delegates to the elected branches, not to the judiciary, responsibility for America's security. The judicial branch, on the other hand, plays a critical role in enforcing those provisions of the Constitution that protect our basic liberties, including "the freedom of speech" and the freedom not to be "deprive[d]" of "liberty . . . without due process of law."[4]

So what happens when security and civil liberties collide? If the President and Congress, trying to strike a balance, come to one conclusion, can the Court rebalance those imperatives and come to another? And if the Court is to decide on the merits of what the right balance is, how is it to go about that job?

Over time, as I've said, the Court's approach to these questions has changed. During the Civil War, when Abraham Lincoln imprisoned civilians, censored the press, established military tribunals, and suspended the writ of habeas corpus, the Court tended in the direction of deference. Similarly, during World War I, when various American presidents curtailed ordinary civil rights for reasons of military necessity, the Court simply did not respond.

Alternatively, the Court has sometimes agreed to consider such a matter on the merits, only to decide in the end that the President's authority to act in the interests of security is so broad that almost any challenge will be decided in his favor. This was the approach just before and during World War II. Like the first approach, it leaves little room for Court protection of civil liberties.

In more recent times, however, the Court has asserted a stronger check on presidential authority. In several cases arising out of the detention of enemy combatants at Guantanamo Bay, it has held that even when security is at issue, the Constitution does not give the President a blank check to curtail civil liberties.

This Part will show the Court steadily more willing to intervene and review presidential decisions affecting national security, even to the point of finding a related presidential action unconstitutional. What is notable is that this progression toward assertiveness has occurred even as threats to national security have become more international, indefinite with respect to manner, and uncertain with respect to time. Indeed, threats today are less likely to arise out of a declaration of war by another sovereign power and more likely to be posed by stateless international terrorist networks. They are also more likely to last for many years, perhaps indefinitely. The change in the Court's approach together with the change in circumstances is, I would argue, no mere coincidence.

But if the Court is no longer prepared to give the President a blank check, just what kind of check is it prepared to give him? To answer that question, the Court will have to know a great deal more about the threats themselves and about how other nations are responding to them. Greater willingness to come to grips with the underlying, fundamental constitutional problems thus necessarily implies a greater willingness to understand and take account of both the world and of the law beyond our borders. It also implies a readiness to meet the various challenges of doing so.

CHAPTER 1

Silence

Cicero and His "Political Question" Counterpart

"THE LAWS FALL SILENT"

Cicero set forth what would eventually become one of the best-known legal principles concerning the role of courts during wartime. Two thousand years ago he wrote, *"Silent enim leges inter arma,"* which I should like to translate as "When the cannons roar, the laws fall silent." When the senator wrote those words, he was responding to civil strife that had erupted in Rome, where armed gangs had taken control of the streets. They were never punished, for their leaders had been elected to public office. Still, we see the point of Cicero's remark: When the security of the state is threatened, do not expect the laws to apply. To what extent has that principle governed the actions of American courts?

Consider the principle in the context of the American Civil War. At the very outset, President Lincoln suspended the writ of habeas corpus.[1] That ancient writ traditionally allows anyone in detention to challenge the lawfulness of his confinement by getting word to a judge that he is being held, in his view, without legal authority. And the judge can then tell the jailer, the local sheriff, say, to "bring me the body." Questioning both the jailer and the prisoner, the judge can discover the legal basis, or the lack thereof, for the prisoner's detention. It would be difficult to point to a more important legal protection against arbitrary imprisonment.

President Lincoln's suspension of the writ in effect allowed his military to arrest civilians arbitrarily, without court review. He had seen firsthand a pressing need for such an extraordinary measure. On the way to his inauguration, he had been forced to sneak through Baltimore under cover of night in order to avoid a pro-secession mob, while transferring from one train station to another.[2] Lincoln knew that Union troops from the West and the North would have to negotiate the same station transfer on their way south. And he feared the effect this might have on their ability to travel, on the city of Baltimore itself, and on the State of Maryland, which itself stood on the brink of secession.[3]

By suspending the writ, Lincoln intended to allow Northern troops to arrest disloyal Baltimore citizens. And that is just what they did. Early on the morning of May 25, 1861, on the orders of General William H. Keim, they arrested John Merryman, who had been a ringleader in anti-Northern riots that spring, and held him at Fort McHenry, a nearby post under the command of General George Cadwalader.[4] Merryman immediately asked a nearby federal court to issue a writ of habeas corpus. And the court's judge, Supreme Court Chief Justice Roger Taney, sitting as a local circuit judge, agreed to do so.[5]

At first glance, Lincoln's actions to stop judges like Taney from issuing the writ might seem constitutional, for the Constitution authorizes suspension of the writ of habeas corpus "when in cases of rebellion or invasion the public safety may require it."[6] But this grant of authority appears in Article I, which deals with Congress's powers, not in Article II, which addresses the powers of the President. Hence, Taney concluded, the President, by acting without congressional authority, had violated the Constitution.[7]

President Lincoln's reaction to the court's decision is well known. He did not release John Merryman. Neither did he appeal the ruling, as he might have done. Rather, he defended his right to take decisive unilateral action. A few weeks after Merryman's arrest, he asked Congress, "Are all the laws, but one, to go unexecuted, and the government itself go to pieces, lest that one be violated?"[8] A week later Attorney General Edward Bates presented Congress with a report justifying Lincoln's decision to suspend the writ of habeas corpus.[9]

Still, the same day as the Bates report, Merryman was released on bail, and Lincoln did not prosecute him. And two years later Congress itself suspended the writ of habeas corpus, thereby curing the constitutional defect. The controversy about the President's powers fizzled out without any definite resolution.[10]

Merryman's detention, however, is but one of many examples of how President Lincoln suspended or sidestepped constitutional protections of civil liberty in the name of national security. He also authorized his generals to censor the press, to prevent citizens from speaking vociferously against the war (accusing the President of "malfeasance," for example), to arrest suspected supporters of the enemy, and, often, to hold prisoners without trial irrespective of whether ordinary courts where they might have been tried were open and functioning. The generals exercising this authority did so by general order; they did not need to prove that, say, hostilities required their actions. In this way, they imprisoned about thirteen thousand citizens during the war.[11] Secretary of State William H. Seward once told a British minister,

> I can touch a bell on my right hand and order the imprisonment of a citizen of Ohio; I can touch a bell again and order the imprisonment of a citizen of New York; and no power on earth, except that of the President, can release them. Can the Queen of England do so much?[12]

This attitude reflects that of many American presidents during wartime. During World War I, the Wilson administration successfully prosecuted distributors of leaflets urging resistance to the draft. It barred leftist magazines from using the mails. And it jailed Eugene V. Debs, the leader of the American Socialist Party (who subsequently received nearly one million votes in the presidential election of 1920 while incarcerated).[13] During World War II, President Roosevelt ordered the internment of more than seventy thousand Americans of Japanese origin, an action that the Supreme Court upheld.

Roosevelt's attorney general, Francis Biddle, once said that "[t]he Constitution has not greatly bothered any wartime President."[14] During war, the executive and legislative branches typically believe that the foreign threat—not the preservation of civil liberties—is the paramount concern. And at times throughout American history, the judiciary has agreed. While the Civil War raged, with the exception of *Merryman*, the courts did not meaningfully interfere with presidential or legislative decisions.

Once the Civil War was over, however, the Court was in a position to take a different view, and in 1866 it heard the case of *Ex parte Milligan*. Two years earlier, just before the war's conclusion, a Northern general stationed with his troops in Indiana had arrested Lambdin P. Milligan and four other civilians. The general charged them with conspiring to foment an insurrection designed to help the South. He set up a special military tribunal, which tried the accused, convicted them, and passed a sentence of death. The defendants asked an ordinary federal court to hear their claim that the army could not try American citizens in a special military court, at least not when conditions in the area were peaceful and ordinary civil courts were open. The case eventually reached the Supreme Court.[15]

Urging the Court to deny the defendants' claim, the government's lawyer took a page from Cicero and argued that "[t]he officer executing martial law is at the same time supreme legislator, supreme judge, and supreme executive. As necessity makes his will the law, he only can define and declare it."[16] The government maintained that the Constitution's provisions protecting basic human rights are "peace provisions . . . and, *like all other conventional and legislative laws and enactments, are silent amidst arms, and when the safety of the people becomes the supreme law.*"[17]

The Court unanimously rejected this claim. All its members agreed that the Constitution's protections applied and that Milligan must be released. A minority of the justices added an explanation to the effect that Congress had not enacted legislation permitting military trials for civilians, implying that the result might have been different under such circumstances.[18] The majority, however, held that the Constitution did not permit military trials of American civilians in places where, and at times when, ordinary civil courts were open, whether or not Congress enacted laws authorizing such proceedings.[19]

Milligan, then, represents something of a retreat on the part of the Court from the absolutism of Cicero, and a willingness to enforce constitutional protections in the face of a claim by the executive that the laws should be silent "amidst arms." Still, it bears emphasizing that the case was decided only after the war had ended and relative normalcy had returned. We should not be surprised to find a different judicial attitude in later cases decided in the heat of battle, such as the World War II case of *Korematsu*. If *Milligan* signaled to the executive branch that there were limits to what the Court would permit in the name of wartime necessity, it was something less than a full or permanent flight from Cicero.

"THE POLITICAL THICKET"

The doctrine of the "political question" is more specific and better developed than Cicero's maxim as crisis jurisprudence, but as applied to questions of national security, it is nonetheless in the same spirit. It provides a technical legal basis for courts to refuse to consider the lawfulness of presidential action taken pursuant to either his wartime or his foreign affairs powers. Indeed, by walling off many of the President's wartime and foreign affairs decisions from review, it is but one step removed from Cicero.

The doctrine says that in certain instances, the Constitution gives not to the courts but to other branches of government the power to decide whether an action violates the Constitution. In this way, the laws, including the Constitution, do not necessarily fall "silent." They still apply to the government action in question. But it is for Congress or the President, not the courts, to determine what the law requires given the national security threat.

The doctrine has a venerable provenance. In 1803 Chief Justice John Marshall wrote in *Marbury v. Madison:* "By the constitution of the United States, the president is invested with certain important political powers, in the exercise of which he is to use his own discretion, and is accountable only to his country in his political character, and to his own conscience."[20]

The Court has since invoked the doctrine in both wartime and foreign relations cases. During the War of 1812, for example, the President called up the New York State militia for service. Jacob Mott, a member of the militia, refused to comply. He was court-martialed and convicted of refusing to report for duty. He appealed, and his case came to the Supreme Court.[21]

Mott conceded that the Constitution gives Congress the power to "provide for calling forth the militia, to execute the laws of the Union, suppress insurrections, and repel invasions."[22] He agreed that Congress had enacted a statute stating that

> whenever the United States shall be invaded, or be in imminent danger of invasion from any foreign nation or Indian tribe, it shall be lawful for the President of the United States to call forth such number of the militia of the State or States most convenient to the place of danger, or scene of action, as he may judge necessary to repel such invasion.[23]

But, Mott argued, the President had failed to establish the presence of an "imminent danger of invasion." Hence he had not met the statutory requirement. And since the Constitution gave him no independent power to call up the militia, Mott argued his call-up was impermissible.[24]

The Court rejected Mott's claim, not because it agreed with the President about the risk of invasion, but because it thought this risk was the kind of question that the Constitution denied the Court the power to decide. Justice Joseph Story wrote that

> the power to call the militia into actual service is certainly felt to be one of no ordinary magnitude. But . . . it is, in its terms, a limited power, confined to cases of actual invasion, or of imminent danger of invasion. . . . [I]s it to be considered as an open question . . . to be contested by every militia-man who shall refuse to obey the orders of the President? We are all of opinion, that the authority to decide whether the exigency has arisen, *belongs exclusively to the President*, and that his decision is conclusive upon all other persons.[25]

The Court further developed the "political question" doctrine during the 1840s, in a case concerning the government of Rhode Island.[26] The petitioners had argued that the new state constitution—under which their rivals had claimed authority and called upon the federal government for military support—violated the federal Constitution's guarantee of a "republican form of government."[27] But the Supreme Court held that the matter was a "political question," grounding its decision in the idea that the political branches should have unfettered power over national security matters. Referring back to Mott's case, Chief Justice Taney explained why the Court could not second-guess a determination by Congress or the President as to the legitimacy of a state's government:

> After the President has acted and called out the militia [in support of one group alleging to be the true state government], is a Circuit Court of the United States authorized to inquire whether his decision was right? Could the court, while the parties were actually contending in arms for the possession of the government, call witnesses before it and inquire which party represented a majority of the people? If it could, then it would become the duty of the court (provided it came to the conclusion that the President had decided incorrectly) to discharge those who were arrested or detained by the troops in the service of the United States or the government which the President was endeavoring to maintain. If the judicial power extends so far, the guarantee contained in the Constitution of the United States is a guarantee of anarchy, and not of order.[28]

The same theme would be expounded by the Court into the twentieth century, in *Chicago & Southern Airlines, Inc. v. Waterman S.S. Corp.*, a case involving the award of an international airline route.[29] A statute had given the courts the power to review route awards to airlines by the Civil Aeronautics Board. The Court, however, held that this power did not apply when the President himself had approved the final decision. That is because, as Justice Robert H. Jackson wrote, the

> President, both as Commander-in-Chief and as the Nation's organ for foreign affairs, has available intelligence services whose reports neither are nor ought to be published to the world. It would be intolerable that courts, without the relevant information, should review and perhaps nullify actions of the Executive taken on information properly held secret. Nor can courts sit in camera in order to be taken into executive confidences. But even if courts could require full disclosure, the very nature of executive decisions as to foreign policy is political, not judicial. Such decisions are wholly confided by our Constitution to the political departments of the government, Executive and Leg-

islative. They are delicate, complex, and involve large elements of prophecy. They are and should be undertaken only by those directly responsible to the people whose welfare they advance or imperil. They are decisions of a kind for which the Judiciary has neither aptitude, facilities nor responsibility and have long been held to belong in the domain of political power not subject to judicial intrusion or inquiry. We therefore agree that whatever of this order emanates from the President is not susceptible of review by the Judicial Department.[30]

Not surprisingly, then, during the Vietnam War, lower courts invoked the "political question" doctrine in refusing to decide whether Congress had properly authorized the Cambodian bombing or the war itself.[31] And the Supreme Court did not intervene.[32]

Many of these decisions—particularly the Vietnam cases—involve challenges to the lawfulness of a war itself. They do not necessarily prevent federal courts from deciding whether a presidential action violates an individual's civil liberties, a different question. But in any event, during the past half-century, the "political question" doctrine has gone into decline, having reached its jurisprudential high-water mark in 1946, in *Colegrove v. Green*.[33] There the Court decided that the doctrine prevented it from reviewing a claim that Illinois had unconstitutionally redrawn its voting districts as to ensure that some counties (typically rural ones) received representation disproportionate to their numbers, with the effect that each voter in the more populous districts now exercised less political influence than a voter in the less populous districts with the same congressional representation. The Court held that it *"ought not to enter this political thicket"* and that the remedy for unfairness in districting was for the electorate "to secure State legislatures that will apportion properly, or to invoke the ample powers of Congress."[34]

Less than twenty years later the Court would overturn *Colegrove*. In *Baker v. Carr*, it did indeed enter the "political thicket," deciding the constitutional question at issue and ultimately interpreting the Equal Protection Clause as obligating legislatures to draw districts according to the "one person, one vote" principle.[35] The *Baker* Court would still acknowledge, however, that the "political question" doctrine remained valid outside the realm of electoral apportionment.[36] In particular, it would continue to apply where there was "a textually demonstrable con-

stitutional commitment of the issue to a coordinate political department[,] . . . a lack of judicially discoverable and manageable standards
for resolving" the question, and where the Court could not decide the
issue presented "without an initial policy determination of a kind clearly
for nonjudicial discretion."[37] In other words, the doctrine apparently
continued to have force in matters of war and national security.

But since *Baker,* the Court has hesitated to apply the "political
question" doctrine even to cases involving foreign affairs. In 1979, for
example, several members of Congress petitioned to the effect that the
President could not, without the consent of Congress, withdraw from
a treaty with Taiwan.[38] The Court debated whether it had the power
to decide the case. Some justices maintained that it could not, for the
case presented a political question.[39] Others pointed out that the Court
frequently decides whether the Constitution limits the President's or
Congress's powers.[40] Still others wrote that, even if the Court could
sometimes determine the boundaries of congressional or presidential
authority, it would not be prudent to do so in this case.[41] Ultimately,
the Court refused to decide even whether a political question presented
itself. Instead, it dismissed the case in a per curiam order, without hearing oral arguments or addressing the underlying issue.[42]

More recently the Court considered a case questioning the lawfulness of a long-standing State Department policy specifying that the
birthplace of an American citizen born in Jerusalem be given as "Jerusalem" rather than "Israel or Jordan" in his passport.[43] The courts were
asked to review this policy in light of a congressional statute requiring
the State Department to describe the birthplace as "Israel" if the citizen
so wished. Did the statute unconstitutionally interfere with the President's power to conduct foreign affairs?[44]

The lower courts had decided that the case presented an unreviewable political question.[45] But the Supreme Court held to the contrary.
All the justices but one (and I was the one) considered the matter of
deciding what the statute meant and whether it was constitutional to be
"a familiar judicial exercise."[46] My colleagues believed the courts should
not avoid the question by invoking the "political question" doctrine.[47]
They consequently sent the case back to the lower court for a decision
on the merits.[48]

Though alone, I saw the case differently. "In the Middle East," I
wrote, "administrative matters can have implications that extend far

beyond the purely administrative."[49] The secretary of state had argued that requiring her to stamp the word *Israel* on a passport would represent an "official decision by the United States to begin to treat Jerusalem as a city" under Israeli sovereignty.[50] She maintained that upholding the statute would have significant foreign policy implications (a conclusion that others denied). Because of our inability to know the answer to this kind of dispute, I concluded that the merits of the case raised a political question, which the other two branches should resolve between themselves.[51] What matters for our purposes, however, is that the other members of the Court disagreed with me. They thought that, even there, the doctrine did not prevent the Court from reviewing the merits of this foreign policy-related question.

The upshot is that neither the classical view of Cicero nor the "political question" doctrine prevents today's Court from reaching, and deciding the merits of, many questions in which security and civil liberties collide. But there are other doctrines, embodied in other cases, that have had much the same effect.

CHAPTER 2

A Second Approach

"The President Wins"

The Court is not limited to following Cicero or the "political question" doctrine when believing that the President should have a free hand in security matters. It can simply hear the case and determine that the Constitution applies, but then interpret the Constitution as granting the President broad discretion in the name of, say, security or foreign affairs—to the point that the President and Congress almost always win. This was the approach just before and during World War II, most notably in the cases of *Curtiss-Wright* and *Korematsu*. But even during those years, the doctrine was not absolute. Indeed, the Court suggested in one case, *Ex parte Quirin*, that the President's authority was not unlimited. And as we shall see, after the war, the Court began to impose more serious limits upon the President's exercise of his security powers.

UNITED STATES V. CURTISS-WRIGHT EXPORT CORPORATION

In *Curtiss-Wright*, the Court considered the breadth of the President's foreign affairs power. The case concerned war, but among foreign countries, not including the United States.[1] Still the case is germane, since it presents national security threats. These often originate abroad. And by broadening the presidential foreign affairs power, it also broadens the presidential security power. In *Curtiss-Wright*, the Court held that the scope of the President's foreign affairs power is broad indeed.

In the early 1930s the Standard Oil Company discovered oil in southeastern Bolivia.[2] Bolivia (wrongly) believed it would find yet more oil just to the west in the "Chaco" territory, control of which region Bolivia disputed with Paraguay. As a result of this and other underlying tensions, Bolivia and Paraguay went to war. The war lasted for three years and resulted in more than 100,000 dead.[3]

During the war, the new American president, Franklin Delano Roosevelt, announced his Good Neighbor Policy for Latin America. The United States, he said, would meet its "obligations," "respect[] the rights of others," and honor its "agreements in and with a world of neighbors."[4] Other nations should in turn do the same. Some thought the Good Neighbor Policy obliged us to take action in Latin America to help resolve disputes. In doing so, we would distinguish between aggressors—Hitler's example in Europe came to mind—and their victims. In this hemisphere, we might try to punish aggressors, though through peaceful means.[5]

Pursuant to this policy, in 1933 the President asked Congress for the discretionary authority to impose an arms embargo selectively. Initially, isolationists had enough influence to prevent any such legislation from passing.[6] But by mid-1934, the American public had become aware of the Chaco War. The secretary of state had charged that American arms manufacturers, for "the sake" of their "profits," were helping the belligerents carry on a "useless and sanguinary conflict."[7] And the newspapers began to describe it as a war being fought to help protect Standard Oil's Bolivian investments.[8]

In May 1934 Congress gave the President the authority he sought.[9] It enacted a statute (a "Joint Resolution") that said:

> if the President finds that the prohibition of the sale of arms and munitions of war in the United States to those countries now engaged in armed conflict in the Chaco may contribute to the reestablishment of peace between those countries, and if after consultation with the governments of other American Republics and with their cooperation . . . he makes a proclamation to that effect, it shall be unlawful [*and a federal crime*] to sell . . . any arms or munitions of war in any place in the United States

to the countries now engaged in that armed conflict [but with such "exceptions as the President prescribes"].[10]

On May 28 President Roosevelt issued a proclamation:

> I have found that the prohibition of the sale of arms and munitions of war in the United States to those countries now engaged in armed conflict in the Chaco may contribute to the reestablishment of peace between those countries and . . . I have [made the necessary consultations with, and secured the necessary cooperation of, other countries].[11]

Thus the statute delegated broad discretionary authority to the President to create a federal crime—namely, the selling of arms to the Chaco belligerents. And the President exercised that authority.

Throughout the war, Curtiss-Wright had sold arms to Bolivia, the sales apparently facilitated by side payments to officials in that country.[12] After the proclamation, Curtiss-Wright had mostly ceased the sales, but employees had left a few bombs and crates of weapons inside at least one of those planes that they sent to Bolivia.[13] When the federal government found out, it indicted the company and two of its executives, charging them with having violated the Joint Resolution and the Proclamation.[14]

The trial court dismissed the case. The judge thought that the indictment was unconstitutional. The Constitution, he reasoned, does not permit Congress to delegate to other branches the authority to make criminal laws.[15] The government appealed, the Supreme Court heard the case, and in December 1936 it announced its decision.[16]

At issue was whether the Constitution allowed Congress to delegate to the President the authority to establish a crime. It was more difficult, and more important, for the Court to find an answer to that question in 1936 than it might be today. The political class, as well as the legal profession, were keenly interested in what the Court might say about delegations of authority, especially at that moment, when conflict between the President and the Court had been brewing over how to address a national emergency.

In 1936 the Great Depression was in full swing. Unemployment had risen from just 3 percent in 1929 to nearly 25 percent in 1933.[17] Having pledged to take active steps to deal with the emergency, Roosevelt found that the Supreme Court had become a serious obstacle, for it was finding important New Deal programs to be unconstitutional. The next year the President would send to Congress proposed "court-packing" legislation, which would have allowed him to appoint one new justice for every sitting justice over the age of seventy. The object was to force some of the older anti–New Deal justices to retire, allowing him to appoint new justices more sympathetic to his legislative agenda.[18] And in November, just weeks before the Court heard arguments in *Curtiss-Wright,* the voters reelected President Roosevelt in a landslide. Roosevelt won the popular vote by 28 million to 17 million and carried every state except Maine and Vermont, winning 97 percent of the votes cast in the Electoral College.[19]

Popular will, then, was mostly with Roosevelt that fall, but the Court was deeply divided, with four conservative justices (the "four horsemen": Justices George Sutherland, Pierce Butler, Willis Van Devanter, and James Clark McReynolds), three liberal justices (Justices Louis Brandeis, Harlan Stone, and Benjamin Cardozo), and two "swing" justices (Chief Justice Charles Evans Hughes and Justice Owen J. Roberts). It was the "conservative" majority, with the help of the swing justices, that had struck down key pieces of New Deal legislation, relying on various constitutional doctrines, such as the prohibition against depriving any person of "property without due process of law" and the prohibition against impairing the obligations of contracts.[20]

For our purposes, the most important of these anti–New Deal cases was *A.L.A. Schechter Poultry Corp. v. United States,* decided ten months before *Curtiss-Wright.* In it, the Court struck down the National Industrial Recovery Act, the heart of the first New Deal.[21] The decision relied upon the "nondelegation" doctrine, which limits Congress's authority to delegate its legislative powers to others.[22]

In 1935, in *Panama Refining Co. v. Ryan,* the Court had struck down a statute empowering the President to forbid the transportation in interstate commerce of oil produced in violation of state law.[23] The statute had been intended to provide federal help to states that regulated oil production. But the Court held that the measure to limit "hot oil" delegated too much discretionary power, leaving "the matter to the President without standard or rule, to be dealt with as he pleased."[24] It gave him "unlimited authority to determine the policy and to lay down the prohibition, or not to lay it down, as he may see fit. And disobedience to his order is made a crime punishable by fine and imprisonment."[25]

This was the context in which the Court decided *Schechter* the following year. The federal statute at issue, the National Industrial Recovery Act, had created committees for individual industries, each made up of business, labor, and government representatives. The committees were designed to help end the Great Depression by boosting prices, which each committee had the legal power to do by proposing, and with the President's approval then promulgating, legally enforceable codes of "fair competition."[26]

The Court held unanimously that this act went too far. Although the statute forbade the committees to "promote monopolies or to eliminate or oppress small enterprises," or to create codes that "will discriminate against them," it did not otherwise define the key term *fair competition.*[27] It thus left the committees largely free to "roam at will, and the President may approve or disapprove their proposals as he may see fit."[28] Without a manageable standard, the statute, the Court said, was "an unconstitutional delegation of legislative power," violating those provisions of the Constitution that vest "the legislative power" in Congress.[29] Even Justice Cardozo, who previously had consistently voted to uphold New Deal legislation, agreed with the majority. He thought the statute represented "delegation running riot."[30]

So, if the Constitution forbade the delegations at issue in *Schechter* and in *Panama Refining,* how could it permit the delegation of power to create a federal crime, the issue in *Curtiss-Wright*? After all, the statute's authorization was contingent on nothing more than the President's concluding (after consultation with others) that an arms sales embargo would "contribute to the reestablishment of peace."[31] How was this standard any more definite than those in the laws that the Court had just struck down? In any event, could the justices who had consistently found New Deal legislation unconstitutional—the "four horsemen"—suddenly change course when presented with this "Good Neighbor" legislation? How?

At the end of the day, the Court upheld the delegation. And Justice Sutherland, one of the horsemen, wrote the opinion, which was adopted unanimously. His reasoning was, essentially: *foreign affairs are different.* The Constitution grants Congress the power to enact domestic laws, but "the investment of the federal government with the powers of external sovereignty" does "not depend upon the affirmative grants of the Constitution."[32] Rather, the

> powers to declare and wage war, to conclude peace, to make treaties, to maintain diplomatic relations with other sovereignties, if they had never been mentioned in the Constitution, would have vested in the federal government as necessary concomitants of nationality.[33]

And "[i]n this vast external realm, with its important, complicated, delicate and manifold problems, the President alone has the power to speak or listen as a representative of the nation."[34]

Justice Sutherland was at pains to make very clear how the Joint Resolution differed from the statutes the Court had earlier struck down:

> It is important to bear in mind that we are here dealing not alone with an authority vested in the President by an exertion of legislative power, but with such an authority plus the very delicate, plenary and exclusive power of the President as the sole organ of the federal government in the field of international relations—a power which does not require as a basis for its exercise an act of Congress. . . . It is quite apparent that if, in the maintenance of our international relations, embarrassment—perhaps serious embarrassment—is to be avoided and success for our aims achieved, congressional legislation which is to be made effective through negotiation and inquiry within the international field must often accord to the President a degree of discretion and freedom from statutory restriction which would not be admissible were domestic affairs alone involved. Moreover, he, not Congress, has the better opportunity of knowing the conditions which prevail in foreign countries, and especially is this true in time of war. He has his confidential sources of information. He has his agents in the form of diplomatic, consular and other officials. Secrecy in respect of information gathered by them may be highly necessary, and the premature disclosure of it productive of harmful results.[35]

In the Court's view, George Washington, John Marshall, and Joseph Story all had claimed similarly broad presidential foreign affairs powers.

Justice Sutherland did sound one note of caution, though: those powers, "of course, like every other governmental power, must be exercised in subordination to the applicable provisions of the Constitution."[36]

The upshot is that foreign affairs are different. The delegation to create a crime was constitutional. And so the action against Curtiss-Wright must proceed. As it happened, though, with World War II looming on the horizon, the government realized it would need Curtiss-Wright as an aviation contractor. And so it decided to settle the case. The company and the executives paid fines, and their energies were applied to manufacturing aircraft rather than to criminal defense.[37] This resolution notwithstanding, the Court's broad interpretation of the President's constitutional foreign affairs powers remained the law.

KOREMATSU

The Court took its broadest view of the President's war powers (and its narrowest view of its own power to protect individual liberties) when, during World War II, it decided cases involving the Japanese internment. It upheld as constitutional the President's removal of 112,000 persons of Japanese origin, including 70,000 American citizens, from their homes on the West Coast and subsequent internment in camps for much of the war.[38] It is perhaps not surprising that the Court, having taken a highly expansive view of the President's authority over foreign policy in *Curtiss-Wright,* would take an even broader view of his authority to conduct a war. Nevertheless, today *Korematsu* counts for many as one of the three worst Court decisions in U.S. history, the other two being *Dred Scott* and *Plessy v. Ferguson.*[39] If we are to ask how the Court could reach such a decision, we must understand the background facts and circumstances.

On December 7, 1941, the Japanese bombed Pearl Harbor, and in the aftermath of the bombing many Californians feared a Japanese invasion. The press, after initially urging them "not" to "get rattled," began to support the removal of "all Japanese whether citizens or not" from California,[40] with state officials soon adding their voices to the chorus. General John DeWitt, in charge of the Sixth Military District (which included California), told the War Department that he, too, feared invasion, that Japanese persons in California had signaled valuable targeting information to submarines offshore, that they had committed acts of sabotage, and that he could not distinguish the loyal from the disloyal, and therefore he advised that all be removed.[41] For the most part, the War Department and California state officials (including Earl Warren, then attorney general), supported DeWitt's recommendation.[42] (Warren would later say he very much regretted his actions.[43]) The Justice Department, including the FBI (and its director, J. Edgar Hoover), opposed removal, thinking it unnecessary, logistically difficult, a civil rights horror, or all three.[44]

Nonetheless, in February 1942, President Franklin Roosevelt signed Executive Order 9066, delegating to military commanders the power to designate "military areas" and to impose restrictions on those living in those areas, thereby allowing the relocation of persons of Japanese ancestry.[45] Soon thereafter Congress ratified the order with a statute that made it a crime for anyone knowingly to "enter, remain in, leave, or commit any act in any . . . military zone . . . contrary to" applicable "restrictions."[46]

In early March, General DeWitt designated the western portions of California, Oregon, and Washington as special "military area[s]."[47] He then imposed a curfew upon Japanese living in these areas, who, for the time being, were ordered to remain where they were. He followed that with an order in effect telling them to report to specified "assembly centers," such as the Tanforan and Santa Anita racetracks near San Francisco and Los Angeles, respectively. From these centers they were sent to internment camps in the eastern parts of California and the intermountain states. By June, more than seventy thousand American citizens of Japanese ancestry (and another forty thousand Japanese who were not American citizens) were living in camps. There they would remain, forbidden to return to California, until 1944, when the war was nearly won.[48]

Most of those affected by an internment order did not seek to contest its legality, but a few did. Fred Korematsu was among those few. An American citizen, Korematsu was born of Japanese parents in Oakland, California. He'd studied at Los Angeles City College, worked as a welder, and tried to join the navy (which rejected him for medical reasons). But most important for our purposes: he refused to report for relocation.[49]

When he was arrested, he explained why he resisted and sought to challenge his removal. Here are his words:

Assembly Camps were for: Dangerous Enemy Aliens and Citizens; These camps have been definitely an imprisonment under armed guard with orders shoot to kill. In order to be imprisoned, these people should have been given a fair trial in order that they may defend their loyalty at court in a democratic way, but they were placed in imprisonment without any fair trial! Many Disloyal Germans and Italians were caught, but they were not all corralled under armed guard like the Japanese—is this a racial issue? If not, the Loyal Citizens want fair trial to prove their loyalty! Also their [*sic*] are many loyal aliens who can prove their loyalty to America, and they must be given fair trial and treatment! Fred Korematsu's Test Case may help.[50]

Meanwhile, Ernest Besig, the director of the northern California chapter of the American Civil Liberties Union, had read about Korematsu's arrest in the newspaper. Besig visited Korematsu in the San Francisco County Jail and offered to represent him.[51] And Korematsu accepted, eager to go "forward on the basis of his own conviction" that the removal order was unjust.[52] He lost his case in the trial court. He lost again in the court of appeals. After further procedural ups and downs, the Supreme Court heard the case in October 1944.[53]

By that time, much had happened. In June 1943 the Court had upheld the constitutionality of the curfew in *Hirabayashi v. United States*.[54] The majority found that the wartime emergency, the Constitution's grant of war powers to the President and to Congress, and the consequent need for judges to defer to military decisions provided adequate legal support for the military's curfew. The Court explicitly refused to "sit in review of the wisdom" of the wartime activities of the other branches,[55] finding it could not "substitute its judgment for theirs."[56] At most it could ask only whether, "in the light of all the relevant circumstances" as seen at the time, there was "a reasonable basis for . . . imposing the curfew."[57] And the then-present risks of invasion, sabotage, and espionage, taken together, provided just such a "reasonable basis."[58]

Still, by 1944, with the war in the Pacific nearly won, the risk of Japanese invasion was virtually nonexistent. And even the Justice

Department believed that General DeWitt had gone too far.[59] Before the orders were given, he had, as mentioned, warned the War Department of his concerns; in that report he claimed, in addition to reports of espionage and sabotage, "hundreds of reports nightly of signal lights visible from the coast, and of . . . unidentified radio transmissions."[60] After DeWitt's report found its way into the press, it drew the notice of two young Justice Department lawyers, Edward Ennis and John L. Burling, who asked the Federal Communications Commission (FCC) and the FBI to look into the claims.[61]

The FCC reported back that a lengthy investigation of the signaling reports found no evidence of their veracity, that many of the reports had come from army privates without training to use the electronic detection equipment, and that General DeWitt had known all this at the time. The FBI came to roughly the same conclusions, while also pointing out that Director J. Edgar Hoover had opposed the internment.[62]

The result was that the Justice Department included a footnote in its Supreme Court brief essentially disowning DeWitt's case for the internment.[63] Charles Horsky, the lawyer for the ACLU (which had filed an amicus brief), drew special attention to the "extraordinary footnote" during oral argument and made clear that the Court could not rely upon DeWitt's claims.[64]

By October 1944, few in the federal government believed it important to maintain internment. The Justice Department wished to end it. Even the War Relocation Department allowed that it saw no reason to prolong the arrangement. (In that way, the case resembled *Milligan,* in which the Court had held, *after the war was over,* that military trials of civilians during the war were unconstitutional.) But this view was not unanimous. California state officials still thought it would be unpopular to permit the Japanese to return home. And the President favored postponing any decision until after the November election. It was in this context that the Court heard and decided Fred Korematsu's case.[65]

On December 18, 1944, the Supreme Court released its decision. By a vote of six to three, it decided against Korematsu and in the government's favor. Justice Hugo Black, writing for the majority, accepted the government's argument that the Court need not decide whether the internment was constitutional; it need only decide the constitutionality of the military order excluding Korematsu (and others) from any area within northern

California but for the assembly center at the Tanforan racetrack.[66] The Court did not explain why this distinction mattered. More to the point, it held that the order was similar enough to the curfew previously upheld in *Hirabayashi* to warrant the same constitutional treatment.[67]

The Court again cited the emergency situation, the difficulty (according to the military) of distinguishing the "loyal" from the "disloyal," and the need to "repos[e] confidence . . . in our military leaders" as factors justifying the action.[68] Justice Black added, "[W]e cannot—by availing ourselves of the calm perspective of hindsight—now say that at that time these actions were unjustified."[69] Other justices whom history properly characterizes as "liberal," including Chief Justice Harlan Stone, Justice William O. Douglas, and Justice Wiley Rutledge, joined the opinion, as did Justice Stanley Reed. Justice Felix Frankfurter joined the opinion while also writing separately to say that the proper standard was that of "reasonably expedient military precautions in time of war," and he believed that the orders in question met that standard.[70]

Three justices dissented. Justice Owen Roberts made clear that the government's efforts to distinguish "exclusion" from "internment" made no sense. The military orders at issue required the Japanese not just to leave their homes but to report to specified locations that they were not free to leave. To pretend otherwise, he wrote, would be to "shut our eyes to reality."[71]

Justice Murphy meticulously dismembered the government's justifications for the orders and subsequent actions: There was no evidence of signaling, sabotage, or the like, and the military knew it at the time; there was no evidence of subversive activities or divided loyalties; the loyal/disloyal line could have been drawn individually, as both Britain and the United States had done with respect to, for example, individuals of German origin; there was no reason to think that the military and intelligence agencies did not have the situation well in hand; and in any event, the military reports justifying the internment were filled with racial assumptions without support in any sociological or other serious literature or experience. In a word, Murphy saw in those military orders little but racial prejudice.[72]

Justice Robert Jackson, also dissenting, argued that the Court could not have known in early 1942 whether the orders were justified. Military decisions, "in the very nature of things," are "not susceptible of intelligent judicial appraisal."[73] But that being so, the Court should enforce ordinary constitutional standards.[74] In an emergency, the President may direct the military to violate ordinary constitutional standards. But that should do the country no lasting harm, for, by the time the Court hears the question, the emergency will be over and the Court can strike the order down. And so the Court should refrain from any opinion that ratifies emergency action. Such an opinion would "lie[] about like a loaded weapon ready for the hand of any authority that can bring forward a plausible claim of an urgent need."[75]

In my own view, Justice Frank Murphy was right. He demonstrated persuasively that the internment had been based on racial prejudice, not specific evidence, and that the Court should have said so. Years later Congress enacted a resolution apologizing for what the country had done—but apologies, while welcome, do not undo injuries.[76]

So what happened to civil liberties? How could the Court have reached such a decision? The question is a fair one, particularly since the majority included Justices Black, Douglas, Frankfurter, and Reed, all of whom later joined the unanimous *Brown v. Board of Education* decision, striking down racial segregation as unconstitutional. The most convincing, or perhaps charitable, explanation that I can find is that the majority, while thinking the government wrong in *Korematsu* itself, feared that saying so would only lead to other such cases in which the government was right, and that the Court would have no way of telling one kind from the other. Someone has to run a war. In this case, it would either be FDR or the Court. Seeing the folly of the latter choice, the Court elected not to question the President's actions. This is an argument, baldly put, for broad, virtually uncheckable war powers. But as we have seen, it resembles what many presidents may actually have thought in time of war.

Is that how the Court reasoned? We cannot be certain. We know that Justice Sutherland struck a similar note in *Curtiss-Wright*. If we take that case seriously when foreign affairs are at issue, then the President must surely enjoy yet broader powers when there is a threat to national security, and he is equipped with both foreign affairs powers *and* war powers to confront it. Moreover, in *Korematsu*, Congress with its ratification had supplemented the President's war powers with its own. Consequently, if the government was wrong about executive power in *Korematsu*, that would suggest that the government had also been wrong in *Curtiss-Wright,* and that the Court might need to retreat from that holding.

EX PARTE QUIRIN

A third case, also decided during World War II but two years before *Korematsu,* further demonstrates the Court's approach at the time of considering challenges to wartime policies but deferring to presidential or congressional power. As in *Curtiss-Wright* and *Korematsu,* the Court in *Ex parte Quirin* sided with the President. But the opinion here was less absolute than *Curtiss-Wright* had been or *Korematsu* would be. In word and deed, the Court suggested the existence of important constitutional limitations on presidential and congressional action. And those limitations concerned individual liberties.

Six months after the United States entered World War II, a group of Nazi saboteurs, all members of the German army, traveled by submarine from Germany to the East Coast of the United States. Though all were born in Germany, at least one of the eight was an American citizen.[77]

On June 13, 1942, four of the saboteurs landed at Amagansett Beach, New York; four days later the remaining four landed near Jacksonville, Florida.[78] As trained, they took off their uniforms, buried them, put on civilian clothes, and walked inland, intent on carrying out a Hitler-inspired plan to destroy war production facilities and weaken the American will to fight.[79]

Unfortunately for the would-be saboteurs, a Coast Guardsman spotted the New York team and reported their activity. At about the same time, two of them, George Dasch and Ernest Burger, decided to abandon the plan. Dasch, who "spoke nearly flawless American English," went to the FBI and told them the story.[80] After several days of confessing and finally showing the agents $82,000 in cash, Dasch persuaded them he was telling the truth. The FBI then rounded up the remaining infiltrators, and by June 27 all eight were in custody and had confessed.[81]

President Roosevelt, Attorney General Francis Biddle, Secretary of War Henry Stimson, and other high government officials decided that a special military tribunal should try the prisoners. FDR's orders naming the members permitted the military commission to receive any evidence that "a reasonable man" would consider to have "probative value," and required the commission to send the trial record directly to the President for review; they also forbade the federal courts from considering any judicial action filed by any person charged with a law of war violation before a military tribunal.[82]

The military commission's first meeting would take place at the Justice Department on July 8, 1942.[83] On August 3 it would return guilty verdicts, sentencing all eight defendants to death.[84] Historians tell us that by the very next day the President had reviewed the lengthy transcript and approved capital sentences for six of the eight.[85] On August 8 those six were executed. The President commuted the death penalty to prison terms for the two remaining convicts, Dasch and Burger. Imprisoned during the war, they were subsequently deported to Germany.[86]

In July, however, before the trial had even taken place, a defense lawyer, Colonel Kenneth Royall, tried to prevent it, filing a petition for habeas corpus in the District of Columbia trial court. He argued that trial before a military commission violated the Constitution.[87]

On July 28 the judge, referring to the President's order prohibiting federal courts from considering the matter, denied the petition.[88] He also referred to *Ex parte Milligan,* the Civil War case discussed earlier, in which the Court had held that the Constitution forbids trial by special military court when the ordinary courts are open. But, the trial judge said, he "did not consider" it "controlling in the circumstances" of the petitioners.[89]

After interrupting its summer recess specifically for this purpose, the Supreme Court heard arguments on July 29 and 30.[90] And the next day, on July 31, the Court issued a short per curiam decision resolving the question. It said that the "President is authorized to order" the offenses "tried before a military commission," the "military commission was lawfully constituted," the "petitioners [we]re held in lawful custody[] for trial before the military commission," and the "motions for leave to file petitions for writs of habeas corpus [we]re denied."[91]

The chief justice added that the Court had "fully considered the questions raised," that it had "reached its conclusion," and that it would enter judgment "in advance of the preparation of a full opinion which necessarily will require a considerable period of time for its preparation."[92]

When the Court finally released its full opinion on October 29,

1942, the saboteurs had long been executed. In it, Chief Justice Stone explained the Court's view that the trials were constitutional. Justice Murphy did not participate, but otherwise the Court was unanimous.[93]

On its face, *Ex parte Quirin* seems simply to present a further affirmation of the President's broad, virtually unreviewable wartime powers. After all, the Court took only a few days to decide the case and did not even release an opinion at the time of decision, as it almost always does.[94] Moreover, one defendant was an American citizen. Six other defendants were executed before the Court could even write its opinion. Thus the case might be considered a harbinger of the opprobrious *Korematsu* and in retrospect even more extreme.

As troubling, a desire to protect the Court as an institution may have influenced the proceedings. According to Justice Murphy's notes from the preargument conference, Justice Roberts told his colleagues that "[Attorney General] Biddle has real[] apprehension that [the] commission may enter [an] order and [that the] president will order men shot despite proceedings in this court." "That," the chief justice responded, "would be a dreadful thing."[95]

Nonetheless, the case may be seen as having had some positive implications for the protection of civil liberties. There are two good reasons to believe that the Court did not abdicate its authority to review presidential actions even in wartime. First, recall that the President's trial order forbade the federal courts from considering any petition filed by a person tried before the military commission.[96] Indeed, the district court had denied the defendants' habeas corpus petitions on this ground.[97] Chief Justice Stone's opinion, however, makes clear that the Court could and would hear the appeal, despite the President's order. It would indeed review the constitutionality of trial by a special military commission.[98]

The Court could have found considerable precedent to do the contrary. There is support for Cicero's approach in various authorities. In the eighteenth century, for instance, Blackstone had written that "alien enemies have no rights, no privileges, unless by the king's special favor, during time of war."[99] And British courts had later said that this phrase means that

a man, professing himself hostile to this country, and in a state of war with it, cannot be heard if he sue for the benefit and protection of our laws in the courts of this country.[100]

Indeed, of the thousands of prisoners of war held in the United States during the two world wars, few if any even tried to obtain access to the courts to argue that their detention was illegal.[101]

Blackstone's principle, however, is less absolute than it sounds. An enemy alien "hostile to this country" might come to court to defend himself should he be sued in respect to, say, ownership of property or inheritance.[102] In the event, the Court decided the matter without reference to Blackstone or the other authorities. Its opinion simply stated that *"neither the Proclamation nor the fact that [the defendants] are enemy aliens forecloses consideration by the courts of petitioners' contentions that the Constitution and laws of the United States constitutionally enacted forbid their trial by military commission."*[103]

Second, recall that in *Ex parte Milligan* following the Civil War, the Court found unconstitutional the use of a special military tribunal as long as ordinary courts were open.[104] The district court had pronounced *Ex parte Milligan* irrelevant, since it involved the trial of an American citizen, *not* an enemy soldier. The Court could have taken the same line in *Quirin*, in which all but the one American defendant were German nationals. As to that one, it could have said that his actions placed him in the same category as the foreign combatants.

But that is not what the Court said. Rather, it carefully distinguished *Ex parte Milligan* on several different grounds. Congress here had provided legislative support for the President's decision by "authoriz[ing] trial of offenses against the law of war before" military "commissions."[105] Indeed, the legislation had made clear that those engaging in such behavior might be punished as "war criminals."[106] Nothing of the kind was at work in *Milligan*.

Moreover, the laws of the United States, like those of many other nations as well as international law, had long recognized "by universal agreement" that a "spy" or other "enemy combatant who without uniform comes secretly through the lines for the purpose of waging war by destruction of life or property" is a belligerent who is "generally deemed not to be entitled to the status" of a "prisoner[] of war" but that of an "offender[] against the law of war subject to trial and punishment by military tribunals."[107] Further, "[c]itizenship in the United States of an enemy belligerent does not relieve him from the consequences of a belligerency which is unlawful because in violation of the law of war."[108]

In addition, the *Milligan* defendants had been charged with a crime for which the Constitution guarantees a defendant a trial by jury. The crime of which the *Quirin* defendants were accused carried no such guarantee. Indeed, it "has never been suggested in the very extensive literature of the subject that an alien spy, in time of war, could not be tried by military tribunal without a jury."[109] And nothing in Article III, the Fifth Amendment, or the Sixth Amendment enlarged the right to trial by jury in this respect.[110]

Finally, Milligan "was not an enemy belligerent."[111] He was not "associated with the armed forces of the enemy."[112] Rather, he "was a non-belligerent"[113] and thus "not subject to the law of war save as—in circumstances found not there to be present and not involved here—martial law might be constitutionally established."[114]

There is more to this effect, but the positive implications of *Quirin* respecting the Court's readiness to review executive action in time of war should be clear. In finding that federal courts have the constitutional authority to consider a petition for a writ of habeas corpus, even when presented by an alien enemy and even despite a President's proclamation, the Court in fact took a decisive step away from Cicero. *Quirin*, then, is not just one more case finding broad authority for the President to narrow or to abandon ordinary individual liberties when he believes the exigencies of war or security emergency require it. Rather, Chief Justice Stone's October opinion points to a different, more flexible approach.

CHAPTER 3

A Third Approach

"The President Goes Too Far"

During World War II, the Court found in the Constitution great leeway for the President to take action to protect the nation's security, and President Roosevelt readily embraced that power. Indeed, he understood it in a very broad sense, declaring, for example, that even absent congressional authorization for actions necessary to "stabilize" the wartime economy and tame inflation, he would nonetheless "accept the responsibility" and "see to it that the war effort is no longer imperiled by the threat of economic chaos."[1] The President, he added, "has the powers . . . to take measures necessary to avert a disaster which would interfere with the winning of the war. . . . When the war is won, the powers under which I act will automatically revert to the people of the United States—to the people to whom those powers belong."[2] *Korematsu, Quirin,* and even *Curtiss-Wright* all unambiguously support Roosevelt's view of presidential power.

After the war, however, the Court's approach began to change. In the *Steel Seizure* case, decided during the Korean War that was soon to follow, and in the Guantanamo cases, decided during the present "War on Terror," the Court read the Constitution as denying the President that blank check.[3] And the Court was itself to determine whether the President had gone too far.

Of course, the new approach could raise problems of its own. If the President's powers were not unlimited, how were the limits to be determined? And once determined, how could the limits be implemented? Such questions, which the Court had been able to evade entirely under the older, almost entirely deferential approach, are at the heart of this book. For if the Court is to read the Constitution as cabining the President's security powers, it takes upon itself an obligation at least to understand the nature of the problem that led the President to curtail civil liberties; it must become aware of the choices that faced the President. It must inform itself, therefore, of circumstances and realities not ordinarily within its purview. How is the Court to obtain the necessary information—particularly when that information, as with many of today's ongoing terrorist threats, is gathered from beyond our borders?

After all, as Justice Robert Jackson wrote, the "President, both as Commander-in-Chief and as the Nation's organ for foreign affairs, has available intelligence services whose reports neither are nor ought to be published to the world. It would be intolerable that courts, without the relevant information, should review and perhaps nullify actions of the Executive taken on information properly held secret."

The *Steel Seizure* case illustrates the kind of conflict that can arise between a President, charged with the duty of protecting the nation's security, and the Court, charged with the obligation to keep presidential action within constitutional limits. To understand that conflict, we must examine it from both the President's and the Court's point of view. The Court must understand why the President has taken the action at issue, and that understanding may be difficult to come by. In this sense, the *Steel Seizure* case is particularly instructive, and this chapter will be devoted to considering it in some detail.

President Harry S. Truman seized the nation's steel mills on April 8, 1952, in the midst of the Korean War.[4] He did so to avert a strike that he believed would risk serious harm to our military, making good on his predecessor's commitment to "see to it that the war effort is no longer imperiled by the threat of economic chaos."[5] Within a few weeks, however, to the President's surprise, the Supreme Court held that the Constitution denied him the power to take such action.[6] A comparison of the two competing institutional points of view in this case will help us better to understand the challenges that face today's Court in its attempt to review executive action during times of national emergency.

BACKGROUND

In late June 1950 the North Korean Army invaded South Korea. The United States, acting under the authority of a United Nations resolution, came to South Korea's aid. By late 1951 China had entered the fray, American troops were fighting on the Korean Peninsula, and diplomats were trying to negotiate a solution.[7]

The war caused much of American industry to shift its productive capacity toward meeting military needs, and as so often happens in wartime, when the government adds so substantially to aggregate demand in the economy, there was a surge of inflation. By January 1951, seven months after the war had begun, the wholesale price index had jumped about 15 percent.[8] Congress responded with legislation empowering the President to seek wage and price controls.[9] Pursuant to that power, President Truman created two new administrative agencies, the Wage Stabilization Board and the Office of Price Stabilization,[10] both located in the Defense Department, under the Office of Defense Mobilization. The head of that office was Charles E. Wilson, former president of the General Electric Corporation and nicknamed "Electric Charlie" (to distinguish him from "Engine Charlie" Wilson, the secretary of defense and former head of General Motors).[11]

Of the Wage Stabilization Board's eighteen members, six were drawn from labor, six from industry, and six from the general public.[12] The board could receive dispute referrals from the President or from either party in a labor dispute. Its mandate, however, was limited to mediation; it did not have the power to impose a settlement. In the case of a presidential referral, however, it could send a report of its findings to the White House, proposing what it deemed fair and equitable terms.[13]

For our purposes, it is important to understand why Congress did *not* empower the board to impose settlement terms. For one thing, Congress shared the view of most Americans that collective bargaining and a decentralized system for determining wages were desirable and efficient. That arrangement forced labor and management each to decide its priorities and to aim for the best result that the other side could also live with. Most agreed it was a better way to set wages than the obvious alternatives: unilateral action by labor, by management, or by the government.[14]

Congress and the public also recognized, however, that with free collective bargaining sometimes come strikes, and with strikes, lost wages and lost production output. Sympathy for workers tends to wane quickly when a labor action means no milk, no school, or no public transit. How much more so during wartime, when a strike in a vital industry can potentially threaten national security. And so the public may express support for legislation allowing the government to forbid certain strikes, or, as happens in some foreign countries, oblige the parties in certain key industries to submit to compulsory arbitration.[15]

But compulsory arbitration is no panacea for labor discontent. It may impose terms a few managers dislike, but equally, it may lead to a settlement that perhaps hundreds of thousands of workers find intolerable, spurring them in the end to the very action that arbitration was intended to avoid. When, for instance, New Zealand adopted compulsory arbitration late in the nineteenth century, the law worked well as long as the arbitrators decided largely in labor's favor. But when a new government appointed arbitrators more sympathetic to management, the system broke down. As one observer wrote, "the workers startled the government and the country by refusing to accept the award and going out on strike."[16] In response, the government arrested the workers, brought them to court, and had them "duly fined," but it "could find nothing to levy upon but a wash boiler and a skillet."[17] The same chronicler adds that "nothing more comical was ever seen. . . . [T]he unfortunate government . . . [wrung] its poor hands and order[ed] the men to go back to work, and the men just laughed and continued their strike."[18] New York State would have a similar experience in the twentieth century with its so-called Taylor Law: despite prohibiting strikes by public service workers, it could not prevent a fourteen-day walkout by 50,000 schoolteachers or a nine-day work stoppage by 10,000 sanitation workers.[19]

It is important to keep these practical realities in mind as we consider what the President or Congress did as against what they might have done at the time of the steel seizure. Congress had enacted laws providing for mediation,[20] waiting periods,[21] and fact-finding boards,[22] and with the Taft-Hartley Act it even gave the President authority in the event of a national emergency to obtain an injunction delaying a strike for up to eighty days, to provide a cooling-off period.[23] But tellingly, Congress itself has only twice imposed a settlement, once in 1916, when it ordered terms to which railroad workers had already agreed anyway,[24] and once in 1963, when it imposed compulsory arbitration to prevent a pending railroad strike.[25] So it should come as no surprise that Congress gave the Wage Stabilization Board the power to recommend, but not to impose, a settlement. To do more would have been courting trouble.

The Office of Price Stabilization enjoyed, by contrast, a freer hand to develop a complex set of regulations determining whether or when to allow a firm to raise its prices.[26] It could impose its decisions, and that too should come as no surprise. The relatively few individuals subject to these regulations, the fact that enforcing a court order against them rarely met with difficulty, and the public outcry that was sure to greet an industry's refusal to follow mandatory rules all emboldened Congress to delegate power to set binding prices, while in the case of wages delegating only the power to recommend.

Nevertheless, by 1951, when the United Steelworkers' contract expired, many union leaders feared that the national climate was turning against labor. The less friendly Republicans were poised to take the White House in the upcoming election, having captured Congress in 1946.[27] And even though the Democrats had taken it back in 1948 and Truman was reelected, the party hadn't managed to repeal Taft-Hartley, a law that labor felt undermined in various ways its ability to organize workers. The United Steelworkers union represented 500,000 members.[28] It had not had a full contract renegotiation since 1947.[29] Now it was seeking considerable improvements in wages and working conditions. The several large steel companies employing the union's membership were highly profitable, but they were willing to consider meeting labor's demands only if they could obtain compensatory price increases.[30] At the time, however, the government had a strong interest in maintaining wartime steel production along with wage and price stability. It was against this background that the threatened strike and steel mill seizures took place.

THE STRIKE THREAT

In October, three months before the United Steelworkers' contract expired at the end of 1951, the union advised its rank and file that it would not renew the old contract. It was seeking significant wage increases.[31] President Truman warned against unsettling the nation's wage and price stabilization program. But in November the union set forth twenty-two demands.[32]

In addition to a 15-cent-per-hour average raise, the union sought changes in job classifications and in wage discrepancies by region, as well as extra pay for afternoon shifts, significant increase in overtime and weekend pay, more paid holidays, easier vacation-eligibility rules, a guaranteed annual wage, a union shop, and various other nonremunerative changes.[33] The parties estimated the cost of these changes differently, but the range fell roughly between 30 and 60 cents per hour.[34]

Hewing to the industry line that any concession to labor should be tied to a price hike, the president of Bethlehem Steel said publicly that he saw no justification for higher wages and that he would have "no offer to make."[35] Meanwhile, government price office officials judged industry profits high enough to pay for a 40-cent-per-hour increase without a compensatory price increase.[36]

Wage Stabilization Board officials thought that the matter would be resolved through ordinary collective bargaining. But they were wrong. November and early December passed without signs of progress in negotiations. Finally, the union's Wage Policy Committee called for an industrywide strike, to begin on December 31, 1951.[37]

President Truman became alarmed. In his memoirs he would write that Defense Secretary Robert Lovett had long "point[ed] out" that a steel "strike" that "halt[ed] production" would "endanger" the "national defense program."[38] And so the President referred the dispute to the Wage Stabilization Board. He also asked the union to "postpone" the strike,[39] and on January 3, 1952, a special union convention complied, pledging not to walk off the job until forty-five days after the board began hearings. (Later, the union provided further time for the board to write a report.)[40]

At that point, the parties looked to the Wage Stabilization Board's standards, which said, in essence, "Go back two years to January 1950. If wages were then satisfactory, adjust them upwards to account for sub-sequent inflation."[41] As to fringe benefits, improvements would be per-missible as long as they did "not exceed the prevailing industry or area practice, as to either amount or type."[42]

The parties agreed that in the two-year period between January 1950 and late 1951, prices had risen by about 14 percent (23 cents per man-hour), and about halfway into this period, in December 1950, the steelworkers had received a wage increase of about 10 percent (16 cents per hour).[43] But they agreed on little else.

By management's calculation, 14 percent minus 10 left 4 percent (or 7 cents, subtracting 16 from 23 cents). The workers were entitled to no more than that difference.[44]

But the union objected, claiming that compensation two years ear-lier, in January 1950, was *not* "satisfactory," since it reflected a "no-strike" clause and other government measures to keep wages down and prevent truly free bargaining.[45] Moreover, the November 1950 raise had been intended to offset earlier, not subsequent, inflation, which was consid-erably greater.[46] Since then, prices had risen by 8.3 percent (15 cents per hour), which the union considered[47] to be the least to which its mem-bers were entitled. It also pointed to rising productivity, to agreements approved in other industries, and to unusually high industry profits.[48] It calculated that the total cost to management of granting all of labor's demands to be about 35 cents per hour.[49]

Sticking to their stated maximum offer of 7 cents per hour, the steel companies introduced an alternative inflation measure that took account of, for example, special holidays. Higher-than-average wages were compensation enough, they claimed, for lower fringe benefits,[50] and higher pay for nights and weekends was unjustified in an industry obliged to work around the clock.[51] As to their profits, they admitted they were high in gross terms, but the government taxed much of them away. Management estimated the total cost to the companies of meet-ing all the demands to be about 56 cents per hour.[52]

To make the arguments I have roughly summarized, the parties sub-mitted hundreds of documents, filled thousands of pages of transcript with testimony, and ventured endless comparisons with other indus-tries.[53] For the board, the questions were still many. Were steel profits so high? In fact, they were higher than in some industries but lower than in others. Did steelworkers "deserve" significantly better fringe benefits?

Again, theirs were better than those in some industries but worse than in others.[54] To what extent should workers benefit from improvements in productivity? What were the established understandings of wage relationships within the industry? Did the fact that steel was a leading American industry entitle the workers to higher wages (as a reward for the industry's performance) or lower wages (lest a "pacesetting" industry's wage hikes lead to matching increases, and inflation, throughout the economy)?

For several months, the board wrestled with these (and other) nearly unanswerable questions. In March 1952 it made its recommendations.[55] At the outset, it allowed that its writ was to consider whether an agreed-upon wage increase was permissible, not to choose between the parties. It added that wartime mobilization meant that real living standards might decline, as it was impossible to offer workers complete inflation protection. Nonetheless, it recommended a general wage increase of 17.5 cents per hour (roughly 11 percent), consisting of an immediate increase of 12.5 cents per hour, to be followed six months later by a further increase of 2.5 cents per hour and a still further increase of 2.5 cents per hour six months after that.[56] It approved some but not all of the union's fringe benefit demands.

The chairman wrote that the board's recommendations represented "its best estimate of what the parties would have agreed to had their negotiations been completed without Government intervention."[57] He added that the board had "recommended moderate adjustments" in those fringe benefits that "were relatively low as compared with established practice in American industry generally."[58] All the board's public members and labor members supported the recommendations; all the industry members dissented.[59]

The steel companies replied almost immediately that they would not comply with the board's recommendations, at least not without the compensatory price increase they had sought all along. Clarence B. Randall, chairman of Inland Steel, told the press that the "recommended increases" would increase "direct employment costs by 30 cents per employee hour," and "based upon past experience," that would increase "total costs of the companies by about 60 cents per employee hour." That, he added, meant an increase in "steel production" costs of "$12 a ton."[60] The Office of Price Stabilization meanwhile had decided that the industry was entitled to an increase of $3 per ton and no more.[61] Another steel company executive said that he thought a strike was inevitable.[62]

The President straightaway convened his top wage and price officials. Two unfortunate press reports immediately followed. The first quoted "Electric Charlie" Wilson, head of the Office of Defense Mobilization, saying that the wage board's recommendations, if put into effect, "would be a serious threat in our year-old effort to stabilize the economy."[63] The second had a top union official, David McDonald, saying that the steelworkers' union had "a rather friendly gentleman in the White House."[64]

In fact, Wilson had argued to the President that the only way to avert a strike was to give the companies their $12 price increase.[65] The President's reluctance, along with Wilson's subsequent exclusion from some key meetings, then led Wilson, in March 1952, to resign,[66] writing the President that he could not "accept public responsibility for major stabilization actions which I cannot control."[67] These events left the general public with the impression that the board's recommendations were too expensive.[68]

In the meantime, the union announced it would accept the board's recommendations, agreeing to postpone its strike by two more weeks, until April 8, 1952. But when the board then offered the union lesser increases believed to be worth about 14.5 cents per hour (not the 17.5 cents initially proposed), the union rejected the offer and called a strike, beginning on April 9.[69]

THE PRESIDENT'S CHOICES

What was the President to do? He had just announced he would not seek reelection, so for the most part he could put purely political considerations to the side. Still, his choices were not appealing.

First, he might do nothing and let the strike occur. Eventually economic self-interest would lead the parties to reach an agreement. The President and his "principal advisors," however, agreed that inaction was not an option. As Truman would tell it in his memoirs:

The secretary of defense "stress[ed] the situation in Korea," explaining "that our entire combat technique . . . depended on the fullest use of our industrial facilities. . . . Any curtailment of steel production, he warned, would endanger the lives of our fighting men."[70]

The "Chairman of the Atomic Energy Commission[] expressed grave concern over the delay which any lack of steel would mean for the major expansion of facilities for atomic weapons production."[71]

The administrator of the National Production Authority said that "power plants, railroad construction, shipbuilding, machine-tool manufacture, and the like, all would come to a halt if the steel mills closed down. He pointed out that it would depend on the inventory situation how soon the steel shortage would make itself felt in the manufacturing plants, and in certain types of ammunition there was virtually no inventory stock on hand."[72]

The secretary of commerce said that "a ten-day interruption of steel production would mean the loss of 96,000 feet of bridge and 1,500 miles of highway"; only "twenty-one of the ninety-eight ships then under construction . . . could be completed"; and major aircraft manufacturers "would have to halt their assembly lines within sixty days."[73]

The secretary of the interior "said that the maintenance and expansion of facilities in the petroleum, gas, and electric-power utility fields depended on steel materials," given that "[c]oal mines and coke ovens require steel for any number of accessory, but essential, uses."[74]

The secretary of state said that a strike "would seriously undermine" our allies' "faith in our ability to aid them in critical moments." It was even possible that "Russia would believe us so weakened by an extended strike as to invite further aggression, and there might be other 'Koreas.'"[75]

President Truman concluded that he "had to act to prevent the stoppage of steel production, which would imperil the nation."[76]

Second, he might invoke the Taft-Hartley Act and ask a court to enjoin the strike for eighty days. The union, however, had already postponed its strike for more than ninety days. Would it not have been unfair to force a further strike delay?

Strikebreaking injunctions, moreover, had an unsavory history. Before World War II, management had used them to weaken or to destroy unions, accounting in part for organized labor's loathing of Taft-Hartley.[77] To invoke the act now could well enrage the labor movement. The union consequently might refuse to cancel its strike call; workers might stage wildcat strikes or call in sick or find other ways simply to ignore the injunction.[78]

Third, the President could direct the price agency administrators to give the steel companies the increase they sought. But the Office of Price Stabilization had already made public its report explaining that the industry was entitled to no more than $3 per ton;[79] and even that was possible only owing to a special law, the Capehart Amendment, which allowed the rise on the basis of certain earlier rises in costs.[80] As to the office's ordinary standards for justifying a price increase, these required a firm's profits to fall below 85 percent of profits during its best three post-war years. The wage board's recommendations would cost the industry a yearly average of $4.67 per ton; but the industry's 1947–49 profits had averaged close to 20 percent on stockholder investment. Given a $3-per-ton rise in price, the wage recommendations would still leave the industry with hefty profits.[81]

The industry's argument that after-tax profits should be the guide was rejected out of hand. (Taxes, like death, were deemed inevitable.) So too, despite an abundance of supporting facts and figures, was its claim that the wage increase would cost it $12 per ton.[82]

Most important, the office director had written that a price increase as high as $12 per ton would have a host of negative knock-on effects. Violating "all our standards," it would encourage other industries to seek similar treatment and so undermine the "health of our entire economy."[83]

President Truman shared this concern about seriously damaging the government's price stabilization efforts; for this reason, he was willing to countenance a small increase (of about $4.50), but the steel firms refused it.[84]

Fourth, the President might try personally to persuade the companies to accept the wage board's recommendations by meeting with them or, failing that, by using "strong-arm" tactics, like threats of anti-trust or securities fraud investigations. Indeed, when presidents tried them in the 1960s, such tactics would prove effective.[85] But in the 1950s, with his popularity declining, this President worried that strong-arming industry might haunt his party in the coming presidential campaign. He would try his powers of personal persuasion, but the companies remained unmoved.[86]

Fifth, the President might ask Congress to act. He hesitated to try this, being uncertain how Congress would respond, owing again to the forthcoming election. Truman knew that Congress, reflecting its constituents' divided views about individual labor-management disputes, often preferred compromise.[87] Besides, time was running out. Though he could not count on Congress to fix the problem, he would eventually ask it to ratify his final decision with legislation.[88] Which brings us to his sixth option, the one Truman took.

Sixth, he could simply seize the steel mills. It would mean that the American flag would fly above the plants while the existing executive staff and workers remained in place. Unlike an injunction, a seizure would not freeze current wages; the government could insist upon an immediate increase, thus allowing production to continue while bargaining with management dragged on. Changing the terms of employment in the workers' favor would also put pressure on the companies to compromise further, increasing the likelihood of reaching a contract agreement.[89] And it had worked before: Lincoln had seized companies during the Civil War and Wilson during World War I. To prevent similar work stoppages just prior to and during World War II, Roosevelt and Truman had undertaken some fifty-nine of the eighty-five presidential seizures in the nation's history, and Truman alone would implement twelve more in the war's immediate aftermath.[90]

Truman warned negotiators in New York on Tuesday, April 8, that barring a settlement by four p.m., he would take "extraordinary action."[91] After meeting with his advisers and concluding that the companies would not accept a price increase of $4.50, he told the secretary of commerce, Charles Sawyer, that he would have to seize the mills.[92] At ten-thirty that evening the President announced publicly that steel "is vital to the defense effort," that a work stoppage would harm our "soldiers at the front in Korea," and that the steel companies, all highly profitable, were insisting upon "outrageous" price hikes. It was not simply a matter "between the Government and a few greedy companies" but a threat affecting everyone. "If we gave in . . . you could say goodbye to stabilization," for "prices would start jumping up all around us." At "midnight," he said, "the Government will take over the steel plants," after which "[b]oth management and labor will then be working for the Government."[93]

There immediately followed an executive order directing the secretary of commerce to "take possession of and operate" the steel companies.[94] Truman simultaneously sent a message to Congress stating that "immediate Congressional action" was not "essential," but it would be "very desirable" to have legislative ratification of the seizure.[95] Secretary Sawyer issued the seizure orders.

The immediate reactions were much as foreseen. The union's president, Philip Murray, wrote the secretary that he had ordered members "to continue at work."[96] Inland Steel's president, Clarence Randall, issued a statement strongly arguing the companies' position while accusing "Harry S. Truman, the man," of acting "without the slightest shadow of legal right"; of having "seize[d] private property" and so indulging in a form of "tyranny" that the Constitution "was adopted . . . to prevent."[97] Press and congressional reactions were primarily hostile.[98]

THE COURTS' PERSPECTIVE: THE LOWER COURTS

The morning after the seizure, the steel companies filed a lawsuit. They asked Judge Alexander Holtzoff, a federal district judge sitting in the District of Columbia, to issue a temporary restraining order that would leave the companies in control of the mills while they litigated the President's authority to seize them.[99] Judge Holtzoff denied the request. He wrote that, without "vital reason," he would not "nullify an order of the President of the United States, promulgated by him to meet a nation-wide emergency."[100] He added that if the seizure turned out to be unlawful, the companies could eventually obtain damages from the government.[101]

A few days later the President sent another letter to Congress, in which he said that while he found seizure "thoroughly distasteful," he thought the "available alternatives" were "even worse." A Taft-Hartley injunction would in a sense have only triggered what was already in train—namely, fact-finding and a strike delay. But while accomplishing the delay that way would have helped the companies, the workers properly would have resented it. Truman asked Congress, "in the light of the critical situation which confronts this country and the whole free world," to "indicate by legislation . . . what *should* be done."[102] The Senate passed a bill that would have cut off funding for the seizure, but this was purely symbolic, as the seizure required no funds anyway.[103]

On April 20 Secretary Sawyer announced the wage increase.[104] That brought the companies back into court. They asked a different federal court judge, Judge David A. Pine, to issue preliminary injunctions that would block the government from acting on Truman's executive order or at the very least forbid it from changing the conditions and terms of employment.[105]

At an April 24 hearing, Assistant Attorney General Holmes Baldridge and Judge Pine discussed the President's constitutional authority to seize the mills and to raise wages. Here is the key element in that exchange:

MR. BALDRIDGE: We say that when an emergency situation in this country arises . . . [and] something has to be done about it and has to be done now, and there is no statutory provision for handling the matter, that it is the duty of the Executive to step in and protect the national security and the national interests. We say that Article II of the Constitution, [which] provides that the Executive power . . . shall reside in the President, that . . . he shall be Commander-in-Chief of the Army and of the Navy . . . [is] sufficient to permit him to meet any national emergency that might arise, be it peace time, technical war time, or actual war time.

THE COURT: So you contend the Executive has unlimited power in time of an emergency?

MR. BALDRIDGE: He has the power to take such action as is necessary to meet the emergency.

THE COURT: If the emergency is great, it is unlimited, is it?

MR. BALDRIDGE: I suppose if you carry it to its logical conclusion that is true. But I do want to point out that there are two limitations on the Executive power. One is the ballot box and the other is impeachment.

THE COURT: Then, as I understand it, you claim that in time of emergency the Executive has this great power.

MR. BALDRIDGE: That is correct.[106]

On April 29 Judge Pine ruled that the executive could not seize the mills. He pointed out that no statute authorized the action; that the Constitution granted the President no inherent emergency power that would allow him to do so; and that a later damage payment would not compensate the companies for their losses. He issued an injunction requiring the secretary of commerce to return the mills to their owners.[107] The companies had won what Bethlehem Steel counsel Bruce Bromley described as "the whole hog."[108]

Events then moved quickly. The government immediately appealed.

The next day the court of appeals issued a stay. Three days after that, on May 3, the Supreme Court (over the objection of Justices Felix Frankfurter and Harold Burton) exercised its power to take the case before the court of appeals could reach a final decision. It also issued an interim order permitting the seizure to continue, though without the wage increases—a fact that destroyed the companies' incentive to negotiate a settlement. All parties filed their briefs by May 10, and the Court then quickly heard argument on May 12 and 13.[109]

THE COURTS' PERSPECTIVE: THE SUPREME COURT DECISION

On June 2, three weeks after hearing oral argument, the Court announced its decision, finding that President Truman's seizures had violated the Constitution. The vote was six to three.

Justice Hugo Black wrote in the Court's opinion that the Constitution does not grant the President "lawmaking" power. Rather, the Founders "entrusted the lawmaking power to the Congress alone in both good and bad times."[110] Clearly Congress had passed no law authorizing the President "expressly" or by implication to "take possession of property as he did here."[111] Nor did the Constitution grant the President, in his role as "Commander in Chief of the Armed Forces," the power "as such to take possession of private property in order to keep labor disputes from stopping production."[112] Thus the President, in seizing the mills, acted beyond his constitutional authority.

The four other justices who joined this opinion found it incomplete. Justice Frankfurter, for example, wrote that "the considerations relevant to the legal enforcement of the principle of separation of powers" were "more complicated and flexible than may appear from what Mr. Justice Black has written."[113] For his part, Justice William O. Douglas reasoned that the heart of the matter was that the mill owners must receive compensation for the seizure of their property; since only Congress could raise the revenues necessary to pay compensation, only Congress could authorize the seizure.[114]

Justice Robert Jackson added what history has shown to be the most important concurring opinion, in which he set forth an important, now well-known analysis dividing presidential action into three categories:

Category one: "When the President acts pursuant to an express or implied authorization of Congress, his authority is at its maximum, for it includes all that he possesses in his own right plus all that Congress can delegate."[115]

Category two: "When the President acts in absence of either a congressional grant or denial of authority, he can only rely upon his own independent powers, but there is a zone of twilight in which he and Congress may have concurrent authority, or in which its distribution is uncertain. . . . In this area, any actual test of power is likely to depend on the imperatives of events and contemporary imponderables, rather than on abstract theories of law."[116]

Category three: "When the President takes measures incompatible with the expressed or implied will of Congress, his power is at its lowest ebb, for then he can rely only upon his own constitutional powers minus any constitutional powers of Congress over the matter. . . . Presidential claim to a power at once so conclusive and preclusive must be scrutinized with caution."[117]

Justice Jackson went on to argue that presidential power to seize the mills fell within the third category, action congressionally proscribed. Congress had "never authorized the seizure here."[118] Rather, it had implicitly forbidden the President to take that action by creating "statutory policies inconsistent with this seizure."[119]

Justice Frankfurter agreed. He conceded that the Court should not rule "on a constitutional issue" if the case might "be decided without even considering delicate problems of power under the Constitution."[120] But he saw no way to resolve this case without considering the constitutionality of the seizure. That being so, he found, like Justice Jackson, that the case fell into category three. When Congress passed the Taft-Hartley Act, it had considered giving the President emergency seizure power, but it had not done so.[121] In a lengthy appendix, Justice Frankfurter listed almost one hundred instances in which presidents had seized companies during wartime, but he claimed that only three occurred "in circumstances comparable to the present," too few to show an "inherent" presidential power to seize.[122] Justice Burton seemed to agree with Justices Jackson and Frankfurter, for he wrote to emphasize that with Taft-Hartley, Congress had "prescribed for the President specific procedures, *exclusive of seizure,* for his use in meeting the present type of emergency."[123]

Justice Tom Clark agreed with the Court's result, but he did not join Justice Black's opinion. He said only that the President, to deal with an emergency, should have followed the procedures set forth in Taft-Hartley, the Defense Production Act, or the Selective Service Act.[124]

How convincing are these reasons? Did Congress in fact forbid the President to seize the mills? In a dissenting opinion (joined by Justices Sherman Minton and Stanley Reed), Chief Justice Fred Vinson said that he could find no such thing. Indeed, while numerous statutes called for war-related steel production, no statute prohibited the President from using an inherent power of seizure to ensure that production continued during an emergency.[125]

True, the Taft-Hartley Act addressed the problem of emergency strike action directly, providing a set of tools that the President could use to avert a strike during an emergency (including the eighty-day injunction and referral to a fact-finding board); seizure was not one of them. Still, nowhere was it forbidden; the act said nothing implicitly or explicitly to limit any inherent presidential wartime authority.[126] Senator Robert A. Taft, one of the law's sponsors, did tell the Senate that the law's authors had decided not to list seizure because they did not think the President should exercise that power.[127] But though an important senator and son of a former President, Taft was just one among the ninety-six senators in the 80th Congress.

At the same time, two other statutes explicitly gave the President the power to seize private property. The Selective Service Act authorized him to place orders for defense-related matériel and, if necessary to ensure the orders were filled, to seize the firms.[128] Likewise, the Defense Production Act gave him the power to condemn property for defense purposes, while specifying a complex set of procedures that the executive must follow to ensure payment of just compensation.[129] If the President could have used the authority granted by these statutes, he chose not to, being on the one hand uncertain whether the Selective Service Act provision applied to strikes and on the other short of the time necessary to comply with the Defense Production Act's condemnation procedures.[130] For our purposes, however, what matters is that neither statute says anything about restricting the President's use of any inherent power. One could read them as endorsing the use of inherent power in an emergency in which time does not permit compliance with the statutes' procedures as easily as one could read them to forbid that use. But why infer congressional hostility rather than indifference? The legislative context suggests that the seizure fell within Justice Jackson's second, more ambiguous category, not his third.[131]

What about the security-related emergency? In his executive order, the President had found that "a work stoppage would immediately jeopardize and imperil our national defense and the defense of those joined with us in resisting aggression, and would add to the continuing danger of our soldiers, sailors, and airmen engaged in combat in the field."[132] To avert these dangers, it was "necessary that the United States take possession of and operate the plants, facilities, and other property [of the steel industry]."[133]

The secretary of defense, the chairman of the Atomic Energy Commission, the administrator of the National Production Authority, the secretary of commerce, and the secretary of the interior all filed detailed affidavits with the Court setting forth facts and figures supporting the same conclusions, which they'd already presented to the President (as his memoirs attest). How could the Court have believed that the emergency, which included threats to our armed forces, was not real?[134]

Moreover, Chief Justice Vinson listed many instances of presidential action to deal with an emergency absent explicit statutory or constitutional authority, ranging from Lincoln's calling up of troops at the start of the Civil War, and President Hayes's use of federal troops during the Railroad Strike of 1877, down to President Roosevelt's sending forces to occupy Iceland, President Truman's action to repel aggression in Korea, and several of the labor relations-related seizures listed in Justice Frankfurter's opinion.[135]

The Court may have thought that, were the emergency to become severe, Congress would act. But President Truman believed that he could not rely upon Congress. Time was short, the politics unfavorable, and the risks of military harm too great. Indeed, as Chief Justice Vinson pointed out, Congress, without ever denying the facts set forth in the cabinet's affidavits, had not yet reacted to the President's two messages sent several weeks before.[136]

If the opinion is hard to comprehend in terms of the legalistic tit-for-tat, a broader perspective may be helpful. The Court was aware of the sway of Cicero's dictum; of *Curtiss-Wright*'s affirmation of broad inherent presidential powers in wartime and over foreign affairs; and of how *Korematsu*, and other cases, had found almost limitless presidential power during wartime. But the Court was also alert to the unhappy consequences of some of those cases, particularly *Korematsu*, which may have inspired it to change direction. If so, we can understand this case to be of fundamental importance as an instance of the Court asserting an authority to impose a limit upon the scope of the President's emergency wartime powers.

In doing so, the Court could not expect to, and indeed did not, find much guidance about imposing such limits from the history of the founding or that of presidential action. Neither the examples of the Founders nor those of later history clearly indicated whether, or how, the Court should impose limits.

Alexander Hamilton once wrote that the "EXECUTIVE POWER" that the Constitution vests in the President is broader than its subsequent grant of power "to take care that the laws be faithfully executed."[137] Reading this, Thomas Jefferson wrote to James Madison: "For God's sake, my dear Sir, take up your pen . . . and cut him to pieces."[138]

President Theodore Roosevelt once said that it was "not only" the President's "right but his duty to do anything that the needs of the nation demanded unless such action was forbidden by the Constitution or by the laws. . . . I did and caused to be done many things not previously done by the President and the heads of the departments. I did not usurp power, but I did greatly broaden the use of executive power."[139]

To this, President William Howard Taft replied that

the President can exercise no power which cannot be fairly and reasonably traced to some specific grant of power or justly implied and included within such express grant. . . . There is no undefined residuum of power which he can exercise because it seems to him to be in the public interest.[140]

As we have seen, President Franklin Roosevelt told the nation that should Congress fail to give him the power to fight wartime inflation,

I shall accept the responsibility, and I will act. . . . The President has the powers . . . to take measures necessary to avert a disaster which would interfere with the winning of the war. . . . This total war . . . makes the use of the executive power far more essential than in any previous war. . . . And when the war is won, the powers under which I act will automatically revert to the people of the United States—to the people to whom those powers belong.[141]

We should expect presidents to make broad assertions of presidential authority, especially during an emergency, when in the rush of immediate events they face immediate problems requiring immediate solutions. The Court, by contrast, playing a different institutional role, can and must take a longer view, looking back to the Founding, across the nation's history, and sometimes into the unforeseeable future. No matter how limited an opinion the justices try to write, their holdings will be taken as precedent, perhaps for a very long time.

Justice Jackson himself referred to these institutional differences during oral argument, when the government attorney pointed out that the justice had, as attorney general, supported President Roosevelt's seizure of the North American Aviation plant during a strike, for which he had no specific statutory authority. Jackson replied candidly, "I claimed everything, of course, like every other Attorney General does. It was a custom that did not leave the Department of Justice when I did."[142] He might have cited Assistant Attorney General Baldridge's statement to Judge Pine, claiming that presidential emergency powers were virtually unlimited, but he did not. In fact, much in Justice Jackson's opinion suggests that he saw a need to check such assertions.

Judges are inevitably creatures of their times, and the *Steel Seizure* justices had just seen totalitarian regimes destroy individual liberty in Europe. While they did not necessarily fear the rise of an American dictator, knowledge of what had happened to other democratic societies must have been sobering.

Thus the most important features of the majority opinion and concurrences are likely those that express a general concern about concentration of power.

Jackson spoke directly of the experience of foreign nations with provisions for emergency powers. He pointed out that "Germany, after the First World War, framed the Weimar Constitution" in a way that permitted the president "to suspend any or all individual rights if public safety and order were seriously disturbed or endangered." And once "Hitler persuaded President Von Hindenberg to suspend all such rights," they "were never restored." The Allied powers presented a crucial contrast.

The French Republic also provided for an emergency government; but what it referred to as a "state of siege" could be authorized only by parliament. Great Britain similarly "fought both World Wars under a sort of temporary dictatorship," but it, too, was "created by legislation."[143]

This experience, he said, indicates "that emergency powers are consistent with free government only when their control is lodged elsewhere than in the Executive who exercises them."[144] The President's actual power is vast. As Woodrow Wilson pointed out, if the President "rightly interpret[s] the national thought and boldly insist[s] upon it, he is irresistible."[145] And so Jackson found it difficult to believe that "this country will suffer if the Court refuses further to aggrandize the presidential office, already so potent and so relatively immune from judicial review."[146] "No one," he wrote,

> perhaps not even the President, knows the limits of the power he may seek to exert in this instance, and the parties affected cannot learn the limit of their rights. We do not know today what powers over labor or property would be claimed to flow from Government possession if we should legalize it.[147]

The American constitutional "technique" for dealing with emergencies is for Congress to enact a statute that expands "normal executive powers," and Congress has done so many times.[148]

If the reader can find no clear legal line, no specific limit, in the Court's opinion, perhaps that is as the Court intended. According to his own notes on the justices' conference after oral argument, Justice Jackson believed that the Court should affirm the issuance of the injunction while "doing [as] little damage as possible." He found the President's position "untenable"; Justice Douglas recalls Jackson's complaining that "the Department of Justice has been demoralized. The crowd that wants to claim everything has taken over."[149]

Perhaps it is unsurprising that the Court should have imposed limits without defining their precise nature. Justice Jackson opened the second paragraph of his opinion with these words:

> A judge … may be surprised at the poverty of really useful and unambiguous authority applicable to concrete problems of

executive power as they actually present themselves. Just what our forefathers did envision, or would have envisioned had they foreseen modern conditions, must be divined from materials almost as enigmatic as the dreams Joseph was called upon to interpret for Pharaoh. A century and a half of partisan debate and scholarly speculation yields no net result but only supplies more or less apt quotations from respected sources on each side of any question. They largely cancel each other. And court decisions are indecisive because of the judicial practice of dealing with the largest questions in the most narrow way.[150]

In my own view, the *Steel Seizure* case, even if read narrowly, represents a major change in the Court's approach to the President's emergency powers. Occasionally a prior case—*Milligan,* some of the language in *Quirin*—had pointed to court-enforced limits. But in the *Steel Seizure* case, the Court both held that limits existed and analyzed the matter in detail. Its conclusion: better the indeterminacy of Pharaoh's dreams than a judicial ratification of presidential emergency power without limits.

AFTERWORD

On June 2, 1952, immediately after the Court announced its decision, the President ordered Secretary Sawyer to release the mills to their owners. The unions immediately went out on strike. Over the next few weeks negotiators and government officials met at the White House. The Office of Price Stabilization said it would authorize a $5.20-per-ton increase (including $4.50 then required by the Capehart Amendment plus $0.70 to account for an increase in freight costs). And the parties agreed on most, but not all, issues.[151]

In the meantime, the President appeared before Congress, asking for legislative authority to seize the mills, which, as he had predicted, Congress refused to give.[152]

On the strike's fifty-first day, Secretary of Defense Lovett announced that the loss of steel production had caused more harm than the worst possible enemy bombing raid. Two days later the parties settled, on terms very similar to those the wage board had originally suggested: a wage increase of 16 cents per hour and fringe benefits costing another

5.4 cents per hour. The government approved a $5.20-per-ton price increase, 30 cents less than the $5.50 Charles Wilson had suggested several months before.[153]

The strike led some plants to stop production of mortars and artillery shells,[154] at a cost of 16 to 20 million ingot tons of steel that might have been used to create more munitions.[155] There was diminished production in other industries dependent upon steel, and the action undercut the government's wage and price stabilization policies, in addition to idling about a million workers.[156] Yet a study conducted in 1953 by the government's National Production Authority concluded that the stoppage had "had surprisingly little effect upon the economy as a whole." Even the vital industries rebounded, with the government reporting that "deliveries of planes, tanks, guns and ammunition for defense reached a new peak in July," and "defense-rated" steel shipments, which accounted for about half of all steel shipments, rose continuously. The report concluded that the steel strike had a "very minor effect . . . upon defense-rated shipments."[157]

Most observers believe that the catastrophe the administration feared did not come to pass. Perhaps that was because companies producing defense-related goods had made conservative estimates, emphasizing the risks of harm. Perhaps, too, human ingenuity found ways around steel-production bottlenecks, with employers and employees acting imaginatively, devising solutions to threatened shortages. If the Court thought that the emergency was not a serious one, it turned out to be right. But the administration had acted in good faith in raising the alarm. And no judge could have disbelieved its calculations at the time.

Ultimately, what appears to have led to the holding was not a discrediting of the administration's factual assertions about steel production, or even the Court's own factual conclusions. Rather, it was a discomfort on the part of several justices with the way presidential power had been exercised, perhaps reminding them of the circumstances of *Korematsu*. Marking an important shift in its national security jurisprudence, the Court in *Steel Seizure* asserted it was now in the business of reviewing the President's wartime authority, on which it would hereafter enforce limits.

CHAPTER 4

"No Blank Check"

Guantanamo

In 2004, 2006, and 2008 the Court decided four cases arising out of the detention of enemy combatants at Guantanamo Bay Naval Base in Cuba. The cases required the Court to balance competing constitutional interests, security needs, and civil liberties protections. How did the Court proceed? The *Steel Seizure* case showed that the more closely the Court would oversee a presidential decision regarding security, the more urgent the need to understand the President's perspective. That such understanding might be difficult to obtain did not lead the Court to return to *Curtiss-Wright*, to simply reaffirm presidential action, or to revert to earlier decisions inspired by Cicero. Rather, in the years following *Steel Seizure*, the Court had shown itself ready to follow the path there marked out, as when it protected the *New York Times*'s decision to publish classified material from the Pentagon Papers during the Vietnam War.[1]

By the time of the Guantanamo cases, too, there had been a broader change in perception of the federal judiciary's role in American society, on the part of both the Court and the general public. That change supported greater federal court efforts to protect civil liberties, even when the effect was to limit the President's security-related powers. Since 1954 and *Brown v. Board of Education,* the Court had helped to end legal racial segregation in America. It had presided over a "due process" revolution, applying protections of the Bill of Rights to restrictions imposed not just by the federal government but by the states as well: it had insisted that criminal defendants be represented by counsel, that police inform arrested persons of their constitutional rights to remain silent and to have a lawyer, and that the press enjoy greater freedom deciding what to print.[2] Thus the Supreme Court came to be seen as an institution engaged in interpreting and enforcing such constitutional protections, amid a consensus that this was a proper role for it.

At the same time, the need for nation-states to protect basic individual liberties, and to rely on national (or international) court systems in doing so, had also become a priority throughout much of the world. In 1949, following World War II, the United States signed conventions in Geneva providing basic protections for prisoners of war, which have since been ratified by 196 nations.[3] More than that: in 1948 the United Nations adopted the Universal Declaration of Human Rights, which outlines fundamental freedoms guaranteed to all persons.[4] The Council of Europe created a Human Rights Court in Strasbourg in 1959, which has since adjudicated more than ten thousand claims of human rights violations made by citizens of almost fifty nations.[5] Also during the postwar period, the United States and hundreds of other nations signed conventions on torture, genocide, and the rights of children;[6] nations created regional human rights courts with authority to hear cases arising in North America, South America, and parts of Africa;[7] and countries with new constitutions—for example, Poland, South Africa, and India—wrote human rights protections into them, authorizing courts to enforce those rights.[8] All this indicates a widespread public acceptance of the role of courts as guarantors of basic freedoms.

In the years leading up to the Guantanamo cases, the move in American legal doctrine toward increased protection of constitutional order and basic liberties came to include protection in times of national security threat. As we have seen, Cicero had lost his influence, and the force of the "political question" doctrine had largely dissipated (even though the Court would refuse to decide whether the Vietnam War was constitutional). *Steel Seizure* had made it clear that even during a military conflict, the President's authority to act was not absolute.

This is the background of the Guantanamo cases. They show the Court determined to enforce a Constitution that does not give the President a blank check. Civil liberties would now be understood to have a weight that needed to be balanced against security. To appreciate the grounds for, and importance of, these conclusions, we must examine the four cases.

UNDERLYING CIRCUMSTANCES

The background facts are well known. In September 2001 a group of Al Qaeda terrorists hijacked four commercial airplanes, with which they managed to destroy New York's World Trade Center and to demolish a portion of the Pentagon. In so doing, they killed nearly three thousand Americans.

As a result, Congress authorized the President to use "all necessary and appropriate force against those nations, organizations, or persons he determines planned, authorized, committed, or aided the terrorist attacks . . . or harbored such organizations or persons."[9]

Shortly thereafter, the President sent American troops to Afghanistan to fight against the Taliban government and the Al Qaeda forces it had harbored. During the fighting (which would continue for more than thirteen years), and in subsequent conflicts in Iraq and elsewhere, the American military captured and screened thousands of suspected members of the Taliban, Al Qaeda, and other terrorist groups. Military authorities sent almost eight hundred of those captured to a detention camp located on the American naval base at Guantanamo Bay, Cuba. The military questioned them there and initially kept the vast majority imprisoned. Since 2004, the government has released many of the detainees. Still, as of 2015, about 120 remain confined.[10]

The government considered Guantanamo to be a facility located outside the United States. Largely for that reason, the authorities believed that the detainees would not have "the opportunity to contest their detention in the U.S. courts."[11] But lawyers for the detainees soon began to challenge that proposition.

By early 2002, advocates of the detainees—at times their lawyers and at times relations—began appearing on their behalf as "next friends," petitioning federal courts to issue writs of habeas corpus. The petitioners argued that federal authorities were holding the prisoners in violation of the Constitution and the laws of the United States.[12]

Most of the lower courts denied the petitions, often on grounds familiar since the Civil War: variations on the theme that a court lacks the legal power to compel the military to release an alien prisoner held outside the sovereign territory of the United States.[13]

The courts did not uniformly answer the questions presented, taking various positions on such questions as: Do the federal courts possess the power to issue a writ of habeas corpus to a Guantanamo detainee? Can the President put a captured terrorist suspect on trial before a special military tribunal? What kind of procedural rights, if any, does the Constitution provide a prisoner who claims he is not an enemy combatant but, say, a peaceful Afghan farmer? Cases presenting these questions slowly made their way to the Supreme Court.

RASUL AND HAMDI

The Court decided the first two Guantanamo cases in 2004. In *Rasul v. Bush* a group of detainees from Kuwait and Australia, captured in Afghanistan, claimed that they were not enemy combatants but humanitarian aid workers whom the American army had imprisoned by mistake. The question presented was whether courts had the power even to consider the prisoners' claims.[14]

Why would they not have that power? The detainees claimed that their jailer, the executive branch, was holding them contrary to federal law. As we have seen, U.S. judges have long had the power to issue a writ of habeas corpus, ordering the executive branch, like the English kings of old, to release an unlawfully held prisoner. If, upon examination, a judge should find the circumstances of Rasul's detention unlawful, why should he not have the power to order his release, in accordance with (in the words of the Magna Carta) "the law of the land"?

The problem was that Congress had enacted a statute saying that writs of habeas corpus could be granted by Supreme Court justices, by individual district courts, and by individual circuit judges *"within their respective jurisdictions."*[15] The government argued that these words imposed a geographic restriction on the issuance of the writ to the judge's specific districts; Guantanamo Bay, Cuba (where no federal judge sits), was in no judge's jurisdiction. In addition to the statute, the government pointed to the fact that the petitioners were aliens, which, as earlier cases had all shown, had also put their claims beyond the power of the Court to consider.[16]

In the second case, *Hamdi v. Rumsfeld*, an American citizen, brought up in Saudi Arabia, was captured by American forces during fighting in Afghanistan. After being held captive in Afghanistan and Guantanamo Bay, he was eventually transferred to a naval prison in Virginia, then moved again to another in South Carolina. He, too, claimed to be not an enemy combatant but a relief worker. The government responded with a written statement, signed by an army official, attesting that Hamdi had been "affiliated with a Taliban military unit," had "received weapons training," had "engaged in battle," and had "surrender[ed] his Kalashnikov assault rifle" to the Northern Alliance forces who captured him.[17]

Both sides agreed that Hamdi, as an American citizen held in the United States, could file a habeas corpus petition in a federal district court and that, if he was being held contrary to law, the court could provide appropriate relief.[18] But was the navy holding Hamdi unlawfully? That depended upon whether the government had provided him sufficiently fair procedure and given him a fair chance to make his case.

The Court issued its decisions in both cases on the same day, June 28, 2004. In *Rasul*, the Court, by a vote of six to three, rejected the President's claim that 28 U.S.C. § 2241, the relevant habeas corpus statute, imposed a geographical limitation preventing any federal judge from issuing a writ of habeas corpus to detainees held in Guantanamo Bay; the Court held, rather, that the statute authorized judges in the jurisdiction where the respondent, the President, lived—namely, the District of Columbia—to hear the case.[19] In reaching this conclusion, Justice Stevens, writing for the Court, emphasized the historical purpose of the writ as a protector of liberty. He quoted Justice Jackson:

> Executive imprisonment has been considered oppressive and lawless since John, at Runnymede, pledged that no free man should be imprisoned, dispossessed, outlawed, or exiled save by the judgment of his peers or by the law of the land. The judges of England developed the writ of habeas corpus largely to preserve these immunities from executive restraint.[20]

Rejecting the idea that "enemy combatants" fall outside the statute's scope, Justice John Paul Stevens pointed to *Quirin*, the case in which the Court considered habeas petitions filed by the German saboteurs who had landed in the United States by submarine during World War II. A military tribunal had tried and convicted them. But it was ordinary

federal courts that heard their habeas corpus challenges, assuming jurisdiction irrespective of the fact that they had been found to have violated the laws of war.[21] Justice Stevens also referred to peacetime cases in
which alien citizens had been "permitted to resort to the courts for the
redress of wrongs and the protection of their rights."[22]

The Court further held that Cuba's possession of legal "sovereignty"
over Guantanamo did not prevent the federal courts from hearing the
case. Referring to English cases, the Court found that the reach of the
habeas writ depends "not on formal notions of territorial sovereignty,
but rather on the practical question of 'the exact extent and nature of
the jurisdiction or dominion exercised in fact'" by the government.[23]
And international agreements with Cuba make clear that the United
States "exercises complete jurisdiction and control over the Guantanamo Base." The United States has the right, under these agreements,
to continue to exercise full control permanently, if it wishes.[24]

A World War II case, *Johnson v. Eisentrager,* posed a more difficult
problem. There the Court had held that it could *not* consider the habeas
corpus petitions filed in the United States by twenty-one German citizens convicted of war crimes by a military commission in China, and
imprisoned in occupied Germany. The government argued that this
case amounted to binding precedent.[25]

The *Rasul* majority concluded, however, that the present case was
different. Each prisoner in *Eisentrager*

(a) [was] an enemy alien; (b) ha[d] never been or resided in
the United States; (c) was captured outside of our territory and
there held in military custody as a prisoner of war; (d) was tried
and convicted by a Military Commission sitting outside the
United States; (e) for offenses against laws of war committed
outside the United States; (f) and [was] at all times imprisoned
outside the United States.[26]

In *Rasul,* the Court said, factors (d), (e), and (f) were missing. The petitioners had not been convicted of war crimes (or even appeared before
any tribunal), and they were imprisoned at Guantanamo, which is not
"outside the United States."[27]

Finally, the Court made clear that it held only that the detainees
could bring their claims to court; it did not say who would win.[28]

Justice Anthony Kennedy, concurring in a separate opinion, made two important points: First, unlike the location of the prison in *Eisentrager* (Germany), Guantanamo Bay "is in every practical respect a United States territory, and it is one far removed from any hostilities."[29] Second, the detainees "are being held indefinitely, and without benefit of any legal proceeding to determine their status."[30] He approached the problem with a sliding scale. "Perhaps," he said, "where detainees are taken from a zone of hostilities, detention without proceedings or trial would be justified by military necessity for a matter of weeks; but as the period of detention stretches from months to years, the case for continued detention to meet military exigencies becomes weaker."[31]

Three justices dissented, arguing that since Cuba possessed legal "sovereignty" over Guantanamo, Guantanamo was a "foreign land." American and English courts, they said, had not issued, and should not issue, writs of habeas corpus on behalf of aliens in foreign lands.[32] They added that the most direct precedent, *Eisentrager*, required the Court to side with the government.[33] And, they said, the majority's contrary view would have permitted millions of World War II enemy combatants to file habeas corpus petitions in American courts. In the future, the Court's holding would allow numerous others to do so, and so the Court had risked seriously interfering with the President's ability to conduct a foreign war.[34]

The Court also decided the second case, *Hamdi*, against the government.[35] As an American citizen held in a military prison in South Carolina, Hamdi had every right to file a habeas corpus petition. But was his detention against the law of the United States? Can the President, in time of hostilities, detain an American citizen as an "enemy combatant"?

A majority of five members thought yes. Though an American citizen, Hamdi was fighting against the United States.[36] In *Quirin*, the Court had upheld the imprisonment of an American citizen fighting for the German army, who had come back to the United States during wartime bent on sabotage.[37] Thus, under *Quirin*, Hamdi could be held as an "enemy combatant." But the detention of an enemy combatant, according to the laws of war, "may last no longer than active hostilities."[38]

Four members of the Court disagreed, concluding that the President could not hold an American citizen as an enemy combatant. Two of the four thought the President lacked the statutory authority to do so,[39] and two thought he lacked the constitutional authority.[40] The latter two, Justices John Paul Stevens and Antonin Scalia, thought that the government could not simply detain an American citizen who was also an enemy combatant. Rather, it must bring him to trial for criminal behavior, or it must release him.[41]

A second question in *Hamdi* pertained to due process. The majority, as I have just said, held that the government could detain, for the duration of hostilities, an enemy combatant who was also an American citizen. But was Hamdi really an enemy combatant? Again, he had denied the government's factual contentions, claiming he had engaged only in peaceful activities. The question therefore arose, "[W]hat process is constitutionally due to a citizen who disputes his enemy-combatant status[?]"[42]

The government argued that "'[r]espect for separation of powers and the limited institutional capabilities of courts in matters of military decision-making in connection with an ongoing conflict' ought to eliminate," or at least minimize, a court's consideration of "any individual process."[43] Courts could perhaps review "whether legal authorization exists for the broader detention scheme," but they should not second-guess individual detention decisions; and if they did, it should be only under a highly deferential standard of review—asking whether "some evidence" supported the executive's decision.[44]

The Court denied the government's claims. Justice Sandra Day O'Connor wrote for a plurality of four members, with two of the concurring justices agreeing with the due process portion of her opinion, thus providing six votes for its holding.[45] In rejecting the government's due process argument, Justice O'Connor spelled out the general problem that the Court faces when security needs and civil liberties conflict. The Constitution recognizes, she wrote, that "core strategic matters of warmaking belong in the hands of those who are best positioned and most politically accountable for making them,"[46] and courts must take account of legitimate military concerns, such as the need for commanders in battle to focus upon the war, not upon burdensome litigation back home.[47] But the Constitution also establishes as "fundamental" a "citizen's right to be free from involuntary confinement by his own government without due process of law."[48] Consequently, the Court must "weigh the opposing governmental interests against the curtailment of liberty that such confinement entails."[49] Doing so, Justice O'Connor said, leads to the conclusion that the executive cannot "erode[]" the "fundamental . . . right to notice and an opportunity to be heard."[50] Those rights must be "granted at a meaningful time and in a meaningful manner."[51] And a "citizen-detainee" challenging his classification as an enemy combatant must "receive notice of the factual basis for his classification, and a fair opportunity to rebut the Government's factual assertions before a neutral decisionmaker."[52] As for other elements of due process, "enemy combatant proceedings may be tailored to alleviate their uncommon potential to burden the Executive at a time of ongoing military conflict."[53]

The government's more extreme position (i.e., that courts can review only entire detention schemes but not individual detention determinations), Justice O'Connor added, "cannot be mandated by any reasonable view of separation of powers."[54] It "serves only to *condense* power into a single branch of government." Referring to *Steel Seizure,* she concluded that the Court had "long since made clear that *a state of war is not a blank check for the President when it comes to the rights of the Nation's citizens.*"[55]

HAMDAN

In 2006 the Court considered a third Guantanamo case, that of *Hamdan v. Rumsfeld.*[56] Salim Ahmed Hamdan was a Yemeni national captured in Afghanistan and confined at Guantanamo Bay. The government brought him to trial before a special military commission, charging him with conspiracy—that is, conspiring with other members of Al Qaeda to attack civilians, to commit murder, and to engage in terrorism.[57] In particular, the government alleged that Hamdan had acted as "bodyguard and personal driver" for Osama Bin Laden, had transported Al Qaeda weapons, had driven Osama Bin Laden to Al Qaeda training camps, and had received weapons training.[58] The question before the Supreme Court was whether the government could lawfully try Hamdan before a special military commission created by executive order.[59] Such a commission could (in the interests of "national security") provide less procedural protection for defendants than ordinary courts—say, by excluding a defendant from its proceedings so that it could privately hear and consider certain evidence.[60]

By a five-to-four vote, the Court held that the government's use of these special military commissions was unlawful, the opinion referring back to *In re Milligan,* the case about a military trial of Indiana civilians, which the Court had decided just after the Civil War. Chief Justice Salmon P. Chase then wrote that, but for instances of "controlling necessity," the power during war to "institute tribunals for the trial and punishment of offences" belonged to Congress, not to the President acting without delegated authority.[61]

Indeed, Congress had not enacted any statute directly authorizing the President to use such a commission for Guantanamo prisoners. The statute most directly in point said only that the jurisdiction of "courts-martial" was "not exclusive," while adding that "military commissions" could be used "in respect of offenders or offenses that [1] *by statute or* [2] *by the law of war* may be tried by . . . other military tribunals."[62] As to the first, both parties agreed that the conduct charged—namely, participating in a conspiracy that took place in Afghanistan or other foreign countries—violated no statute. And after examining in detail the history of military commissions, the Court concluded that the *"law of war"* did not permit "military tribunals" where the crime in question consisted of a conspiracy that took place *before* hostilities had even begun outside any "theater of war."[63]

Moreover, the Uniform Code of Military Justice said that courts-martial procedures and military commission procedures shall "insofar as practicable" be "uniform" and similar to those of ordinary criminal courts.[64] The Court pointed out procedural divergence in the rules the President was attempting to follow: commission rules permitted conviction on the basis of evidence that the defendant had not seen, while courts-martial rules did not. The majority said that the government had not justified this nonuniformity.[65]

Four members of the Court said that in addition, the military commission procedure violated an international treaty provision: Common Article 3 of the Geneva Conventions, which applies to a "'conflict not of an international character,'"[66] prohibits the carrying out of criminal sentences "'without previous judgment pronounced by a regularly constituted court affording all the judicial guarantees which are recognized as indispensable by civilized peoples.'"[67] The denial of Hamdan's right to "be present for his trial and . . . privy to the evidence against him," at least where "not justified by any evident practical need," violated that provision.[68] The fifth member of the majority, Justice Kennedy, wrote that he thought it unnecessary to decide the treaty question.[69] In a word, the majority found for the detainee—but on statutory, not constitutional, grounds.

BOUMEDIENE

Decided in 2008, the fourth case, *Boumediene v. Bush*,[70] was the most important by far. That is because Congress, reacting to *Rasul*, repealed the very statutes the Court had found to allow a detainee to petition for a writ of habeas corpus, substituting for them a prohibition against such petitions.[71]

The case arose when several Guantanamo detainees, including Lakhdar Boumediene, filed a petition in a federal district court seeking release and claiming that they were not enemy combatants at all. Believing that *Rasul* permitted it to consider Boumediene's petition, the court agreed to do so. In the interim, however, Congress in 2006 enacted its new law, saying that[72] "no court, justice, or judge shall have jurisdiction to hear or consider . . . an application for a writ of habeas corpus filed by or on behalf of an alien detained . . . at Guantanamo Bay, Cuba." The lower courts consequently dismissed Boumediene's petition,[73] whereupon the Supreme Court agreed to decide whether the statute was constitutional.

Article I of the Constitution contains the relevant language: the "Privilege of the Writ of *Habeas Corpus shall not be suspended,* unless when in Cases of Rebellion or Invasion the public Safety may require it."[74] Congress had been facing neither "rebellion" nor "invasion" when passing the statute of 2006, but even so that didn't necessarily mean the petitioners were entitled to the "Privilege of the Writ." In *Rasul,* the Court had decided that the Guantanamo detainees were entitled to the protection of a specific congressional statute.[75] Absent that statute, were they entitled to the constitutional protection? This all may sound technical, but it is not. The question is simply whether the Constitution itself protects aliens detained as enemy combatants at a military base, allowing them to challenge the lawfulness of their detention.

In another five-to-four decision, the Court held that it does, and the reasoning was mostly an elaboration of *Rasul*. Justice Kennedy, writing for the majority, first stressed the fundamental importance of the writ,[76] citing its role in English history as the guarantor of a primordial right enshrined in the Magna Carta (namely, the right not to be "imprisoned . . . except . . . by the law of the land");[77] he mentioned how Black-stone had called it the "stable bulwark of our liberties,"[78] providing, in Alexander Hamilton's words, a safeguard against "arbitrary imprison-ments, . . . [the] most formidable instruments of tyranny."[79]

Second, Justice Kennedy considered historical practice. The gov-ernment argued that English courts would issue the writ on behalf of aliens detained in places where England was "sovereign."[80] Now, the American lease says that Cuba retains "ultimate sovereignty" but also stipulates that the United States exercises "complete jurisdiction and control" over the base as long as it wishes.[81] Practical rather than legalis-tic sovereignty seemed to be the operative principle historically, Justice Kennedy concluded, insofar as "a categorical or formal conception of sovereignty does not provide a comprehensive or altogether satisfactory explanation for the general understanding" of the "issuance of the writ outside England."[82] In the present case, practical considerations argued strongly for considering the United States sovereign in Guantanamo Bay.

Third, Justice Kennedy referred to *Eisentrager,* the case in which the Court had refused to consider habeas corpus petitions filed by German citizens convicted of war crimes, and he reiterated *Rasul*'s reasons for finding that case distinguishable.[83]

In determining the reach of the constitutional privilege of habeas corpus, he argued in conclusion, the detainees' status, the "nature of the sites where apprehension and then detention took place," and the "prac-tical obstacles inherent in resolving the prisoner's entitlement to the writ" were all relevant.[84] History, precedent, and practical considerations all favored the detainees here. And so the Court held that the protection of the writ of habeas corpus extended to the petitioners.[85]

The four dissenting justices argued that the constitutional privilege belonged only to (1) American citizens, and (2) noncitizens located in places where the United States was sovereign, which in their view did not include Guantanamo.[86] They further believed that the Detainee Treatment Act did not actually suspend the writ, for a provision allowed one court, the Court of Appeals for the District of Columbia Circuit, to review a determination that a detainee was an enemy combatant. At least, the chief justice argued in dissent, we should wait to see how the lower courts interpret that provision.[87]

The majority, however, countered with what it saw as inadequacies in the nature of this appellate review provision.[88] And it further noted that the "cases before us . . . do not involve detainees who have been held for a short period of time" while awaiting the government's decision.[89] Rather, in some cases, *"six years have elapsed without the judicial oversight that habeas corpus or an adequate substitute demands."*[90] This did not mean that "a habeas court should intervene the moment an enemy combatant steps foot in a territory where the writ runs."[91] But here "there has been no showing that the Executive faces such onerous burdens that it cannot respond to habeas corpus actions" within a "reasonable period of time."[92]

In holding that Congress must permit a judicial determination as to the lawfulness of detention of these alien detainees, confined during time of hostilities,[93] the Court went beyond *Milligan*. For unlike that post–Civil War case, *Boumediene* involved noncitizens and was decided while hostilities continued. The Court also went beyond the *Steel Seizure* case. Unlike in that case, Congress here had enacted a specific law denying power, not to the President, but to the courts, to intervene in a national security strategy. Asserting its duty under the Suspension Clause, the Court in *Boumediene* roundly rejected the notion that it could be prevented from hearing the challenge.

OBSERVATIONS: THE HOLDINGS

Taken together, *Rasul, Hamdi, Hamdan,* and *Boumediene* took the government's side on two matters. The Court reaffirmed the constitutional power of the executive branch (authorized by Congress) to detain enemy combatants "during active hostilities," as in all previous wars.[94] It also held that the executive could detain an American citizen fighting against the country as an enemy combatant.[95]

Otherwise, the Court held for the detainees across the board: the habeas corpus statute did give Guantanamo prisoners the right to bring court cases contesting their detention as unlawful.[96] In the event that a detainee, whether alien or citizen, contested his status as "enemy combatant," the executive must provide him the basic elements of due process (an impartial decision maker, a fair chance to present and hear proofs and arguments, etc.).[97] The Court further found that the executive lacked the statutory power to conduct trials of enemy combatants before special military commissions,[98] and also that Congress lacked the constitutional power to suspend the "privilege" of habeas corpus for Guantanamo detainees without meeting the requirements of the Suspension Clause; detained aliens could therefore petition the courts for release.[99] In sum, the decision said that even amid serious security threats, the Constitution does not give the President (or Congress) a blank check to determine the response.

In the context of earlier foreign affairs and war powers cases, the Guantanamo cases call for two more general observations. First, they continue the shift further away from Cicero ("the laws fall silent") and toward an attitude expressed during World War II by the British judge Lord Atkin:

> In this country, amid the clash of arms, the laws are not silent. They may be changed, but they speak the same language in war as in peace. It has always been one of the pillars of freedom, one of the principles of liberty for which . . . we are now fighting, that the judges . . . stand between the subject and any attempted encroachments on his liberty by the executive, alert to see that any coercive action is prohibited in law.[100]

While this change was under way in *Steel Seizure*, it is dramatically more evident in the Guantanamo cases. *Steel Seizure* dealt with the President's authority in primarily domestic matters, but the Guantanamo cases concern the political branches' authority to manage international affairs during an active conflict. To appreciate the transformation, let us consider the fate of a few of the once reliable legal authorities in this area.

What happened to Blackstone's idea that "a man, professing himself hostile to this country, and in a state of war with it, cannot be heard if he sue for the benefit and protection of our laws in the courts of this country"?[101] That sentiment, which appears extensively in *Quirin* and *Eisentrager*, lies dead and buried at Guantanamo.

What happened to Attorney General Francis Biddle's view, "The Constitution has not greatly bothered any wartime President"?[102] Those days are perhaps over.

What happened to Justice Robert Jackson's view in *Korematsu* that "in the very nature of things military decisions are not susceptible of intelligent judicial appraisal"? What happened to the idea that the Court should restore constitutionality only after, perhaps long after, the war is over?[103] The latter was simply set aside; the former is now subject to case-by-case consideration.

What happened to President Lincoln's stirring defense of the suspension of habeas corpus: "Are all the laws, but one, to go unexecuted, and the government itself go to pieces, lest that one be violated?"[104] *Milligan* supports that reasoning insofar as it matters that the Court did not decide it until the Civil War was over. But the Court decided the Guantanamo cases with the war still in progress. Indeed, some judges pointed to that fact, and in particular to the war's six-year duration, as a reason for deciding the case.

As to the "political question" doctrine, as expressed in *Curtiss-Wright* and *Korematsu,* the Guantanamo cases did not overrule these decisions directly, but it is as if they (and also *Steel Seizure*) drained those earlier cases of their persuasive force—though like icebergs lurking underwater, they may perhaps reemerge another day.

Second, while it is easy to criticize the Guantanamo decisions for saying too little, the way in which the Court resolved these cases has much to recommend it, both in what it specifies and what it does not. The *Boumediene* majority did set forth guidelines respecting the reach of habeas corpus beyond our shores. It pointed out that the detainee's "citizenship and status" were relevant, as were "the adequacy of the process through which that status determination was made," the "nature of the sites where apprehension and then detention took place," and the "practical obstacles inherent in resolving the prisoner's entitlement to the writ."[105] Subsequently, the D.C. Circuit Court of Appeals, applying these factors, would hold that the writ's privilege did not extend to Bagram Air Force Base in Afghanistan, which was too near an active battlefield.[106] *Boumediene* was instructive, then, even if the Court said little more than that Guantanamo itself was far enough from the battlefield, close enough to the mainland, and sufficiently controlled by the United States to fall within the writ's geographic scope. Similarly, when describing in *Hamdi* the "process" to which the Constitution entitled the detainees, the Court listed only the most basic elements (e.g., neutral decision maker, opportunity to present and to hear proofs and arguments). It left for another day the question of just what others the Constitution might require.[107]

Other justices would have preferred a "bright-line" rule. Some thought that while both citizens and aliens located in the United States fell within the writ's protection, enemy combatants held abroad did not.[108] Some further believed that, in the case of an American citizen, the government was obliged either to try him (though perhaps with relaxed procedural safeguards) or to release him; it was not necessarily so with an alien captured as an enemy combatant on the battlefield.[109]

Such bright-line rules can of course bring clarity to the law, guiding those who would apply it. But the danger always exists that the Court may draw the line in the wrong place without sufficient qualifications and exceptions. Subsequent events may prove it unworkable, if not harmful to the very security interests it means to advance, or needlessly restrictive of civil liberties.

Dissenting justices, for example, would have drawn a bright line distinguishing Guantanamo from Florida, but the distinction would have been tenuous. After all, the United States controls Guantanamo, which is very near Florida and likewise far from the battlefield—why should ninety miles of sea make such a critical legal difference? Recall what happened with the "bright line" the Court drew in *Curtiss-Wright* to help assure the President and Congress that the courts would not interfere in the conduct of a war; as *Korematsu* illustrates, that bright-line assurance may have come at too high a cost to civil liberties.

IMPLICATIONS: BEYOND THE PROLOGUE

The Guantanamo cases reflect the current way the Court sees the balance between security and civil liberty, the culmination of an evolution that may continue. Rather than sit on the sidelines and declare that cases of this kind pose an unreviewable "political question," or take jurisdiction but ultimately find for the President or Congress as a matter of course, today's Court will be more engaged when security efforts clash with other constitutional guarantees. It will listen to the government and consider its arguments, but it will not rubber-stamp every decision.

I do not see this evolution in approach solely in terms of the operation of the constitutional mechanism of checks and balances. True, the Court moved from an attitude of deference to one of scrutiny, and it concluded, beginning with *Steel Seizure* and culminating in the Guantanamo cases, that the other branches had gone too far. But the question remains: Why did that which long had proved acceptable come to be seen as going "too far"? I have already mentioned some of the factors

I believe responsible for the change, including the failure of *Korematsu* and growing public acceptance (after *Brown v Board of Education*) of the Court's role in civil rights protection. But there was another important change as well. The intrusion of the world's realities into our national life no longer seemed, as it once had, such an anomalous thing, justifying anomalous results. *Steel Seizure* (coming during the Korean War and Cold War, and on the heels of World War II) and the Guantanamo cases (coming out of the longest war in American history) were both decided in times when foreign matters, and in particular foreign threats, seemed likely to persist indefinitely. In *Boumediene* several justices emphasized their concern about detention that had already lasted six years, longer than the Civil War or World War II.

If the world seems too much with us, it can hardly help to pretend nothing has changed. Change is upon us and not only in the proliferation of foreign threats. These are merely one particularly worrisome manifestation of the larger reality I have referred to as interdependence, the sum of the ways, both good and bad, in which foreign actors and activity enter into our national life and create problems that we share with other nations.

Interdependence means that, when facing subsequent cases like those discussed so far, the Court will increasingly have to consider activities, both nonjudicial and judicial, that take place abroad. As to the former, the Court will have to understand in some detail foreign circumstances—that is, the evolving nature of threats to our nation's security, and how the United States and its partners are confronting them—in order to make careful distinctions and draw difficult lines. This need for expanded awareness will require the Court to engage with new sources of information about foreign circumstances, in greater depth than in the past. Indeed, by agreeing to decide, rather than avoiding or rubber-stamping, cases involving national security, the Court has implicitly acknowledged a willingness to engage with the hard *facts* about our national security risks.

Second, the Court will find itself looking abroad not only to understand the nature of the threats we face, but to develop an effective approach to addressing them. Other courts and legislatures have faced and are facing similar threats to their nations' peace and safety, and they have engaged in similar projects to those before our Court of balancing security and liberty. The solutions these institutions have fashioned may serve as constructive examples that our Court could put to good use.[110] Consider, for instance, the problem that Justice Clarence Thomas identified in his *Hamdi* dissent, when he pointed out that a confined person's "access to counsel and to the factual basis" for classifying him as an enemy combatant "would not always be warranted." He feared that given such access, the prisoner could disclose classified information, compromise intelligence sources, and ultimately "destroy the intelligence gathering function."[111]

The United Kingdom's government has already dealt with the same problem by specifying that counsel in such cases must be chosen from a list of lawyers with security clearance. Counsel would meet with the client at the outset of the case, but after receiving the government's closed file with all the relevant classified information, any further consultation with the client would require special permission. This system, the government conceded, would deprive the detained alien of the better representation that counsel with full access could provide. But it was found to be the best compromise among the alternatives: no counsel, counsel with no access to classified information, or release of a potential terrorist.[112] The British Supreme Court (then the Law Committee of the House of Lords) suggested that the system could violate the European Convention on Human Rights insofar as "the case against the [detainee] is based solely or to a decisive degree on closed materials" that have not been shown to the defendant, and thus have not been discussed between defendant and counsel,[113] but the system continued to be used.[114]

Similarly, Israel has developed a method that permits its armed forces to detain a suspected terrorist without access to counsel for up to thirty-four days, provided that the government, appearing in court ex parte, can convince the judge that circumstances demand it (e.g., to prevent a terrorist from saying to counsel, "Tell my mother I'm well," which turns out to be code for "Blow up the café").[115] In such a case, however, the government must appear every few days to explain why such detention is *still* warranted. Indeed, courts could mandate that the longer the detention, the more often the government must appear, each time shouldering a greater legal burden of proof.

Spain has a system similar to the United Kingdom's but more restrictive. Once an "incommunicado order" is issued against a terrorism suspect, the defendant can be held in isolated pretrial detention for up to thirteen days. During this time, he cannot designate his own lawyer and must instead be represented by a legal aid attorney, with whom he is not permitted to meet in private.[116]

I do not argue for or against either the British, Israeli, or Spanish system in particular. I simply point out that other democracies with the same commitment to basic human rights have led the way in developing solutions to the problem we face, and that we may learn something from examining their practices rather than considering our own in a vacuum.[117] I am not saying we can or should accept other nations' solutions. I am saying only that their examples can help us to find our own Constitution's answer to what is ultimately an American constitutional problem.

Cases concerning the legality of detention are not the only cases that raise security/civil rights questions. There are others that concern, for example, the legality of electronic surveillance, of data retention, of using certain sorts of evidence to prosecute terrorists, and related issues. Cases presenting a multitude of challenges to the federal government's policies in the "War on Terror" are already percolating through the federal courts and are likely to keep coming. In the Introduction, I mentioned a surveillance case that our Court decided in 2013, involving the government's monitoring of conversations between foreign terrorism suspects and their U.S.-based lawyers. The petitioners argued that the program was unconstitutional, but a majority of the Court found that they lacked standing to bring their claim.[118] While none of the opinions referred to practices outside our country, an amicus brief had highlighted the approach of the European Court of Human Rights with respect to surveillance of similar conversations.[119] Consulting this or other sources of foreign practices, while not determinative, could prove useful.

Referring to examples from abroad is by no means new. Recall that in his concurring opinion in *Steel Seizure,* Justice Jackson defended his views about the proper balance between congressional and presidential power in a democracy by citing systems in Europe. Studying the experience of other democracies may help our judges work out cases of their own, and better see ways in which to align the efforts of our country with those of our foreign allies combating the same threats.

As I mentioned above, future security/liberty cases will also require the Court to look abroad to obtain a more detailed understanding of the threats themselves. The Civil War and World War II were traditional wars of national survival. The current terrorist threats are different. Al Qaeda, for example, threatens many different kinds of harm, ranging from biological and chemical weapons, to logistical support for insurgents fighting a traditional government, such as Syria, to the bombing of civilians.[120] A terrorist group may consist of many loosely affiliated cells, comprising a network any of whose parts may work out its own ways to destabilize hostile governments or kill their citizens.[121] Consider the transformation of Al Qaeda over the past decade and a half since 9/11: Once its strongholds were in Afghanistan and Pakistan and the organization maintained a relatively well-organized hierarchy. Today terrorists fighting in its name or under the banner of its ideology have often barely spoken with their "home office" for direction; yet they launch deadly, self-initiated attacks, whether on troops at Ottawa's Parliament, against police officers in New York City, on fellow American soldiers in Texas, or on journalists in Paris.[122] Such threats may continue, in similar or idiosyncratic forms, over many years. They must be considered in their particularity.

Korematsu illustrated that it can be highly destructive of civil liberties to understand the Constitution as giving the President a blank check. Such deference could prove even more destructive of rights during a "war" against more diffuse security threats over longer periods of time. By the same token, it hardly seems the moment to tie the hands of the President or Congress too tightly when they are facing an amorphous threat and perpetrators whose malign intent may be impossible to know until they strike. When no two dangers are alike, there is also danger in hindering the speed and flexibility of response.

Between those two unappealing options—the blank check and an entrammeled executive—lies case-by-case review. But as I say, in electing to become involved in the evaluation of security threats, the Court assumes a considerable burden to inform itself of a vast and multiplying array of circumstances and actors. The temptation to generalize may be strong but must be avoided: bright-line rules are ill suited to a "war" the shape of which we can discern only dimly. In the immediate aftermath of 9/11, for example, few could have foreseen that Al Qaeda would not conduct another successful attack against the United States in the next thirteen years.[123] The inability of courts to predict accurately the nature of future risks, either to security or to civil liberties, argues strongly that judges should proceed case by case.

The world has changed so fast that even the usefulness and persuasiveness of formerly absolute factual distinctions such as those at issue in the Guantanamo cases can no longer be taken as given. There is, of course, a traditional and critical legal difference between a citizen and an alien, for instance. But in a world of extensive travel and immigration, of worldwide commerce, and of the Internet, the "foreignness" of an alien is not quite what it used to be. Likewise, North Africa, Europe, Midway, and the Philippines all seemed much more remote during World War II than they do today. Perhaps so did Guantanamo. None are as foreign as they once were. In what category, then, should we place an American citizen in a far-off place, like Yemen, who plots attacks against the United States and communicates with operatives via the Internet, as the radical cleric Anwar al-Awlaki did before his death in 2011?[124] If it can be hard to tell how the law should differentiate between citizens abroad and aliens present in American territories, then courts may well reflect that uncertainty, hesitating (as in *Hamdan*) to create clear, essential differences distinguishing those who do from those who do not have protected rights to enjoy basic human liberties.

As our Court has moved away from Cicero and toward Lord Atkin, it has inevitably and properly sought the help of lawyers with special, sometimes technical expertise, which they put to use when asking two traditional questions. The first is *why?* Why is it necessary here to limit the usual rights protections? What is it specifically about our national security need that requires this particular limitation? If security considerations prevent the government from explaining in public, it may be feasible (I take no view) to present information to the judge *in camera*. No matter what the security consideration, the government has to satisfy a neutral decision maker that the restriction is justified. The second question is *why not?* Why can the government not satisfy its security need in a less restrictive way?

These questions, as I say, are traditional. But as the Court seeks to evaluate security matters, the answers are likely to grow more technical and more laden with foreign details with which those asking the questions will have to reckon. The government is typically well prepared and understands both the need for and the potential consequences of what it asks. Its briefs are helpful, but the Court cannot rely upon the government alone. It will need a record and briefs that reflect informed analyses by lawyers for all sides as well as neutral parties.

The technological dimensions alone make this a difficult goal to achieve. In 2013, for example, the President's Review Group on Intelligence and Communications Technologies brought together academic and government experts to review the practices of the intelligence community after the unauthorized release of information by Edward Snowden.[125] Critics thought the review group short on technologists and heavy on lawyers and policy experts.[126] One advocacy group wrote, "An informed and competent technical understanding is critical to the oversight function of U.S. government surveillance programs. A lack of technical understanding in existing oversight bodies has already resulted in substantial material defects in these programs."[127] I do not say the critics were right, but I do agree about the need for technical understanding.

The point is obvious. Often for both bench and bar, "informed and competent technical understanding is critical."[128] Traditionally, judges, lawyers, and academics have helped to satisfy this kind of need through explanation, research, criticism, and discussion, each with the others. Insofar as the Guantanamo cases reflect likely future demands for specialized knowledge, of international as well as national practice, this kind of communication among segments of the legal profession is particularly important. This is not to say that such communication will solve the problem. Obviously it will take more than technical information to answer the constitutional questions fully, but we should not understate its importance, particularly when these problems concern the separation and division of power. Through "checks and balances," the Constitution protects us against abuses of power that can, among other noxious effects, threaten individual liberty. And the need for such protection is not likely to diminish over time.

I mention this because there is reason to suppose that the public today may well lack confidence in traditional efforts within the branches (and for that matter, between the executive and legislative branches) to check abuse. There is, for example, the well-publicized concern about intelligence agencies collecting too much private information about American citizens. Most people recognize the need to gather data relevant to terrorism, but what is to prevent the government from going too far? At one time, the public might have looked with confidence to the congressional intelligence committees to monitor executive branch intelligence agencies. But today the public may lack the necessary confidence in Congress. As to the judicial branch, a special federal court has jurisdiction over intelligence-gathering procedures. But that fact is of limited comfort to the public, since that court's proceedings (involving the equivalent of police applications to wiretap suspected criminals) are often necessarily secret.[129]

The executive branch has not fared much better. Despite the recent proliferation of executive agencies designed to oversee intelligence gathering—the NSA's Office of the Inspector General, the President's Intelligence Advisory Board, and the (bipartisan) Privacy and Civil Liberties Oversight Board, to name just a few—the public remains skeptical. According to a recent Pew Research Center report, Americans feel as if they have "lost control" over their personal information. Some "70% of social networking site users say that they are at least somewhat concerned about the government accessing some of the information they share without their knowledge."[130] And "80% of adults 'agree' or 'strongly agree' that Americans should be concerned about government's monitoring of phone calls and internet communications."[131]

Insofar as the public sees the Court as one of the few remaining bulwarks against abuse, the Court of necessity may find itself more involved in security-related matters. But that involvement will help build confidence in our public institutions only if the Court can reach sound conclusions. And it can do so only if it understands the security side as well as the civil liberties side of the equation. That, it seems to me, is the major institutional challenge imposed by the new global realities. The Guantanamo cases represent the future of our legal system, from which, I believe, there is no going back. If so, the past is prologue.

PART II

At Home Abroad

The Foreign Reach of American Statutory Law

W e have seen how the effort to preserve individual liberties has led to a change in the Court's approach to the law. I have suggested that this evolution owes as much to the changing nature of the world as to the predictable cycles of self-correction one might expect to see in a system of constitutional government.

In an intensely interdependent world facing global threats that are likely to last a generation or more (particularly terrorism), special security needs are no longer as intermittent or short-lived as they once were. In such circumstances, for the Court to avoid constitutional questions for security reasons, as it was long used to doing, is to concede to the President as a matter of course the extraordinary powers he was intended to wield only under extreme conditions of wartime; it is also to accede to a diminished version of the basic liberties guaranteed by the Constitution. Rather than rubber-stamp the President or simply wait for a more propitious time to rescue individual rights, then, the Court has adopted a new approach of greater engagement with security requirements. And this new approach has obliged it to extend its awareness and understanding to places and circumstances traditionally beyond its ken, in order to obtain knowledge about foreign factual and legal conditions, policies, and institutions. It is a new burden for the Court but not likely a passing one. It is more nearly the way we live now.

If Part I showed the Court responding indirectly to a changing world on account in part of changes in constitutional interpretation and in part of changes in the world, in Part II the changing world itself is the direct and driving force behind changes in American law. Here the examples are not constitutional but statutory. They raise problems of how American statutes should be interpreted. Determining a statute's geographical reach, for instance, or whether a foreign person can bring a lawsuit in an American court, are not new problems. But solving them in an interdependent world is full of new challenges.

To find answers today, the Court must increasingly consider foreign and domestic law together, as if they constituted parts of a broadly interconnected legal web. In this sense, the old legal concept of "comity" has assumed an expansive meaning. "Comity" once referred simply to the need to ensure that domestic and foreign laws did not impose contradictory duties upon the same individual; it used to prevent the laws of different nations from stepping on one another's toes. Today it means something more. In applying it, our Court has increasingly sought interpretations of domestic law that would allow it to work in harmony with related foreign laws, so that together they can more effectively achieve common objectives. Since there is no Supreme Court of the World, national courts must act piecemeal, without direct coordination, in seeking interpretations that can dovetail rather than clash with the working of foreign statutes. And so our Court does, and should, listen to foreign voices, to those who understand and can illuminate relevant foreign laws and practices.

Two sets of examples will illustrate the kind of change now taking place and the sorts of answers our Court has found so far. Chapter 5 focuses on American commercial statutes and the legal questions about their foreign reach. To what extent does American law govern commercial activities that take place abroad in large part? To what extent must courts take account of foreign law and related practices when interpreting the reach of an American statute? The increased importance of a worldwide marketplace, the heightened economic interdependence of nations, and the greater acceptance among nations of a regulated free market as an economic norm have changed the way in which our Court answers such questions, shifting the emphasis from the mere avoidance of direct conflict toward enabling analogous foreign and domestic statutes to work harmoniously together.

Chapter 5 presents four examples, one from the law of antitrust, one from the law of "discovery," one from the law of securities, and one from the law of copyright. Together these illustrate how, guided by "comity," the Court pursues such legal harmony. They also illustrate, inevitably, the Court seeking and using a broader, more worldly-wise understanding and knowledge.

Chapter 6 considers a less mundane matter: the extraterritorial application of a U.S. statute providing damages for violations of human rights. To what degree are the doors of the American courthouse open to foreign victims of serious human rights violations abroad? The need to protect fundamental individual rights is widely accepted, not only in the United States but throughout the world. But can a citizen of a foreign country obtain compensation in an American court for torture suffered elsewhere? Our discussion will trace the life of the Alien Tort Statute and its rediscovery by civil rights advocates after World War II. Examining Court cases interpreting this statute, we shall see how institutional difficulties arising out of foreign circumstances complicate efforts to apply the statute even to the least controversial human rights norms. And as in the commercial cases of Chapter 5, we shall see how the Court is better equipped to determine the extraterritorial reach of the Alien Tort Statute when it can ask the basic question that modern "comity" poses: How is our domestic statute best interpreted to work together with those laws and practices of other nations that also seek to enforce human rights norms?

Finally, it bears emphasizing that while new applications of American law have intensified the need for better understanding of foreign activities and laws, "understanding" is no more than that. A more harmonizing understanding and application of American law to foreign activities is not the same as American courts deciding cases on the basis of foreign law.

Regulating International Commerce

When a case concerns foreign events or foreign persons or foreign property, a court has to decide which nation's laws apply. In answering that question, it will follow principles that also determine the reach of its own nation's laws. During the Middle Ages, for example, if a Roman citizen brought a suit in Florence against a Florentine citizen, claiming that the Florentine had damaged property in Rome belonging to the Roman, the court would apply the body of rules known as the "statutist" system. Under that system, physical location—whether of a piece of property, a person, or a marriage—determined legal status and rights; because this was such a simple and readily ascertainable rule of decision, the laws of different cities and nations could work together in harmony, minimizing conflict. Thus in our medieval scenario, the court would likely decide that Roman, not Florentine, law determined the rights and remedies of someone who owned property in Rome, and it would have done so even if the owner had been Florentine.[1]

The statutist rules worked well as long as most people remained in one place for most of their lives. But as historians tell us, with the development of trade and travel, there began to develop more complex systems for determining the reach of a nation's laws, as well as for choosing what law applied to which transactions. In the seventeenth century, for example, Dutch law pragmatically modified the simpler statutist rules so that they took better account of the needs of merchants doing business in more than one town.[2]

In time, the same thing would happen in America, with courts and legal commentators developing their own complex set of doctrines for determining what law should apply to a given conflict and particularly whether it should be American law. For this purpose, the courts have used a variety of principles, such as interest-balancing and the so-called "rule of reasonableness," as well as interpretive rules such as "the presumption against extraterritorial application" (of U.S. statutes) and "comity," the judicial practice of taking into account the interests of other nations, to guide American jurists' analysis.[3] But doctrines and rules inevitably have exceptions, and their presumptions do not always answer the question at hand. That is particularly so where commerce is concerned.

Recently, we have witnessed an enormous further expansion in world commerce. In the past forty years, world trade has doubled from about 15 percent to more than 30 percent of global economic output, growing (in constant 2005 dollars) from $18.1 trillion to $55.9 trillion.[4] America's imports have increased from 6.4 to 16.8 percent and exports from 6.7 to 13.5 percent of GDP, which in total has increased from $4.98 trillion to $14.5 trillion (in constant 2005 dollars).[5] Almost a third of personal expenditures on consumer goods go toward foreign-made products.[6] More than 23 million Americans travel abroad each year.[7] Electronic communication is continual and instantaneous. And major businesses are often made up of networks, connecting divisions located in many different countries, each of which reacts to and plans with the others second by second.[8]

Consequently, just as the growth of trade forced late-medieval nations to modify or abandon the statutist system, so today we find ourselves in the midst of legal change. Commercial cases are more complex, with ambiguous jurisdictional boundaries to be determined, and their outcome can have a significant impact upon international commerce overall. While each case turns upon an interpretation of a particular statute, viewing them together we can generalize about changes in the Court's interpretive approach.

For one thing, as mentioned, the Court no longer seeks only to avoid direct conflicts among laws of different nations; it seeks, rather, to harmonize the enforcement of what are often similar national laws.

For another, where the Court might previously have found a rough understanding of foreign statutes sufficient to decide a case, it now finds it necessary also to try to understand foreign legal practices, and often foreign and international business practices, in greater detail. It has had to learn something of foreign regulatory practices, foreign enforcement practices, foreign procedures, and sometimes even foreign marketing practices, in order to find a satisfactory interpretation of a domestic statute.

As in Part I, here, too, the need for foreign information itself raises the question of how the Court can best obtain and make sense of it. We rely upon briefs filed by the parties and by other interested persons, including the executive branch, of course, but also foreign governments. These may refer us to academic sources on the subject, such as restatements, treatises, and journal articles. Are these sufficient? The four cases in this section are intended to illustrate how the Court contends with these issues.

EMPAGRAN: ANTITRUST LAW

American antitrust laws prohibit companies from entering into agreements that restrain trade or create anticompetitive market structures, such as monopolies. In 1890 Congress passed the most venerable antitrust law, the Sherman Antitrust Act.[9] Among other things, the act forbids competing firms from fixing prices and imposes criminal penalties upon those who do.[10] It also permits persons injured as a result of unlawful price-fixing to sue the fixers for treble damages as well as attorney's fees.[11]

Although the Sherman Act says nothing about its own geographical scope, American antitrust authorities have long understood it as applying to at least some activity taking place abroad. Thus in the early 1900s the Justice Department sued a group of American banks and other companies, including a Mexican corporation, for monopolizing the importation and sale of sisal, a type of fiber, in the United States by concentrating all buying and selling of sisal in Mexico in one agent.[12] Similarly, the government's famous antitrust case against Aluminum Company of America (Alcoa) in the 1940s concerned activities that took place, in great part, outside the country.[13] And so did the government's antitrust case in the 1950s and 1960s against a group of Swiss and American watchmakers;[14] an action against General Electric and other companies involved in the manufacture of electric lamps;[15] and one against a group of quinine manufacturers—foreign drug companies that had entered into cartel agreements in Europe, resulting in higher prices for their quinine in the United States.[16]

But when does the Sherman Act apply to activity taking place abroad? The cases I have just mentioned all involved a mix of foreign and domestic conduct, which taken as a whole helped produce monopolies and higher prices in the United States. What about a price-setting agreement between an American banana company and the government of Costa Rica, made in Costa Rica, considered on its own? In 1909, while noting that it was a crime to fix prices, the Court found that the Sherman Act did *not* apply to that arrangement, because the "improbability of the United States attempting to make acts done in Panama or Costa Rica criminal is obvious."[17]

It was in the Alcoa case that Judge Learned Hand, one of America's great judges, developed a standard that for decades would guide interpretation of the reach of the statute. The Sherman Act, he found, *does* apply to actions taking place abroad provided that those actions have the intent to affect and do affect market activities or prices in the United States.[18] Certainly U.S. law, even criminal law, applies to those who throw stones or shoot bullets or send defective goods into the United States, even if the perpetrators stand just across the border when they do so.[19] Foreign price-fixers who meet Judge Hand's two conditions are no different. But instead of defective goods, they send goods with improperly inflated prices.[20]

It eventually became apparent, however, that this widely adopted standard of Judge Hand's did not answer the question of applicability in every case. The antitrust laws are too complicated and the circumstances in which potential violations can arise too varied, as are the combinations of nationalities of persons affected.[21] Suppose, for example, Timberlane, an American logging company cutting trees in Honduras, sues Bank of America, complaining that the bank conspired with various Honduran entities to keep Timberlane from milling its lumber in Honduras, thereby diminishing competition in the Honduran lumber export business and resulting in higher prices in the United States. Do the American antitrust laws cover this conduct, even under Judge Hand's limited, two-part test?

In the late 1970s and early 1980s, the Court of Appeals for the Ninth Circuit, repeatedly considering precisely this case, came to the conclusion that the laws did not apply.[22] The first time the court confronted the case, it crafted a "rule of reason" for resolving the dispute.[23] It began by noting that there "is no doubt that American antitrust laws extend over some conduct in other nations."[24] But that fact "does not mean" that American law "embraces all."[25] After all, extraterritoriality is "a matter of concern for the other countries involved," and those "nations have sometimes resented and protested . . . broad assertions of authority by American courts."[26] The court determined that to trigger the application of American antitrust law, the foreign activity must not only have some "actual or intended" effect on American commerce (as Judge Hand had specified), but that the "interests of . . . the United States" must also be "sufficiently strong, vis-à-vis those of other nations."[27] To carry out this "interest-balancing" analysis, courts should take account of such matters as

> [1] the degree of conflict with foreign law or policy, [2] the nationality or allegiance of the parties and the locations or principal places of businesses or corporations, [3] the extent to which enforcement by either state can be expected to achieve compliance, [4] the relative significance of effects on the United States as compared with those elsewhere, [5] the extent to which there is explicit purpose to harm or affect American commerce, [6] the foreseeability of such effect, and [7] the relative importance to the violations charged of conduct within the United States as compared with conduct abroad.[28]

In short, a more complicated analysis for a more complicated world.

When confronted with *Timberlane* a second time, on appeal, the Ninth Circuit applied its new framework. It observed that Honduran law permitted the very practices that Timberlane was objecting to (i.e., agreements, even among competitors, to "allocate geographic or market territories, to restrict price or output, [or] to cut off the source of raw materials");[29] that the effect of the anticompetitive activity on American lumber markets was minimal;[30] and that the potential for "conflict" with "Honduran economic policy and commercial law" was great and outweighed the negative economic impacts at home.[31] All things considered, then, American antitrust laws should not apply, and the plaintiffs should not be permitted to proceed with their case.[32]

The Ninth Circuit's test has its strengths and weaknesses. On the one hand, it is arguably an improvement over Judge Hand's test in *Alcoa*, in that it takes account not only of the effects of extraterritorial conduct on U.S. markets, but also of the potential for conflict between U.S. economic policy and foreign economic policy should American law apply, as well as of the relative interests of each nation in having its domestic law supply the rule of decision. On the other hand, the test is complex, opening the door to broad judicial discretion, and thus it creates unpredictability. How will courts determine the existence, degree, and force of these seven factors? How will they weigh them, one against the other? Indeed, commentators argued, the approach in *Timberlane* would produce nothing but uncertainty among foreign governments and their exporting businesses as to just what they could do abroad without facing the wrath of American antitrust law and its treble damages.[33] This was surely not good for trade.

In the early 1980s, as other courts were grappling with cases like *Timberlane* and attempting to create their own frameworks for resolving the overseas-application question,[34] Congress enacted an amendment to the Sherman Act intended to provide clarity.[35] The new provision started by saying that the Sherman Act "shall *not* apply to conduct involving trade or commerce . . . with foreign nations,"[36] but it went on to create exceptions. According to one, the Sherman Act would apply when conduct taking place abroad has a "direct, substantial and reasonably foreseeable effect" on domestic commerce and also is of a kind (say, price-fixing) that would "give rise to" a Sherman Act "claim."[37] Another exception made the act applicable when the overseas conduct involves "import trade or import commerce."[38]

The revised statute established that, at a minimum, something similar to Judge Hand's two-part *Alcoa* test had to be satisfied for the Sherman Act to apply to foreign conduct: there must be a "direct" effect on U.S. commerce, and that effect must be "reasonably foreseeable," to permit a claim.[39] But the 1982 amendment still left open many questions. For one, it did not say whether courts should also apply comity frameworks, as the Ninth Circuit had done in *Timberlane*.[40] For another, when, under the "actual or intended effects" standard, does foreign activity affect *enough* American commerce for the effect to be "actual"? And when can the foreign actor be assumed to have been on notice, so the effect could be deemed "intended"? Finally, the amended statute said nothing about what happens when a party is injured by anticompetitive conduct that inflates prices in foreign markets but *also* has adverse effects on U.S. markets. These questions, especially the last, are among those that brought the *Empagran* case before our Court.

Empagran involved a worldwide vitamin cartel. Its members were vitamin manufacturers, many of which were headquartered in Europe but some of which were U.S.-based.[41] Cartel members sold vitamins to distributors throughout the world. And they fixed their prices, for which the U.S. Justice Department prosecuted many cartel members during the 1990s. Twelve companies and thirteen individuals pleaded guilty, paying the government millions in criminal fines. Soon domestic distributors that had paid the inflated prices for vitamins from these companies began to bring civil cases seeking treble damages and attorney's fees for the overcharges. Several of these suits were settled, resulting in payments by the vitamin companies of over $2 billion.[42]

Empagran focused on a group of vitamin distributors that had yet to obtain damages in U.S. civil litigation. Domiciled in foreign countries—namely, Ecuador, Panama, Australia, and Ukraine—they had bought vitamins for delivery outside the United States.[43] Importantly, the plaintiffs in *Empagran* had not alleged that they purchased any vitamins within the United States, or engaged directly in any U.S. transactions.[44] And for purposes of the Supreme Court argument, they were willing to assume that their injury—that is, the overcharges for vitamins they bought—was caused solely by the conspiracy's negative effects on foreign commerce.[45] Nonetheless, the distributors believed they should be able to sue under the Sherman Act because the cartel had engaged in illegal price-fixing that had also caused substantial damage to U.S. commerce—precisely what the Sherman Act specifies. The fact that the injuries arose from buying overpriced vitamins *abroad* rather than in the United States was of no moment, they contended. Here was a global cartel that had artificially raised prices in the United States, meeting the essential criterion. Why should the distributors not be able to bring their case in an American court and obtain compensation? In a sense, why should American courts not allow them to sue when they were hurt by the very activities that American law makes criminal?

The Court would ultimately hold (a quarter century after *Timber-*

lane) that the distributors could not go forward with their claims.[46] The antitrust laws, according to the holding, did not cover foreign distributors in their positions—namely, entities that seek damages for injuries caused in foreign commerce, when the adverse effects on foreign commerce (caused by the defendants' activities) are independent of any adverse effects on U.S. commerce.

How did the Court arrive at this conclusion? There is a canon of interpretation that is often used in these sorts of cases, and it applies a "presumption against extraterritoriality"—that is, a presumption against the foreign application of an American statute.[47] But that canon did not help, since all conceded that the Sherman Act sometimes does apply extraterritorially. The question was not whether it applies to foreign conduct but when and where it does so.

The language of the statute was not much help. It says that the act covers "conduct involving trade or commerce . . . with foreign nations" that (1) has a "direct, substantial and reasonably foreseeable effect" on American commerce, and (2) "give[s] rise to" a Sherman Act "claim."[48] The cartel's conduct satisfied the first condition, for it directly affected American commerce (it raised vitamin prices here) and that effect was certainly foreseeable (indeed, it was the cartel's object). The conduct had also given rise to a "claim" in the United States, as the Justice Department had brought criminal proceedings against several of the *Empagran* defendants and American distributors had brought civil claims against them as well. So the language, taken literally, seemed to apply.

But the fact remained that these plaintiffs, companies based in Ecuador, Panama, Australia, and Ukraine, were injured *independent* of any effect that price-fixing had had on American commerce. Does the statute mean, therefore, to exclude them as plaintiffs, or does it regard the cartel members rather as pirates, the sort of malefactors who (as the next chapter will show) have long been considered enemies of all mankind and treated accordingly? Put simply: Can anyone hurt anywhere in the world by price-fixing "pirates" sue for damages in the United States, as long as Americans have been hurt as well (and at least some bring suit)? The statute simply does not say.

To resolve the question and interpret the statute in a way consistent with congressional intent, the Court relied heavily upon the concept of "comity." Courts have long invoked it in cases that present potential conflicts among the laws of nations, because it is reasonable to assume that Congress seeks to avoid such conflicts where possible. The Supreme Court "ordinarily construes ambiguous statutes to avoid unreasonable interference with the sovereign authority of other nations."[49] At least one member of the Court, Justice Antonin Scalia, has identified this approach to statutory construction as equivalent to the internationally accepted principle of "prescriptive comity," which holds that states should avoid the unreasonable application of their statutes to persons or activities abroad, out of respect for foreign jurisdiction.[50] In *Empagran*, the Court applied the doctrine broadly. It asked whether it was reasonable to apply the Sherman Act to "foreign conduct insofar as that conduct causes independent foreign harm that alone gives rise to a plaintiff's claim."[51] The answer the Court ultimately came to was no; the application of the statute in such circumstances would cause unnecessary "interfer[ence] with a foreign nation's ability independently to regulate its own commercial affairs."[52]

In fact, the meaning of "comity" has shifted more than once over its long history. During the Middle Ages, with the expansion of trade and commerce, it began as a principle for resolving conflicts that arose between local jurisdictions.[53] At that time, it primarily meant a rule of deference to the host forum's law, rather in the way the statutist system looked to physical location to determine applicable law. In the eighteenth and nineteenth centuries, comity grew into a more permissive doctrine employed by courts to justify giving effect to the laws of foreign countries when desirable and not at odds with public policy.[54] In contemporary times, scholars have described comity as a doctrine rooted in respect for state sovereignty.[55] It is "a traditional diplomatic and international law concept used by States in their dealings with each other. Short of legal obligation, States respect each other's policy choices and interests in a given case without inquiring into the substance of each other's laws. Comity is widely believed to occupy a place between custom and customary international law."[56]

When American courts employ the "comity" doctrine today, they often do so according to a "rule of reasonableness." Would it be reasonable for an American court to exercise jurisdiction over these foreign parties and their conduct, or would it not? A book about current law, written or reviewed by current scholars, *The Restatement of Foreign Relations Law*, directs courts to ask this very question.[57] Rather like the court in *Timberlane*, it prescribes a host of factors by which courts should determine whether to exercise jurisdiction over a person or matter—including whether there is a territorial link between the activity and the regulating state, the connections between the person responsible for the activity and the regulating state, the character of activity at issue, the nature of the parties' justified expectations, whether regulation of the activity would be consistent with international traditions, the interests of other states, and the likelihood of conflicts.[58]

Thus the Court in *Empagran* concluded it would not be "reasonable" to apply American antitrust laws "to foreign conduct insofar as that conduct causes independent foreign harm and that foreign harm alone gives rise to a plaintiff's claim."[59] Doing so would risk interference with foreign nations' abilities to regulate their internal economic affairs, and for an "insubstantial" gain to the American system.[60] When the conduct giving rise to the claim has affected only foreign commerce, why should American law supplant foreign law? After all, many nations now have their own antitrust policies and enforcement agencies. On this basis, we should hesitate to interfere with, for example, Canada's or Great Britain's or Japan's own determination about how best to protect Canadian or British or Japanese customers from anticompetitive conduct.

The amicus briefs filed in *Empagran* underscored the international conflicts that could arise should U.S. antitrust laws be applied. Some emphasized that more and more nations had adopted or strengthened their laws against price-fixing in the preceding decades.[61] I had seen this happening firsthand. In the late 1960s, while working for the Antitrust Division of the Justice Department, I would occasionally attend meetings of antitrust enforcers of the Organization for Economic Cooperation and Development (OECD). The United States always seemed the most enthusiastic about stopping anticompetitive behavior, such as price-fixing and mergers between competitors. France and Italy, by contrast, seemed hesitant, believing that mergers would increase the competitiveness of their firms vis-à-vis American ones; and the Japanese seemed altogether unenthusiastic, their authorities convinced that government intervention and guidance on behalf of business interests (instead of freely competitive markets) would lead to a stronger economy. Those days, however, are no more. Today the antitrust authorities in all these countries and others, too, firmly apply laws against most price-fixing. Some of the briefs in *Empagran* argued that this, in fact, was a strong reason for applying American law anyway. It is now highly reasonable, they said, to collect damages from a price-fixer wherever you find him.[62]

Other briefs, however, showed that, while anti-price-fixing measures have become common, enforcement regimes vary by nation in important ways. The United Kingdom and the Netherlands, for instance, told the Court that a ruling against Empagran could undermine the "leniency" or "amnesty" programs that they, the European Union, and other nations had developed.[63] Those programs encouraged companies to blow the whistle against international cartels and to inform their governments about conspiratorial activities. The British-Dutch brief warned that "proposed expansion of United States jurisdiction over private treble damages claims" would prevent their shielding whistle-blowers from the threat of American treble damages, thus making the leniency programs "less attractive to whistle-blowers." American jurisdiction would thereby have an "adverse effect on international cartel enforcement."[64] They added that "[e]nforcement officials from Germany and the United States agree."[65]

The government of Japan highlighted different concerns. It told the Court that it had "a bilateral antitrust cooperation agreement" with the United States;[66] that this agreement constituted part of a "network of international relationships among national antitrust authorities";[67] that an international "Council" supervising much of that network "recognize[d] the need for member countries [including the United States] to use moderation and self-restraint in the interest of cooperation in the field of anticompetitive practices";[68] that "no comparable network" through which consultation with "private U.S. antitrust lawyers" or "with U.S. courts having jurisdiction over global class actions" was possible;[69] and that "neither national governments nor national courts [were] well suited to supervising and resolving the conflicts that would result" from permitting the *Empagran* action to go forward.[70]

The United States filed a brief agreeing with these foreign nations. It stated that expansive jurisdiction in *Empagran* would not only threaten the United States' own amnesty programs for whistle-blowers but would also "undermine" cooperative relationships developed with foreign antitrust authorities in recent years.[71] It further pointed out that in 1986 the OECD (of which the United States is a member) had recognized "the need . . . to give effect to the principles of international law and comity and to use moderation and self-restraint in the interest of co-operation in the field of anticompetitive practices," the same point made by Japan.[72] And it reminded the Court that in September 1991 the European Union and the United States had signed an "Antitrust Co-operation Agreement" that was designed to promote enforcement co-operation by creating a system of notifications and requests, through which authorities from each country ask their counterparts abroad to initiate enforcement proceedings against violators.[73] If suits like *Empagran* could proceed in an American court, the United States warned, such collaborative regimes could be threatened. The solicitor general wrote: "If our foreign counterparts fear that the fruits of their cooperation ultimately will be used to support follow-on treble damage actions in the United States that they perceive as inappropriate, cooperation may be strained, to the overall detriment of international cartel enforcement."[74]

The Court ultimately found these considerations convincing. It concluded that "even where nations agree about primary conduct, say, price-fixing, they disagree dramatically about appropriate remedies."[75] Applying American law, with its treble damages remedies, could permit the citizens of foreign nations "to bypass their own less generous remedial schemes, thereby upsetting a balance of competing considerations that their own domestic antitrust laws embody."[76] And that could in turn jeopardize the cooperative arrangements that the United States had forged with other countries, by eroding the goodwill and mutual respect upon which those programs depend. Accordingly, the Court held, it would not be "reasonable"—that is, consistent with comity—to permit foreign firms suffering independent foreign injury abroad to sue under American law.[77]

For present purposes, three aspects of the finding are important. First, the international nature of commerce and of efforts to regulate it led the Court not only to consider the need to avoid conflict between the substantive rules of different nations but also to ponder in some detail the differing procedural methods through which different nations enforce similar rules. The Court also took account of executive branch agreements seeking to coordinate enforcement efforts with many of those nations.

Second, the Court sought, not simply (in a value-neutral way) to avoid conflict among different national laws, but also to promote the smooth operation of an international business regulatory system. It described its use of the term *comity* as an effort to "take account of the legitimate sovereign interests of other nations . . . [by helping] potentially conflicting laws of different nations work together in harmony—a harmony particularly needed in today's highly interdependent commercial world."[78]

Third, the Court reached its conclusion with the help of briefs filed by those who understood international practice. The executive branch explained how international cooperation agreements worked, why they were important, and how they could be undermined by a holding for the plaintiffs. Several foreign nations, and the antitrust authorities of the European Union, did the same.

INTEL: DISCOVERY

We have just seen the Court taking account of foreign enforcement procedures in determining the proper interpretation of an antitrust statute. But taking account of foreign procedures is often easier said than done, as the case of *Intel Corp. v. Advanced Micro Devices* illustrates.[79] It concerned the rules of discovery—that is, those allowing one party in a case to obtain documents and testimony from others—and one American statute specifically designed to permit a person to obtain discovery material for use in foreign tribunals. What seemed a simple statute at first in fact bristled with interpretive difficulties.

The case began in October 2000, when Advanced Micro Devices (AMD), a company that does business throughout the world, filed a complaint with the antitrust law enforcers of the European Commission (EC), claiming that its competitor Intel Corporation, another worldwide company, was violating Europe's antitrust laws. Calling on the European enforcement authority, the Directorate-General for Competition (DG-Competition), to investigate, AMD urged it to seek discovery of a set of documents that Intel had produced in a private antitrust case brought by another competitor in a federal district court in Alabama, documents then being kept under seal by that court.[80]

The European authorities decided they did not need the documents for their investigation, at which point AMD decided it would try of its own accord to get them for the DG-Competition (and perhaps have a look at those documents itself). Consequently, AMD asked a federal district court located in northern California, near the corporate head-quarters of both companies, to order Intel to produce the documents.[81]

How could a court in northern California order Intel to produce documents from federal litigation in Alabama? After all, there was no case involving AMD and Intel in California, or in Alabama, or any-where else in the United States for that matter. AMD pointed to a statute that, in its view, gave the California district court the authority to order that the documents be produced. The statute said:

> The district court of the district in which a person resides or *is found* may order him to give his testimony . . . or to *produce a document* . . . for *use in a proceeding in a foreign or international tribunal,* including criminal investigations conducted before formal accusation. The order may be made *pursuant to a . . . request made[ ] by a foreign or international tribunal or upon the application of any interested person.*[82]

AMD declared itself to be just such an "interested person"; Intel, it added, is "found" in the district of northern California; the DG-Competition is a "foreign . . . tribunal"; and AMD wanted the documents for use in a "proceeding" in that tribunal. Thus the district court "may order" Intel to produce the documents.[83]

The court was not so certain. For starters, it thought that the DG-Competition was not a "tribunal" under Section 1782.[84] This find-ing the Court of Appeals for the Ninth Circuit reversed,[85] concluding that because its activities led to "quasi-judicial" proceedings in certain instances, they were not purely administrative in nature. Accordingly, the DG-Competition could be considered a "tribunal."[86] The Ninth Circuit also rejected Intel's request that the court impose a threshold obligation on AMD, requiring that it show that the documents being sought in the United States would also be discoverable in the foreign jurisdiction in which they would be used. Two other courts of appeals had adopted that type of foreign discoverability rule, but the Ninth Cir-cuit declined to do so.[87] The stage was thus set for the Supreme Court to interpret the statute.

The case presented the Court with four technical interpretive questions: (1) Was the DG-Competition a "tribunal" under Section 1782? (2) Was AMD an "interested person"? (3) Was the European Commission's investigation a "proceeding"? (4) Did the statute permit AMD to obtain the documents if it could not do so (a) under the law of the foreign jurisdiction in which they would eventually be used, (b) under American law in an analogous domestic case, or (c) both?[88]

The Court answered those questions in light of the statute's history. For more than 150 years, American courts had helped foreign courts obtain information, normally by responding to what were called "letters rogatory"; these were requests from foreign diplomats asking an American court to take testimony to be used in a proceeding overseas.[89] Congress codified these practices in an authorizing statute that was passed in 1948 and subsequently expanded in 1965 and again in 1996. The amendments of 1965 were significant. They reflected the work of an expert commission that Congress created in light of the "extensive increase in international commercial and financial transactions" (as of 1958!); its mission was to "investigate and study existing practices of judicial assistance and cooperation between the United States and foreign nations with a view to achieving improvements."[90] The amendments of 1965 authorized U.S. courts to compel not only the testimony of witnesses but also the production of documents or other physical evidence sought in any "proceeding in a foreign or international tribunal."[91]

The Court in *Intel* thought that the statute's language, read in light of this history, called for a broad interpretation. But it recognized that this conclusion was not obvious. Two opposing briefs framed the problem. The European Commission filed an amicus brief in which it called for a narrow interpretation of § 1782.[92] Acknowledging that its filing was "highly unusual,"[93] the EC said it had decided to share its views only because a broad interpretation of the statute "would directly threaten the Commission's enforcement mission,"[94] place its "competition law enforcement programs . . . in jeopardy,"[95] and risk "unacceptable consequence[s]."[96] The EC went so far as to warn that an expansive interpretation would "undermine[] international comity" and "offend the sovereign interests of the United States' foreign policy partners."[97]

On the other hand, the amicus brief filed by the U.S. Department of Justice argued that the statute foresaw a broad interpretation.[98] It described the statute's history, referring to articles by Professor Hans

Smit, chair in the early 1960s of the commission that drafted the 1965 amendments, and it suggested alternative ways that district courts could deal with the EC's objections and concerns.[99]

The Court, having received these views, turned to the specific questions presented. First, was the DG-Competition a "tribunal"? The EC had argued no: It operates as an investigative body, not a judicial one. It decides whether to bring cases, rather like an executive branch agency such as the Justice Department's Antitrust Division. Its proceedings are not adversarial. It can eventually decide to make findings of a violation, rather as the American Federal Trade Commission can. But if it does, those findings are subject to judicial review.[100] And most important, to hold, over its objection, that the DG-Competition is a "tribunal" would permit businesses, anxious to obtain confidential information describing practices from competitors, to bring "pretextual" complaints before the EC and file document requests in the United States.[101] This would threaten the EC's confidentiality rules, its systems of prosecution, and in particular its "leniency program," whereby a "whistle-blower," such as a cartel member, can submit incriminating information to the EC on condition that it not be disclosed.[102] Perhaps in the early 1960s, when European antitrust enforcement was less vigorous, these EC interests were less important. But today, the EC said, they are "vital."[103] The EC added that it had no problem obtaining the information it needed without the statute. It could do so either by ordering firms doing business in Europe to produce it, or by asking the U.S. Department of Justice for help under its cooperation agreements.[104]

But what was the Court to do about the statute's language and history? It was fairly clear from both that Congress had intended it to reach foreign proceedings resembling those in an American administrative agency.[105] The text refers to "tribunals," not just courts, and it makes clear, for example, that the statute covers requests by prosecutors who are simply investigating prior to an indictment.[106] If similarity to an American agency were determinative, the DG-Competition would seem to qualify: like the Federal Trade Commission, its job is to investigate potential violations of European competition laws and make recommendations to the EC, all of which are reviewable by courts. Moreover, the DG-Competition was only one among many thousands of foreign entities affected by § 1782. Perhaps it did not want the documents sought by AMD to be produced, and perhaps it did not want to call itself a "tribunal." But what about the other entities?[107]

The EC warned that if § 1782 were interpreted to authorize discovery here, the statute would then apply to "virtually *every* administrative agency action, regulation, investigation, license, or permit anywhere in the world, so long as the action is ultimately subject to judicial review."[108] And Congress could not have intended district courts to be clearinghouses of information for use in *all* such proceedings. It was a good point, though drawing a line was admittedly difficult. What is the legal standard for separating some overseas proceedings from others? And how is the Court, which has only limited knowledge of foreign administrative entities, to find the right rule? Perhaps the Court could defer to an entity's own self-characterization (that is what I argued in dissent);[109] but doing so invites inconsistency. In the end, the Court held that the DG-Competition was a "tribunal," but it did not lay down an absolute rule or framework for classifying foreign entities in the future.[110]

Second, was AMD an "interested person"? AMD was not a litigant overseas. It simply called the DG-Competition's attention to possible antitrust law violations by Intel and submitted evidence. But the Court acknowledged that AMD also had a right to "proceed to court if the Commission discontinues the investigation or dismisses the complaint."[111] Moreover, Professor Smit had written that the phrase "any interested person" is "intended to include not only litigants ... but also ... any other person ... [who] merely possesses a reasonable interest in obtaining the assistance."[112] The Court concluded that AMD fell within the scope of the phrase.[113]

Third, was the EC's investigation a "proceeding"? The Court said yes. An investigation is not an "adjudicative" proceeding, but it is a proceeding nonetheless. Congress indicated that it expected the statute to extend to investigations.[114] And the Court rejected the view that the section "comes into play only when adjudicative proceedings are 'pending' or 'imminent.'"[115] Rather, the statute "requires only that a dispositive ruling by the Commission, reviewable by the European courts, be within reasonable contemplation."[116]

Fourth, what about some kind of limiting rule, for example, to exclude instances of a private person seeking discovery to which he would not be entitled under the law of the foreign jurisdiction in which it was to be used, or under domestic law in analogous circumstances? Dissenting, I favored such a rule, lest the statute permit, for example, a private citizen to obtain information relating to a foreign criminal prosecutor's decision *not* to prosecute, or a housing developer to obtain information designed to help secure a British Housing Authority grant.[117] The DG-Competition strongly favored such a rule, too.

But there were strong reasons against interpreting the statute in this way. For one thing, the statute, as the Court pointed out, says nothing about discoverability abroad. Moreover, it only permits, it does not require, a court to order the production of documents. In any individual case, a district court can take into account foreign countries' objections to compelled production and either narrow or decline § 1782 requests to prevent international discord. Further, a foreign discoverability rule of the type requested by Intel would invite litigation in case after case asking whether foreign law would, in a given instance, permit document production of the kind at issue. Such a limiting principle could become considerably more difficult to apply than might at first appear.

At the same time, the Department of Justice argued that there was little need for a limiting principle. District courts could refuse to issue an order in a case in which the DG-Competition had problems.[118] And that is just what the Court said. It emphasized that "a district court is not required to grant a § 1782 discovery application simply because it has the authority to do so."[119] The court "may take into account the nature of the foreign tribunal, the character of the proceedings under way abroad, . . . the receptivity of the foreign government or . . . agency" to our "judicial assistance," and the burdens likely imposed.[120] In sum, the Court held that the statute has a broad scope, but individual courts should limit its reach where reasonable, on a case-by-case basis.[121]

Was this a sound compromise? The European Commission did not think so. It pointed to several defects in a case-by-case approach. For one thing, "a district court can weigh fairly the complex interests of a foreign sovereign," only if the court "is made aware of those interests."[122] But "there is no system for providing" the EC "with notice" of a case.[123] For another, when notified, the EC will have to waste "scarce resources" arguing to a U.S. court that it should not enforce a private party's request.[124] Further, different judges may develop different approaches, producing "unpredictability and uncertainty."[125] Finally, "each adverse" district court decision "will be a potential irritant in relations between . . . important allies"; it will produce "interference with the normal conduct of international cooperation between the Commission and United States law enforcement authorities" and risk substituting "international friction" for "international comity."[126] The Department of Justice did not deny the problem, saying that these considerations "may ultimately provide the basis for developing general" supervisory "rules to channel the district court's discretion."[127] But the Court should not do so now, without the benefit of additional lower court experience and the views of other foreign governmental entities.

For present purposes, what lessons should we draw from the Court's opinion? First, to decide the case—which required interpreting the text of an American statute—the Court had absolutely no choice but to examine (and endeavor to understand) the details of foreign legal procedure. Section 1782 spoke of "proceeding[s]," "tribunal[s]," and "interested person[s]" abroad. To apply those terms to a particular factual circumstance, the Court needed to know something about foreign practices and rules. If the *Empagran* case had brought the Court into new territory—requiring it to understand not only substantive antitrust law overseas but also the rules and practices involved in the *administration* of that law—*Intel* went one step further. Now the Court needed to understand even more technical rules and systems for administering the law abroad, and to distinguish between a judicial forum, an administrative forum, and the like, in foreign countries.

Second, examining these matters is a far more difficult task than one might imagine. The Court is not expert in foreign legal systems.

Third, predictions about likely consequences may prove important. Which route was likely to produce the greater set of difficulties: (1) an absolute limiting rule, which would lead to litigation about when, and whether, foreign law permits the production of documents of the kind at issue; or (2) a case-by-case *discretionary* approach, which would empower district courts to make sensitive determinations about when to limit discovery but would threaten the harms that the EC feared? The truth is that the Court could not be certain which approach was preferable. It had little directly relevant legal experience upon which to draw. It opted for the discretionary case-by-case approach, but time will tell how workable that approach turns out to be.

Fourth, we need better ways of learning about the necessarily relevant foreign realities. In this case, we received government briefs only from the EC and the U.S. Department of Justice. The Court relied upon these briefs, as well as on a commentary written in the early 1960s by a well-informed professor of international procedure. Was this enough? As the Court noted, we could not be sure whether the EC's view—that American discovery would not greatly aid its work abroad and that a narrow reading was thus appropriate—was widely shared by other foreign entities.[128] Did we know enough to decide the case?

This "information gap" may be closing. The legal profession has three parts, the judges, the lawyers, and the academics. When the system works well, it works iteratively. The judges decide cases on the basis of the bar's briefs, which in turn rest, not just upon experience, but also upon research, articles, and treatises written by academics, and the academics base their work in part upon court decisions, amalgamated and criticized in light of research, which in turn feeds back to the bench through the bar, in principle producing better decisions. Perhaps this system, along with increased understanding of the ever more international demands of legal practice, will close the "information gap." But at the moment I pose my question: How can we better answer the multinational procedural questions of the kind that *Intel* presents?

MORRISON: SECURITIES REGULATION

Morrison, a securities case, provides another excellent example of the effect of a changing world marketplace upon the interpretation of an important American statute.[129] The one in question authorizes the Securities and Exchange Commission (SEC) to promulgate rules prohibiting securities fraud.[130] In the 1930s the SEC issued its most famous rule, Rule 10b-5. Echoing the language of the statute, this rule forbids "any person" from making any materially false statement or otherwise engaging in fraud "in connection with the purchase or sale of any security."[131] Does the rule apply to fraudulent activities taking place abroad?

There are many ways to answer this question. A court could look to whether (and how much of) the fraudulent activity took place in the United States versus abroad; it could assess whether (and how many of) the deceived buyers or sellers live in the United States versus other countries; or it could consider whether the exchanges on which the securities were traded are located in the United States or abroad. We will turn to some of these specifics later, but for present purposes, the basic point is that the Court's *approach* to the bigger question (where does Rule 10b-5 apply?) has shifted over the years. And it has done so in response to the changing nature of foreign securities markets.

To understand how the law has changed, we must first consider securities cases decided in the 1960s and 1970s, particularly in New York by the Court of Appeals for the Second Circuit and even more particularly the opinions of Judge Henry Friendly. Those cases had considerable influence, because the legal community has long thought that the Second Circuit (and the esteemed Judge Friendly) understood securities law and securities markets especially well.

Although the circuit set forth its views in a series of cases, an epitome is found in *IIT v. Cornfeld*, a case decided in 1980 by a panel consisting of Judges Friendly, James Oakes, and Jon Newman, all well-respected jurists.[132] The facts are complicated, but I can simplify them. The plaintiff was IIT, an investment trust organized under Luxembourg law and managed by a company that was incorporated in Luxembourg but operated out of Switzerland. Of IIT's 150,000 "fund holders" (whom we can treat as shareholders), only 200 resided in America. At the company's height, it had approximately $375 million under management, 40 percent of which was invested in American securities.[133]

The investors sued in the name of the trust, IIT itself, claiming they had been defrauded (or more accurately, that IIT had been) when the trust bought securities in several companies owned or controlled by an American, John King. IIT's shareholders claimed that King's entities made many false statements designed to inflate the projected valuations of their companies; that IIT had consequently paid far too much for those entities' securities; and that when the truth came out, IIT's value declined significantly, losing approximately $35 million.[134]

Did Rule 10b-5 apply? In answering that question, the court distinguished among three different kinds of securities that IIT had purchased from King's companies: (a) 200,000 shares of common stock in a publicly traded firm called King Resources Company (KRC), incorporated in Maine; (b) a convertible note issued by a private company called The Colorado Corporation (TCC), largely owned by King himself; and (c) Eurodollar bonds issued by a special subsidiary of KRC called King

Resources Capital Corporation (KRCC), which was based in Netherlands Antilles.[135]

The Second Circuit held that Rule 10b-5 plainly applied to the first two sets of securities. Both the shares and convertible notes were "securities of American companies," and the transactions, or purchases of them, had been "fully consummated" in the United States.[136] Specifically, in the case of the KRC common stock, the shares had been purchased for IIT in the over-the-counter market by an American brokerage firm, Lipper, and then been placed in a custodial account in The New Bank's office in New York City. The TCC notes, purchased in Denver, were placed in the same custodial account. Accordingly, the only thing "foreign" about these transactions was that "purchaser [IIT] was a foreigner and the orders were transmitted from abroad."[137] But that fact could not change the result. There was no reason to deny a foreign buyer the protection of American laws where the securities and the sales were all basically American in nature.

So far, the answer seems easy. But what about the third category of securities, involving the KRCC bonds (called "debentures")? Here there were considerably more foreign elements to the fraud: the debentures were of a Eurodollar offering, they were the obligations of a foreign corporation (KRCC, the wholly owned subsidiary of KRC, with its headquarters in Netherlands Antilles), and IIT bought the bonds in the European aftermarket. While much of the fraudulent conduct occurred in America or was consummated by Americans, these securities were foreign, as were the transactions and the company that the securities obliged.[138]

The court held that Rule 10b-5 still applied. Why? The easiest part to deal with was the foreign subsidiary. The court found that KRC's Netherlands Antilles unit served no significant business purpose. It had been "inserted into the total offering simply because European investors were reluctant to purchase debentures issued directly by an American corporation," but it "had no operating assets, the debentures issued by it were guaranteed by KRC, and they were convertible into KRC common stock."[139]

But what about the Eurobonds themselves? Were they not foreign? The court thought not, or at least not entirely. For one thing, the offering of those bonds had been part of a larger, "closely coordinated" bond offering by KRC, the parent company. That is, the sale by KRC of

$15 million in KRCC debentures had followed a primary offering of $25 million in its own debentures (i.e., American securities sold in the United States) and had been "an integral part of th[e] financing" of the broader scheme.[140] Furthermore, almost all the work on the KRCC bond issuance was done in the United States: The prospectus was written in the United States. The accounting work was done in the United States. And little if any of this necessary work was done abroad.[141] The upshot: A foreign buyer, a nominally foreign seller (but one integrally connected to an American company), a foreign transaction, nominally foreign securities, and American fraud; it all amounted to sufficient relation to America to fall within the scope of Rule 10b-5.

The most important part of *IIT v. Cornfeld*, for purposes of the present discussion, is the way the court approached the problem. It proceeded in a piece-by-piece, totality-of-the-circumstances fashion, determining the degree of the American connection after considering the details of each aspect of the overall transaction. Thus, after finding that the sale of the first set of securities (the 200,000 shares of common stock in KRC) was "fully consummated within the United States," the court went on to say that the presence of this factor, like *"the presence or absence of any single factor . . . [wa]s not necessarily dispositive."*[142] It stated. "[W]e do not mean to suggest that either the American nationality of the issuer or consummation of the transaction in the United States is either a necessary or sufficient factor" to trigger the application of Rule 10b-5.[143] But if both factors were present, that "point[ed] strongly toward applying" the American law.[144]

The court also referred to the statute's intent. It said that "Congress would have been considerably more interested in assuring against the fraudulent issuance of securities constituting obligations of American rather than purely foreign business."[145] But when the securities "in substance were American," as the court concluded was the case for the KRCC debentures, Congress would have intended its antifraud laws to apply. It was unlikely that "Congress intended to allow the United States to be used as a base for manufacturing fraudulent security devices for export, even when these are peddled only to foreigners."[146]

Finally, the court referred to a case in which the fact that "many acts of deception had occurred in the United States" led to application of Rule 10b-5, even though the buyer had bought stock in a foreign company and bought it abroad.[147] The court did not believe that "if fraud had been committed in the United States . . . , American courts would look away."[148]

So Rule 10b-5's application depended upon a mix of factors; it might well prohibit fraud in connection with securities prepared at home but bought and sold abroad; and it would protect foreign buyers. What would other countries think of this application of Rule 10b-5 to sales of foreign securities within their borders? The Second Circuit considered the possible reaction of Luxembourg, the country where IIT had its headquarters, went bankrupt, and was the subject of bankruptcy court proceedings. And the court said: "The primary interest of Luxembourg is in the righting of a wrong done to an entity created by it. If our anti-fraud laws are stricter than Luxembourg's, that country will surely not be offended by their application. . . . The defendants with whom we are here concerned acted in the United States and cannot fairly object to having their conduct judged by its laws."[149]

But was the Second Circuit right about this? And even if so, would the same conclusion necessary hold in future cases?

Over the next two decades, the Second Circuit and federal appellate courts throughout the country continued to use multifactor tests to determine the applicability of Rule 10b-5 abroad. Each circuit would develop its own particular formula, but the basic questions asked concerned the place where the conduct occurred, the effects of the activity on American securities markets, and the nationality of the purchasers, sellers, and securities exchanges. In assessing these factors, as in *IIT*, courts would put considerable weight not only upon the country where the securities were actually ordered or purchased, but also upon the one where the fraudulent misrepresentations were made. Still, courts were not identical in their analyses; some valued the "effects" on U.S. markets more than any other factor, while others prioritized the degree of U.S.-based wrongdoing.[150] And as cases involving foreign securities or foreign purchasers became more common (as financial markets became more integrated), commentators began to criticize the lack of consistency across American jurisdictions regarding Rule 10b-5's application abroad.[151]

THE PRESENT: *MORRISON*

Let us now return to *Morrison,* the case our Court heard in 2010.[152] In 1998 National Australia Bank, the largest bank in Australia, had bought HomeSide Lending, a mortgage servicing company with headquarters in Florida. Because HomeSide earned money by administering mortgages—that is, sending homeowners monthly mortgage bills and collecting payments—the longer a mortgage lasted, the more money HomeSide made. HomeSide used models to calculate its profitability, based in part upon assumptions about interest rates, refinancing, and the typical duration of mortgages. These assumptions turned out to be faulty, overstating HomeSide's likely profits.[153]

In mid-2001 National Australia Bank announced that the value of HomeSide's business was less than it had thought earlier, and it wrote that value down on its books by about $2.25 billion. As a result, the bank's share prices fell precipitously. Bank officials blamed the overvaluation and write-down on an unexpected fall in interest rates, which had driven more mortgage holders to refinancing and early repayment than the models had predicted.[154]

Some of the bank's shareholders, however, had a less innocent explanation. They thought that HomeSide executives had deliberately manipulated the models and that bank executives were aware of this but took no action. A group of Australians who had bought shares of National Australia Bank on the Australian stock exchange in 2000 and early 2001 (meaning after the acquisition of HomeSide Lending but before the write-down) sued the bank for fraud. They brought their lawsuit in New York City, claiming a violation of Rule 10b-5.[155]

Now we have foreign purchasers (i.e., Australians), foreign shares (i.e., shares in National Australia Bank listed on the Australian stock exchange), a foreign transaction (i.e., bank share purchases executed in Australia and other countries), but an American fraud involving an American company. Does Rule 10b-5 apply when conduct contributing to securities fraud takes place within the United States, but the sales affected by the fraud take place abroad? The lower courts thought not and dismissed the case. According to the Second Circuit panel, while U.S.-based activity can indeed trigger federal jurisdiction over securities transactions consummated abroad, the domestic activity here was too marginal to count.[156] Finally, the Supreme Court agreed to consider the question.

All the justices agreed that the fraud, the purchases, the securities, and the parties, when taken together, were too closely connected to Australia and too little connected to the United States to trigger application of the SEC's rule.[157] The interest of the case, for present purposes, however, does not lie in the result. Indeed, the Second Circuit had come to the same conclusion. Rather, what's notable is the reasoning adopted by the majority and by the concurring justices to determine whether the American statute applied.

Two justices, while agreeing with the conclusion that Rule 10b-5 did not apply in this instance, would have used something like the Second Circuit's framework for deciding the question. Justice Stevens summarized the approach as involving two inquiries: (1) whether the wrongful conduct (or "substantial acts in furtherance of" it) occurred in the United States, and (2) whether the wrongful conduct "intended to produce and did produce detrimental effects within the United States."[158] If either condition was satisfied, an investor could sue for damages in federal court under Rule 10b-5. This approach, Justice Stevens explained, was developed and "refined" by the Second Circuit "over several decades and dozens of cases, with the tacit approval of Congress and the Commission and with the general assent of its sister Circuits."[159] It was crafted in light of the statute's text and purpose, and it reflected that text and purpose. Surely Judge Friendly and his colleagues on the Second Circuit were "aware that United States courts cannot and should not expend [their] resources resolving cases that do not affect Americans or involve fraud emanating from America."[160] But they were also aware that Congress intended its securities laws to reach *some* frauds with an international component, and they carefully developed a test that captured that congressional intent.[161]

Accordingly, this minority would have proceeded on something like a case-by-case basis, looking to a multitude of factors—such as the nature of the U.S.-based conduct and its relationship to the overall fraud, and the effects of the fraud on domestic markets or investors—to determine if the rule applied. Even if the case involved foreign investors buying shares on foreign exchanges, these concurring justices would have favored such an approach.[162]

The majority of the Court, however, took a different approach. It interpreted § 10(b) of the Exchange Act, and the SEC's corollary Rule 10b-5, as containing clear guidelines as to territorial scope. Namely, Rule 10b-5 applies "only in connection with" either (1) the "purchase or sale of a security listed on an American stock exchange" or (2) the "purchase or sale of any other security *in the United States.*"[163] Since none of the plaintiffs had purchased or sold National Australia Bank's securities on a domestic exchange or consummated their purchases or sales within the United States, the rule did not apply.[164] And that was the end of the matter.

The holding represented a significant change from the case law that had governed in most federal circuits. The Court substituted a simple principle for a case-by-case approach: instead of weighing various factors to assess the fraud's overall connection to the United States, it simply looked to the location of the securities transaction in question. Unlike the Second Circuit and many others, the Court did not seek to ascertain what Congress would have intended in respect to application of the securities laws to that specific circumstance. Given the bright-line finding, it seems unlikely that the Second Circuit could have applied Rule 10b-5 to KRCC's Eurobond debentures had *Morrison* been the law at the time.

The Court provided several reasons for making this significant change. First, it set forth a fairly common criticism of approaches such as that taken by the Second Circuit. Compared to a bright-line rule, the multifactor test is vague, is difficult to apply, and threatens inconsistent results. How is one to decide whether Congress "wished the precious resources of United States courts . . . be devoted" to protecting foreign stock purchasers rather than "leav[ing] the problem to foreign countries"?[165] Does it make a difference whether those who buy abroad are American or themselves foreign? Is the fact that fraudulent conduct takes place within the United States a sufficient basis to apply the rule? How can courts administer a test that identifies several different factors as relevant but not determinative? As we saw in Part I, multifactor tests, and many common law decisions, are subject to such objections.

Second, the Court invoked the presumption against the extraterritorial application of statutes: that is, the "longstanding principle of American law that legislation of Congress, unless a contrary intent appears, is meant to apply only within the territorial jurisdiction of the United States."[166] Examining the language of the statute, it found that nothing "affirmative[ly]" suggested that Congress intended extraterritorial application.[167] Hence it concluded that § 10(b) of the Securities Exchange Act, the section that authorizes Rule 10b-5, did not apply extraterritorially.

But how does turning to this presumption answer the question? Everyone agrees that some of the conduct at issue—namely, the fraudulent conduct—took place within the United States. Doesn't that fact trigger application of the statute? To answer that question, one must look at the statute's purpose, not just its language. That is perhaps why the Court conceded that the "presumption here (as often) is not self-evidently dispositive."[168]

Third, the Court emphasized the one basic purpose of the securities statutes—namely, ensuring the integrity of American financial markets. More specifically, the Court explained, the goal of federal securities laws is to protect investors undertaking purchases and sales of securities within the United States—either by buying or selling securities listed on American exchanges, or by otherwise engaging in securities transactions within U.S. territory. Rule 10b-5, in particular, is designed to prevent fraudulent misrepresentations to investors when they engage in such transactions. By limiting § 10(b) and Rule 10b-5's reach to purchases or sales occurring within the United States, the Court believed it was effectuating what Congress intended.[169]

Fourth, and for our purposes most important, the Court said that the "probability of incompatibility with the applicable laws of other countries is so obvious that if Congress intended such foreign application 'it would have addressed the subject of conflicts with foreign laws and procedures.'"[170] Underscoring that thought, it wrote:

> [F]oreign countries regulate their domestic securities exchanges and securities transactions occurring within their territorial jurisdiction. And the regulation of other countries often differs from ours as to what constitutes fraud, what disclosures must be made, what damages are recoverable, what discovery is available in litigation, what individual actions may be joined in a single suit, what attorney's fees are recoverable, and many other matters.[171]

The Court then produced a list of amicus briefs filed by foreign entities. They included the governments of Australia, France, and the United Kingdom, financial institutions and businesses from France, Germany, and Switzerland, and European and international associations. The Court said that "*all* [these briefs] complain of the interference with foreign securities regulation that application" of Rule 10b-5 abroad "would produce, and urge the adoption of a clear test that will avoid that consequence."[172]

What about Judge Friendly's contention that if "our anti-fraud laws are stricter than Luxembourg's, that country will surely not be offended by their application"?[173] That assurance, the Court decided, was no longer warranted. There "is no reason to believe that the United States has become the Barbary Coast for those perpetrating frauds on foreign securities markets," the Court wrote (while adding that "some fear that it has become the Shangri-La of class-action litigation for lawyers representing those allegedly cheated in foreign securities markets").[174]

The Court did not make much of the word *comity*, as it had done in *Empagran*. But its arguments, reflecting the amicus briefs, accept the importance of the principle as defined in terms of the need for harmonizing enforcement schemes throughout the world. As with overseas antitrust laws and regulation in *Empagran*, the *Morrison* Court well appreciated that foreign securities laws and regulation had become quite complex and highly developed by the year 2010. And importantly, those legal regimes were not identical to that in the United States. Switzerland, for instance, has created a comprehensive system of securities regulation involving a central regulator, the Swiss Financial Markets Supervisory Authority, registration requirements, antifraud prohibitions, administrative investigations, and civil penalties. But Swiss law does not authorize securities fraud class actions, and it has a different standard for judging the "materiality" of disclosures and a different method for calculating damages.[175] The French regime has its own variations: it does not allow opt-out class actions and grants recovery in securities cases only upon a showing of negligence.[176]

With the maturation of many different regulatory systems for securities markets, there arose an increased need for both procedural and substantive coordination; a demand for legal certainty in each system; and a dearth of good reasons for using American antifraud law to police the world. In a word, the reality of global financial markets and their modern-day regulation argued for an American system that worked in harmony with others. Such harmony, the Court thought, required an interpretation that was more definite about the statute's territorial scope. That is what the amicus briefs tried to tell the Court in *Morrison*.[177] And the *Morrison* Court ultimately agreed.

KIRTSAENG: COPYRIGHT

Now let us turn to a final example of a case in which the Court has wrestled in recent years with the reach of an American commercial statute. This case, mentioned at the very outset of this book, concerned the federal Copyright Act and whether one of its provisions applied to a commercial dealing conducted outside the United States. As with *Empagran, Intel,* and *Morrison,* the facts here illustrate the reality of modern-day commerce: national markets are now so interconnected and integrated that the most ordinary commercial transactions can involve a host of different activities and entities across the globe. The case shows how the nature of those international business practices and the large amount of commerce involved can significantly affect the Court's interpretation of a primarily domestic statute. In the absence of comity concerns like those at issue in *Empagran* and *Morrison* (a potential clash between American enforcement priorities and those of foreign countries) the Court has been more willing to apply a domestic statute to foreign activities.

In 1997 Supap Kirtsaeng, a citizen of Thailand, received a scholarship from his government permitting him to study in the United States.[178] After undergraduate work in mathematics at Cornell, he completed a Ph.D. in the field at the University of Southern California. He subsequently returned to Thailand to teach for ten years, a condition of his scholarship.[179]

While he was still in the United States, Kirtsaeng had noticed that many of his textbooks were far more expensive than the foreign export editions of the same books, also in English, which were on sale at bookstores in Thailand. He therefore asked friends and family in Thailand to buy him copies and ship them to the United States, which they did. Kirtsaeng kept some of the copies for himself and sold the rest to students and to others. With the proceeds he would reimburse his family and friends and keep the rest as profit.[180]

In 2008 John Wiley & Sons, an academic textbook publisher, sued Kirtsaeng for copyright infringement. Wiley published and sold textbooks in the United States.[181] But the firm also sold foreign editions of those textbooks—the same English-language text, but printed and sold abroad—through its wholly owned foreign subsidary, John Wiley & Sons (Asia) Pte Ltd. The foreign editions sold at lower prices, and each copy contained a notice stating that the book was "[p]rinted in Asia" and "authorized for sale in Europe, Asia, Africa, and the Middle East only and may not be exported out of these territories."[182] Thus there were two equivalent versions of Wiley's textbooks: a higher-priced one "printed and sold in the United States," and a lower-priced one printed and sold in Asia. The second contained a notice making clear that the copy was not to be taken into the United States without Wiley's permission.[183]

After a trial in federal court, the jury found that Kirtsaeng had brought copies of eight Asian editions of Wiley's books into the United States without Wiley's permission and resold them to persons here. This constituted copyright infringement. The jury assessed damages against Kirtsaeng of $75,000 per work, or $600,000 total.[184] Kirtsaeng lost his first appeal, and then the case came to the Supreme Court.[185]

The question in the case was important for domestic and international commerce. Federal copyright law covers a vast range of products. Not only books but also articles in journals and on the Internet, films, music, video games, and television programs are copyrighted. So, too, are software components of automobiles and other consumer products, as well as the designs and even words on the labels of those products. And many of these copyrighted items are sold internationally. Indeed, briefs suggested that hundreds of billions, perhaps trillions, of dollars of commerce was involved. Thus, whether John Wiley did or did not have the legal right to keep Supap Kirtsaeng from importing Wiley's cheaper foreign editions of its textbooks into the United States, and reselling those editions here, mattered to manufacturers and consumers both in the United States and throughout the world.

At the same time, the legal question, like most statutory questions we resolve, was highly technical. The Copyright Act gives a copyright owner an "exclusive right" to "distribute copies . . . to the public by sale or other transfer of ownership."[186] But it then limits that right by stating that the "owner of a *particular copy* . . . *lawfully made under this title* . . . is entitled, without the authority of the copyright owner, to sell or otherwise dispose of the possession of that copy."[187] In other words, a bookstore taking books on consignment from a publisher cannot sell copies of, say, *Catch-22*, without the publisher's permission. The publisher, as the owner of the copyright, has that "exclusive right." But once you, an ordinary customer, buy a copy of *Catch-22* from the bookstore, you can do with it what you wish. You can give it away or resell it to a friend. The publisher's exclusive right to dispose of that copy of *Catch-22* has been limited by your purchase of it. This limitation is known as the "first sale" doctrine. It is also sometimes referred to as "exhaustion," in that the first sale of the copy "exhausts" the copyright holder's exclusive rights vis-à-vis that copy.

The question before the Court concerned copies of textbooks that were manufactured and sold abroad. John Wiley (Asia) was in the business of printing English-language textbooks in which John Wiley & Sons, its American parent corporation, held copyrights (having obtained them from the authors through assignments, licenses, and permissions).[188] John Wiley (Asia) then sold (or consigned) the textbooks it printed to Thai bookshops. Kirtsaeng asked his parents and friends to buy English-language textbooks from Thai stores and send them to him for resale in the United States at a higher price.[189] The Court had to determine: Does a "first sale" of a copy in Thailand (say, to Kirtsaeng's parents) trigger the "first sale" doctrine? If so, Kirtsaeng could do what he wanted with the copy—he could resell it to friends or others. If not, he had violated the Copyright Act.

Well, why should the "first sale" doctrine not apply given these facts? The statutory language I italicized several paragraphs above suggests a possible problem: the "first sale" doctrine applies to "a particular copy ... *lawfully made under this title*."[190] (The word *title* here refers to the Copyright Act itself, an American statute.) So, was Kirtsaeng's copy, lawfully manufactured in Thailand and originally sold lawfully to a customer there, "made under this title"? If not, Kirtsaeng certainly could not distribute the copy in the United States, and he also could not import it in the first place. A different provision of the act says that importing a copy without permission of the copyright owner violates the basic exclusive "right to distribute."[191] But if the copies here were "lawfully made under this title," such that the "first sale" doctrine was triggered, limiting Wiley's exclusive rights in those copies with respect to both their importation and distribution, then Kirtsaeng's actions were indeed lawful.[192]

Do the words *lawfully made under this title* refer, geographically, to books published or printed in the United States only? If so, the liberating "first sale" provision does not apply to Kirtsaeng's situation, for the copies he acquired and resold were made abroad. And in that case, when Kirtsaeng brought them into the United States, he violated the law. Or do those words refer more broadly to books published or printed in conformity with the American law's requirements, even if those books were physically made or printed abroad? If so, Kirtsaeng was home free.

Ordinarily, when deciding difficult textual questions, courts look to text, history, tradition, precedent, purpose, and consequences. In my own view, most of these traditional considerations did not point to a clear answer. Consider the text. What does "under this title" mean? Should we give it a *geographical* interpretation, referring to location (that is, the United States), or a *non*geographical interpretation, referring to copies wherever made but made "in accordance with," or "in compliance with," the Copyright Act?[193]

At first blush, the geographical reading may seem more natural. After all, a violation of the Copyright Act—say, by distributing or importing a copy without permission— typically takes place in the United States. And so to ask whether a book made or sold abroad was made or distributed "in conformity with" the provisions of the American act is to ask a hypothetical question that may be hard to answer.

On the other hand, some provisions of the act do seem to apply abroad. It says, for instance, that works "subject to protection under this title" include unpublished works created abroad,[194] as well as works "first published" in any of the nearly 180 nations that have signed a copyright treaty with the United States.[195] Thus a manuscript lying in the desk drawer of its Irish author in Dublin would seem to be covered, as would a video recording of a ballet performance first made in Japan and now on display in a Kyoto Gallery.[196] And if the act applies to materials originally written or otherwise created abroad, why would it not apply to copies of a book manufactured and sold abroad with the copyright holder's permission?

What about the Copyright Act's history? The Court pointed out that the "first sale" doctrine is a common law doctrine with deep roots. In the early seventeenth century, Sir Edward Coke, a great English judge, explained that the common law wisely forbade a seller of "a horse[] or of any other chattel" from imposing upon a buyer a condition forbidding the buyer to resell that property, for such a restriction on alienation would be "against Trade and Traffi[c], and bargaining and contracting betwee[n] man and man."[197] Conditioning a first sale on a requirement that there be no subsequent sales would indeed prevent competition in the marketplace; trying to enforce those conditions, courts would face serious administrative difficulties, like tracing horses or other goods back to their original owners.[198] The same is true of copyrighted commodities today. But if history argued for the deep roots of the "first sale" doctrine in American common law and its importance for economic efficiency, it did not yield a determinative answer to the precise questions in the case.

What about the Copyright Act's purposes? It is easy to say that the "first sale" doctrine, as applied within the United States, serves the purposes just mentioned—encouraging competition in buyers' markets and saving judges from burdensome chain-of-custody investigations. But that does not tell us whether Congress intended the doctrine to apply when the first sale takes place abroad. In fact, applying the doctrine in such circumstances would make it harder for American and foreign publishers of the same book to divide territories, selling their books in separate territories. And perhaps Congress wanted to encourage that kind of division, as it would likely help American publishers to keep prices, and thus revenues, higher in the United States. But the majority pointed out that Congress had just repealed the "manufacturing clause," which had previously required that books sold in America be printed in America.[199] Was this not evidence that Congress favored free trade and consequently wanted the "first sale" doctrine to apply to foreign sales? Or is it that Congress favored *some degree of* free trade, perhaps leaving a "no first sale" doctrine as a still-desirable remnant of a more protectionist past?

As in many cases, the majority thought these traditional arguments leaned somewhat in one direction, here in favor of Kirtsaeng. And the dissent thought the contrary.

The majority also thought that some of the strongest arguments in Kirtsaeng's favor rested upon commercial consequences, particularly those combining foreign and domestic considerations. It pointed to a brief of the American Library Association telling us that collections here contain at least 200 million books published abroad.[200] Many of these were printed and bought outside the United States; many were still under copyright protection (which now can last longer than a century).[201] Were libraries therefore obliged to obtain permission to distribute these books?[202] Suppose they had difficulty finding, or reaching, the foreign copyright holder?

Technology companies reminded us that "automobiles, microwaves, calculators, mobile phones, tablets, and personal computers" all contain copyrighted software programs or packaging.[203] If the "first sale" exception did not apply to foreign-manufactured and foreign-sold goods, an American car dealer could not import for resale a car made and sold abroad without first obtaining permission from the holders of each copyright on each piece of automobile software.[204]

Retailers told us that over $2.3 trillion worth of foreign goods were imported in 2011. American retailers buy many of these goods after a first sale abroad. Many bear copyrighted labels, logos, and instructions. Would retailers find themselves subject to suits for infringement?[205]

Used book dealers explained that they have operated since the days of Thomas Jefferson and Benjamin Franklin under the assumption that the "first sale" doctrine applies to books published and printed abroad. And what were travelers to do when they wish to buy a dozen or more copies of a foreign book overseas, to give to friends at home (who might give them away to others)?[206]

Art museum directors told us that they often display works by foreign artists, on loan from foreign museums, which in turn might have received the work by donation or sale from a foreign artist or collector. Must the American museums obtain permission from the copyright holders before they "display" the work, even if the artist or copyright holder donated or sold the work to the foreign museum? And suppose the museums do not know who that copyright owner is?[207] (Ownership of Picasso's works was, for many years, the subject of legal disputes among his heirs.)

In a word, the untoward commercial consequences were too many and too grave, weighing heavily against an interpretation restricting the "first sale" doctrine to articles or items published and/or initially sold in the United States.

The dissent pointed out that in some areas of the country, their interpretation ("no first sale" doctrine abroad) had been the law, and the "parade of horrible[]" consequences feared by the majority had not taken place.[208] The dissenters thought there were other ways to minimize or to prevent such harms. Other parts of the Copyright Act could be invoked so that retailers, manufacturers, museums, and other entities in the United States did not need to obtain permission from copyright holders to reproduce or resell copyrighted works brought into the United States.[209] And, the dissent argued, the majority's interpretation, by preventing the division of international markets into distinct sales territories, would also have negative consequences. It would prevent writers and publishers, whom copyright law seeks to protect, from maximizing their profits.[210]

But ultimately these latter arguments did not carry the day. The size of international markets, their interdependence, as well as the abundance of products mixing foreign and domestic components, all made the predictions of adverse consequences plausible. At the same time, neither the dissenters nor any other member of the Court had enough information to counter the majority's argument with an estimate of how much copyrighted material was subject to international market division agreements. Nor could we easily reckon the likely importance to consumers or to producers of maintaining the separate markets.

The Court's opinions make clear that market divisions permit manufacturers or publishers to discriminate in pricing. A publisher, for example, might sell the same book for a high price in one market, America, and for a low price in another market, Thailand, without fear that some Kirtsaeng will buy at the low price and resell at the high price, thereby undermining the two-tier pricing arrangement. But from the perspective of copyright law, is that good or bad? The publisher will make more money, but copyright law does not necessarily aim to maximize publisher profits at all costs. The consumer may, or may not, be better off, depending upon whether the alternative for the publisher is higher prices abroad or lower prices at home. But in the absence of information about how the markets actually work, neither the majority nor the dissent could say more than "it depends."

Market divisions are, furthermore, forbidden throughout the European Union. The most one could say in their defense is that the key international treaty on intellectual property (the TRIPS agreement) leaves the matter up to each nation to decide for itself. And the United States has favored treaty provisions permitting discrimination and market divisions where foreign trade is at issue, such as among publishers, each of which came from a different foreign nation.[211]

Ultimately, the fear of adverse consequences (at least when coupled with what I have called traditional arguments) prevailed. By a vote of six to three, the Court held that the "first sale" doctrine applies whether that first sale takes place at home or abroad. Kirtsaeng won.

For present purposes, I would draw lessons from the Court's decision in *Kirtsaeng* similar to those drawn in the three other cases I have discussed. First, the "parade of horribles" did not seem imaginary to the majority in large part because we, like other Americans, are aware that our dependence upon foreign trade has grown, that American businesses have ever more components coming from aboard, that the amount of commerce flowing here through foreign channels is continuously increasing, and that throughout the world, communication grows only more rapid. Thus when retailers told us they feared lawsuits based upon copyrighted labels, when libraries asked, "What about our huge foreign collections?," when technology experts feared a requirement demanding resale permission for each piece of software in highly technical equipment, their concerns rang true, and the Court was not prepared to dismiss them as minor.

Second, to resolve the case satisfactorily, the Court had to understand in some detail the interaction of foreign and domestic markets. It needed to appreciate the way sales of items abroad would have an impact upon Americans. Indeed, as I have suggested, that information may have constituted the most important feature of the case.

Third, sources of information on the foreign matters at issue were plentiful. We received the information I have described from associations of commercial and nonprofit entities with high economic stakes in the matter. The publishers, with an opposing interest, explained their side of the question well, but they did not have (and probably no one has) detailed information that could have demonstrated the need for market divisions. The United States filed a brief favoring their side,[212] but there were few explanations from anyone about how the "first sale" doctrine (or lack thereof) has worked in other countries and what has occurred if and when it was abolished.

OBSERVATIONS

These four commercial cases discussed do not show a uniform tendency by the Court to expand or to retract the reach of American statutes. In the antitrust case, the Court narrowed the scope of the statute; in the securities case, it did the same. In the discovery case, the Court expanded the reach of the statute; in the copyright case, it did the same. If the cases illustrate anything uniformly, it is the Court's practice of taking into account the relevant international effects of its decisions. Those effects have always been important when the Court decides cases involving foreign parties or activities. But they seem to have become more important and to play an ever larger role as the international marketplace itself becomes more important and its parts more interdependent.

The cases also demonstrate that in order to interpret American statutes, the Court must be reasonably familiar with foreign legal and commercial practices. It could not answer the statutory questions presented by applying a legal rule of thumb, such as the presumption against the extraterritorial application of statutes. To interpret the reach of an American antitrust statute, an American discovery statute, an American securities regulation, and a "first sale" copyright defense, the Court had to go well beyond any invocation of a presumption. And doing so demanded plunging into details, often of foreign procedure as well as of substance. The ways in which American procedures interact with those of foreign nations were highly relevant to the Court's decisions across the varied areas of the law considered here.

Further, when interpreting the statutes, the Court sought not simply to avoid conflict but also to harmonize analogous American and foreign law so that the systems, taken together, could work more effectively to achieve common aims. The Court said as much in *Empagran*. The disagreement between the majority and the dissent in *Intel* concerned not the validity of this objective, only whether it could be better achieved through a rule limiting the reach of the discovery statute more absolutely, or through a case-specific approach, leaving the matter to be worked out by district courts. In the securities and copyright cases, the Court was less explicit about harmonizing across borders, but the reasoning and holdings in those cases are certainly consistent with that end.

The Court's changing approach tracks a similar change in its conception of comity—from one emphasizing the more formal objective of simple conflict avoidance to the more practical objective of maintaining cooperative working arrangements with corresponding enforcement authorities of different nations. It is also consistent with the efforts in the executive branch to harmonize regulatory rules with foreign authorities.[213] Those efforts, along with the absence of ideological division on the Court relating to these, are indicative of a change in tune reflecting changes in the world.

Finally, the cases suggest that the judicial need for information about foreign practices, rules, laws, and procedures is only likely to grow. Judges need not be expert in the laws of every nation. Indeed, few if any are expert in all branches of American law. Rather, they expect lawyers and other members of the profession, through their briefs to the Court, to supply information on what is legally relevant. It is also helpful to receive briefs from other nations as well as pertinent foreign associations. Still, there remains, as these cases illustrate, an uncertainty on the part of judges where foreign law and practice is concerned. How are we to find out all we need to know? This knowledge gap is a problem to which I shall return.

CHAPTER 6

Opening the Courthouse Doors

The Alien Tort Statute and Human Rights

We now turn to a statute that helps to protect basic human rights. The citizens of most nations believe that goal to be important. They also believe that the rule of law is necessary to achieve it. The "rule of law," however, is a very general objective, and it takes hosts of subsidiary legal institutions, statutes, rules, and customs in order to make the defense of human rights a reality. The statute before us, the Alien Tort Statute (ATS), is one such implementing statute. But interpreting it to help achieve its objective has proved difficult, in large part because of the foreign implications of any interpretation.

We shall consider the ATS in detail. As in Chapter 5, doing so will illustrate the need to understand foreign practices and to find an interpretation that helps to harmonize them. But we shall also see why this isn't as easily done as with a commercial statute.

FILARTIGA

On March 29, 1976, in Asunción, Paraguay, seventeen-year-old Joelito Filártiga was kidnapped and tortured to death. His father, Dr. Joel Filártiga, was a civil rights leader, the director of a rural health clinic, and a well-known opponent of Alfredo Stroessner, the dictator of Paraguay. Early the following day, at three a.m., police officers awakened Joelito's sister, Dolly, and took her to the nearby house of Américo Peña-Irala, a neighbor and high-ranking police officer. Peña-Irala showed Dolly Joelito's body. As Dolly fled, he shouted after her, "Here you have what you have been looking for for so long and what you deserve. Now shut up."[1] Dolly said that she replied, "Tonight you have power over me, but tomorrow I will tell the world."[2]

The family subsequently brought several legal actions against Peña-Irala in Paraguay's courts. At various points Dolly, her mother, and the family's lawyer were arrested and threatened. The legal actions went nowhere.[3]

In mid-1978 Peña-Irala sold his house in Asunción, left Paraguay, and came to New York City. Dolly was living in Washington, D.C., at this point. Learning that Peña-Irala was staying in Brooklyn, she found a lawyer and brought a lawsuit against Peña-Irala in federal court, seeking $10 million in damages.[4]

Dolly's claim for damages was based on a statute that Congress had enacted in 1789: the Alien Tort Statute. The statute is deceptively simple. It says: "The district courts shall have original jurisdiction of any civil action by an alien for a tort only, committed in violation of the law of nations or a treaty of the United States."[5]

Dolly's suit said that the torture and murder of her brother was a "tort"—that is, a civil wrong causing injury, and furthermore a tort that violated the "law of nations." In addition, she, a citizen of Paraguay, was an "alien," and her suit for damages was a "civil action." Hence the federal court had "jurisdiction"—that is, the authority to hear her case, hold Peña-Irala accountable, and award her damages.[6]

But the matter was far from simple in fact. For one thing, Dolly Filártiga's action was without legal precedent. Congress had enacted the ATS in 1789 for a special reason. Five years earlier, in 1784, in Philadelphia, a former French army officer, Charles de Longchamps, angry at the French consul general, François Barbé-Marbois, and wanting to dishonor him, had struck Marbois's cane as he walked in the street.[7] France protested and sought to extradite de Longchamps, but Pennsylvania refused to send him back to France. In the meantime, the Continental Congress stood by, doing little or nothing. While recognizing that de Longchamps's action (by physically interfering with a foreign diplomatic official) violated international law, the Congress saw that, legally speaking, it was up to Pennsylvania to decide what to do. The

Congress could only ask the secretary of foreign affairs to apologize to the French and to explain the legal problem. Pennsylvania would later prosecute de Longchamps, but Congress remained embarrassed on the world stage by its lack of legal authority.[8]

A second incident reinforced this concern. In 1787 a New York City police officer entered the house of the Dutch ambassador and arrested a servant. The Dutch government complained to Secretary of State John Jay (who would later become the first chief justice of the United States). As a result of the complaint, the mayor of New York arrested the police officer,[9] but as the mayor wrote to Jay, "neither Congress" nor the state "legislature" had "yet passed any act respecting a breach of the privileges of Ambassadors; so that the . . . punishment depend on the common law [and] . . . the law of nations."[10] While the breach of the law of nations qualified at the time as a "breach of the common law," the Continental Congress again remained embarrassingly impotent to address this foreign relations fiasco and ensure that the violator was sanctioned.

Soon after the Constitution was ratified and the federal government given new powers, Congress enacted the ATS, likely with these incidents in mind. The ATS provided foreign citizens with a right of action in American courts so that they could sue for violations of the law of nations—that is, the unjustified striking with a cane, or the unauthorized raiding of the home—and bring their abusers to justice.

But there was evidence that Congress intended the statute to go beyond protecting only foreign officials in the United States. In 1794 a group of Americans joined a fleet of French privateers in a raid on the British colony of Sierra Leone. The British ambassador protested, demanding that the Americans be held accountable. In reply the American attorney general, William Bradford, wrote that since the raid took place outside the United States, the United States could not punish it as a crime.[11] But he added (using the language of the recently enacted Alien Tort Statute), "[T]here can be no doubt that the company or individuals who have been injured by these acts of hostility have a remedy by a *civil* suit in the courts of the United States[,] jurisdiction being expressly given to these courts in all cases where an alien sues for a tort only, in violation of the laws of nations, or a treaty of the United States."[12]

Thus the early history of the statute suggests that it was aimed at protecting not only foreign officials from assault but also foreign persons from the universally unlawful actions of privateers and pirates. That the statute would offer the latter protection is not surprising, for at the time much of the world considered a pirate to be a "common enemy of mankind." Any country that caught one could hang him and turn over to the pirate's victims any of his assets seized.[13]

There followed 160 years of silence, when virtually no one used the ATS. We can find no more than a handful of cases referring to it, most involving privateers or the slave trade.[14] In 1975, however, the well-respected judge Henry Friendly considered a claim for fraud brought under the statute in New York City by a group of British investors against a company incorporated in the Bahamas. The investors pointed out that they were "aliens" and argued that, since virtually every nation forbids fraud, the Bahamian company's fraud violated the law of nations. Thus the ATS entitled them to damages in the United States.[15]

Judge Friendly wrote that the statute "must be narrowly read" lest American courts become embroiled in foreign matters beyond their constitutional power to decide.[16] He added that the statute forbids only violations of "those standards, rules or customs ... affecting the relationship between states or between an individual and a foreign state."[17] The "Eighth Commandment 'Thou shalt not steal'" was *not* one of these universal standards or customs.[18] The ATS, Judge Friendly said, is "old but little used." It is a "kind of legal Lohengrin; ... no one seems to know whence it came."[19] The court of appeals ordered the claim dismissed.

Now let us return to Dolly Filártiga's case. The trial court, recognizing that it must construe the law of nations narrowly, found that international law did not govern a nation's (i.e., Paraguay's) treatment of its own citizens. And it consequently dismissed the claim.[20] Dolly appealed to Judge Friendly's court, which had just held that international law did not prohibit fraud. Now that court had to decide whether the Alien Tort Statute gave Dolly the right to recover damages for the murder by torture of Dolly's brother.

Taking a new and different attitude toward the ATS, the court held that it did permit Dolly to press her claim. The court wrote:

> In light of the universal condemnation of torture in numerous international agreements, and the renunciation of torture as an instrument of official policy by virtually all of the nations of the world ... we find that an act of torture committed by a state

official against one held in detention violates established norms of the international law of human rights, and hence the law of nations.[21]

This holding now may appear reasonable to us, almost to the point of being self-evident. But at that time it was turning the statute in such a radically new direction that the court felt obliged to explain in detail some fairly complex matters.

How, for example, are we to determine the content of the law of nations? The Second Circuit referred to an 1820 case in which the Supreme Court had said that the law of nations "may be ascertained by consulting the works of jurists, writing professedly on public law[,] . . . by the general usage and practice of nations[,] or by judicial decisions recognizing and enforcing that law."[22] It also referred to another Supreme Court case in 1900 reaffirming that "the general assent of civilized nations" may produce "a settled rule of international law": the existence of that "assent" may be ascertained through "customs and usages," and the existence of those "customs and usages" may in turn be determined by referring "to the works of jurists and commentators who by years of labor, research and experience, have made themselves peculiarly well acquainted with the subjects of which they treat"—though their works, the Court warned, should be taken "not for the speculations of their authors concerning what the law ought to be, but for trustworthy evidence of what the law really is."[23] The Second Circuit also pointed to the statute of the International Court of Justice, which lists sources of international law, including "international conventions," "international custom," "general principles of law recognized by civilized nations," "judicial decisions," and "the teachings of the most highly qualified [experts]."[24]

But how do we know that the law of nations prohibits a nation from torturing its own citizens? Again the appeals court produced a thorough reply: treaties, declarations, the "usage of nations, judicial opinions and the works of jurists" all show that it does.[25] All members of the United Nations "pledge themselves to take joint and separate action . . . for the achievement of the purposes set forth in Article 55 [of the United Nations Charter]," and Article 55 in turn says the organization "shall promote . . . universal . . . observance of[] human rights."[26] The 1948 Universal Declaration of Human Rights, set forth in a General

Assembly resolution (and now, according to scholars, "an authoritative statement of the international community"),[27] says that "[n]o one shall be subjected to torture."[28] The General Assembly has declared this precept a "basic principle[] of international law."[29] Numerous other international treaties and declarations also forbade torture. Furthermore, the State Department, as well as scholars of the subject, had found that "no government has asserted a right to torture its own nationals."[30]

The court then cautiously added that "[t]he requirement that a rule command the 'general assent of civilized nations' to become binding upon them all is a *stringent* one."[31] It is only "where the nations of the world have demonstrated that the wrong is of mutual, and not merely several, concern, by means of express international accords, that a wrong generally recognized becomes an international law violation within the meaning of the statute."[32] The prohibition against torture is precisely such a "clear and unambiguous" rule, based upon international agreements as well as international practice.[33]

The court concluded that the ATS should be construed not "as granting new rights to aliens but simply as opening the federal courts for adjudication of the rights already recognized by international law."[34] Today "humanitarian and practical considerations have combined to lead the nations of the world to recognize that respect for fundamental human rights is in their individual and collective interest. . . . Among th[ose] rights . . . is the right to be free of physical torture."[35] And "for purposes of civil liability, the torturer has become like the pirate and slave trader before him *hostis humani generis,* an enemy of all mankind."[36]

The court of appeals' decision left Dolly Filártiga free to pursue her case and to prove her facts in the lower court, which she did, eventually winning a $5 million judgment. (Her father, Joel Filártiga, also received approximately $5 million, bringing the total damages to over $10 million.)[37] She was unlikely to collect the judgment, for Peña-Irala had returned to Paraguay after the original district court decision dismissing Filártiga's claim. Still, she said, "I came to this country in 1978 hoping simply to look a killer in the eye. With the help of American law, I got so much more."[38]

The Second Circuit's holding in *Filartiga* does not seem controversial—at least not at first blush. Its reasoning is simple, and support for the legal result seems fairly solid. The court showed at some length just how and why it could find that the "law of nations" bars torture, and that the ATS permits an alien to obtain compensation for a violation of the "law of nations." But as is sometimes true in the law, what initially seems simple and clear is later found to harbor serious uncertainties, to lack clarity, and to generate legal and practical problems going forward. That is just what occurred after *Filartiga*.

Filartiga had suddenly shown human rights lawyers and others that they might use the ATS to help victims. There soon followed a stream of human rights cases—about 80 suits resulting in published circuit court opinions over the next three decades, and about 150 suits filed since 1993 against corporations.[39]

Some of those lawsuits presented facts almost identical in kind to those in *Filartiga*. The plaintiffs basically asked district courts, and then courts of appeals, to adopt *Filartiga*'s reasoning. And that is what courts did when, for example, Philippine victims of the Ferdinand Marcos regime sued the deposed president and his family in Hawaii, where they had taken refuge.

Let us consider, in particular, a lawsuit brought by the mother of Archimedes Trajano. Archimedes had attended a public meeting held in the Philippines in 1977, where the speaker was Imee Marcos-Manitoc, daughter of the president. After asking a hostile question, Archimedes was taken away, tortured, and murdered by Philippine military intelligence personnel. Several years later, in 1986, Ferdinand Marcos, his family, and former high-ranking officials left the Philippines and moved to Hawaii. The month after they arrived, Archimedes's mother, Agapita, a citizen of the Philippines but a resident of Hawaii at the time, filed a lawsuit against Marcos and eventually the Marcos estate in federal court.[40] In February 1994 a jury awarded her, and other plaintiffs with somewhat similar claims, $1.2 billion in damages (a figure that eventually grew to almost $2 billion).[41]

When the Marcos estate appealed, the Court of Appeals for the Ninth Circuit upheld the award,[42] writing that the case was virtually identical to *Filartiga*. The Second Circuit had there said that the ATS covered "violations of international law" that were, in the Ninth Circuit's words, *"specific, universal, and obligatory."*[43] And it decided to "join the Second Circuit in concluding that the Alien Tort Act . . . creates a cause of action for violations of specific, universal and obligatory international human rights standards which 'confer[] fundamental rights upon all people vis-a-vis their own governments.'"[44] Like the Second Circuit, the Ninth Circuit found that the facts satisfied those conditions.

Subsequently, victims or their representatives won cases claiming torture against a host of foreign leaders and officials from other countries. There were, for example, cases against an Argentine general,[45] against a former local official of Ethiopia's military dictatorship,[46] against a Guatemalan minister of defense,[47] and against the former mayor of Beijing.[48] Sometimes the victory was merely symbolic, for the defendant did not have the money to pay. And sometimes the defendant did not appear in court, so the plaintiff won by default.[49] Yet even in those situations, the victim could feel the vindication of prevailing law.

But torture is not the sole gross abuse of human rights. Over time victims of other forms of abuse began to bring cases under the ATS. As those cases entered the courts, the legal and practical issues surrounding application of the statute to overseas activities became more complicated. As happens with many legal principles, those that seemed to work well in *Filartiga* and the *Marcos* litigation began to be stretched toward the limits of their own logic.

For one thing, lawyers and courts began to apply the statute to misdeeds other than easy-to-recognize torture.[50] From the beginning, courts had found it difficult to distinguish torture from other gross human rights abuses, such as slavery, genocide, summary executions, and disappearances. Does the statute apply to these other kinds of abuse? Which are equally heinous and when? And what about other rights to which the Universal Declaration of Human Rights refers—for example, the right to be free of "arbitrary arrest, detention, or exile," the right to be free of "arbitrary interference with . . . privacy, family, home or correspondence, []or attacks upon . . . honour and reputation," the right to "freedom of movement," "to marry," to free "thought," to free "expression," "to social security," "to work," and so forth?[51] What about the right to be free from child labor?

How well does the circuit courts' test work—namely, that the right must be "specific, universal, and obligatory" in order for it to fall within the jurisdictional scope of the ATS? That test may seem more concrete than it is. After all, what is not "specific, universal, and obligatory" about a right to marry, about a right to freedom of movement, or about a right to freedom from arbitrary arrest or detention? And what can that test tell us about the difference between, say, a summary execution and an ordinary murder, a "disappearance" and an ordinary kidnapping, or slavery and absolutely abysmal working conditions?

These kinds of issues began to come to the surface. In one case, the Second Circuit upheld a complaint claiming that, during the Bosnian civil war, the head of the Bosnian Serb rebel forces had not just ordered torture but had also ordered or participated in summary executions, genocide, and war crimes against non-Serb civilians.[52] In another case, a trial court upheld a claim that the assassination of an archbishop in El Salvador was a crime against humanity.[53] Lawyers have brought cases claiming serious environmental harms. Although most have been dismissed, one trial court decided that degradation of the environment (caused by pollution crossing an international boundary) could violate the ATS, because international tribunals have applied a legal principle of *sic utere*, under which an owner of property cannot use that property in a way that harms others.[54]

Another complication was that the courts began to expand not only the categories of actions that might give rise to suit under the statute but also the categories of those persons or entities who might be sued. A consensus emerged that certain acts of *nonstate* actors, including acts of torture, do not fall within the statute under the prevailing law of nations.[55] But what about the actions of a defendant who does not act on behalf of a formally recognized state as such but for a political entity or quasi-national group that resembles a state? In *Karadzic,* the Bosnian case mentioned earlier, the Second Circuit held that a Bosnian Serb political entity, the self-declared Republic of Srpska, "satisfie[d] the criteria for a state, for purposes of those international law violations [i.e., torture] requiring state action," because it was "alleged to control defined territory, control populations within its power, and to have entered into agreements with other governments."[56] Meanwhile, that same court— and others—held that numerous other abuses did not even *require* state action to qualify as violations of the law of nations in suits under the ATS, because international law condemned such conduct even when perpetrated by private individuals.[57] Other courts disagreed, however, and the disagreement continues.[58]

The courts also had to consider the extent to which a defendant must be personally involved in the crime in order to be liable. What about an accomplice—one who aids and abets a government official or entity in committing a crime? When faced with this type of question, most courts found that an accomplice—say, someone who furnishes a gun to the assassin of the archbishop—aids and abets a violation of the law of nations and consequently can be made a proper defendant under the ATS.[59]

Once the courts had established that aiding and abetting a violation could make one liable under the statute, human rights victims began to see a particularly fruitful way to expand the scope of the law: suing corporations. Doing so might lead entities doing business in countries that violated human rights to pressure those countries into changing their ways. In any event, suits against corporations had many practical advantages. Corporations often have deep pockets, they or their representatives can be found in the United States, and they might well settle a suit rather than face the publicity accompanying a trial.

Thus a group of residents of Myanmar brought a lawsuit in California against Unocal, a corporation doing business in their country.[60] The plaintiffs claimed, among other things, that Unocal had helped the military subject them to forced labor, as well as murder, rape, and torture—all violations of the ATS. Allowing the case to go forward, the Ninth Circuit held that a defendant corporation violates the ATS by providing "knowing, practical assistance or encouragement that has a substantial effect on the perpetration of the crime."[61] Unocal settled the case.[62]

In other cases, plaintiffs would claim that the defendant corporation had, for example, helped governments violently repress peaceful protesters, violently suppress labor unions, commit genocide, practice apartheid, or use dangerous herbicides in foreign countries. The number of suits against corporations grew rather rapidly. One source says that "plaintiffs have filed some 180 ATS cases against corporations; of those, 155 (85%) have been filed since 1993, with 136 coming since 2000 (76%)."[63]

As the source adds, many of these cases were dismissed.[64] Indeed, a source published in 2004 reports that of thirty-eight brought against corporate defendants under the statute as of that date, only five survived motions to dismiss.[65] Nonetheless, the bringing of such cases may still help plaintiffs, at least if the corporation offers the plaintiff a settlement. And this began to occur with greater frequency, especially after 2004.[66]

PROBLEMS

There are other reasons why the statute is not as easy to apply as it may initially have appeared. There is a host of what I should call ordinary problems of legal interpretation. How are courts to apply the basic legal standard *"in violation of the law of nations"*? As I asked before, when does a murder, an arrest, detention, suppression of protesters, low pay, or environmental harm qualify as a violation of international law? Does being fully aware of a country's violent suppression of human rights and still doing business there make a firm liable to pay damages to a human rights victim? If not, what in addition is required to impose liability?

We have also seen the difficulties that arise when courts wrestle with the question of who can properly be named a defendant in a tort suit under the statute. If "state action" is required for certain claims to be cognizable, such as torture, when does a paramilitary, separatist, or terrorist group that controls significant territory or population qualify as a "state"? And if the victim is to sue state actors, which ones are actually subject to suit—given the Foreign Sovereign Immunities Act and the immunity enjoyed by heads of state?

These are not the only questions. Is there, for example, a time limit on bringing a lawsuit? Can a victim of Nazi oppression sue Ford Motor Company for actions that a foreign subsidiary of Ford took under the Nazis?[67] To what extent are World War II atrocities subject to compensatory lawsuits? What about atrocities in colonial Africa?

In which court should the victim sue? Suppose the law of the foreign nation in which the offense took place now permits compensation for this kind of violation and its court system seems to work fairly well. Is the victim obliged to bring any claim for compensation in that country? What about a foreign corporate defendant with a subsidiary doing business in the United States? When the basis of the lawsuit is the company's overseas conduct (meaning *not* any conduct in U.S. territory), must the victim bring suit in the nation (say, the Netherlands, France, or the UK) where the corporation has its headquarters or principal place of business? (As we shall see, in a case decided in 2014, the Court held that plaintiffs could *not* use the presence of a subsidiary to sue the parent corporation under the ATS, when the basis of the lawsuit was overseas conduct and the parent did not have headquarters, a principal place of business, or operations "so substantial and of such a nature as to render the corporation at home in that State.")[68]

In general, should a court applying the ATS see itself as simply applying a kind of foreign law, in this case international law, or should it see itself as applying American common law that incorporates bits and pieces of international law but is still the law of the United States?

Of course, it is fair to ask whether these problems are any more difficult than those that federal courts typically face when interpreting other statutes or constitutional provisions. Few statutes, after all, are perfectly clear. What counts as a "restraint of trade" as forbidden by the antitrust laws? What kind of behavior violates a pension fund fiduciary's basic legal duty to act with "prudence"? And what about constitutional language, such as "the freedom of speech," "equal protection of the laws," or the "liberty" that cannot be taken from "any person" without "due process of law"? What do these phrases finally mean, and how do they apply? In this sense the ATS is perhaps not so special.

Those who oppose broad application of the statute, however, have argued that there is indeed something special here, in fact four special things—all of them connecting our judicial system, including the Supreme Court, to the courts and legal systems of the rest of the world.

1. *Legitimacy.* The first unique feature concerns a basic constitutional principle. If that principle is theoretical, it nonetheless reflects a theory that most Americans intuitively understand and believe important. Recall the first seven words of the Constitution: "We the people of the United States."[69] Remember, too, James Madison's important distinction between the American government and the governments of European kings. The American Constitution, he wrote, is a "charter[] of power granted by liberty," not (as in even enlightened European nations) a "charter[] of liberty ... granted by power."[70] In the United States, it is the people, not a central authority, who are the source of legitimate federal power.

Thus Americans are unlikely to consider an exercise of governmental authority fully legitimate unless they can trace the source of that exercise back to the people themselves. We can easily trace congressional statutes back to the people through our system of federal elections, which put in place the representatives who write the statutes. We also can trace federal judges' interpretations and applications of federal law back to the people, perhaps less directly but no less surely, through the judges' appointment by an elected President and confirmation by the Senate. The Constitution itself is the product of "We the people." Although the Founders wrote it at a particular time—namely, the eighteenth century, we can conceive of the "people" as those who ratified it and as those who live under it, giving it legitimacy through their acceptance of it, both then and now. And the public has, in the course of more than two hundred years, accepted this kind of explanation.

Now consider the "law of nations" to which the ATS refers. Who are the people who give substance to that law? American judges do, to some extent. But this answer is incomplete. The statute, as interpreted in *Filartiga*, tells those judges to look for, and to ratify, the work of international courts, foreign courts, and scholars.[71] And who are those latter individuals and institutions? More specifically, what is their connection to the "people of the United States"? How can we draw a line of authority from what they say back to the "people of the United States"?

This may not be too serious a problem when an American court decides fairly technical matters—say, of commercial law, or of family law involving both the United States and another country. But the ATS reaches further. It concerns basic human rights—rights that our own Constitution protects, yet more rights than that. The critics' concern is that, when American judges apply the interpretations and understandings of foreign scholars and foreign institutions in the process of adjudicating ATS claims, then these sources of law, which themselves have no direct connection with "We the people," will come to influence the interpretation and application of our *own* American laws, whether they be tort laws, criminal laws, or constitutional laws. Given the number of potential cases, the nature and breadth of their subject matter, and the likely practical consequences, is the American judiciary's reliance upon, and application of, foreign sources of law in ATS cases ultimately undemocratic?

2. *Capacity.* Critics ask another question: Are courts, indeed American courts, the right institutions to determine systematically when and where not only individuals, but also corporations, have violated the

"law of nations"? Plaintiffs have filed ATS claims against oil companies, gas companies, mining companies, banks, financial services institutions, food service companies, and agricultural companies. They have alleged extremely harmful conduct, including, among other things, that defendant companies have emitted highly toxic chemicals; caused other serious environmental harm; helped governments compel their citizens involuntarily to work in company factories; and helped governments suppress, imprison, torture, or kill their citizens.[72]

But will the facts bear out these claims? More important, what happens if the facts show that *something* occurred, indeed something bad, but not *quite* as bad as, or not quite like, what the plaintiffs originally set forth? Suppose the defendants reply, for example, that they took steps to render any chemical emissions less toxic; that the environmental harm was not much worse than that caused by many American companies operating in the United States; that even if pay and working conditions were pretty undesirable, they were not bad enough to amount to, say, "forced labor" or "slavery." And suppose they add that even if soldiers treated citizens badly, the company itself did little to encourage them, or whatever it did was under compulsion or threat of expulsion from the country and confiscation of property, at a minimum?

Juries may decide the brute facts, such as who said what to whom and who took what physical actions on what occasions. But it is judges who instruct the jury. And it is the judge who will decide first whether the facts (as the jury might find them) show a violation of the "law of nations" under the ATS.

Are judges the right people to make these findings? In most nations, regulators, not judges, play a major role in deciding many such questions: When are factory emissions too toxic? What are minimally acceptable labor conditions? When is it permissible for companies to stand by, or to cooperate in, violations of laws forbidding, say, environmental harm? One reason regulators tend to answer these questions in the ordinary course of things is that, by and large, they tend to be the best informed to do so. Local regulators generally know better than judges or other officials—and especially better than judges of other nations, such as American judges—how to weigh alternative harms to their country, that of, say, tolerating poor labor conditions versus that of discouraging such conditions at the possible cost of some foreign investment. Meanwhile, the rules of the American judicial system are, compared to those of many nations, favorable to plaintiffs, and the expenses of litigation can impose pressure on defendants to settle. Especially when a corporation's conduct is borderline—that is, when it *arguably* gives rise to liability under the ATS, but not definitively—the pressure on the company to settle will be high. And those are precisely the cases in which the corporate conduct is better assessed by local regulators than by American judges.

3. *Interference.* A third criticism: Decisions by American judges about aliens suffering from human rights violations abroad can interfere with America's foreign relations. Imagine a citizen of Tibet coming to New York City and filing an ATS suit against China, claiming violation of basic rights. The State Department would likely ask the court to dismiss such a case, as it has done in several cases.[73] And courts often grant such State Department requests.[74]

Foreign relations can be implicated in other ways, too. The South African government, for example, has used its Truth and Reconciliation process as a means for moving the nation beyond the recriminations of apartheid. It has negotiated with many foreign corporations that did business with the government during the apartheid years. And it has reached agreements involving various forms of payment that would, in South Africa's view, not be so onerous as to force the companies to depart. That same post-apartheid government, fearing that ATS litigation against these corporations might unravel its negotiated settlements, filed briefs in several American courts, asking for the cases to be dismissed.[75]

Similarly, Indonesia, the United Kingdom, Switzerland, Germany, Canada, and Papua New Guinea have filed requests, either with the Department of State or with courts, seeking to have an ATS suit dismissed.[76] At least one knowledgeable commentator has pointed out that "foreign governments—including those of America's closest friends and allies, such as Canada, Britain, and the Netherlands—increasingly" have become "concerned with the effects" of ATS litigation, in part because they fear that American judges will apply an Americanized version of that law that is "untethered to actual international law processes in which their countries could participate."[77] This fear of American international law "hegemony" is the mirror image of the American concern about the "internationalization" of American law, and it is no less real.[78]

4. *Universality.* A fourth criticism goes that what American courts can do, other courts can do, too. There is, as I've said before, no Supreme Court of the World to iron out conflicting rulings. As things stand, a broad interpretation of the ATS would offer relief to plaintiffs beyond what other nations provide, but that does not prevent other nations from changing their approach. What, for instance, is to prevent a Belgian from permitting a victim of, say, America's use of a toxic chemical in Vietnam from suing former secretary of state Henry Kissinger in Brussels? A Spanish court could, likewise, permit a Palestinian refugee to sue a former Israeli cabinet official in Spain, alleging the refugee was deprived of his basic rights. Suits like these have, in fact, arisen.[79] Thus such repercussions should be considered by American courts deciding whether to allow a given ATS suit to proceed. What matters is whether the principle underlying its decision will work well if generalized and applied by other courts in the world. Another aspect of the principle called "comity" is that we cannot normally insist upon a right to enact laws of a kind that we then deny to other similar nations. Still, how best to apply comity in the context of the ATS remains an unresolved problem.

Let me briefly summarize the special issues created in the wake of *Filartiga* by the federal courts' efforts to apply the ATS to a growing variety of claims. First, *legitimacy,* the democratic problem: Is the connection between the content of the law of nations and the American people sufficiently robust and clear? Second, *capacity,* an institutional problem: Are American judges suited to determining the content of a law regulating the conduct of corporations in foreign countries, putatively to protect those countries' interests, or are regulators, including foreign regulators, better suited to that task? Third, *interference,* a foreign relations problem: To what extent will judicial enforcement of the ATS in the United States interfere with America's foreign relations? Fourth, *universality,* a generalization problem: Can American judges, applying the statute, help to create a workable international system were other nations' judges to do the same?

In general, there are three kinds of answers or approaches to the broad questions I have identified about the proper scope of the ATS. First, *let the statute expand.* There is little or nothing to be said for the conduct at issue; the victims deserve compensation; many nations seek to cooperate in protecting against human rights violations; strong enforcement of the statute simply represents an effort by the United States to do its part. What is so terrible about offering compensation to victims of reprehensible behavior?

But how, then, are we to resolve the four major problems previously mentioned? What will happen to American law as judges give force to international agreements and standards in ATS cases? Will judges not inevitably interpret American law, whose language is often similar to that in international human rights documents, as granting the same breadth of protection to aliens as to Americans? And as the interpretation or use of international law gradually influences that of American constitutional and statutory language, will the power of a democratic electorate to shape the meaning of those words gradually shrink?

And what about the effects of judicial ATS decisions on U.S. international relations and policies? Foreign countries—including developing countries with spotty human rights records—have made considerable efforts to encourage businesses to invest in their nations—that is, abroad. The United States is generally supportive of these efforts. Will corporate liability in American courts for activities such as forced labor, child labor, and environmental degradation chase away foreign investment? And if so, what will be the effect on our relationships abroad and on our broader goals of encouraging economic development, education, and democratization in the world's poorest nations?

Second, take the opposite path: *limit the scope of the ATS severely, in one way or another.* The ATS could be interpreted, for example, as limited to behavior contrary to the law of nations in the eighteenth century—namely, "violation of safe conducts, infringement of the rights of ambassadors, and piracy."[80] Yet certainly the language itself permits broader interpretation, as does, arguably, the purpose of the statute; furthermore, since the end of World War II, nations have reached a virtual consensus that torture, genocide, slavery, war crimes, and piracy are beyond the pale. And what about Dolly Filártiga? What about the victims of Ferdinand Marcos? Are we certain we do not want to apply the statute to the conduct those persons suffered? If we ask, "Who are today's pirates?," does anyone doubt that we would find the likes of Peña-Irala and the Marcoses on a list?[81]

I recognize that such an evisceration of the ATS would not leave human rights without international protection, nor its victims without other remedies. In America alone, Congress has enacted another stat-ute, the Torture Victim Protection Act, which allows both aliens and U.S. citizens who are victims of torture outside the United States to bring suits inside the United States for compensation.[82] That act does not apply to corporate defendants, only to government defendants act-ing under the color of law.[83] But there are indications that it does not displace any additional remedies that the ATS may provide.

Elsewhere, the International Criminal Court (ICC), established by a treaty to which 122 countries (though not the United States) are cur-rently parties, helps to protect human rights by threatening criminal prosecution of individuals who have engaged in war crimes, genocide, and the like.[84] It can also order "a convicted person" to pay "reparations" (including "restitution, compensation and rehabilitation") to "victims."[85] The ICC's effectiveness, however, depends heavily upon cooperative efforts of member states, including military efforts, to bring the accused before the tribunal. While military forces helped the ICC's predecessor, the International Criminal Tribunal for the Former Yugoslavia, obtain custody of several of those indicted,[86] the ICC has found it more diffi-cult by itself to obtain custody. In existence for over a decade, it has ini-tiated only twelve cases and reached convictions in but two.[87] Another constraint is that as of the present day, the ICC authorizes criminal jurisdiction only over natural persons—not over corporations. To the extent that human rights victims also seek to hold corporations that contributed to their harms accountable, they cannot do so in the ICC.[88] Still, I suspect that the single factor most decisively keeping Ameri-can courts from returning the ATS to that foggy land from which it emerged is Dolly Filártiga. If asked, "Would you think it better, legally or morally, had the *Filartiga* court reached the opposite conclusion?," most jurists (and most Americans) would surely answer no.

Third, split the difference: *find a middle ground.* But is there one? Courts and commentators have often searched for a set of interpreta-tions that would preserve the usefulness of the ATS while constraining excesses, by which I mean the risks of harm inherent in the four basic problems that critics have raised. To understand the possible middle grounds, and the extent to which we can count them as "middle," I must say more. In particular, it is important to understand the two cases in which the Supreme Court had to grapple with these issues: *Sosa* and *Kiobel.*

THE COURT'S INTERPRETATIONS: *SOSA*

The Supreme Court first interpreted the ATS in 2004. From the perspective of those who favor a broad reading, the facts of the case before the Court were not particularly favorable. It arose out of events that took place in 1985, when Mexican drug dealers kidnapped an American DEA agent then in Mexico. They brought him to a house in Guadalajara, and over a two-day period, they questioned him under torture until his death. One of those present, Humberto Álvarez-Machaín, was a doctor who helped the torturers by keeping their victim alive so that they could continue to ask questions.

A few years later a federal grand jury in Los Angeles indicted Dr. Álvarez for murder. When the Mexican government refused to extradite him, the DEA concocted a plan to bring him to the United States. They hired a group of Mexican nationals who kidnapped Dr. Álvarez in Mexico, held him overnight in a motel, and the next day delivered him by private plane to American agents in Texas. Álvarez was tried for murder and torture in 1992, but the district court ultimately granted his motion for a judgment of acquittal.[89]

Then the tables were turned. After returning to Mexico, in 1993, Dr. Álvarez brought a lawsuit in Los Angeles against José Francisco Sosa, one of the kidnappers whom the DEA had hired to abduct him. The district court ultimately awarded Álvarez $25,000 under the ATS, as compensation for his arbitrary abduction, which the judge concluded qualified as a violation of the "law of nations."[90] The court of appeals affirmed the judgment,[91] and the en banc court affirmed as well.[92] The Supreme Court then agreed to take the case to determine whether liability under the statute stretched so far.

The basic question before the Court concerned what conduct could give rise to liability—and thus lead to compensation—under the ATS. What kinds of abusive activities did the "law of nations" cover? How broad was the ATS's substantive scope? The Court tried to carve out a middle way.

On the one hand, it rejected a claim that would have made the statute close to useless. Sosa, the kidnapper-defendant, had argued that the ATS was purely jurisdictional and depended on the codification of other positive laws in the United States in order to give rise to a cause of action. Sosa pointed out that the statute's text speaks in jurisdictional terms; it says that the "district courts shall have original *jurisdiction* of any civil action by an alien for a tort only, committed in violation of the law of nations."[93] According to Sosa, that means that *if* Congress or perhaps a state legislative body creates a tort for a violation of the law of nations, then a federal district court can hear a case claiming a defendant committed that tort. But no legislative body had created such a tort; hence there was no case to hear.[94]

The Court rejected this argument, pointing out that when Congress passed the ATS in 1789, there were no federal or state statutes creating causes of action for law-of-nations torts. And it is unlikely, the Court reasoned, that Congress enacted the statute expecting it simply to be "placed on the shelf for use by a future Congress or state legislature."[95] Rather, "at the time of [the statute's] enactment the [grant of] jurisdiction enabled federal courts to hear claims in a very limited category defined by the law of nations and recognized at common law."[96]

On the other hand, the Court also rejected a claim that would have said, in effect, "full steam ahead." Dr. Álvarez, the plaintiff, argued that Congress intended to give not just a "jurisdictional grant" but also "authority for the creation of *a new cause of action for torts,*" without specifying what those new claims might be or whether or how they might be limited.[97] The Court said that too broad a "reading" was "implausible."[98] Rather, courts could hear cases claiming torts based upon violations of international law "because torts in violation of the law of nations would have been recognized within the common law of the time."[99]

But just what torts did the statute recognize? The Court, searching for a limited definition, held that the statute encompassed only a "narrow set of violations of the law of nations, admitting of a judicial remedy and at the same time not threatening serious consequences in international affairs."[100] That "relatively modest set of actions" included Blackstone's list: "violation of safe conducts, infringement of the rights of ambassadors, and piracy."[101] As to other torts, the Court concluded that "courts should require any claim based on the present-day law of nations to rest on a norm of international character accepted by the civilized world and defined with a specificity comparable to the features of the 18th-century paradigms we have recognized."[102]

It was important that federal courts "*not* recognize private claims under federal common law for violations of any international law norm with less definite content and acceptance among civilized nations than the historical paradigms familiar when" the statute "was enacted."[103] On this point, the Court cited with approval the reasoning of the court of appeals in *Filartiga:* a torturer could be held liable under the statute because "'the torturer has become—like the pirate and slave trader before him—*hostis humani generis,* an enemy of all mankind.'"[104]

The Court, recognizing the major problems that I have discussed, then added that courts should show "great caution in adapting the law of nations to private rights,"[105] pointing out that unlike in the eighteenth century, when many believed law was "found or discovered" rather than "made or created," today there is a common understanding that it is "made," in this case by judges.[106] Still, "a decision to create a private right of action is one better left to legislative judgment in the great majority of cases," the Court held, particularly when it comes to civil actions, with no criminal prosecutor to exercise discretion in not bringing an individual case.[107] In addition, "attempts by federal courts to craft remedies for the violation of new norms of international law would raise risks of adverse foreign policy consequences."[108] Finally, although Congress had enacted the Torture Victim Protection Act (1991), "Congress as a body has done nothing to promote" private suits other than those involving torture.[109]

These considerations, while demanding "caution," did not require the Court "to shut the door to the law of nations entirely."[110] They were sufficient, however, to deny Álvarez any right of recovery in his particular suit. Surveying international sources, the Court concluded that there was no sufficiently specific norm of international law forbidding abduction across an international boundary, or any such norm forbidding "arbitrary" detention, even where that detention violated the domestic laws of individual nations.[111] The best Álvarez could do was point to the Restatement (Third) of Foreign Relations Law, which says that nations violate international law when they "practice[], encourage[], or condone[] . . . prolonged arbitrary detention."[112] But that was too indefinite and, in any case, did not describe Álvarez's detention.

A concurring opinion (which I wrote) added one further consideration:

> Since enforcement of an international norm by one nation's courts implies that other nations' courts may do the same, I would ask whether the exercise of jurisdiction under the ATS

is consistent with those notions of comity that lead each nation to respect the sovereign rights of other nations by limiting the reach of its laws and their enforcement.[113]

Will the laws of different nations work together in harmony—a matter of ever greater importance in an ever more interdependent world?[114] In the eighteenth century nations agreed not only upon the substantive principle that piracy was a crime but also upon the procedural principle that any nation could prosecute a pirate wherever he might be found.[115] A relatively broad international consensus had also emerged by the time of *Sosa* regarding acts of torture, genocide, crimes against humanity, and war crimes—they were deemed not only to violate the law of nations in a substantive manner but also to be punishable or prosecuted "universal[ly]," meaning wherever the defendant might be found.[116] But I could find "no similar procedural consensus supporting the exercise of jurisdiction" in a case such as Álvarez's, which provided "additional support for the Court's conclusion that the ATS does not recognize the claim at issue here" for arbitrary arrest.[117]

FOLLOWING *SOSA*

Many lower courts seemed to find in *Sosa* a green light, not a note of caution. In the years to follow, the trends that preceded the decision grew. Corporate defendants were named in an increasing number of suits,[118] plaintiffs continued to push the boundaries on what types of civil claims could be brought, and district courts and courts of appeals allowed many suits to proceed. For instance, the Court of Appeals for the District of Columbia Circuit permitted a case in which the plaintiffs claimed that a corporation, ExxonMobil, aided and abetted Indonesian soldiers who tortured, killed, and detained for a prolonged period of time Indonesian citizens.[119] A panel of the Court of Appeals for the Ninth Circuit permitted a lawsuit in which the plaintiffs sought to hold a mining company liable for helping the government of Papua New Guinea commit war crimes, crimes against humanity, as well as racial discrimination—despite the State Department's urging that the court dismiss the case.[120] The Second Circuit permitted a plaintiff to sue a group of corporate defendants, including banks, oil companies, and car companies (including Ford and General Motors), for having aided and abetted the apartheid regime in South Africa,[121] this despite the South African government's pleas that such suits would interfere with the South African Truth and Reconciliation process. The U.S. State Department recommended dismissal on the same basis.[122] But the Second Circuit did not order dismissal. Rather, it sent the case back to the district court to determine whether the suits should be dismissed for prudential reasons, such as international comity or the "political question" doctrine.[123] The district court said no, and many of the suits could proceed.[124]

Then the Second Circuit heard the case of *Kiobel v. Royal Dutch Petroleum Co.* The plaintiffs were citizens and former residents of Nigeria, and their claims related to the oil exploration activities of Shell Petroleum Development Company (SPDC)—a subsidiary of Royal Dutch Shell—in the 1990s in Ogoniland, located in the Niger delta. When villagers objected to the environmental degradation caused by SPDC's activities, the company sought local protection. According to the plaintiffs, SPDC conspired with Nigerian military and police forces to suppress local resistance through killings, rapes, beatings, floggings, denials of medical care, the burning of houses, the destruction of whole villages, and many other horrors. Throughout, the plaintiffs said, SPDC acted hand in glove with the military, helping directly to bring about these results in some instances, with knowledge in others, and benefiting from them all.[125]

The primary question before the Second Circuit was whether the corporations named were proper defendants in an ATS case. That court of appeals, like many other lower courts, had previously held that international law authorizes liability for a defendant who, like the man who hands a gun to the archbishop's assassin, aids and abets another in a violation of the law of nations.[126] That court had also held that judges, when filling in the ATS's details, should look to international law, not to domestic law, as their source.[127] Accordingly, the question for the Second Circuit in *Kiobel* was whether, under customary international law, a corporation could be held liable for aiding and abetting a violation of the law of nations.

The court said no. Corporate liability for "offenses against the law of nations"—that is, for violations of human rights—is not recognized by customary international law.[128] Surveying international sources, the Second Circuit panel concluded, "customary international law has steadfastly rejected the notion of corporate liability for international crimes, and no international tribunal has ever held a corporation liable for a violation of the law of nations."[129] Hence American courts could not do so in suits brought under the ATS, because those claims "fall outside the limited jurisdiction provided by the ATS."[130]

One judge concurred only in the judgment. He wrote that while international law is the proper reference point for what constitutes a substantive violation of the law of nations—that is, for what kind of conduct the ATS covers—it is domestic law that supplies the rule as to who can be held civilly liable for such violations.[131] The concurrence agreed that international law tends to exclude corporations from criminal liability for human rights abuses because, unlike individuals, they are paper entities. But that "in no way supports the inference that corporations . . . can incur no *civil compensatory liability* to victims when they engage in conduct prohibited by the norms of international law."[132] Rather, international law "leaves the manner of enforcement, including the question of whether there should be private civil remedies for violations of international law, almost entirely to individual nations," and "the United States, through the ATS, has opted to . . . dra[w] no distinction . . . between violators who are natural persons and corporations."[133] The concurring judge agreed, nevertheless, that the case should be dismissed, finding that the complaint lacked allegations supporting a reasonable inference that the company acted with the purpose of bringing about the terrible human rights abuses described.[134]

KIOBEL

Thus the stage was set for the second appearance of the ATS in the Supreme Court. In 2011 the Court agreed to hear the *Kiobel* case, and after receiving a first round of briefs and hearing oral argument, it directed the parties to argue a further issue: "Whether and under what circumstances the [ATS] allows courts to recognize a cause of action for violations of the law of nations occurring within the territory of a sovereign other than the United States."[135] Ultimately, the Court would not decide the original question of corporate liability. Instead, it would answer this further question about extraterritorial conduct. The five-to-four decision is brief and at first blush seems absolute. It speaks to "not whether" the plaintiffs have stated a proper violation of the law of nations but whether an ATS claim can "reach conduct occurring in the territory of a foreign sovereign."[136] And the answer is mainly no: the ATS does not cover activity that takes place abroad.

The majority began by invoking the law's presumption against extraterritoriality: unless a statute gives a "'clear indication of an extra-territorial application, it has none.'"[137] That presumption is important, for it helps "'protect against unintended clashes'"[138] between U.S. law and the laws of other nations, and it prevents courts from "'impinging on the discretion of the Legislative and Executive Branches in managing foreign affairs.'"[139] Looking to the ATS's text and history, the majority found "nothing" to suggest that Congress intended to rebut the presumption against extraterritorial application.[140] "[T]here is no indication that the ATS was passed to make the United States a uniquely hospitable forum for the enforcement of international norms."[141] To the contrary, the majority wrote, the First Congress (which enacted the statute) would have wanted its "fledgling Republic" to be *embraced* by the international community, not rejected by it.[142] And protests against ATS lawsuits by Canada, Germany, Indonesia, Papua New Guinea, South Africa, Switzerland, and the United Kingdom underscored the potential for international discord were the statute to be given the overseas reach the plaintiffs sought. The concerns of other nations were not just theoretical.[143]

Nor are these concerns diminished even if, as the lower courts held in the *Marcos* litigation, only "specific, universal, and obligatory" norms fall within the statute's scope. Norms that meet these definitions still require the elaboration of detail for the bringing of civil claims—that is, who is a proper defendant, what is the statute of limitations, and what is the proper court for filing the claim (namely, is there an exhaustion rule). Answering each of those questions "carries with it significant foreign policy implications," for different countries may have different rules on these procedural matters.[144] In short, allowing ATS suits for extraterritorial conduct—even for conduct substantively prohibited overseas—can nonetheless create international discord.

So would this ruling mean the end of Dolly Filártiga's lawsuit? She'd complained of conduct that took place outside the United States and the defendant was a foreigner. Nonetheless, Dolly need not give up hope. By hedging on two key points, the majority left open the possibility of suits like hers, along with an indeterminate range of others. First, the opinion made clear that the case before the Court did not involve defendants who were "U.S. citizens."[145] It left open, without resolving or even addressing, the question of whether aliens might sue *American* defendants under the statute for a violation of the "law of nations" abroad. Second, at the very end of the opinion, after specifying that "all the relevant conduct [in *Kiobel*] took place outside the United States," the Court added these key words: *"And even where the claims touch and concern the territory of the United States, they must do so with sufficient force to displace the presumption against extraterritorial application."*[146] The "touch and concern" phrase is not further defined. What does it mean? The Court notes that "[c]orporations are often present in many countries," and "mere corporate presence" (presumably in the United States) will not "suffic[e]."[147] But what would suffice for a claim to "touch and concern the territory of the United States ... with sufficient force" if the conduct occurred abroad? The Court does not say; here the opinion ends.

Four members of the Court (including me) joined a concurring opinion, saying that Congress had intended the statute to apply to activities taking place abroad, in certain circumstances. After all, the statute "was enacted with 'foreign matters' in mind," and its text "refers explicitly to 'alien[s],' 'treat[ies],' and 'the law of nations.'"[148] Its purpose was to address those "'violations of the law of nations, admitting of a judicial remedy and at the same time threatening serious consequences in international affairs.'"[149] And "at least one of the three kinds of activities that we found to fall within the statute's scope, namely piracy, normally takes place abroad."[150] For these reasons, the concurring opinion would have found the presumption against extraterritorial application to be out of place when it came to the ATS.

Instead, we believed that Congress intended the statute's jurisdictional reach to match its substantive grasp. And (as in *Sosa*) we would have looked to customary international law to help determine both. In looking "to international jurisdictional norms to help determine the statute's jurisdictional scope," we pointed out that international law would authorize jurisdiction over a law-of-nations violation in three instances: (1) when the violation occurred within that state's territory, (2) when the defendant was a national or citizen of the state, and (3) where the conduct substantively affected an important national interest of the state.[151] As to the third, a state's "interest in not becoming a safe harbor for violators of the most fundamental international norms" is a "national interest" that would justify our hearing a case.[152]

Applying these principles to the present case, we found that jurisdiction under the ATS did not cover Royal Dutch Shell's conduct: it had all occurred abroad, in Nigeria, and the defendants were foreign corporations, whose only presence in the United States consisted of an office in New York City primarily concerned with selling the company's stock.[153] The nature of the claims, combined with the defendant's minimal and indirect American ties, made it too "farfetched to believe . . . that this legal action helps to vindicate a distinct American interest, such as in not providing a safe harbor for an 'enemy of all mankind.'"[154] Accordingly, we agreed for this narrow reason that the plaintiffs' claim should not proceed.

There were other concurring opinions written by justices who joined the majority opinion as well as its conclusion.[155] Two justices read the majority's "touch and concern" language as offering little or no room for any case that arose out of facts taking place abroad.[156] A fifth member of the majority, Justice Kennedy, wrote that the "opinion for the Court is careful to leave open a number of significant questions regarding the reach and interpretation of the Alien Tort Statute."[157] He added that "cases may arise with allegations of serious violations of international law principles protecting persons, cases covered neither by the [Torture Act] . . . nor by the reasoning and holding of today's case; and in those disputes the proper implementation of the presumption against extraterritorial application may require some further elaboration and explanation."[158]

Thus four justices thought the ATS could cover acts taking place abroad, provided that the perpetrator sought refuge in the United States. The majority opinion left open the possibility of future suits premised on overseas conduct—namely, those involving U.S. defendants, and those that involve claims that "touch and concern" U.S. territory. Justice Kennedy yet more explicitly left the courthouse doors open.

OBSERVATIONS

Where do we stand? Perhaps the Court has crafted a middle ground. Both *Sosa* and *Kiobel* limited the kinds of cases that plaintiffs can bring under the Alien Tort Statute. But they did not directly deny the legal legitimacy of Dolly Filártiga's case or of the cases of the victims of Ferdinand Marcos. And such cases continue to lie at the heart of modern ATS litigation. Virtually the entire world decries the torture and murder they involved, agreeing that international law forbids governments from that kind of conduct and that its perpetrators are common enemies of mankind. The *Kiobel* majority did not refute any of those points. And because the defendants in *Filartiga* and *Marcos* had taken refuge in the United States, the opinions in *Kiobel* appear to have preserved those cases' holdings.

Four members of the Court in *Kiobel* wrote that the country has "a distinct interest," warranting application of the statute, "in preventing the United States from becoming a safe harbor (free of civil as well as criminal liability) for a torturer or other common enemy of mankind."[159] According to one justice, determining how the "presumption" against extraterritoriality applies in ATS suits "may require some further elaboration and explanation" in later cases.[160] And the remaining four members of the majority referred to the possibility that the "presumption" might be overcome in cases where the activity "touch[es] and concern[s]" the United States.[161] The door has not been slammed shut to cases like those of Dolly Filártiga and the victims of Ferdinand Marcos.

If the doors remain open, the courts must continue to meet the interpretive and the policy challenges that the ATS poses: Who are today's pirates? Who now are the "common enemies of mankind"? Before *Sosa*, lower courts had said that the statute applied to activities forbidden by an international norm that was *"specific, universal, and obligatory."* *Sosa* says that the statute covers those "norm[s] of international character accepted by the civilized world and defined with a specificity comparable to the features of those three 18th-century paradigms."[162] Which are they? The majority and concurring opinions in *Kiobel* referred to torture, genocide, crimes against humanity, and war crimes. Is that everything?

As a technical matter, the ATS cases make clear that, when federal courts apply the statute, they do not directly apply international law. Rather, they apply American law—namely, federal common law, which picks up some but not all international legal norms (i.e., those norms that satisfy the conditions I have just set out). The conditions are general. Ordinary domestic crimes, such as murder, kidnapping, arbitrary imprisonment, and the like are horrifying, causing serious suffering. But presumably they are not included. Still, a good lawyer can often draft a complaint reasonably claiming that such crimes rise to the level of a violation of the law of nations in some cases. What are those cases?

Who are proper defendants in ATS lawsuits? Again, the *Kiobel* Court made clear that the "mere presence" of a corporation in the United States does not make that corporation a proper defendant. What more is necessary? Are American corporations, with headquarters in the United States, proper defendants? What about foreign corporations conducting major business activities here? What about foreign corporations that sell in the United States products connected with unlawful activity—for example, oil produced in the Ogoni region of Nigeria?

In which court can a plaintiff pursue the lawsuit? One principle present in the law of the United States (and many other nations) is that of "exhaustion of remedies." How does it apply to the ATS? Does it mean that Dolly Filártiga could not bring her lawsuit unless she first tried to sue Peña-Irala in Paraguay (or unless she showed a suit there would be futile)? Does it mean that the plaintiffs in *Kiobel* should first have brought their lawsuit in the Netherlands, where the corporate defendants maintain their principal place of business?

Another legal principle, called *forum non conveniens,* means that a court can dismiss a case when the plaintiff might bring the same case in a "more convenient" forum. Thus American plaintiffs suing a British airline for harm caused in a crash over Italy might have to sue in the United Kingdom or Italy, rather than in the United States. How does this principle apply in ATS actions? The solicitor general, in *Kiobel,* argued that lower courts have jurisdiction to hear some ATS cases, but that they should apply the *forum non conveniens* doctrine "with special vigor" and "presumptively dismiss" a case if "an adequate alternative forum exists."[163]

What about foreign affairs? If the State Department asks the courts to dismiss a case—say, the apartheid litigation—because the litigation interferes with its ability to conduct our foreign relations, should the court do so? Automatically? If not, when? The United States permits prosecutors to decide whether to bring a *criminal* action, but they do not have that kind of authority in *civil* actions for damages. Belgium and Spain, however, have given their prosecutors the authority to dismiss a civil action, and they will do so when they believe it is unjustified or improperly interferes with the conduct of foreign relations.[164]

What about comity? When will an American action generate a legal principle that could not work if generalized internationally? How will the Court know? Do foreign nations, for example, accept the existence of an alien's right to recover damages for serious violations of the "law of nations" committed abroad? Many nations have accepted what foreign relations law calls "universal jurisdiction," and that principle sometimes seems to give an affirmative answer to the question.[165] This jurisdictional principle, however, most commonly applies to criminal prosecutions, not necessarily to civil actions for damages or to instances in which the defendant is a corporation. Nonetheless, a Belgian and a Dutch court have each allowed plaintiffs to recover damages stemming from torture.[166] The International Criminal Court may order a convicted person to pay damages to victims.[167] Can we interpret our statutes so that (if our lead were followed by these other courts) it would keep nations from stepping on one another's toes?

How is the Court to answer these and similar questions? The justices are not experts on the practices of other nations. Lawyers can explain those practices in briefs; in *Sosa* and *Kiobel*, lawyers from the United Kingdom, the Netherlands, Argentina, and France, as well as from the European Union, did so.[168] The State Department can inform the Court through briefs filed by the solicitor general. And of course, experts write law review articles on these subjects, which we can read. But are these sources sufficient? It is a question with which the Court continues to wrestle and whose ultimate answer only future necessities can determine.

What seems more certain is that the ATS, as least as interpreted in *Filartiga* and the Marcos litigation, is here to stay, with three consequences. First, the Court will maintain the rule of law that preserves the ability of some victims of significant crimes abroad to hold their perpetrators accountable. Second, questions about the proper scope and application of the ATS will inevitably continue to arise, and answering them will require the Court to know something of foreign law, foreign practices, and international relations in the field of human rights, in measures perhaps impossible to foresee. Third, the best answers to the many questions I ask about the ATS throughout this chapter may well be provided by Congress. The statute has not been amended in over two hundred years. In the commercial cases surveyed in Chapter 5, the Court had considerably more guidance from Congress about the intended reach of the relevant American statutes, because Congress had legislated those more recently. The Court can do its best trying to shape human rights litigation in the United States through its interpretation of the ATS, as it has done. But as I have said, the statute is old, general, and silent in respect to many critical questions. Only Congress can effectively modernize it.

PART III

Beyond Our Shores

International Agreements

From the interpretation of American statutes, we turn to a subject with more obvious international content—namely, the interpretation of international agreements. The President of the United States has the "power, by and with the advice and consent of the Senate, to make treaties, provided two thirds of the Senators present concur."[1] He can also enter into executive agreements with other nations, which typically require the approval of majorities in both houses of Congress, rather like the enactment of a statute. Finally, the President can issue executive orders authorizing formal or informal arrangements between executive branch agencies and their foreign counterparts. Sometimes he will issue such an order pursuant to general authority that Congress previously gave him—say, in a statute creating a regulatory program. Sometimes he may do so pursuant to authority delegated to him by the Constitution.[2]

Regulators, such as antitrust enforcers or bank regulators, can also enter into less formal "cooperation agreements" with their foreign counterparts.[3] Any or all of these different kinds of international arrangements may turn out, in practice, to control the conduct of American businesses or individuals. And any or all of them could, in principle, lead to legal disputes that reach the courts.

While problems surrounding the interpretation of international agreements have existed since the beginning of the Republic, the interpretive issues that now reach our Court reflect changes in the nature of those agreements. Certainly the President with the Senate more frequently exercises the treaty-making power these days. Our first few presidents would sign one or two treaties per year; today that number has grown by a factor of ten.[4] At the same time, the subject matter has changed. At the nation's founding, treaties almost exclusively concerned war and peace, territory, armaments, trade, and occasionally aliens' property rights. Today they also cover matters once solely of domestic concern, such as individual social and political rights,[5] technical aspects of private commercial contracts,[6] the arbitration of disputes,[7] and even marriage, divorce, and child custody.[8] That is not surprising, for today ordinary travel, communication, business dealings, and even family relationships routinely take place across national borders.[9]

Further, today's treaties are often multilateral and create new organizations. They may delegate to a treaty-based administrative entity a general power to create subsidiary rules and regulations.[10] And the United States (as it has done more than fifty times) may sign further treaties with the treaty-based organizations.[11] Compare the Treaty of Paris, which ended the Revolutionary War, with the United Nations Treaty, signed at the end of World War II. Or contrast the Jay Treaty of the late eighteenth century, governing trade between the United States and Great Britain, with the twentieth-century treaty creating the World Trade Organization, an organization that promulgates rules governing trade among most of the world's nations.

How has the Court's approach to the interpretation of international agreements adapted to these changes? This part will describe cases that help the reader answer that question. They will show changes in degree and in kind. Even more than when statutes are at issue, it has become important to find interpretations that will harmonize the relevant laws and practices of the treaty signatories. It has become more important to find interpretive solutions that are workable, thereby showing that a rule of law itself can work. It has become more important to consider how treaty-based (or agreement-based) rule-making bodies work in practice. And for all these reasons, it has become more important for the courts to understand the details of foreign and international rules, laws, and practices. Specific examples will illustrate what I have in mind.

Chapter 7 concerns the traditional interpretation of a traditional sort of treaty, one governing child custody. Chapter 8 pertains to a kind of treaty becoming ever more common—an international treaty that protects investment by providing for international arbitration. Chapter 9 explores several constitutional issues and other legal problems arising from increased delegation of authority to international bodies created by treaty or created in other somewhat similar ways—say, by executive agreement or by agreement among different nations' regulatory bodies.

CHAPTER 7

Treaty Interpretation

Child Custody

Interpreting treaties is usually a straightforward legal enterprise. The Court will normally proceed in much the same way as when it interprets any other legal text. It begins with the language, which it interprets in light of the treaty's context and purposes; it considers the treaty's drafting history; and it takes account of precedent.

Treaty interpretation will often include consideration of decisions of foreign courts interpreting the same treaty language, and the importance of looking to foreign interpretations is well settled. Indeed, judges who would hesitate to consider decisions of foreign courts when interpreting the American Constitution do not hesitate to consult such decisions when treaties are in question.[1] One particular feature of treaty interpretation is that the Court will often give special weight to the views of the Department of State, which is normally familiar with the drafting process and may understand better than others what the signatories had in mind. State may also have relevant experience with the way particular interpretations have worked out previously in practice.[2]

Other countries tend to follow these same interpretive methods. The Vienna Convention on the Law of Treaties, itself a treaty, sets down general rules for their interpretation. It explains that a "treaty shall be interpreted in good faith in accordance with the ordinary meaning to be given to the terms of the treaty in their context and in the light of its object and purpose."[3] It finds relevant "subsequent practice in the application of the treaty."[4] It provides that "[r]ecourse may be had to supplementary means of interpretation, including the preparatory work of the treaty and the circumstances of its conclusion"[5]—that is, the treaty's historical context and legislative history—in order to "confirm the meaning" suggested by the text alone. And it says that where textual meaning is "ambiguous or obscure," or a more literal interpretation would lead "to a result which is manifestly absurd or unreasonable," those interpreting the treaty can again look to "the preparatory work" of the drafters.[6]

Between 2010 and 2014, our Court decided three cases involving the interpretation of the Hague Convention on the Civil Aspects of International Child Abduction. (One, which was highly technical, I shall not discuss.)[7] The interpretive methods used were those just described. They are straightforward and uncontroversial and do not reflect any recent change in basic method. But they do present questions: Why would three cases involving the same treaty appear in our Court in such a short span of time? Is there something special about that treaty?

In fact, I think those cases *do* illustrate that something new is under way: some activities that used to be predominately local, including family life, now increasingly involve more than one nation. And that fact has required the Court to venture into uncharted legal territories, reckoning with (and at times applying) foreign laws concerning what once were almost exclusively local matters.

Signed in 1980, the Hague Convention on the Civil Aspects of International Child Abduction addresses an old problem. Two parents experience marital difficulties; one leaves and takes their child to a different place; and the remaining parent objects. Does the departing parent have the right to take the child and flee? Who will decide? These questions are familiar to courts both in the United States and abroad. But what is new is that increasingly these disputes cross borders. Even in 1980 the number of marriages, divorces, and child custody battles involving residents of more than one nation had grown to the point that the international community felt the need to respond with the Hague Convention.[8] The trend has only increased in the thirty-five years since.

With more than eighty nations as parties, the Hague Convention reflects a collective effort to provide internationally applicable rules and procedures for resolving cross-border child abduction cases, with the aim of making results more predictable and uniform.[9] When our Court has been called upon to interpret and to enforce the treaty in recent years, it has found the task similar in kind but different in *substance* compared with times past. It has been able to use traditional interpretive methods to discern the meaning of the text and apply it to the controversies at issue, but it has also had to go further. To arrive at the right decision, the Court has found it necessary to learn about the laws, customs, and practices dealing with family matters abroad. Such matters once seemed so essentially local that federal courts rarely considered them, let alone under the rubric of international treaty interpretation. To interpret treaties governing family matters, the Court has had to rely on new and often foreign sources of information.

THE ABBOTTS

Timothy Abbott is British; his wife, Jacquelyn, is American. They were married in the UK in 1992. For professional reasons, Mr. Abbott, an astronomer, moved the family to Hawaii, where, in 1995, their son was born. In 2002 they moved to Chile, where marital discord caused Mr. and Mrs. Abbott to separate, the Chilean courts awarding Mrs. Abbott "daily care and control of the child." Mr. Abbott had requested custody, but the Chilean courts found that the boy was "more emotionally tied to his mother, who has assumed his breeding in a totally satisfactory way."[10] Mr. Abbott was nevertheless awarded visitation rights. And a Chilean statute provides that, where a parent has visitation rights, the other parent cannot take the child out of the country without permission—of either the other parent or a Chilean court.[11]

One day Mrs. Abbott discovered that Mr. Abbott had obtained a British passport for the boy, and she began to fear he would take the child to Britain. She applied for, and obtained, a court order forbidding him from doing so. And then, taking matters into her own hands, she took the child to Texas, where in 2005 she filed for divorce.[12]

Later that same year Mr. Abbott hired a private investigator, who located Mrs. Abbott and the boy in Texas. Mr. Abbott brought a proceeding in a local court, seeking visitation rights and return of the child to Chile. The Texas court agreed to his first request, granting him liberal visitation rights as long as he remained in Texas. But it denied the second. Mrs. Abbott could not work in Chile (because of visa restrictions), and Mr. Abbott was behind in his support payments, and so the court decided that mother and son were better off in Texas.[13]

At this point, Mr. Abbott filed a case in the federal court for the Western District of Texas. He cited the Hague Convention on Child Abduction, which says that the removal of a child "is . . . wrongful" if "it is in breach of rights of custody."[14] The right given him by Chilean law to keep his son in Chile (absent a court order to the contrary) was a right of "custody," he claimed. Hence the federal court must, in the words of the convention, "order the return of the child forthwith."[15] The district court rejected this argument. So did the court of appeals. And so the stage was set for Supreme Court review.[16]

The essential dynamics of the Abbotts' story are familiar. Should the child be returned to where he was, or should he remain where he is? Should his mother have to return to Chile, where she could not work (and might not receive regular child support), or could she remain in Texas with her son? Substitute, say, "Wisconsin" for "Chile," and we have the kind of case that state domestic relations courts, and other state family courts, decide routinely. But here foreign law, indeed international law, had intervened. And the federal courts were asked to determine a matter with which they were not very familiar: What is the scope of the parental "visitation" right under Chilean law, and does it qualify as a form of "custody" under the treaty?

The treaty says that where "a child has been wrongfully removed," a court "shall order the return of the child forthwith."[17] It adds that a "removal" is "wrongful where . . . it is in breach of rights of custody."[18] And it defines "rights of custody" to "include . . . the right to determine the child's place of residence."[19] Meanwhile, as noted above, a provision of Chile's "Minors Law" says that a parent with visitation rights can allow (or refuse to allow) the minor's exit from Chile (although if he or she refuses "without good reason," a Chilean family court can override the objection and grant the parent or minor permission to leave nonetheless).[20] The Court thought that, semantically speaking, if a parent could block the minor's departure from the country, he could in effect "determine the child's place," or at least country, "of residence."[21] And in turn, because the convention provides that removal is "wrongful" when it is in "breach of a right of custody," an American court, when faced with a wrongful removal such as in *Abbott*, must order the child returned "forthwith."[22]

The Court also looked to the purpose of the convention, which is to prevent abductions so that custody disputes might be resolved where they originate, not in some country to which the child is taken. "The Convention is based on the principle that the best interests of the child are well served when decisions regarding custody rights are made in the country of habitual residence."[23] And a broad interpretation of "custody," the Court reasoned, would serve the convention's purpose by discouraging abduction.

A document reflecting the convention's drafting history also supported this interpretation, categorizing Mr. Abbott's Chilean right as a right of custody.[24] The Court then further noted that the U.S. Department of State, whose Office of Children's Issues serves as the central authority under the convention, had long understood the convention "as including" rights such as Mr. Abbott had enjoyed in Chile as being "among the protected rights of custody."[25]

Finally, looking to precedent, the Court found further support in decisions by courts in Britain, Israel, South Africa, Australia, and Germany. All those had taken the view that Mr. Abbott's rights qualified as rights of "custody" under the convention—although courts in France and Canada had not concurred entirely with those judgments.[26] Nonetheless, "[s]cholars agree that there is an emerging international consensus that *ne exeat* rights [i.e., rights to object to a minor leaving the country] are rights of custody," and "most contracting states" have adopted such views.[27]

The three dissenting justices followed the same basic methodology to reach a different conclusion. They began by looking to language.[28] The treaty says that "'rights of custody' shall include rights relating to the care of the person of the child *and,* in particular, the right to determine the child's place of residence."[29] But it does not say that the latter right *alone* is sufficient to describe custody. Nor does it say that a visitation right, subject to judicial veto, to prevent the mother (with virtually full custody rights) from taking the child to a different jurisdiction amounts to a "right to determine the child's place of residence."

As to the purpose of the convention, the dissenters saw it as preventing one parent's removal of a child from the country where the other parent has custody to a country where the abducting parent hopes for a more favorable custody decision.[30] Mr. Abbott might have a right (under the Minors Law and subject to court veto) to stop Mrs. Abbott from taking their son from Chile, but he could determine no other major choice in the child's upbringing—for example, his schooling, his religion, what language he'd learn, what he'd be fed, where specifically he'd live. Was the father's right to visit a child on Saturday afternoons, then, enough to prevent the mother from taking him from Chile? In addition to custody rights, the treaty defines "access rights," which is a "right to take a child for a limited period of time to a place other than the child's habitual residence"[31]—this, the dissenters believed, was more nearly in line with Mr. Abbott's veto. The treaty may preserve his "visitation rights," but does not in any way view them as "custody rights." Under Chilean law, if a visitation right is violated, "the judge may decree the suspension of alimony."[32] But the law does not foresee enforced return. Likewise, the treaty does not view denial of an "access right" as reason for the child's automatic return.

Looking at the same report from the drafting history that the majority had considered, the dissenters found confirmation that the drafters did not intend to grant "the same degree of protection to custody and access rights."[33] And in reviewing the same foreign court decisions that their colleagues had, the dissenters found better and more pertinent reasoning in the minority opinions, which matched their own.[34] As to the views of the State Department, they refused to weigh them as heavily as the majority had, pointing out that the department had presented its conclusion in a single paragraph, without much analysis.[35] They omitted to mention that over time the department had taken different positions on the issue, and the brief offered no particular insight into the views of the treaty framers. In general, the minority found, the department's views were entitled to less legal weight than when a particular interpretation of a treaty would help to avoid conflict with other nations.[36]

So far, then, the case seems to present nothing very special about treaty interpretation. Despite reaching divergent opinions, all the justices used the traditional legal considerations of language, history, purpose, and precedent (and possibly consequences). The tradition of these considerations is venerable indeed. Shakespeare (following *Holinshed's Chronicles*) shows them applied to similar purposes. When Henry V wishes to contend for "the vasty fields of France," he asks the Archbishop of Canterbury and the Bishop of Ely whether his claim to French territory is legally legitimate.[37] The claim comes through his grandfather John of Gaunt ("time-honour'd Lancaster"), son of King Edward III, whose mother, Isabella, was the daughter of the King of France (and wife of Edward II).[38] Can Henry V inherit a claim to land in France from a woman? Or does the Salic Law bar that claim—as an assembly of French notables has announced?

The bishops first examine the text. Pharamond, a legendary king of France, described the Salic Law as follows: "*In terram Salicam mulieres ne succedant* . . . No female should be inheritrix in Salic land."[39] But, the bishops add, "Salic land" refers not to France but to Meissen, the German territory between the Sala and Elbe Rivers.[40] Next they look to history and purpose. The law reflects the fact that, after Charlemagne subdued these territories, he left behind some French settlers, who held "in disdain the German women for some dishonest manners of their life."[41] Hence, to include them in a line of succession risked lack of clarity—one couldn't be sure who the father was.

Finally, the bishops look to tradition and to precedent. In the "Book of Numbers," they say, "is it writ" that "when the man dies, let the inheritance descend unto the daughter."[42] Moreover, Pepin, Hugh Capet, and "Lewis the Tenth," all three being kings of France, took a royal title that descended through a woman.[43]

What is new in *Abbott,* then, is not the method of the Court's majority or its dissenters in answering the legal question presented—the method has been in use for centuries. What is novel is that the traditional approach required the Court to understand not only an international document—namely, a treaty—but a foreign country's laws and customs in an area most *unfamiliar* to federal courts, domestic relations—far less familiar than the laws of succession in one medieval European dominion would have been to the ecclesiastical authorities of another.

As the *Abbott* Court explained, the purpose of the Hague Convention is to secure the best interests of children by ensuring that courts of their home countries make their custody determinations.[44] When a child is abducted from a parent with "rights of custody," the convention directs that he or she be returned "forthwith," so that such a court can retain jurisdiction over the case. The key question, then, for U.S. judges facing abduction petitions is whether the complainant has "rights of custody." If so, the purpose of the treaty will be furthered by a return order.

Everything comes down to "custody," and "custody," in turn, will depend on the laws and practices of a foreign country, an area of relative obscurity to American federal judges. Returning to Mr. Abbott's case, the question was whether his visitation rights gave him enough of a "custody" interest under Chilean law to warrant the child's return. The dissenters thought not. After all, his rights were only those of access, not of deciding how to raise the child.[45] The majority saw it otherwise. Being entitled to bar the child's departure from Chile gave Mr. Abbott a significant right relating to his boy's care and development—he could thus determine "the language the child speaks, the identity he finds, or the culture and traditions [he] will come to absorb."[46] What matters for present purposes is that both the majority and the dissenters had to dive rather deep into Chilean family law to understand what visitation rights in that country connote. And this is one way in which globalization is coming to transform the Court's docket and the nature of its work.

LOZANO

Another recent Hague Convention case also required the Court to learn about family and domestic relations law in foreign countries. *Lozano v. Alvarez* did not involve the laws of one foreign country but rather a procedural practice called "equitable tolling," which, in one form or another, many countries follow.[47]

A man and woman lived in England, enjoying a happy, normal relationship, at least in the man's view. The woman, however, found the man physically violent. Without telling him, she took their child to a women's shelter, where they remained for seven months before going to France and, finally, New York City, where the woman moved in with her sister. According to a therapist, the child adjusted well to life in New York. When, however, the man located the woman in New York about sixteen months after she'd left England, he asked a federal court to order the child returned.[48]

The convention directs that when a court receives such a petition within one year of a wrongful abduction, it should "order the return of the child forthwith."[49] But "where the proceedings have been commenced after the expiration of the period of one year [from the date of wrongful removal], [the court] shall also order the return of the child, *unless it is demonstrated that the child is now settled in its new environment.*"[50] In other words, if return is sought within one year, return is generally ordered. If more than a year has passed, the court should decide whether the child is well "settled." In *Lozano,* the petition came some sixteen months after the fact,[51] making settlement seem the dispositive consideration, but the Court still had a way of returning the child even if it found him settled. It could "toll"—that is, suspend—the mandatory one-year return window in light of the fact that the father hadn't been told his child was leaving with its mother or where they were going.

Experts on child abduction told the Court that, unless the return period was extended, the United States would become a haven for abductors waiting out the time limit.[52] Experts on domestic violence, however, argued to the contrary, viewing the treaty's one-year limitation as a compromise between two competing objectives: the desire, on the one hand, to deter child abductions, and the wish, on the other, to prevent children from being uprooted once resettled elsewhere, particularly when they had been the victims of domestic abuse in their home country.[53]

The Court would ultimately decide that the mandatory return rule should not be "equitably tolled" to account for a parent's inability to locate a fleeing parent or child.[54] After one year has elapsed, a child is too likely to have adjusted to its new home. And the goal of the convention, the Court found, was not to "discourage child abduction" at "any cost" but rather to balance the goal of deterring it with that of promoting the child's best interests.[55]

What matters particularly for our purposes is that in arriving at its decision not to toll, the Court surveyed case law from several other countries to decide whether they would have written such a practice into Article 12. In so doing, the Court concluded that "Lozano ha[d] not identified a background principle of equitable tolling that is shared by signatories to the Hague Convention," and that indeed, intermediate courts in England, Canada, and Hong Kong had all rejected the principle.[56] Foreign courts had also held that the objective of preventing deception by one parent of the other could be advanced by taking concealment into account when determining whether a child was well settled. "Equitable tolling is therefore neither required by the Convention nor the only available means to advance its objectives."[57]

Both of these cases required difficult family law decisions that involved parties and interests spanning several jurisdictions with whose family law practices our federal courts are generally unfamiliar. The Supreme Court therefore considered with particular care the expert views—not only experts on how the treaty was written but also those familiar with child abduction issues and those conversant with the problems of child abuse.

Why would the nations that wrote the treaty want our federal courts to decide cases of family law, rather than our state courts, particularly domestic relations courts, which consider such matters daily? The answer is that treaty interpretation is a matter that normally takes a case into federal court. And nations today cannot easily forgo embodying family law in treaties. There are too many multinational families. There is too much travel. Abduction is all too easy. At the same time, the variation in systems of family law that continues to exist in these countries renders American experience of diminished practical use.

We can expect more such questions of treaty interpretation, as the United States has also entered into treaties concerning adoption and child maintenance.[58] And it is considering joining one concerning child protection.[59] Through treaty interpretation, the federal courts and the Supreme Court will face more and more cases obliging them to become more expert in an area where the subject matter itself is so often individualized and so deeply personal that courts must beware of relying too heavily upon experts. These circumstances do not mean that our Court will become the main forum for such matters; state domestic relations courts will maintain their predominant role. But it does mean that those with a stake in domestic relations law will have to pay particular attention to the consequences of our decisions, to monitor those consequences, and to be ready, willing, and able to seek modifications in the language or substance of international treaties related to child welfare, if they hope to achieve those treaties' beneficent goals.

CHAPTER 8

Investment Treaties

Arbitration

The Internet's growth makes it ever easier for people to do business abroad. At a personal level, an individual can order a taxi for next weekend in a foreign city; a family can rent a vacation house for a week in another country. Such transactions can increase the wealth and well-being of all involved. But they can also generate disputes that are more complicated than those arising from entirely local transactions—disputes that require a fair system for resolving them nonetheless. Here we consider one such system—namely, the system embodied in certain international treaties that compel the parties to submit to arbitration, particularly where the dispute is a complex commercial matter, as when there are parties in more than one nation.

Arbitration, like mediation and other informal methods of dispute settlement, may prove quicker and cheaper and is occasionally informed by more expertise than traditional courtroom litigation. Court-based decision makers, such as judges and jurors, are rarely expert in the technical area involved in a dispute. Indeed, Judge Learned Hand once suggested that in such commercial cases the judge should sit with two masters who are specialists in the field and could help him reach a decision.[1]

During the past few decades, commercial parties and courts have sought ways to resolve commercial disputes with less formality and more expertise; these have included conciliation, mediation, and arbitration. Conciliation and mediation are informal mechanisms that do not bind the parties but help them reach a mutually satisfactory agreement. Arbitration, on the other hand, is binding, with the parties accepting its results in advance.[2] Once the decision is made, it is too late for the losing party to withdraw, as courts will enforce a decision flowing from a binding arbitration agreement.

Congress first passed the Federal Arbitration Act (FAA) in 1925, overcoming what had been judicial hostility to such extrajudicial tribunals.[3] The act authorized the federal courts to recognize agreements to arbitrate and to enforce them and the judgments of their panels.[4] Since that time, in one commentator's assessment, arbitration has "become the primary mechanism … for resolving civil disputes in American society."[5] The American Arbitration Association (AAA), founded a year after the FAA's enactment, now has twenty-two offices overseeing more than 200,000 matters per year.[6] (Federal courts, by contrast, handled only 28,571 contract actions in 2013.)[7] In 2014 AAA celebrated the administration of its four millionth case.[8] As one might expect, arbitration has come to touch many aspects of everyday life. A recent empirical study of businesses dealing directly with consumers found that more than a third employed arbitration agreements (and in some sectors, such as financial services, its use was close to 70 percent).[9]

At the same time, the number of commercial cases resolved through court litigation has fallen.[10] But it's not altogether clear why that should be, since over time arbitration has itself tended to become more formal and elaborate and consequently more expensive. Some have even argued that it no longer offers the major advantages for which it was initially designed, especially speed and cost savings.[11] Others claim that it still holds one: "better" or at least more "expert" judges.[12] Still others, however, believe that by taking cases from the courts, arbitration, which typically yields results not supported by written reasons, deprives the legal system of occasions for judges, through analysis subject to the criticism of others, to maintain and develop sound law.[13] I shall not weigh the merits or demerits of arbitration, particularly commercial arbitration, here, however. Suffice it to say that its growth suggests that many still find it more satisfactory than the available judicial alternatives.

Growth in international commercial arbitration has paralleled that in the domestic variety. But when borders are crossed, arbitration offers the crucially important advantage of forum neutrality—parties can appear before a neutral decision maker without having to be hauled into the other's courts. The practice is therefore particularly popular among investors in developing countries, who are often skeptical of the local court systems. In China, for instance, "arbitration has emerged as the dispute resolution procedure of choice," with the number of disputes submitted to the China International Economic and Trade Arbitration Commission (CIETAC) rising from 37 in 1985 to 1,000 in 1995.[14] At the same time, more and more nations have entered into investment treaties, under which each party promises to protect investors of the other nation from unfair, costly commercial treatment such as expropriation. And these treaties often provide for international arbitration as a method for resolving disputes.[15]

The increased use of international commercial arbitration for resolving disputes, often between a private party and a nation-state, poses difficult questions. Is it desirable to vest so much decision-making authority in tribunals, which, unlike courts, are not even indirectly accountable to any electorate? And if so, how can courts exercise judicial review of arbitral decisions to ensure that awards are fair and consistent with domestic laws, without undermining the efficiency and neutrality of the arbitral system?

The international community has come up with several ways of permitting a degree of judicial review. For one, close to 150 countries have agreed to the framework established by the New York Convention, under which courts can refuse "recognition and enforcement" of an arbitral award if that award is (1) "contrary to the public policy of that country" (in which "recognition and enforcement is sought"); (2) deals with a matter "not capable of settlement by arbitration under the law of that country" (in which enforcement is sought); (3) is made pursuant to an arbitration agreement that itself is invalid; or (4) is made in an arbitration process in which the fairness is undermined by a serious procedural defect.[16] In addition, courts have created their own doctrinal frameworks, layered on top of the New York Convention, for ensuring that the parties intended to arbitrate a matter and that the agreement is therefore valid.

This latter type of judicial backstop was at issue in a case that came before the Court in 2014, *BG Group v. Republic of Argentina*. I shall describe that case, lay out the interpretive framework the Court developed, and illustrate the way the Court drew upon our country's experience with labor arbitration to ground its approach. It remains to be seen whether the Court struck the right balance.

BG Group required the Court to determine whether arbitrators in an international investment dispute had exceeded their powers. It was a challenge very different from those described in Chapter 7, in which the Court, in trying to adjudicate actions pursuant to modern multilateral treaties (such as the child abduction treaty), had to familiarize itself with the intricacies of foreign law in unfamiliar areas. Doing justice to the intent of the child abduction treaty, for instance, meant acquiring some expertise in foreign laws and practices concerning parental visitation and custody. In *BG Group,* however, the challenge was to determine when American judges should *stay out of the matter* for the most part and defer to the independent arbitrators. While both chapters involve the application of international treaties, the treaties call for very different judicial roles.

AMERICAN BACKGROUND: LABOR ARBITRATION

During the 1960s the Court frequently considered issues involving labor arbitration, and that experience would influence its interpretation of statutes and contracts providing for commercial arbitration more generally, including its reading of treaties that provide for arbitration of investment disputes.

The courts were not always the forum of choice for labor disputes. Following World War II, union leaders, businesses, and government had turned to administrative agencies and private arbitrators as a useful way of maintaining industrial accord. Organized labor had developed a particularly strong distrust of federal courts over the earlier part of the century, when the courts had intervened in labor disputes, using federal antitrust law to weaken or destroy trade unions. The first step away from the courts came when Congress created a special regulatory body, the National Labor Relations Board (NLRB). It was to rely heavily upon collective bargaining to ensure fair wages, hours, and working conditions without resort to costly strikes.[17] Business and labor both warmed to arbitration as a speedy, inexpensive, and expert-based system for dispute resolution,[18] and Congress ratified that trend by authorizing federal courts to enforce privately created arbitration contracts.[19] Labor understood that management's acceptance of grievance arbitration as binding was a quid pro quo for its own acceptance of the legally binding nature of "no strike" clauses in labor contracts, which had been intended to prevent wildcat strikes.[20]

In the 1960s and 1970s, the Supreme Court answered a set of questions about labor arbitration in a way that significantly expanded the power of arbitrators to resolve disputes arising under collective bargaining agreements. Answering these questions, as I have said at the outset, would shape judicial attitudes about arbitration more generally.

The questions presented in the Court's early cases were three: First, when a party to arbitration asks a court to review (i.e., confirm, enforce, or set aside) an arbitrator's decision, to what extent should the court second-guess the arbitrator and to what extent defer to him? The Court's answer, given in three labor cases decided in 1960 and collectively known as the Steelworkers' Trilogy,[21] was that the arbitrator is largely autonomous. Reviewing courts must hesitate to upset his interpretation of a contract unless it is wildly off the mark or the contract does not provide for arbitration in the first place. Indeed, courts should give more deference to arbitration awards than they give even to decisions of the relevant administrative agency, the NLRB.[22]

The Court's instruction in one of the trilogy cases was that

the judicial inquiry . . . must be strictly confined to the question whether the reluctant party did agree to arbitrate the grievance or did agree to give the arbitrator the power to make the award he made. An order to arbitrate the particular grievance should not be denied unless it may be said with positive assurance that the arbitration clause is not susceptible of an interpretation that covers the asserted dispute. Doubts should be resolved in favor of coverage.[23]

Thus, for example, a court upheld an arbitrator's reinstatement of a postal worker who had been dismissed for firing a gun at a supervisor's parked car.[24] (The arbitrator had found mitigating factors.) Similar examples abound. As long as the arbitral decision "dr[ew] its essence from the collective bargaining agreement," reviewing courts were to enforce it.[25] Following the Steelworkers' Trilogy, the Court would apply the same basic approach to interpreting the Federal Arbitration Act and to commercial arbitration awards more generally. That is, the Court would direct federal courts to give great deference to an arbitrator's decision.[26]

Second, to what extent can arbitrators determine their own jurisdiction (i.e., their own legal right) to hear a dispute? Suppose the losing party comes to court and argues, "I never agreed to arbitrate, or, at least, I did not agree to arbitrate that kind of question." In *AT&T Technologies*, the Court considered a union grievance arising out of a company's decision to lay off seventy-nine workers.[27] The union said the layoffs violated a provision of the collective bargaining agreement that had created a set order in which employees could be terminated. That set order applied only when a "lack of work necessitates Layoff[s]."[28] The union argued there was no such "lack of work" at the plant, and it sought to compel arbitration on that point. The employer responded that the issue was not arbitrable: while the contract provided a sequence for making layoffs, it left the "lack of work" determination to the employer's sole discretion. Arbitrators had no authority to review such judgments.[29] The question before the Court was whether the parties had agreed to arbitrate disputes about whether there was a "lack of work." Moreover, who was to decide that threshold question: the arbitrator or a federal court?

The Court held that the question was for a court to decide. Arbitration, the Court wrote, is a matter of contractual consent. Without support in a contract for submitting a certain kind of dispute to arbitral resolution, arbitrators lack the power to resolve it and to issue a judgment that would bind the parties.[30] For that reason, the Court held, the matter of "arbitrability"—namely, "whether a collective bargaining agreement creates a duty for the parties to arbitrate the particular grievance" in the first place—is an issue for judicial determination, unless "the parties clearly and unmistakably provide otherwise."[31] The "question of whether the parties agreed to arbitrate is to be decided by the court, not the arbitrator."[32]

These few words provided a bright-line rule, but they have also created enormous difficulty. What exactly is the standard of "arbitrability" under *AT&T Technologies*? Presumably, it has something to do with whether the resisting party agreed to arbitrate the matter. But as commentators have pointed out, the underlying issues invoked can take many forms.[33] The resisting party might argue that the arbitrators lack jurisdiction because the contract's arbitration clause is invalid—for example, because the resisting party never signed the clause, or because someone forged his signature, or because it is contrary to public policy. In making such technical objections, the resisting party may contend that he is thereby raising a question about "arbitrability," and so a court must decide it. Alternatively, the resisting party might argue that the contract *as a whole* is invalid, negating his duty to arbitrate—hence another "arbitrability" issue that only the court can answer. Or a resisting party might argue that while there is a valid contract and a valid arbitration clause, the clause doesn't cover the *particular* issue at hand—say, the question of "lack of work" and layoffs. There again, he will insist it is for the courts to decide.

A resisting party might also cite procedural objections in denying he has a duty to arbitrate. For instance, he might argue that his opponent has somehow waived the right to arbitrate (despite its being clearly set forth in the contract's arbitration clause); or he might assert some other legal barrier, such as a statute of limitations on the underlying claim or a requirement that a party provide certain notice; or he could say that he agreed to arbitrate an issue only once a certain precondition, such as mediation, has been fulfilled, and that this has not yet been done.[34]

When faced with such objections (whose variations seem potentially endless), are courts to decide them on the merits themselves? Or should they defer to the views of arbitrators, who were intended to bear primary responsibility for answering such questions?

In *AT&T,* the Court held that at least with respect to the dispute at issue—namely, whether in their collective bargaining agreement the parties had consented to arbitrate "grievances concerning layoffs predicated on a 'lack of work' determination by the Company"—courts should decide the matter, unless the contract clearly provided otherwise.[35] The legal framework for arbitrability, which would stand until *BG Group* (to be discussed presently), was as follows: questions such as "whether the parties are bound by a given arbitration clause" or "whether an arbitration clause in a concededly binding contract applies to a particular type of controversy" were presumptively for courts to decide. That is because courts should normally assume that the parties would have intended judicial resolution of such issues.[36] But questions about whether *procedural preconditions* to arbitration have been satisfied are for arbitrators to decide. That is because courts should normally assume that parties would have intended arbitrators to interpret and to apply contractual provisions of this kind.[37]

The third type of question the Court first resolved in labor arbitration cases (and later in commercial arbitration cases more broadly) concerns the enforcement of an arbitrator's decision when it is claimed to be in conflict with public policy. In *W.R. Grace,* the Court said that "as with any contract," a court could not "enforce an award that is contrary to public policy."[38] But the Court added that the "public policy" in question "must be well defined and definite[,] and is to be ascertained 'by reference to the laws and legal precedents and not from general consideration of supposed public interest.'"[39] The Court would underscore this latter stipulation four years later when it upheld an arbitrator's reinstatement of a worker discharged for marijuana possession.[40] According to the Court, the lower courts had not identified a clear enough policy against marijuana use while operating heavy machinery to justify invalidating the decision.

The problem in this area is obvious: for courts to wield the "public policy" weapon too often or too finely risks undercutting the autonomy of the arbitrator. And since losing parties will often bet they might win in court, it is to encourage litigation, thereby diminishing arbitration's efficiency advantages. On the other hand, to ignore public policy when reviewing arbitral awards would be to permit potentially outlandish results, undermining arbitration's legitimacy.

For present purposes, the reader need only remember the three basic questions that arose in the Court's labor arbitration cases, and how, in broad terms, they were answered. (1) To what extent are the arbitrator's decisions free from review? Answer: the arbitrator possesses great autonomy, and his decisions will stand unless they deviate wildly from the contract or there was no contract to arbitrate in the first place. (2) Who decides threshold questions about whether arbitration can proceed, such as whether a party actually signed an arbitration agreement or whether a party complied with a precondition to arbitration? Answer: courts decide questions of whether the arbitration agreement applies to the issue in question, and arbitrators decide whether preconditions have been satisfied, unless there is clear evidence in the contract that the parties intended otherwise. (3) How much do courts, ultimate enforcers of an arbitration award, take account of the host country's public policy?

Answer: they take account of it provided the policy in question is concrete and well established.

Developed in the area of labor, this approach would be extended to domestic commercial agreements and to international ones, too, as we shall see. Overall, it strongly favors arbitral autonomy, so that once parties agree to arbitrate a matter, the court's role is very limited, more so than when appellate courts review a typical lower court decision.[41] Though limited, however, the court's role remains vital. Arbitration derives its legitimacy from the consent of the parties. Thus the courts must keep watch over arbitral decisions lest a party find himself compelled to arbitrate a matter whose nonjudicial resolution he never agreed to.

BG GROUP

In 2014 the Court applied the principles just described to a controversy arising under an international investment treaty. In the early 1990s a British firm, BG Group, had received from the Argentine government rights to distribute natural gas in Buenos Aires. At the same time, Argentina enacted laws saying that rates at which distributors like BG Group could sell natural gas would be calculated in U.S. dollars and fixed by the government regulator at levels that would guarantee distributors a reasonable return. A few years later, however, when Argentina suffered an economic crisis, those laws were changed. Under the new rules, gas tariffs would be calculated in pesos, not dollars, and given the exchange rate at the time, this caused distributors like BG Group to suffer heavy losses.[42]

Before BG Group had invested in Argentina, the United Kingdom and Argentina had signed a Bilateral Investment Treaty, in which each promised to treat investments made by nationals of the other "fair[ly] and equitabl[y]" and not to "expropriat[e]" those investments. Believing that Argentina had violated both of those promises with its new tariff law, BG Group sought arbitration, as provided for in Article 8 of the Bilateral Investment Treaty.[43]

Article 8 is complicated. It permits disputing parties to proceed directly to arbitration if they both agree to do so. It also authorizes a party to submit a dispute to arbitration unilaterally if a local court, having heard the matter first, has still not "given its final decision" after eighteen months, or if the local court *has* rendered a decision "but the Parties are still in dispute."[44]

The problem for BG Group was that it never wanted to bring its claim to Argentina's local courts, and so it went right to arbitration instead. The arbitrators decided BG was entitled to do as it had done, since the Article 8 requirement could not be absolute. Suppose, for example, that Argentina had closed its courts to foreign investors; could it then argue that BG Group had not complied with the treaty provision and therefore could not go to arbitration? In fact, Argentina had not blocked BG Group's access to the local courts completely, but it had suspended the execution of those courts' judgments for six months, as well as issuing an order banning firms that had already tried going to the courts (or arbitration) from taking advantage of a special negotiation process it had created precisely to deal with investment problems such as BG Group's. As the arbitrators saw it, Argentina had thus waived its right to the local litigation requirement of Article 8, and so it was proper for them (the arbitrators) to take jurisdiction over the dispute. On the merits, the arbitrators also found in BG Group's favor and awarded it $185 million.[45]

Argentina then went to court to try to have the award set aside, and since the arbitration had taken place in Washington, D.C., the petition was filed in the federal court for the District of Columbia. The district court rejected Argentina's arguments and confirmed the award,[46] but the court of appeals reversed, deciding two questions: First, it was for that court, and not the arbitrators, to determine whether BG Group had complied with the Article 8 requirement. Second, BG Group should indeed have complied with the "local litigation" precondition, and its failure to do so meant that the arbitrators had no business taking jurisdiction. Hence the court held that the award was invalid.[47]

Thus the stage was set for our Court's review. We had to decide whether the circuit court had rightly characterized disputes pertaining to the Article 8 requirement as matters for judges to decide, without deference to the arbitrators, or whether it was for the arbitrators to interpret and apply that part of the treaty in the first instance, and if so, whether their decision in the matter was justifiable. Were they correct in holding that, by impeding BG Group's access to the local courts, Argentina had in effect waived the "local courts" clause?

Given the jurisprudential history set out above, it should not be surprising that our Court held that the matter was one for arbitrators, not judges, to decide. Drawing on the Court's labor arbitration case law, as well as its extension to ordinary commercial arbitration cases, the Court began with a hypothetical, imagining what the parties to a contract would have wanted had a preliminary question about arbitration arisen. Where the dispute is about the meaning and application of a particular *procedural* precondition, the Court explained, we must assume that the parties would have left the matter to the arbitrator. Otherwise judges, determining the application of time limits, notice requirements, and a host of other procedural details, might prevent any arbitration from going forward for basically technical reasons, thus depriving the parties of the quicker, less formal means of resolution that they had originally wanted. On the other hand, where the dispute is about the arbitration contract's very existence, validity, application to a party, or scope (which was not the case here), it was fair to assume that the parties would have intended judges to resolve the controversy.[48]

Applying that framework, the Court held that the meaning and application of the "local litigation requirement" were questions about *when*, not *whether*, arbitration would take place. The issue, then, was not one of substantive "arbitrability"—that is, whether an arbitration agreement had been concluded at all, or whether Argentina and investors such as BG Group were parties to it. Rather, disputes about the local litigation requirement, including the present one, concerned threshold questions of the procedural variety, which arbitrators should decide. Unless something in the treaty or Article 8 "overc[a]me the ordinary assumption" and directed otherwise (which the Court found no evidence of), federal courts should defer to arbitrators' decisions about the local litigation clause. Because the court of appeals had approached the matter *de novo*, that part of its decision was consequently incorrect.[49]

Even so, the Court acknowledged that parties like Argentina are entitled to judicial review of the arbitrators' decision on a procedural point. Though the standard of review will be highly deferential, federal courts should nonetheless determine whether the arbitrators exceeded their powers. Applying such a standard, the Court agreed with the arbitrators that the local litigation requirement was not absolute (that it would not apply if Argentina blocked use of the courts). The Court was less certain about whether Argentina had acted in a way that, in effect, waived its right to local litigation with BG Group. It did stall the courts' judgments for six months, but BG Group still had a year in which to file suit. It also made it difficult for investors to use the courts, thereby losing their right to participate in a contract-renegotiating process, but that also applied to investors who tried to arbitrate. All things considered, the Court said, the arbitrators were not *clearly* wrong. They did not "stray" from the treaty or otherwise "dispense" their own "brand of justice" in holding that the litigation requirement had been waived and that BG Group could proceed directly to arbitration. And given that interpreting this provision of the treaty was basically for the arbitrators to do, their finding was good enough. The Court upheld the arbitral decision and award.[50]

THE TREATY

The Court's application of domestic arbitration case law reflected, as I've said, arbitration law as it was developed in the labor arbitration field. But it was not obvious in *BG Group* that those doctrines *should* apply the same way. In the labor law area, strong reasons, having to do with the desirability of industrial peace, counsel in favor of granting considerable power to arbitrators. But the *BG Group* case was not a labor case. It involved a system of commercial arbitration created by a treaty among sovereign nations. Was it, then, right for the Court to adopt the same presumptions about what the parties likely intended as to who should decide what?

The solicitor general, presumably having consulted with the Department of State, had argued for the U.S. government that the answer was no. He said that the Court's framework for resolving domestic arbitration disputes should be modified in the case of a bilateral investment treaty.[51] The operative question, he said, should be whether preconditions to arbitration included in such a treaty—such as the local litigation requirement in Article 8—are conditions of the sovereign parties' consent to arbitrate with an investor. If so, those provisions should be interpreted and applied by judges, not by arbitrators. That is because they concern the existence and validity of the agreement to arbitrate between a sovereign and a private party.[52] The solicitor general did not say whether he thought the requirement was in fact a condition of Argentina or the United Kingdom's consent. Rather, the government advocated that the Court vacate and remand the decision, sending the case back to the lower court to make that determination.[53]

The Court ultimately rejected the solicitor general's view, applying the usual set of presumptions drawn from domestic arbitration case law to decide the treaty question. Even if "conditions of consent" in investment treaties should be spared the ordinary presumptions, and given *de novo* judicial review categorically, the Article 8 requirement was *not* such a condition.[54] Rather, it was a purely procedural precondition, as the text and structure of the treaty suggested, nowhere calling it a "condition of consent."[55] Further, the treaty provided that the parties could refer a dispute to the International Centre for Settlement of Investment Disputes, or to the United Nations Commission on International Trade Law. And both of those organizations have rules that authorize an arbitration tribunal to be the judge of its own competence to decide an issue.[56]

Suppose, however, that the case had raised a different type of challenge to the use of arbitration. Imagine a case involving an investment treaty that explicitly referred to a precondition to arbitration as a "condition of consent." Trade agreements with such language do exist. Before long our Court may have to decide whether to accept the solicitor general's recommendation in such a case. It may have to determine whether treaties—given that sovereign nations are their signatories—deserve special treatment when they specifically include "conditions of consent" clauses. The Court in *BG Group* observed that the solicitor general had not, *in that case,* presented any particularly compelling reason why the usual presumptions should be relaxed, but it did not resolve the issue conclusively.[57]

Applying the arbitration presumptions from domestic law could also prove difficult given a different kind of challenge to international arbitral awards. Suppose Argentina had claimed some kind of fraud or corruption had existed in its entering into the investment treaty with the United Kingdom. Or suppose it had argued that its Constitution denied it the legal capacity to enter into such a treaty. Or suppose it had claimed that the investment treaty or the arbitration clause itself was "unconscionable" (so unjust as to be unenforceable). These types of objections would all involve what can be seen as substantive "arbitrability," issues that concern the "existence" or "scope" of an arbitration contract and that our case law makes clear are for judges to decide. And if our Court were to resolve *this kind of* objection to arbitration *de novo* (without deference to the arbitrator), doing so could put it into conflict with how courts abroad would resolve a similar question.

Germany, for example, applies a doctrine known as *Kompetenz-Kompetenz,* which basically means that the arbitration panel itself will decide whether it has the power to hear the dispute before it, even in some cases of the kind just mentioned.[58] France, calling the doctrine *competence-competence,* permits the arbitration tribunal to decide virtually any question about its own jurisdiction, including a party's compliance with procedural conditions and whether an arbitration agreement covers the particular kind of dispute at hand, and even whether an arbitration agreement ever existed.[59] (The French courts nonetheless apply an exception in instances where the arbitration agreement "*manifestly* does not exist" or is "*manifestly* null"; in those situations, the arbitrators' decisions about their own authority have no binding effect.)[60]

Our Court may have to decide in due time whether, when confronted with "arbitrability" objections in international cases, it can continue to be guided by U.S. labor cases or whether instead it should follow foreign courts in treating arbitration as a special, autonomous branch of the legal dispute resolution system. In *BG Group,* the Court saw no reason to depart from its conventional, domestic legal framework. But the case was relatively easy in one respect: virtually every nation or arbitration system in the world would have treated the local litigation requirement as a procedural precondition, granting arbitrators primary power to interpret and apply it, just as our Court did. It won't be so simple in future cases involving threshold objections to arbitration where U.S. and foreign law diverge as to which tribunal has primary authority to resolve the objection.

PUBLIC POLICY

BG Group presented only one of the three questions the Court confronted in the earlier labor arbitration cases: the question of who—court or arbitrator—should resolve threshold disputes about whether to begin arbitration. But it isn't difficult to imagine international arbitration cases presenting the other questions discussed: the one about arbitrators' autonomy, and the one about arbitral awards in conflict with public policy.

Let's say an American court is asked to refuse to enforce an international arbitration order on grounds that it is contrary to American public policy. Suppose, for instance, that an American company asks a U.S. court to vacate an arbitration award because a foreign sovereign (in the company's view) committed a regulatory expropriation of its property or denied it fair decision-making procedures. A recent case from the Ninth Circuit involving the Internet and Nazi propaganda is instructive. Though it did not involve arbitration, but rather the enforcement of an ordinary foreign court judgment, it illustrates the *type* of policy-based challenge one might expect to be brought to prevent court enforcement of an arbitration award.

Two groups of Jewish organizations based in France found that Yahoo! exhibited Nazi propaganda on its auction site, which was in turn visible to and usable by French citizens.[61] The organizations sent a cease and desist letter to Yahoo!'s California headquarters, informing it that the sale of the Nazi-related goods on its auction site violated French law. The groups next filed a civil complaint in French court, asking it to ban the material. The court agreed that the display of the Nazi propaganda and artifacts violated French law—specifically, a provision of the French Criminal Code outlawing the exhibition and sale of such items.[62] The court entered an order requiring Yahoo! to block French citizens' access to the offensive materials on its main site, Yahoo.com, and to post a warning on its French site, Yahoo.fr, informing French users that viewing the prohibited materials on Yahoo.com could result in legal action against them personally. The order also imposed a penalty of 100,000 euros on Yahoo! for each day that it failed to comply with the order.[63]

Yahoo! posted the required warning on Yahoo.fr, and it prohibited postings that violated the French Criminal Code from the Yahoo.fr site. It also amended its auction policy on Yahoo.com, barring the sale of "[a]ny item that promotes, glorifies, or is directly associated with groups or individuals known principally for hateful ... acts, such as Nazis."[64] Notwithstanding these measures, the main auction site continued to offer certain items for sale—such as copies of *Mein Kampf*—that were viewable in France and that violated the French court order.

Yahoo! subsequently sought a declaratory judgment from the District Court for the Northern District of California. It wanted a judgment stating that the French court's order was not enforceable under U.S. law, since compliance would entail an impermissible infringement of Yahoo!'s rights under the First Amendment. The district court agreed and issued the order. It concluded that whether or not Yahoo! had the technological capability to block French citizens' access to the materials (an issue in dispute), the requirement that Yahoo! regulate its speech within the United States to curb the exhibition and sale of the materials was inconsistent with the First Amendment.[65] And although the court of appeals ultimately vacated the order for jurisdictional reasons, it reiterated that under California law, as well as the laws of most states and the Restatement of Foreign Relations Law, a "court will not enforce a judgment if 'the cause of action on which the judgment was based, or the judgment itself, is *repugnant to the public policy* of the United States or of the State where recognition is sought.'"[66]

Again, this case concerned a judicial order, but the same problem might have arisen with an arbitration finding, which would have behind it the weight of the New York Arbitration Convention. Signed by close to 150 nations, the convention provides that "[e]ach Contracting State shall recognize arbitral awards as binding and enforce them in accordance with the rules of procedure of the territory where the award is relied upon."[67] Because of this agreement, international arbitration awards are often easier to enforce in foreign nations than are judgments of ordinary courts. But it also provides that a nation may refuse to enforce an order on the grounds that it violates the nation's public policy.[68] As with labor arbitration, courts that are too ready to deny enforcement of awards for public policy reasons can seriously undermine the major benefits of arbitration procedures.[69] At the same time, however, courts that pay little or no attention to their nation's public policies can create, out of arbitration, a procedural method for nullifying those policies. So what is the right balance? How much divergence among nations is appropriate? Does it matter if a party resisting arbitration can choose among three different nations with three different public policies, by (1) bringing a court action (in Nation A) to prevent arbitration from starting, (2) bringing a court action midstream (in Nation B) trying to stop the arbitration from continuing, or (3) bringing an action (in Nation C) after the arbitration trying to prevent enforcement of an award? The lower courts are already beginning to wrestle with some of these questions. And our Court may have to confront them in due time.

As private investment in foreign nations grows, and as more of it is subject to an investment treaty that provides for international arbitration, the Court will face more questions of the kinds discussed above. An investment treaty itself can answer many of them, but often it does not. Other, more general treaties, laying down rules for interpreting arbitration provisions, also might provide answers. But when they do, those provisions, too, require authoritative court interpretation.

BG Group offered the Court a glimpse into this universe of issues that might arise out of international arbitration agreements. As mentioned, it remains to be seen whether the Court should in future continue to apply the labor arbitration framework—particularly if doing so would bring it into conflict with courts in other countries. Also an open question is how U.S. courts should apply the "public policy" exception of the New York Convention so as to avoid serious conflict with other countries or undermining arbitration's advantages.

I can predict only that as economic globalization marches on, such cases are ever likelier to fill our docket. In facing them, I believe we must remember that legal certainty is particularly important to commercial actors. So is uniformity of result across borders. And as international commerce decentralizes, and individuals or small firms become its primary actors (international vacation home rentals being a good example), the virtues of speed and low cost offered by dispute resolution outside the courts will grow together with the other two virtues mentioned.

In these circumstances, courts alone cannot provide all the answers. The best way forward may be for the international community to sign new treaties or agreements specifying the ins and outs of enforcement of arbitration awards, judicial review, and the public policy exception, all as applied to arbitration as well as other dispute-resolution methods. In the meantime, our courts must do their best to honor investors' reasonable expectations, provide legal certainty, and ensure that arbitration continues to serve as an efficient alternative to litigation while also maintaining its legitimacy.

CHAPTER 9

The Treaty Power

Structure

Treaties, of course, play a critical role in defining relationships among different nations and different peoples. The Founders well understood their importance. The Constitution delegates to the President, with the advice and consent of the Senate, the power to make treaties. The Constitution's Supremacy Clause states that together with the Constitution and the laws of the United States, "all treaties made . . . under the Authority of the United States, shall be the supreme Law of the Land; and the Judges in every State shall be bound thereby."[1]

From its beginnings, the Court has faced questions requiring it to reconcile this broad, strong grant of constitutional authority to the President and the Senate with other critical structural features of the Constitution, such as those that place legislative power in Congress, those that leave all nondelegated powers to the states, and those that protect the basic rights of individuals.

Does the Supremacy Clause mean what it seems to say—that treaty provisions automatically become the law of the United States, binding individual citizens without Congress's having to enact an implementing statute? And can a treaty give Congress legislative power that the Constitution otherwise leaves to the states alone?[2] Can the United States enter into a treaty that abridges basic individual rights that the Constitution otherwise protects?[3] If not, just what features of the Constitution trump the authority to make treaties?

After more than two hundred years of constitutional history, these and other structural questions related to the treaty power are still with us, in many cases unanswered. At the same time, the treaty power has become more important in a world of ever more treaties, which govern to an ever greater extent the daily lives of the citizens of interdependent nations. The Union of International Associations, which produces the *Yearbook of International Organizations* and is viewed as having the most authoritative figures on the subject, reports that there were 123 international governmental organizations (IGOs) in 1951, about double that figure (242) in 1971, and about fifteen times as many in 2012, which saw 1,993 IGOs.[4] While some of these organizations were created by international networks of government representatives or by "public-private" initiatives, a great many were created pursuant to treaties. And the United States has entered into at least seven hundred new formal treaties since World War II.[5]

America has felt the effects of this transformation. In its report to Congress for fiscal year 2012, the State Department identified one hundred distinct international organizations to which the United States had contributed funds.[6] According to the *Yearbook,* the U.S. participates in about 25 percent of the world's functioning international organizations, which currently number about two thousand. Below is a breakdown from the most recent year for which figures were reported.

IGOS AND UNITED STATES PARTICIPATION (2012–2013)*

	"Conventional" International Organizations	Most Relevant International Organizations	All Documented International Organizations
IGOs in which the USA participates	66[7]	423[8]	922[9]
IGOs in the world	262[10]	1993[11]	7679[12]

* *Note:* The first column in the table above shows the number of international organizations falling into "Groups A–D" in the YEARBOOK. Groups A–D, in turn, consist of "fed-

Today's international bodies deal with a wide array of matters, including:

> forest preservation, the control of fishing, water regulation, environmental protection, standardization and food safety, financial and accounting standards, internet governance, pharmaceutical regulation, intellectual property protection, refugee protection, coffee and cocoa standards, labor standards, antitrust regulation, regulation and finance of public works, trade standards regulation of insurance, foreign investments, international terrorism, war and arms control, air and maritime navigation, postal services, telecommunications, nuclear energy and nuclear waste, money laundering, education, migration, law enforcement, sport, and health.[13]

Their aggregate staffing has grown considerably, too, from 65,000 in 1970 to 250,000 in 2010.[14] Many of these IGOs set standards, procedures, and rules that directly or indirectly bind nations and sometimes their citizens.[15] Some also possess their own courts or courtlike bodies. Indeed, Sabino Cassese, a leading authority on global regulatory bodies, writes that just prior to the 1990s "there were only six operative international courts."[16] Between 1985 and 2000, however, "fifteen new permanent adjudicative mechanisms and eight quasi-judicial procedures were introduced."[17]

---

erations of international organizations," "universal membership organizations," "intercontinental membership organizations," and "regionally oriented membership organizations." The YEARBOOK calls this category of IGOs "conventional" international organizations, and the grouping corresponds to what the academic literature dubs "formal IGOs." The second column shows the number of international organizations falling into "Groups A-G" in the YEARBOOK. Groups A-G, in turn, consist of those organizations just listed as well as "organizations emanating from places, persons, or other bodies," "organizations having a special form," and "internationally oriented national organizations" (which in turn are bilateral governmental bodies). *See* 5 YEARBOOK OF INTERNATIONAL ORGANIZATIONS 2012–2013, at 8 fig.1.3 (49th ed. 2013). This broader count of international organizations, I believe, is most useful for our discussion—as it catches the essence of the growth that I discuss. The final column in the table shows the number of *all* international organizations documented by the YEARBOOK, including those that are inactive, dissolved, and proposed. This figure likely has limited value, as it is so expansive as to include defunct and irrelevant organizations.

In such a world, one might characterize the general concerns about the relationship of the treaty power to other structural protections in the Constitution as asking, at least in part: To what extent does the Constitution permit the United States to delegate legislative or adjudicative powers to international bodies created by treaties? To the extent that the Constitution inhibits such delegation, it increases the difficulty of the United States in arriving at cooperative solutions with other countries to shared problems, such as environmental degradation, public health, threats to national security, and the like. If we cannot contribute to these bodies and participate in their work, others will do so nevertheless, and our voice in the effort and its outcomes will be diminished. Further, our nation and its citizens will not necessarily be spared the consequences of those outcomes simply because we were not party to the deliberations.

But are there no constitutional constraints of any kind? If the President and the Senate are totally free to ratify treaties that in turn delegate adjudicative and legislative power to others, then what happens to the Constitution's delegation of primary law-making authority to the federal government? What happens to the principles of democracy, separation of powers, and human rights that our Constitution embodies? With one arguable exception—namely, the case of *Reid v. Covert* (which I shall discuss later)—the Court has not provided a general answer to these kinds of questions. But it has considered a handful of cases in recent years that touch upon the broader concerns—even though they posed more specific questions about the treaty power and its relationship with other structural provisions in the Constitution.

ADJUDICATIVE POWER: *SANCHEZ-LLAMAS* AND *MEDELLIN*

American law promises to a significant extent to take content from, or to be bound by, certain decisions of foreign or international tribunals. To understand the current state of legal affairs as to the binding nature of those decisions, it is useful to consider two recent cases, *Sanchez-Llamas* and *Medellin*. Both focus on the International Court of Justice (ICJ), one among several adjudicative bodies to which the United States, by treaty, has delegated authority to make judgments that bind the parties before it. We have not joined the recently created International Criminal Court (ICC),[18] but we have signed treaties that create other types of adjudicative panels, such as the World Trade Organization Dispute Settlement Body,[19] the North American Free Trade Association Bi-national Panel,[20] and the World Bank's International Centre for the Settlement of Investment Disputes.[21] We have also participated in the creation of many ad hoc tribunals—for example, those adjudicating human rights violations in the former Yugoslavia (ICTY),[22] Rwanda (ICTR),[23] and Cambodia (ECCC).[24] Nonetheless, the ICJ is the best known and most strongly rooted of all international tribunals.

Originally founded in the late nineteenth century, the ICJ was modified by the League of Nations after World War I. Following World War II, it was readopted by the United Nations, and its organizational framework and governing procedures were set forth in an annex (the "ICJ Statute") to the United Nations Charter of 1945. The United States signed and ratified the charter that same year.[25]

The U.N. Charter provides that "[e]ach Member of the United Nations undertakes to comply with the decision of the [ICJ] in any case to which it is a party."[26] The annex provides that the ICJ can hear disputes only between nations, not individuals,[27] and that its jurisdiction in any particular case will depend upon the consent of the party-states.[28] States can provide consent in either of two ways: generally in respect to any question arising under a treaty or general international law, or specifically in disputes arising under a separate treaty.[29] Even with party consent, Article 59 of the ICJ Statute specifies that the "decision of the Court has no binding force except between the parties and in respect of that particular case."[30]

Sanchez-Llamas and *Medellin* concerned the ICJ's interpretation of a doctrine of American criminal law called the "procedural default" rule. It is a rule that, with exceptions, basically says that a criminal defendant forfeits, and cannot raise on appeal, a claim of trial court error that he did not first raise in the trial court. In two earlier cases, *LaGrand* and *Avena*, the ICJ considered this rule in the context of a treaty that requires the United States to allow an arrested foreign person communication with his nation's consular authorities. Because the ICJ's holdings in the earlier cases created the basis for its later decisions in *Sanchez-Llamas* and *Medellin*, I will begin with a discussion of *LaGrand* and *Avena*.

The treaty at issue in all four cases is the Vienna Convention on Consular Relations,[31] signed in 1963 by 170 nations, including the United States. (The Senate ratified it six years later.) Among other things, the convention provides that if "a national" of one State is "arrested or committed to prison or to custody pending trial" or is otherwise "detained," then the "competent authorities" of the arresting State "shall, without delay, inform the consular post" of the arrested person's nation (if the arrested person "so requests").[32] Moreover, the arresting "authorities shall inform the person concerned without delay" of these rights.[33] In a word, the convention says, "tell an arrested foreign person that he has a right to consult his nation's consul."

The convention also says that the "rights referred to ... shall be exercised in conformity with the laws and regulations of the [arresting] State, subject to the proviso ... that [they] ... must enable full effect to be given to the purposes for which the rights ... are intended."[34]

In 1969 the United States joined a related Optional Protocol.[35] It provides that "[d]isputes arising out of the interpretation or application of the Convention shall lie within the compulsory jurisdiction of the International Court of Justice."[36]

Germany brought the *LaGrand* case before the ICJ in March 1999, while the protocol was in force. (The United States has since withdrawn from it, in 2005.[37]) Two German nationals, Karl and Walter LaGrand, had been arrested in Virginia in 1982 and charged with murder and rape. They were jointly tried, convicted, and sentenced to death. Karl LaGrand was executed on February 24, 1999. When Germany brought the case, Walter LaGrand was about to be executed.[38]

Germany said that neither man had been told of his right to communicate with the German consul until long after their trial. This failure, Germany said, violated the Vienna Convention provision that an arrested person be "informed" of the right "without delay." The failure, Germany concluded, required a new trial for Walter, reparations ("in the form of compensation and satisfaction") for the execution of Karl, and a guarantee by the United States to Germany that it would not repeat its "illegal acts."[39] The ICJ issued an interim order on March 3, directing the United States to "take all measures at its disposal to ensure that Walter LaGrand is not executed pending the final decision in these proceedings."[40] Virginia nonetheless executed him later that same day.[41]

Germany continued to litigate its case in the ICJ. It asked the court to declare that the United States had violated Article 36 (by failing to tell the LaGrands of their consular rights).

At this point, Germany and the ICJ had to grapple with Virginia's "procedural default" rule, under which the LaGrands should have raised their Vienna Convention Article 36 notification problem during their trial. The rule is not absolute. It excuses a failure to object at trial if the defendant had a good excuse—if, for example, the defendant (and his lawyer) did not know about the prosecutor's error. The "procedural default" rule, then, is not a catch-22. It does not bar a defendant from later complaining about police misbehavior that (say, because of police misbehavior) he could not have known about at the trial, such as the failure to advise a defendant of Article 36.

In the LaGrands' case, neither defendant had raised the issue of the United States' failure to notify them of their consular rights during their state trial, direct appeal, or state postconviction proceedings.[42] Rather, the defendants made this claim for the first time in their federal habeas corpus proceedings—which took place only after a German consular official became aware of their case in 1992. The federal court refused to hear the claim, saying that the LaGrands had no excuse. They should have raised the claim earlier. The court of appeals agreed.[43]

The United States pointed this out to the ICJ, saying that the "procedural default" doctrine was reasonable. Germany replied that the rule, as applied here, was unfair, for it "had 'made it impossible for the LaGrand brothers to effectively raise the issue of the lack of consular notification after they had at last learned of their rights.'"[44]

The ICJ agreed with Germany. While recognizing that the U.S. federal government had done much to inform local police of their legal obligations, it also found that its efforts to publicize this duty had not always worked. Incidents of failure to inform arrested foreign persons of their rights were many, and the penalties were often serious, including death.[45] As to the "procedural default" rule, the ICJ held that "[i]n itself, the rule does not violate" the convention.[46] Rather—and here is the critical language in the ICJ's opinion—"[t]he problem arises *when* the 'procedural default' rule does not allow the detained individual to challenge a conviction and sentence by claiming . . . that the competent national authorities failed to comply with their obligation to provide the requisite consular information 'without delay,' thus preventing the person from seeking and obtaining consular assistance."[47]

And just when is that? The ICJ did not specifically say, in concluding that that was what happened to the two defendants in *LaGrand*.[48]

The upshot, said the ICJ, was that the United States had violated its convention obligations. It then added that "an apology" to Germany was "not sufficient" as remedy.[49] Rather, the United States had to follow through with its commitment to "ensure compliance by its competent authorities at the federal as well as at the state and local levels with its obligation" under the Vienna Convention, through better training.[50] And if, despite such training, U.S. authorities were in future to deprive defendants of their consular notification rights, the United States had to do more—it had to provide "review and reconsideration" of the defendant's conviction and sentence. Namely, "where the individuals concerned have been subjected to prolonged detention or convicted and sentenced to severe penalties[,] . . . it would be incumbent upon the United States to allow the review and reconsideration of the conviction and sentence by taking account of the violation of the rights set forth in the Convention. This obligation can be carried out in various ways. The choice of means must be left to the United States."[51]

Accordingly, while the holding may have been too late for the LaGrands, U.S. courts in the future would have to "review and reconsider convictions and sentences" that were imposed following a lack of consular notification, even if the claim was first brought in a federal habeas corpus proceeding.[52]

The second important ICJ precedent involving the Vienna Convention and its interaction with the American "procedural default" rule is the case of *Avena*,[53] brought in the ICJ by Mexico in early 2003. It claimed that the United States had violated the Vienna Convention by failing promptly to notify fifty-two Mexican nationals of their right to speak to the Mexican consul after their arrests. The defendants had been tried and convicted of murder in nine different states, had been sentenced to death, and were at the time being held on death row.[54]

The ICJ agreed with Mexico in respect to fifty-one of the individuals in question,[55] finding that the Vienna Convention imposed "a duty upon the arresting authorities" of a signatory state to tell an arrested individual about his right to communicate with his nation's consul at least "as soon as it is realized that the person is a foreign national."[56] Since American authorities had not done so in the case of the fifty-one Mexican citizens until long after "the time of arrest" (and in some cases never), they had failed to satisfy the convention's requirements.[57]

But what about the "procedural default" rule? If American courts had done no more than refuse to grant relief to defendants who had failed to raise the question of their Vienna Convention rights on time, *and who lacked any good explanation of that failure*, then why was the United States in violation of the convention? After all, the convention itself says that its "rights" are to "be exercised in conformity with the laws and regulations" of the arresting state (here the United States), as long as these laws and regulations "enable full effect to be given to the purposes for which the rights . . . are intended."[58]

In dealing with this argument, the ICJ repeated what it had said in *LaGrand*—namely, that a "procedural default" rule does not "itself" violate the convention but instead might *sometimes* lead to a violation when its application would "not allow the detained individual to challenge a conviction and sentence by claiming . . . national authorities failed to comply with their obligation to provide the requisite consular information 'without delay.'"[59] The ICJ added that if not telling the arrested person about his right to contact the consul "precluded" the accused's lawyer "from being in a position to have raised the question of a violation . . . in the initial trial," the "procedural default" rule could not save a country from a finding of violation.[60] In such a case, the "procedural default" rule would prevent U.S. courts from giving "full effect" to the "purposes for which" the convention rights were "intended."[61] The ICJ noted that many of the cases at issue in *Avena* were still being judicially reviewed in the United States, making it "premature for the Court to conclude at this stage that, in those cases, there is already a violation."[62] But in respect to those cases where review was complete, violations existed, according to the court.[63]

The ICJ then addressed the issue of remedy. It held that "the appropriate reparation in this case consists in the obligation of the United States of America to provide, by means of its own choosing, review and reconsideration of the convictions and sentences of the Mexican nationals" (whose cases had been finalized).[64] This review should be undertaken "to ascertain[] whether in each case the violation . . . caused actual prejudice to the defendant."[65]

Arguably, the ICJ's holdings in *LaGrand* and *Avena* were straightforward and called for a simple enough fix. Under the Vienna Convention, the United States is obliged to tell arrested foreign nationals that they have a right to contact their nation's consul. In many instances, including some involving the death penalty, American arresting officers failed in this obligation. Therefore, the United States violated the treaty, and in light of this breach, its courts should "review" the cases "by means of [their] own choosing" to see whether each arrested person was prejudiced as a result of the failure of local authorities to inform the defendant of his Vienna Convention rights.

Despite the seeming simplicity of these proposed remedies, however, the ICJ's analysis created a special difficulty for our Court. It surfaced not in the *LaGrand* or *Avena* proceedings themselves but in the related cases of *Sanchez-Llamas* and *Medellin*, which reached the Supreme Court several years later. The difficulty concerned the ICJ's efforts to analyze—and as some members of our Court would come to find, override—the American "procedural default" rule. This legal doctrine is highly complex; filled with legal twists and turns, it is often difficult to understand. It would be particularly difficult for a foreign court or an international tribunal to fully appreciate how it works. But one group of judges does understand it well, as it is part of the bread and butter of their daily criminal work. Those judges are federal judges, including justices of our Court. State prisoners, including many sentenced to death, raise questions every week that require us to decide how the "procedural default" rule works and whether it bars consideration of the merits of a prisoner's legal claim.[66] The ICJ in *LaGrand* and *Avena* had attempted to interpret the doctrine's operation in the cases of several American criminal defendants, and to determine whether its application ran afoul of the defendants' rights under international law. But did the ICJ get the technical analysis about the "procedural default" rule right? And even if so, did it have the authority to tell U.S. courts to provide "review and reconsideration" to several otherwise final criminal judgments and potentially excuse those defendants' procedural defaults in the interests of international law? Those were among the questions before the Court in *Sanchez-Llamas* and *Medellin*, to which I will now turn.

SANCHEZ-LLAMAS (THE CASE OF MARIO BUSTILLO)

The *Sanchez-Llamas* case, which the Court heard in 2006, involved a defendant named Mario Bustillo.[67] Bustillo, a national of Honduras, was convicted of using a baseball bat to murder a man named James Merry outside a Popeye's Restaurant in Springfield, Virginia.[68] Though several witnesses had identified Bustillo as the bat wielder, he claimed throughout his criminal proceedings that a different man, Sirena, had been the actual killer.[69] At trial, Bustillo produced two different witnesses who testified that he did not commit the murder, one of whom specifically alleged that Sirena did.[70] Still, the jury convicted Bustillo, and he was sentenced to thirty years in prison.[71]

At the time, the Honduran consul knew nothing about Bustillo's situation. The police never told Bustillo of his Vienna Convention rights, and he did not communicate with the consul at any point before or during his trial.[72] While Bustillo's case was pending on appeal, however, his new attorney discovered the police's mistake, and at this point contact was first made with the Honduran consul.[73] The consul subsequently provided Bustillo with valuable assistance, which helped to establish Sirena's full name and whereabouts.[74] He also filed an affidavit stating that had he known of the matter earlier, he would have tried to help Bustillo during his trial.[75]

Bustillo did not raise the issue of his Vienna Convention rights at trial or during his first appeal of his conviction.[76] It was not until the state courts conducted a state habeas corpus proceeding—a collateral proceeding that takes place after the direct appeal to determine whether some basic error (for example, an inadequate lawyer) took place below and was not caught during the trial or at the first appeal—that Bustillo finally brought the issue up.[77]

The Virginia courts ruled that Bustillo made his Vienna Convention claim too late, saying he should have raised the issue at his trial or during his first appeal.[78] This procedural default would have been excused if he had good cause for his failure to do so and had suffered prejudice on account of it.[79] Bustillo did allege good "cause" for the delay, namely, that his lawyer during the criminal proceedings was inadequate. But looking into the matter, the state habeas judge rejected Bustillo's claim. He found that the lawyer had been adequate, and the appeals courts agreed. Hence Bustillo could turn only to the U.S. Supreme Court for relief.[80]

Bustillo pointed out to our Court that the state (and the federal government) admitted that government authorities had violated the Vienna Convention by failing to provide timely notification of his right to contact the Honduran consul.[81] The United States had even formally apologized to Honduras for its error.[82] But what about the "procedural default" rule? Did Bustillo not forfeit his claim by failing to bring it up on time? No, Bustillo's lawyer told our Court. Granted, the convention says that the rights it provides must "be exercised in conformity with the laws and regulations" of the United States (of which the "procedural default" rule is one).[83] But those "laws and regulations" must "enable full effect to be given to the purposes" for which the rights are "intended."[84] And in the cases of *LaGrand* and *Avena,* the ICJ had decided that American "procedural default" rules did *not* give "full effect" to those purposes when the government's failure to inform a defendant of his consular notification rights "may have precluded counsel from being in a position to have raised the question of a violation . . . in the initial trial."[85] Under such circumstances, the Court had held, application of the rule prevented courts "from attaching 'legal significance'" to the government's violation of the convention.[86] Right or wrong, Bustillo argued, that was the ICJ's interpretation of the Vienna Convention, and the United States was obligated to follow it by a separate treaty.[87] Hence American courts were required to ignore the "procedural default" rule and permit Bustillo to make his (winning) Vienna Convention argument.[88]

Our Court rejected this claim. And however technical the "procedural default" rule may sound, the reason for allowing its application in the face of Bustillo's challenge did not rest on technicalities. In the first place, the Court said, the relevant treaties (and treaty-created rules) did *not* require the United States to follow the ICJ's treaty interpretations in all cases.[89] To the contrary, Article 59 of the ICJ Statute stipulates that the ICJ's decisions have "no *binding* force except between the parties and in respect of that particular case."[90] Moreover, each member state of the United Nations has agreed to comply with ICJ decisions only "in any case *to which it is a party.*"[91] Thus the ICJ decisions in *LaGrand* and *Avena* may have binding force with regard to the individuals whom Germany and Mexico, respectively, represented in those cases, but not in other contexts. Bustillo was not represented in the ICJ; his case did not appear there. Hence no ICJ decision was binding on American courts in respect to Bustillo.[92]

The Court nonetheless recognized that this was not the end of the matter. For even where ICJ interpretations of treaties are not binding, American courts must give them "respectful consideration."[93] Thus we arrive at what is likely the most important question in the case: Why, under this standard of "respectful consideration," did Bustillo still lose?

The "respectful consideration" concept is important because it reflects an effort to achieve uniformity in treaty interpretation.[94] For this purpose, the ICJ is a natural point of reference for domestic courts throughout the world, being specially charged with the duty to interpret numerous treaties and having special expertise in international law. Its decisions consequently serve as authority well beyond any particular case before it.[95] (In fact, the U.S. government conceded as much in its *Avena* briefing.)[96] And in at least half a dozen Supreme Court cases and many lower court cases as well, American courts have looked to the ICJ for guidance in interpreting treaties.[97]

Others outside the United States have also advocated the use of standards such as "respectful consideration" where relations between international and national courts are at issue. The United Kingdom, for example, has enacted the Human Rights Act, which requires its courts to treat the European Convention on Human Rights as binding internal law.[98] The act also instructs British courts to "take into account" relevant decisions of the European Court of Human Rights (ECHR)—the Strasbourg court entrusted with enforcing the convention—when interpreting convention provisions.[99] According to Lord Irvine, who, as Lord Chancellor, was responsible for drafting the act,[100] these were words designed to ensure that the British Supreme Court "should have considered and respectful regard for decisions of the ECHR, but neither be bound nor hamstrung by that case-law in determining Convention rights domestically."[101] Thus, if the British Supreme Court were convinced that the Strasbourg court was wrong, it could apply its own interpretation of the convention's language. Then Strasbourg, appreciating the long experience of the British courts in the area, might in turn be persuaded to rethink its position. In this way, a dialogue between national and international courts could develop, facilitating improvement in the law as judges converge on more convincing approaches.

The majority in *Sanchez-Llamas* may have been engaged in a similar exercise. It conceded that it owed "respectful consideration" to the ICJ's decision.[102] But it had found the ICJ's analysis, of the American "procedural default" rule and its interaction in both *LaGrand* and *Avena*, with the Vienna Convention to be clearly wrong. The ICJ had held that the rule could not be enforced when it would "'preven[t] [courts] from attaching any legal significance'" to an Article 36 violation and foreign governments from assisting defendants in their criminal proceedings.[103] But how, the Court asked, does the rule block consideration of a Vienna Convention violation any more than do other procedural rules, such as statutes of limitations or rules that make a decision final once a case is closed?[104] Those, too, preclude consideration of and redress for a Vienna Convention violation, unless the matter is raised in time. Yet many countries follow them. Reading the "full effect" proviso so broadly (as the ICJ had done) would invalidate a vast swath of national judicial practices, leaving "little room for Article 36's clear instruction that Article 36 rights 'shall be exercised in conformity with the laws and regulations of the receiving State.'"[105] Indeed, the majority might have put the point directly this way: Since "procedural default" rules contain exceptions designed to prevent injustice, what is the problem with applying them? Why, or how, does their application prevent American courts from giving "full effect" to the purposes of the Vienna Convention?

The dissent in the case (which I wrote) argued that "respectful consideration" of the ICJ's decisions required a different result. In our view, the majority had overlooked the ICJ's actual words.[106] They did not say that the convention trumps all or most applications of a "procedural default" rule. Rather, they said that a "procedural default" rule cannot bar assertion of a Vienna Convention claim where "the failure" of the state "to inform" the defendant about his rights was itself responsible for the defendant not being "in a position to have raised the question of a violation . . . in the initial trial."[107] In other words, you cannot expect a defendant to protest something he does not know about. If you have not told him he has such a right (and he does not independently know about it), how can you expect him to exercise it? The "procedural default" rule thus does prevent the United States from giving "full effect" to Vienna Convention rights but only where it is the arresting authorities' failure to inform the defendant of his rights that prevents him from raising the issue in time. *Avena* does not say that a defendant who knows of his rights, or who has a lawyer who does, can successfully ask a court to waive the "procedural default" rule.[108]

Did the United States' Vienna Convention violations in *LaGrand* and *Avena* prevent the defendants or their lawyers from raising the claim of violation in time? The ICJ opinions do not say. But neither do they say that the defendants in those cases automatically win. They simply ask the United States to provide "review and reconsideration" in each case "by means of its own choosing."[109] They do seem to say, I must concede, that review must be for purposes only of determining whether the failure to inform prejudiced the defendant, for example, by leading him to accept a far less able lawyer than a consul might have found for him. Yet the ICJ did not preclude review of the timeliness question either.[110] All in all, the ICJ opinions don't explore the underlying circumstances as well as they might have in respect to the critical issue of procedural default. But the *Sanchez-Llamas* majority read their language too literally and consequently found the ICJ's interpretation of the Vienna Convention clearly wrong. The dissent tried to interpret the ICJ's opinions in a way that might have reconciled them both with the Vienna Convention and with American law, thereby showing "respectful consideration" with broader force.

Unfortunately, many learning of these cases will not be conversant enough with the American procedural law or the specific point about which the ICJ and the Supreme Court disagreed. They may therefore conclude that *Sanchez-Llamas* stands for the proposition that ICJ decisions do not bind the United States, in the sense that American courts need not follow the rules of law the ICJ enunciates. In fact, the case is more complex and subtle than that conclusion, a point that should not escape notice.

MEDELLIN

Medellin is the second Supreme Court case in which the ICJ's decisions in *LaGrand* and *Avena* became a central issue. And like *Sanchez-Llamas*, *Medellin* posed deeper questions about the ability of foreign courts—created pursuant to a treaty ratified by the United States—to issue judgments that have binding force domestically. Can the United States, by treaty, outsource such authority to foreign tribunals? Or is the treaty power more limited, demanding that Congress enact implementation before such international delegation can occur?

The facts of *Medellin* are as follows. On June 24, 1993, Texas police found the bodies of two young girls who had been brutally raped and murdered. Early in the morning of June 29 police arrested José Medellín, whom they suspected of having committed the crime.[111] Medellín had lived in the United States since childhood, but he was a Mexican national.[112] The police told him of his rights under the U.S. Constitution to remain silent and to have a lawyer, but they did not mention his Vienna Convention right to contact the Mexican consul. Within three hours Medellín had confessed and given the police a detailed written account of the crime. He was subsequently convicted of the murders and sentenced to death.[113]

Medellín's lawyer did not complain about the state's Vienna Convention mistake at trial or during the first appeal. And the state appeals court affirmed Medellín's conviction.[114] Then Medellín initiated a postconviction state court habeas corpus proceeding—again, a special proceeding that looks for important errors at the trial. It was there, for the first time, that he raised the Vienna Convention problem.[115] But the state postconviction court told him he was too late, having had no good reason for not mentioning the problem earlier. Thus the "procedural default" rule barred Medellín from pursuing his Vienna Convention claim. But according to the judge, a claim would have made no difference anyway, as Medellín had "failed to show that any non-notification of the Mexican authorities impacted on the validity of his conviction or punishment."[116]

Medellín initiated another postconviction habeas corpus proceeding, this time in federal court. The federal judge went over the same ground and reached the same conclusion: the doctrine of procedural default prevented Medellín from asserting his Vienna Convention claim. But even if it did not, he had suffered no prejudice as a result of the Vienna Convention violation.[117]

So it seemed as if Medellín was out of luck. As it turns out, however, he was one of the fifty-one individuals whom Mexico represented before the ICJ in the *Avena* case.[118] The ICJ reached its decision while he was in the midst of appealing his federal court habeas corpus proceeding to the federal appeals court. As we know, the ICJ said that the United States must "provide, by means of its own choosing, review and reconsideration of the convictions and sentences" of Mexican nationals, including Medellín.[119] Accordingly, he was entitled to full consideration of whether the police's failure to inform him of his Vienna Convention rights in a timely manner caused him "actual prejudice" in his criminal trial, regardless of the "procedural default" rule.[120] Would the Mexican consul, for example, have provided Medellín with a better lawyer?[121]

Medellín got nowhere with this argument in the federal appeals court, which decided it did not have to follow the ICJ's ruling.[122] But he then asked our Court to hear the case.[123] In the meantime, the President of the United States, George W. Bush, wrote a memorandum stating, "I have determined . . . that the United States will discharge its international obligations under the decision of the International Court of Justice in [*Avena*], by having State courts give effect to the decision in accordance with general principles of comity in cases filed by the 51 Mexican nationals addressed in that decision."[124]

In light of this memorandum, Medellín immediately asked the Texas state courts again to review his case, this time looking directly at whether he had been prejudiced by the Vienna Convention failure.[125] But the Texas Court of Criminal Appeals refused, believing that neither the ICJ decision nor the President's memorandum legally required it to reconsider the case.[126] At that point, our Court agreed to hear the case. Why did the ICJ's decision not bind the Texas courts? Why did they not have to provide one additional hearing about "prejudice"? After all, that is what, in effect, the United States had promised, wasn't it?

The Supremacy Clause in Article VI of the Constitution says that "all Treaties made . . . under the Authority of the United States, shall be the supreme Law of the Land; and the Judges in every State shall be bound thereby."[127] As summarized at the outset of this chapter, the Vienna Convention is a treaty that was made in part under the authority of the United States. The convention says that a nation's "law and regulations must enable full effect to be given to the purposes for which" the Vienna Convention's "rights . . . are intended."[128] The United States signed a second treaty, the Optional Protocol, which says that "[d]isputes arising out of the interpretation or application of the Convention" shall be submitted to the "compulsory jurisdiction of the International Court of Justice."[129] And a third treaty, the United Nations Charter, says that every signatory nation "undertakes to comply with the decision of the International Court of Justice in any case to which it is a party,"[130] and that an ICJ judgment has "binding force . . . between the parties in that particular case."[131] In *Avena*, the ICJ had interpreted the Vienna Convention as requiring the United States to reexamine Medellín's case "by means of its own choosing."[132] And the President of the United States had chosen state court reexamination.[133]

There may be many steps in the chain of legal obligations, consisting of (1) Article VI of the Constitution, plus (2) the Vienna Convention, plus (3) the Optional Protocol's conferring of authority in the ICJ to interpret the Vienna Convention, plus (4) the U.N. Charter requirement to adhere to the ICJ, plus (5) the ICJ decision in *Avena*, plus (6) the President's proclamation about how to comply with *Avena*. But those six steps add up to a legal obligation in Texas court, do they not? QED.

The Court, by six to three, held otherwise.[134] And in reaching that decision, it answered a question with broad ramifications for the status of international law in U.S. courts. The majority said that the United States need not follow the ICJ decision because that decision did not bind the courts of the United States.[135] The treaties at issue may bind the nation as a matter of international law, but they did not bind the nation's courts as a matter of domestic law.

Why not? Look again at Article VI of the Constitution. It says that "treaties," like the Constitution and like federal statutes, are the "supreme Law of the Land" and "Judges in every State shall be bound thereby."[136] How can the Court escape that language?

The answer is that there are treaties and there are treaties: some, called "self-executing," take effect automatically as domestic law, while others, "non-self-executing treaties," do so if and only if Congress enacts a statute making them part of domestic law. In the former case, a treaty provision becomes domestic law once the Senate ratifies it by a two-thirds vote. In the latter case, a treaty provision becomes domestic law only if the House of Representatives also votes in favor of the provision.

The Court did not create this distinction in *Medellin*. We can trace its roots to the time of the Founding. For example, in 1796, a British creditor who had lent money to a Virginian complained that a Virginia statute, enacted during the war with Britain, prevented the debtor from paying him back.[137] The statute said that those owing money to British creditors must repay not the creditors but a state fund. (Virginia, then, would keep the money.) The state law violated a provision of the Paris Peace Treaty of 1783, which said that "creditors . . . should meet with no lawful impediment to the recovery of the full value . . . of all *bona fide* debts."[138]

The Supreme Court held that the treaty trumped the Virginia statute—even though Congress had not enacted any law on the subject. Justice James Iredell (and subsequently the greatest early constitutional commentator, Justice Joseph Story) pointed out that some treaty provisions were automatically "executed," taking effect at once, while others were "executory," requiring them "to be carried into execution" by each signatory nation "in the manner which the Constitution of that nation prescribes."[139] Before adoption of the American Constitution, all American treaties, like all British ones, would have been "executory," taking effect as domestic law only with congressional (or parliamentary) action. But after the adoption of the Constitution, which made treaties part of the "supreme Law of the Land," further congressional action was not always necessary, and certainly not in respect to a minor, technical matter such as debt collection.[140]

Thirty years later Chief Justice John Marshall further developed the standard for self-execution. He wrote that the Supremacy Clause made a treaty "the law of the land . . . to be regarded in courts of justice as equivalent to an act of the legislature," and it "operates of itself without the aid of any legislative provision" *unless it specifically contemplates execution by the legislature and thereby "addresses itself to the political, not the judicial department."*[141]

Applying Marshall's distinction to today's world, treaties on matters such as military assistance, foreign aid, and mutual cooperation of various kinds appear to "address[] . . . the political department[s]" and thus require legislation to incorporate them into domestic law. But at least some treaties on matters such as extradition, trademark infringement, immunity from state taxation, land ownership, and inheritance can arguably take effect as domestic law without further legislative action.[142]

Whether the relevant treaties were self-executing was the question in *Medellín*. And answering it was what separated the Court majority from the dissenters. The majority thought that the language of the applicable treaties indicated that the signatories had left the matter of execution to Congress.[143] The U.N. Charter, for example, says that each member nation *"undertakes to comply* with the decision" of the ICJ in "any case to which it is a party."[144] The majority read that language as "a *commitment* on the part of U.N. members to take *future* action through their political branches to comply with an ICJ decision."[145] It found support for its view in the charter's provision permitting members to submit instances of noncompliance to the Security Council, a body whose actions depend upon political decisions taken by its members.[146] It added that it had found no instance in which other nations treat ICJ decisions as binding on their courts.[147] And it said that, since ICJ judgments "may interfere with state procedural rules, one would expect the ratifying parties to the relevant treaties to have *clearly* stated their intent to give those judgments domestic effect, if they had so intended."[148]

The dissent argued that the same words in the text of the charter—"*undertakes to comply* with the decision"—indicate a firm obligation, addressed (where a nation's constitution so permits) to a nation's courts and not just to its political branches.[149] Referring to twenty-nine cases in which the Supreme Court had found that a treaty provision was self-executing, the minority argued that the treaty language in each was similar to the treaty language at issue here.[150] But the argument did not rely only on the treaty's explicit language; after all, a clear statement of self-execution is not necessarily something onc would expect in a treaty between countries with different constitutional arrangements and different processes for translating international obligations into domestic law.[151] The dissent therefore looked to the substance of the issue, concluding that a treaty provision is more likely to be addressed to the courts than to the political branches of government if it (1) involves subject matter traditionally within the province of the judiciary, (2) sets forth definite standards that judges can readily enforce, (3) does not require the creation of a novel kind of legal claim, and (4) is not likely to engender constitutional controversy.[152] These criteria were satisfied for the treaties involved in the *Medellin* case. Finally, the dissent pointed to the Vienna Convention's "notification provision," which is itself self-executing, and also to the parties' agreement (in the Optional Protocol and U.N. Charter) to accept as final ICJ judgments interpreting that provision. What sense would it make, the dissent asked, to make a self-executing promise, and to agree to accept as final a judgment interpreting that promise, only to find that the promise does not bind our courts without further legislation?[153]

Naturally, since I wrote the dissent, I am persuaded by its reasoning, but that is beside the point. The Court's majority opinion is authoritative, not the dissent. So it is more important to consider the significance of that opinion.

Medellin is less technical than it sounds. The case considers when Congress must, and when it needn't, enact a law in order to make a treaty's provisions enforceable in American courts. The majority opinion reads texts and describes standards in a way that makes automatic incorporation of such provisions more difficult.

Does that decision mean that treaties never, or hardly ever, will take effect here automatically? The Court did not say that Congress must always enact implementing legislation. Nor did it lay down detailed rules for how it would interpret other treaties in the future. Rather, it noted that the question of self-execution depends on the "language of the treaty."[154] It observed that courts have "held that a number of the 'Friendship, Commerce, and Navigation' Treaties cited by the dissent are self-executing."[155] And it provided a general standard: whether a treaty is self-executing requires deciding whether "a treaty's terms reflect a determination by the President who negotiated it and the Senate that confirmed it that the treaty has domestic effect."[156]

Does the general standard set forth in *Medellín* mean that a judicial judgment, in particular an ICJ judgment involving an individual, will not be domestically enforceable unless and until Congress enacts a statute specifically making it so? That does seem a fair implication of the opinion (although the Court pointed out that Medellín was asking for enforcement of a criminal law judgment that affected state law, not for enforcement of "a foreign-court judgment settling a typical commercial or property dispute").[157] Even so, that requirement means only that the House of Representatives must be brought into the matter. And a President who has persuaded two-thirds of the Senate to ratify a treaty he has signed shouldn't find it impossible to obtain the support of a majority in the House.

Does that mean it will be possible to regularly secure congressional approval for domestic enforcement of decisions of foreign tribunals, such as the ICJ's decision in *Avena*? I find this a difficult question to answer. Congress could enact a law ratifying ICJ judgments—or judgments of other treaty-based tribunals—wholesale. Or it could provide that certain subsets of those judgments automatically become part of domestic law.[158] It has certainly done the former in respect to judgments of arbitration tribunals, making them automatically enforceable in American courts.[159]

But will Congress authorize automatic judicial enforceability of all ICJ judgments, or even of all judgments concerning a particular subject matter? I believe that that is possible, but it will require careful consideration and drafting. After all, ICJ decisions could include politically sensitive judgments better suited for political branch enforcement, such as treaty interpretations about military hostilities, naval bases, handling of nuclear materials, and the like. And Congress might not want *this* kind of ICJ judgment to take effect automatically. The statutory language would have to be narrowed accordingly, selecting and specifying in advance the kinds of judgments suited for direct judicial branch enforcement from those requiring political consideration.

Although such an approach would have its challenges, the alternative of waiting for Congress to authorize the enforcement of ICJ (or other international court) opinions judgment by judgment bears its own risks. Congress may hesitate to spend the legislative time necessary to ratify judgments that have little general importance. (Ironically, these are likely the least politically contentious judgments.) But fearing political controversy, it may also hesitate to ratify ICJ decisions that are quite important.

Nor will those who write treaties, particularly multinational treaties, find it simple to respond to *Medellin*. In principle they could make a treaty self-executing by inserting specific language to that effect. But that will not be easy. Different nations, after all, have different systems for incorporating treaties into domestic law. In the United Kingdom, parliamentary action is still always necessary to make a treaty binding domestically. That requirement may not be so onerous in a parliamentary system, where the executive and legislative powers are typically controlled by the same political party, and domestic legislation often flows from executive decisions as a matter of course. But in nations like the United States and the Netherlands, incorporation can be a heavier lift. Sometimes it can happen without further legislative action, but as discussed, that depends upon the nature of the treaty and its language.¹⁶⁰ Given that different nations have different systems for the incorporation, it might be difficult for treaty writers to agree on specific "domestic effect" language.

So the most practical way of incorporating treaty provisions into domestic law may remain congressional action. And that may well involve a predictive piecemeal approach—that is, before relevant cases (and controversies) can come up, Congress would set forth categories of treaties or of international tribunal judgments (entered pursuant to treaties) that would be self-executing in U.S. courts. It might not be such a bad solution. To bring the House of Representatives, the most politically responsive body, into the treaty-enforcing process does make it more democratic.

Years ago Secretary of State Elihu Root said that "a court of international justice with a general obligation to submit all justiciable questions to its jurisdiction and to abide by its judgment is a primary requisite to any real restraint of law."[161] *Medellín* may show that this aim is harder to achieve than one might previously have thought. True, it does leave enforcement of the great political questions—those of armies, navies, territories, war, and peace—just where it found them: in the hands of the political branches. But it also places less politically significant questions, such as those involving the technicalities of criminal procedure, in the same hands. Consequently, it will be more directly and more often, sometimes in a political context, that Americans will have to ask themselves, at least respecting such technicalities often important to everyday life, where they stand with regard to our keeping promises generally, and to our abiding by decisions of an international tribunal that we have promised to follow in particular.

LEGISLATIVE POWER: *BOND*

A case the Court decided in 2014, *Bond v. United States,* centered on a different potential sort of conflict between the Constitution's treaty power and its structural requirements. While *Sanchez-Llamas* and *Medellín* showed the treaty power clashing with the Constitution's separation of powers (i.e., the question of whether the Senate and the President could effectively bypass the House of Representatives by making a treaty that delegated binding law-making authority to foreign tribunals, and what language would be necessary in the treaty to evidence such an intent), *Bond* involved a conflict between the treaty power and the Constitution's federalism provisions (i.e., the question of whether the Senate and the President could effectively bypass the states and make a treaty covering matters not otherwise within Congress's Article I powers).

Bond concerned the Chemical Weapons Convention, an international agreement that the United States ratified in 1997.[162] Among other things, it provides that each state party undertakes never, under any circumstances:

(a) To develop, produce, otherwise acquire, stockpile or retain chemical weapons, or transfer, directly or indirectly, chemical weapons to anyone;

(b) To use chemical weapons;

(c) To engage in any military preparations to use chemical weapons;

(d) To assist, encourage or induce, in any way, anyone to engage in any activity prohibited to a State Party under this Convention.[163]

The term *chemical weapons* is defined to include "[t]oxic chemicals and their precursors, except where intended for purposes not prohibited under this Convention."[164] The convention then defines the term *toxic chemical* as "[a]ny chemical which through its chemical action on life processes can cause death, temporary incapacitation or permanent harm to humans or animals."[165] And it defines "Purposes not Prohibited Under this Convention" as "[i]ndustrial, agricultural, research, medical, pharmaceutical or other peaceful purposes."[166]

Congress subsequently enacted a statute that repeats this language virtually word for word and applies it directly to the activities of individuals in the United States.[167] The statute forbids any person from using a "chemical weapon" as defined by the convention,[168] making violations criminal and strictly subject to lengthy prison terms.[169]

In 2006 Carol Anne Bond, a microbiologist, learned that her husband was having a love affair with one of her closest friends, Myrlinda Haynes, who was carrying the child of Bond's husband. Carol Anne Bond sought revenge. She stole a vial of an arsenic-based compound from her employer, and also obtained a vial of a different chemical used in printing photographs, and spread a mixture of both on Haynes's car door, mailbox, and doorknob, hoping that Haynes would touch them and develop a painful rash. Unfortunately for Bond, the chemicals turned bright red and were easy to spot. Haynes touched them only once, suffering a minor chemical burn on her thumb. And she called the police.[170]

The local police referred Haynes to the post office, whose inspectors placed surveillance cameras around Haynes's home and eventually discovered the perpetrator—namely, Bond—opening the mailbox and applying chemicals inside Haynes's car. Federal prosecutors indicted Bond for possessing and using a chemical weapon in violation of the federal statute that implemented the Chemical Weapons Convention. She entered a conditional guilty plea, reserved her right to appeal, and was sentenced to six years' imprisonment and five years' supervised release.[171]

On appeal, Bond argued that the statute did not apply because she fell within the exception to the "toxic chemical" definition applicable to chemicals used for "peaceful purposes." She also claimed that Congress lacked the power to enact the statute because the act was not, in the Constitution's words, a "necessary and proper" means "for carrying into execution" the Constitution's treaty-making powers. The court of appeals rejected these arguments, and the case made its way to the Supreme Court.[172]

Many of those on Bond's side urged the Supreme Court to overrule an important statement about the treaty-making power. Justice Oliver Wendell Holmes, Jr., had made that statement in *Missouri v. Holland*, decided in 1920.[173] In *Holland*, the Court considered a treaty negotiated with Great Britain covering migratory birds. Previously, Congress had enacted a statute regulating the hunting of those birds, but courts had found it unconstitutional because, in their view, Congress lacked the necessary power to regulate bird hunting, that being one of those many undelegated powers that the Tenth Amendment reserved to the states. When, subsequently, the United States entered into a treaty with Great Britain, promising to regulate the hunting of migratory birds, Congress enacted a new statute, this time under the Constitution's provisions (1) authorizing the President, with the Senate, to make treaties, and (2) authorizing Congress to make all laws "necessary and proper for carrying into execution" all powers that the Constitution "vested" in the federal government.[174]

The state of Missouri challenged the constitutionality of the new, treaty-based hunting statute. It argued that both treaty *and* statute were invalid because they invaded the powers reserved to the states under the Tenth Amendment.[175] Writing for the Court in *Missouri v. Holland*, Justice Holmes rejected in a single sentence the idea that the federal statute could be independently unconstitutional. "If the treaty is valid," he wrote, "there can be no dispute about the validity of the statute under Article I, Section 8, as a necessary and proper means to execute the powers of the Government."[176] So the case boiled down to the constitutionality of the treaty. On that issue, the Court also rejected the claim that the treaty was invalid simply because it mirrored an earlier *statute* that may have been unconstitutional under the Tenth Amendment. Justice Holmes wrote: "It is obvious that there may be matters of the sharpest exigency for the national well being that an act of Congress could not deal with but that a treaty followed by such an act could, and it is not lightly to be assumed that, in matters requiring national action, 'a power which must belong to and somewhere reside in every civilized government' is not to be found."[177]

The Tenth Amendment's restraints applied differently, and less restrictively, where the implementation of a treaty was at issue. The Court then found that regulating the flow of migratory birds served "a national interest of very nearly the first magnitude," and there was "nothing in the Constitution that compels the Government to sit by while a food supply is cut off.... It is not sufficient to rely upon the States."[178]

Holmes was not writing on a totally blank slate. Nearly twenty years earlier, in *Neely v. Henkel,* the Court upheld a federal extradition order sending to Cuba an individual accused of committing a crime there.[179] It found that the "power of Congress to make all laws necessary and proper for carrying into execution ... all [powers] vested in the government of the United States ... includes the power to enact such legislation as is appropriate to give efficacy to any stipulations which it is competent for the President by and with the advice and consent of the Senate to insert in a treaty with a foreign power."[180] Indeed, in 1842 the Court wrote in *Prigg v. Pennsylvania* that, although the "power is nowhere in positive terms conferred upon Congress to make laws to carry the stipulations of treaties into effect," it has "been supposed to result from the duty of the national government to fulfill all the obligations of treaties."[181]

The view of the Constitution expressed in *Holland*—that is, that it authorizes the President and the Senate to make treaties in areas beyond Congress's enumerated powers, and that it also authorizes Congress to pass laws that were necessary and proper for carrying those treaties into effect—had long been opposed by advocates of "states rights." In the 1950s, Senator John Bricker proposed a series of constitutional amendments that would have sharply curtailed the treaty power. One would have provided that any treaty violating the Constitution shall have no effect;[182] another, more sweeping amendment would have provided that a treaty "shall become effective as internal law in the United States only through legislation which would be valid in the absence of treaty."[183]

The executive branch strongly opposed the Bricker amendments, claiming that they would "shackle the federal government"[184] and force the President to represent "49 governments in its dealings with foreign powers" rather than one.[185] And the State Department listed eighty-four treaties negotiated over the prior three decades that it feared the Bricker amendments would invalidate.[186] The amendments failed to pass Congress.[187]

Now let us return to *Bond*. It raised the same difficult issue as *Holland*—the need to reconcile the Constitution's seemingly uncabined treaty power with its reservation of legislative powers to the states. Should the Tenth Amendment, or other structural features of the Constitution, be construed to limit the possible subject matters of treaties? Should the Necessary and Proper Clause be construed as limiting Congress to passing certain kinds of implementing legislation for treaties, but not others?

With one exception, the Court had not fully addressed these questions over the decades that had passed since it had decided *Holland*. Given the ever-growing importance of treaty making, had the time now arrived to provide answers? Should the Court reexamine *Holland*'s single sentence?

The Court decided not to do so. Instead, it simply construed the federal statute at issue—the one making use of "chemical weapon[s]" a crime (with a "peaceful purpose" exception)—as not reaching Bond's conduct. The Court reasoned as follows: We normally interpret congressional legislation in light of certain presumptions. One such presumption is that Congress does not, without saying so, intend to "'radically readjust[] the balance of state and national authority.'"[188] And prosecution of minor crimes such as Bond's is normally within the province of state governments.

To bring Bond's crime within the federal statute, the Court added, would give the statute's words an absurdly broad meaning. Both the Chemical Weapons Convention and the implementing legislation speak of "chemical weapons." But the use of chemicals that gave rise to Carol Bond's prosecution—smearing them on the doorknob of a romantic rival to raise a rash—is not the sort of use "that an ordinary person would associate with instruments of chemical warfare."[189] To hold otherwise would make "[a]ny parent ... guilty of a serious federal offense ... when, exasperated by the children's repeated failure to clean the goldfish tank, he considers poisoning the fish with a few drops of vinegar."[190] The government's reading of the statute, the Court said, would "alter sensitive federal-state relationships, convert an astonishing amount of traditionally local criminal conduct into a matter for federal enforcement, and involve a substantial extension of federal police resources."[191] The Court would not "presume Congress to have authorized such a stark intrusion into traditional state authority."[192] Hence it held that Bond's crime did not fall within the scope of the statute.[193] In a word, Bond won her case—but without the Court expressing a view about whether Congress could enact a statute that, but for a treaty, would lie outside its constitutional powers. Nor did it decide whether the President and the Senate could enter into a treaty in conflict with the Tenth Amendment or exceeding Congress's enumerated powers.

Three members of the Court, however, wrote separate opinions in which they expressed views about the underlying *Holland* questions. Justice Scalia emphasized that the Constitution says that Congress shall have the power to pass laws "necessary and proper for carrying into Execution ... [the] *Power* to make Treaties."[194] Laws that "execut[e]" the *power* to make treaties are not those that implement treaties once made.[195] Rather, they are laws that, for example, "appropriate[] money for hiring treaty negotiators, empower[] the Department of State to appoint those negotiators, [or] form[] a commission to study the benefits and risks of entering into the agreement."[196] Justice Scalia feared that the effect of Holmes's contrary interpretation, if unaddressed, would work a "seismic" change to the Constitution's structure.[197] Modern treaties, he added, "'touch on almost every aspect of domestic civil, political, and cultural life.'"[198] Those treaties consequently could let Congress regulate virtually anything, a grant of plenary power at odds with the Constitution's delegation to the legislature of only limited, specifically defined powers.

Justice Thomas added that the treaty power was itself limited. The Constitution does not grant the federal government the power to enter into treaties "to regulate purely domestic affairs."[199] Rather, treaties must be limited to what James Madison called the "'regulat[ion of] intercourse with foreign nations.'"[200] And because the "Treaty Power is limited to matters of international intercourse," any regulation of local matters "*must* relate to intercourse with other nations . . . (including their people and property), rather than to purely domestic affairs."[201] The main point is that the "Treaty Power has substantive limits."[202] "In an appropriate case," he "would draw a line that respects the original understanding of the Treaty Power. . . . Given the increasing frequency with which treaties have begun to test the limits of the Treaty Power, that chance will come soon enough."[203]

The third concurring justice, Justice Samuel Alito, added that "insofar as the Convention" obligates the United States "to enact domestic legislation criminalizing conduct of the sort at issue in this case, which typically is the sort of conduct regulated by the States, the Convention exceeds the scope of the treaty power."[204]

The result is that *Missouri v. Holland*, with its broad interpretation of the Constitution's Necessary and Proper Clause and broad understanding of the treaty power, remains the law. The federal government retains broad authority to make treaties, and those treaties may authorize Congress to enact laws concerning subjects that the Constitution normally leaves to the states. By that view, the states would have to look to the Senate, not to the courts, to maintain their independent lawmaking authority. When a proposed treaty goes too far, the Senate may refuse ratification. After all, 34 out of 100 senators (perhaps representing only a small percentage of the population) can block ratification of a treaty. Moreover, the Senate can insist upon reservations to the treaty, which can prevent its being applied in a manner opposed by as few as one-third of senators.

Would the concurring justices' position cut back Congress's lawmaking authority significantly? Less than it might appear. That is because, as interpreted since the 1930s, the Constitution gives Congress vast legislative authority, irrespective of the existence of a treaty. The Commerce Clause, for example, authorizes Congress to regulate even the growing of wheat on a local farm for home consumption, or even the growing of marijuana in a local hothouse for similar purposes, on the reasoning that activity of this *kind*, when considered *cumulatively*, can affect interstate commerce.[205]

In recent decisions, the Court has reduced the enormous breadth of the Commerce Clause power since the New Deal, finding, for example, a lack of congressional authority to regulate gun possession in local schools.[206] But it is hard to imagine an international treaty regulating matters without a significant effect on "interstate" or "foreign" commerce.

The question raised in *Bond,* and the expressed views of one-third of the Court, nonetheless illustrate the broader concern identified at the beginning of this chapter. What are the constitutional limits upon the treaty power, including on Congress's authority to implement a treaty through legislation? What *should* they be, given the Constitution's structural provisions and its concerns with federalism, separation of powers, and democratic accountability?

I've mentioned one exception to the Court's long silence about these matters. In *Reid v. Covert,* it held that a treaty cannot limit an individual's criminal procedural rights guaranteed by the Fifth and Sixth Amendments. Writing for the Court, Justice Hugo Black said that the "Court has regularly and uniformly recognized the supremacy of the Constitution over a treaty."[207] But concurring justices in *Bond* thought that constitutional limits to the treaty power go beyond a prohibition on limiting constitutionally guaranteed individual rights. They thereby focused upon both the question of whether a treaty can enlarge Congress's legislative powers, and also the latitude of the President and the Senate to enter into a treaty, including one delegating law-making authority to others.

European courts have already faced this kind of question directly. Through treaties, their nations have delegated vast law-making authority to international bodies—for example, the European Union. Do their national constitutions permit this kind of delegation?

Consider as examples several questions faced by the German Constitutional Court.

Are the European Union treaties, which delegate broad regulatory power to EU institutions, consistent with the German Constitution? One EU regulation requires private parties to lodge a deposit to guarantee, in effect, that when they obtain an import or export license, they will in fact engage in those activities. Does this regulation violate the German Constitution's guarantee of "basic freedom of trade and occupation"?[208]

Does a 2010 European Union treaty establishing the European Stability Mechanism, which in turn obligates countries like Germany to fund the Eurobond defaults of other EU members, violate the German constitutional provision giving the federal parliament the authority to determine budgetary expenditures?[209] (The French Constitutional Court considered a virtually identical case.[210])

Does the 2007 Lisbon Treaty, amending the basic structure of the European Union in order to expand the "European Parliament's competence in the area of lawmaking," among other things, violate the German Constitution's Basic Law and protection of democratic self-determination for German citizens?[211]

In all these instances, the German court found Germany's treaty-based membership in EU affairs to be constitutional. But in each, it articulated important reservations. In the case concerning export licenses, the court held that the deposit requirement was valid under the German Constitution only if the EU rules were interpreted to allow for exceptions "in cases in which the import or export did not take place because of circumstances beyond the control of the importer or exporter."[212] In the case concerning the European Stability Mechanism, the treaty establishing that body was found valid as a matter of domestic law (and thus could be ratified by Germany) only "if at the same time it ensured under international law that . . . no provision of this Treaty may be interpreted in a way that establishes higher payment obligations for the Federal Republic of Germany without the agreement of the German representative."[213] (The French Constitutional Court reached a very similar result in a 2012 decision.[214]) In the case about the Lisbon Treaty, the German court held it was constitutional—and capable of ratification—only if interpreted in a way such that "the Federal Republic of Germany retains substantial national scope of action for central areas of statutory regulation and areas of life."[215]

As these cases show, the European courts have considered—and are continuing to consider—the scope of their nations' treaty-making powers in the context of treaty-based delegations of legislative and regulatory authority to supranational bodies, EU institutions. The *Bond* case presented the related question of the scope of the treaty power in the U.S. Constitution, as it relates to the delegation of (additional) legislative authority to Congress itself. But our Court did not address that question. For their part, the European courts have found uneasy compromises. They read their constitutions as providing a check on their nations' powers to enter into treaties, while interpreting that check as rarely binding.

OBSERVATIONS: DELEGATION OF LAW-MAKING AUTHORITY

Bond and *Medellin* skirt the edges of a basic legal question. *Bond* might have considered (but did not) the President's power to enter into a treaty that broadens Congress's constitutionally limited authority to legislate. *Medellin*, while answering a different question, set forth an answer that will limit, as a practical matter, the ability of international adjudicative bodies to bind our courts. That question, which the European courts faced more directly, asks what limits domestic courts should impose on the treaty-making power or, more specifically, upon the power to delegate to treaty-based organizations the authority to make rules that have the practical effect of law.

Issues related to this basic question are likely to arise with increasing frequency. For one thing, the number of rule-creating international organizations has increased rapidly. They range from the well-known World Trade Organization (WTO), NAFTA, and the Basel Committee on Banking Supervision, to the less familiar Codex Alimentarius, International Sanitary Standards Organization, and International Olive Oil Council. They include organizations established by treaty (e.g., the WTO and NAFTA), those established through intergovernmental efforts to coordinate domestic regulators (e.g., the International Organization of Securities Commissions), and those established by hybrid groups of state and nonstate actors, like the International Organization for Standardization (ISO), the Internet Corporation for Assigned Names and Numbers (ICANN), and the International Conference on Harmonisation of Technical Requirements for Registration of Pharmaceuticals for Human Use (ICH).[216] (I note that the figures on international organizations presented at the beginning of this chapter, drawn from the *Yearbook of International Organizations*, do not seek to provide an accurate count of IOs that are "standard setting." The ones reported in the corresponding table are variously above and below the actual number in that regard; they include federations of national organizations that may not necessarily promulgate rules, but omit certain public-private international bodies that *do* act as standard setters.)

Many of today's international organizations have a structure that facilitates rule making. According to Sabino Cassese, that structure tends to include "[1] a collegial body, usually referred to as an assembly, in which all of the participants—states, other national organizations, and international organizations—are present; [2] a more restricted collegial body, usually called a council, whose members are elected by the assembly; [3] an executive body, called a secretariat, made up of regular employees of the organization; and [4] committees, generally made up of functionaries" of the member nations who work in the regulatory field.[217]

Some of these rule-making bodies then promulgate regulations and standards that bind member nations, at least as a matter of international law (i.e., a member nation will be in violation of its treaty-based international obligations vis-à-vis other signatory nations if it does not comply with the rule). The Commission for the Conservation of Southern Bluefin Tuna, for instance, sets limits on the number of those fish that member (and some cooperating, nonmember) nations may catch each year.[218] The World Trade Organization provides procedural requirements that a member state must follow before undertaking a trade "safeguard" measure, and it has a committee on safeguards that oversees member states' compliance with those requirements.[219] The NAFTA treaty authorizes binational arbitration panels to review antidumping measures and countervailing duties of member countries, and to issue decisions that are binding on government agencies (e.g., the U.S. Commerce Department) and for which local judicial review is not available.[220] The United Nations Convention on the Law of the Sea requires signatory nations to release arrested vessels on bail and to comply with a host of procedural regulations not contained in the treaty itself but promulgated by staff.[221]

The rules of these international organizations—both treaty-based and non-treaty-based—bind citizens of individual states as a practical matter more often than one might expect. Sometimes international regulatory bodies have enforcement mechanisms that make their determinations binding as a matter of domestic law. For instance, the U.N. Security Council can issue orders directing member states to freeze the assets and restrict the travel of persons designated as financers of terrorism, which members are obligated to do "without delay."[222] The executive board of the Clean Development Mechanism, under the Kyoto Protocol, can determine whether energy projects undertaken by private firms in developing countries are eligible to receive emissions "credits" for reducing greenhouse gases, and those decisions directly impact financing for private firms.[223] The International Civil Aviation Organization (ICAO) issues safety standards that apply to private air carriers. If carriers do not comply with those standards, ICAO rules provide that they can be blacklisted or banned by national bodies, or suspended by the ICAO.[224] The Chemical Weapons Convention established an international organization, the Organization for the Prohibition of Chemical Weapons, which has the power to order inspections of both public and private facilities in member states to ensure compliance with the convention.[225]

In other cases, the rules or regulations issued by international bodies are not formally binding but instead take the form of a strong suggestion or a basis for negotiation. The recommendations of the Basel Committee on Banking Supervision are one such example. But in practice, even those types of rules can bind internally. Member states might chose (or feel obligated) to adopt the international organization's recommendations as a matter of domestic law, or the international organization might be able to shame or goad regulated entities into compliance through application of "sunshine," "sticks," and "carrots"—as has been the case with organizations like the International Labor Organization.[226]

As noted, the international organizations making rules that effectively bind private parties extend well beyond those created by treaty. Consider, for example, the Extractive Industries Transparency Initiative (EITI), a coalition of governments, businesses, and civil society groups that have empowered an international organization to develop a standard for monitoring the use of state natural resources and to issue periodic reports on countries' compliance; the Greenhouse Gas Protocol, an accounting framework for greenhouse gas emissions developed by two international NGOs and now embraced by dozens of governments, industry associations, and businesses; and ICANN, a private nonprofit corporation responsible for maintaining databases of Internet domain names used by private and public parties throughout the world. These bodies are, in effect, international regulators with powers to affect our daily lives. But because they are created by private sector organizations or by coalitions of public and private groups, they often lack the types of procedural controls and accountability mechanisms associated with domestic administrative agencies (e.g., the opportunity for notice and comment on proposed rule makings, the opportunity for pre- or postdeprivation hearings to ensure due process, and judicial review).[227] But putting these instances to the side, we can, for purposes of clarity, focus upon organizations created by treaty, though we must recognize that decisions made by organizations created by executive order, and by public-private organizations, can raise similar issues.

For another thing, it is ever more likely that American firms or individuals or businesses adversely affected by a rule will raise issues of statutory, administrative, or constitutional law. They may, for example, claim that the rule, even if promulgated by an American agency, is in fact the creation of an international body. And that body, when creating the rule, may have failed to apply the legal safeguards that administrative law ordinarily provides, such as transparency, an opportunity to present arguments and to obtain replies, reasoned decision making, and court review that protects against arbitrariness and ensures conformity with the law.

Consider cases that have already arisen. The first, *Department of Transportation v. Public Citizen,* illustrates how a treaty can lead to domestic rule or standard setting that circumvents ordinary requirements under federal law.[228] In the 1980s Congress enacted a statute in effect suspending certificates that permitted Mexican trucks to operate in the United States. In the 1990s Mexico and the United States agreed that, under NAFTA, the suspension would gradually end, and Mexican trucks would be able to operate here. In 2001 a NAFTA arbitration panel concluded that the United States, by failing to phase out Congress's moratorium, had violated NAFTA. The President announced he would lift the moratorium, and the Department of Transportation issued regulations doing so.[229]

A group of environmentalists challenged DOT's regulations on the grounds that the department had not first conducted an environmental impact study on the effect of ending the moratorium, as federal law required for agency actions of this kind.[230] The department responded that it need not conduct the study because NAFTA, the NAFTA panel, and the President's decision, not the DOT regulations, were the "causes" of the coming influx of Mexican trucks. Since DOT (the agency) did not "cause" the potential environmental impact, it need not conduct the study. Nor need NAFTA, its panel, or the President conduct the study, as the environmental impact statute did not apply to them.[231] Our Court accepted this argument. Thus the statutory requirement did not apply.[232] In a sense, the government, through its treaties, had set aside what would otherwise have constituted an important statutory obligation for an agency to follow, before promulgating rules that affected domestic actors.

Another recent case, in the Court of Appeals for the District of Columbia Circuit, suggested, but did not hold, that rule making conducted by an international body pursuant to treaty-delegated authority could run afoul of American constitutional requirements.[233] The treaty in question, the 1987 Montreal Protocol, limited emission of ozone-producing gases, such as methyl bromide. Several years after the treaty took effect, the parties agreed that members (including the United States) should try to end production and consumption of methyl bromide, while still emitting a certain amount for "critical uses." The parties met annually to determine who could emit what gases under this "critical use" exception and to promulgate rules helping to define it further.[234]

In 2004, at their annual "critical use" meeting, the parties authorized the United States to produce and to consume more than seven thousand additional metric tons of methyl bromide for "critical uses."[235] But they specified, through cross-reference to a decision made at an earlier meeting, that the domestic procedure for making more methyl bromide available had to "take into account" that country's "existing stocks."[236] The Environmental Protection Agency (EPA) subsequently authorized more production, but it did not require the use of all "existing stocks" first. And an environmental group challenged this decision as unlawful, arguing that the "existing stocks" language of the Montreal Protocol rules was binding on the EPA.[237]

The D.C. Circuit rejected this argument. It conceded that the Clean Air Act requires the EPA to conform its decisions to the "law." Indeed, the act says that the EPA can permit production of methyl bromide only "[t]o the extent consistent with the Montreal Protocol."[238] But, in the D.C.'s Circuit's view, the decisions made by the parties at their annual meeting, following procedures set forth in the protocol, were not themselves binding "law"; nor did they amount to provisions of the Montreal Protocol itself. Hence the Clean Air Act provisions did not apply.[239] And the EPA did not need to conform its regulations to the decisions of the Montreal Protocol parties at their "critical use" meeting.

The court added that any other holding would pose serious constitutional difficulties: if the annual "critical use" decisions of the Montreal Protocol parties bound the EPA "like statutes or legislative rules ...

then Congress either has delegated law-making authority to an international body or authorized amendments to a treaty without presidential signature or Senate ratification, in violation of Article II of the Constitution."[240] While the court conceded that "[t]he Supreme Court has not determined whether decisions of an international body created by treaty are judicially enforceable,"[241] it nonetheless decided to follow its own other decisions finding that the pronouncements of treaty-created organizations were not binding law.[242] (The Supreme Court reached a similar decision two years later in *Medellin*, although for different reasons.[243])

The D.C. Circuit's reasoning, right or wrong, suggests a dilemma. If the Montreal Protocol's annual rules are "law," subject to domestic court enforcement (say, through the Clean Air Act), then treaty-authorized rule making supplants domestic agency decision making, even if the treaty-authorized process lacks guarantees of fairness that American administrative (or perhaps constitutional) law demands. But if the international rules are not binding—even though Congress enacts language suggesting (though not definitively stating) the contrary, then how is the United States to remain an active participant in worldwide efforts, indeed successful efforts, to curb the use of ozone-destroying chemicals? The D.C. Circuit, through statutory interpretation, avoided confronting the problem directly. I suspect it will return.

A third case arose in the United Kingdom. The 1267 Committee of the U.N. Security Council has the authority, under council resolutions, to compile a list of individuals who provide financial aid to terrorist groups and to order U.N. member nations to freeze their assets.[244] The British Treasury issued orders doing just that. Several persons named brought a legal challenge in the UK. They did not question whether the Treasury orders were needed to bring the United Kingdom into compliance with its Security Council obligations. But they argued that the orders were nonetheless illegal under British law because, among other things, neither the original Security Council determination nor the Treasury orders created "procedures" that would have "enabled designated persons to challenge their designation."[245]

The UK Supreme Court accepted the argument.[246] In doing so, it observed that "the regimes that both Australia and New Zealand have introduced" to comply with the sanctions program were "exacting" but "contain[ed] various, albeit limited, safeguards" to protect fundamental rights.[247] The court also cited a 2008 decision of the European Court of Justice (ECJ), finding that the 1267 Committee's processes for designating terrorists violated the basic rights under the European Convention because affected individuals were not given an opportunity for independent judicial review.[248] The UK Supreme Court thus concluded that the Treasury orders could not be enforced against the defendants under British law, unless modified so as to provide "an effective remedy . . . subjecting th[e] listing to judicial review."[249]

In effect, the UK Supreme Court held that an international regulatory action (i.e., the designating of individuals by the U.N. Security Council) could not be enforced in the United Kingdom as binding law without an additional layer of judicial review and procedural due process.

These three cases ask how the United States—and similar constitutional democracies—shall reconcile the expansion of international regulation with the procedural and substantive safeguards that domestic law typically provides. Commentators have begun to examine similar questions. Some suggest that federal courts in the United States can avoid any constitutional problems by imposing procedural conditions upon the enforcement of rules promulgated by international bodies. That is to say, the courts should "apply constitutional requirements of procedural due process and other generally applicable principles of administrative law" to ensure that affected persons have been adequately represented in those forums.[250] Others suggest that we can avoid delegation problems, and promote American participatory values, if domestic "regulators go through notice and comment *before* engaging in international negotiations with their counterparts."[251] These suggestions strike a common theme: they seek to impose controls of transparency, fairness, and rationality upon those who in effect make the rules. International regulators have begun to respond by adopting various administrative procedural requirements—of transparency, participation, response to criticisms, reasoned decision making,[252] and forms of appellate review[253]—in a word, a fairer, more rational, more public process.[254]

The problem is not new. For centuries those subject to the legal authority of regulators have complained of "too much delegation of authority," "too much unchecked power," and "insufficient review of the lawfulness of regulatory action." At their heart these and similar claims reflect one basic question: Who will regulate the regulators? As the Romans asked: *Quis custodiet ipsos custodes?*[255]

Our courts faced a similar problem in the 1930s. The New Deal created many new federal administrative agencies. What kind of constitutional creature was such an agency? Did the Constitution permit it to make rules? To exercise adjudicative power? When had Congress, in delegating power to an agency, gone too far? How were courts to ensure that the agencies acted with transparency, participation, fairness, and in conformity with the law? The Court responded with decisions, such as *Crowell v. Benson*,[256] that found authority in the Constitution for the agencies to adjudicate, provided the courts could review their factual findings (with deference), their conclusions of law, and certain (no longer critical) constitutional questions afresh. And it added a "nondelegation" doctrine that sought to limit the power Congress could grant an agency, but which today has little force. Congress responded with the Administrative Procedure Act, which created rules designed to ensure agency fairness.[257] And the legal profession responded with an entire field, that of administrative law.

Our Court has said little so far about the comparable field of international organization rule making. *Bond*, to repeat, did not answer the question that had already come up in *Missouri v. Holland*, regarding whether federal law making through treaties can extend to subjects that are outside of Congress's enumerated powers. Nor did it confront the question of whether Congress can enact implementing legislation for a treaty that might exceed its express grants of authority. *Medellin*, as I've said, provided an answer (to a different question) that might affect the power of the President and the Senate to create domestically binding rules through treaties—by requiring that certain language now be included in every treaty in order for it to be self-executing without implementing legislation. But as the two environmental cases just discussed make clear, Congress can give rule-making authority to an agency in a variety of ways that do not fall afoul of *Medellin*. And so delegation of rule-making authority to international agencies can and does continue, with the Court having set relatively few parameters to date. In my view, it is not a bad thing that the Court so far has said little.

It is often wise in a democracy such as ours for the Court to wait for the public, perhaps through other parts of government, to experiment with different approaches. As Tocqueville recognized nearly two centuries ago, the American public likes to consider issues through debate. That debate takes place at bar meetings, in specialized journals, in the general press, before administrative agencies and legislative committees, and in a host of other ways. Debate leads to experiments, with rules, with regulations, with statutes, and experiments are often revised. Our Court, particularly in constitutional matters, often works best when it comes in last, considering whether the solutions reached elsewhere fall within the wide bounds of that which the Constitution permits.

Finally, the problem itself, at a basic level, is particularly difficult. There are only a few international bodies with authority to review the legality and fairness of decisions made by international organizations. And there is no international supreme court with authority to work out conflicts among them. At the same time, there is, from the perspective of American law, a dilemma. If, through treaty, we delegate too much rule-making authority to unsupervised international bodies, what becomes of the assurances of fairness that the Constitution provides or, for that matter, of the "legislative" power that the Constitution grants to Congress? But if we severely restrict the power to enter into treaties or other international agreements that delegate rule-making power to international bodies, how can we cooperate with others? How can we coordinate, for example, the enforcement actions of different nations? How can we possibly solve the international problems of environment, trade, and security that so directly affect us but which we cannot solve alone?

The fact is that we need international cooperation and the agreements that help to maintain it. We cannot simply withdraw from international efforts to resolve the commercial, environmental, and security problems of an increasingly interdependent world. We cannot, in our own interest, stand on the sidelines while the rest of the world participates in the making and shaping of decisions that directly affect us. That is why I believe we shall yet have to work out what bodies, national or international, should review the fairness, transparency, and legality of findings of international regulators. And we shall have to determine how they do so.

For present purposes, I can draw one firm conclusion: the growth of rule-making international organizations provides the clearest example of the need on the part of the courts and the legal profession to understand both the legal and the practical realities elsewhere in the world if we are to preserve our basic American values.

CHAPTER 10

Postscript

Home Alone: A Political Discussion

We have now closely considered cases exemplifying the influence of foreign circumstances generally and foreign law in particular on decisions of the Supreme Court. Whether they deal with constitutional, statutory, or treaty-based questions, these cases show how routinely American interests extend beyond the water's edge, obliging the Court, in turn, to extend its range of legal and practical reference beyond what has been its custom, in order to arrive at sound judgments. These cases seem to me the right context in which to consider an argument frequently made when the very idea of foreign law as an influence on American courts raises its head. It is an argument I have deferred considering until now, since it is too often made without much context in our political discourse and even in court opinions. It concerns the practice of "cross-referencing" foreign cases—that is, referring in opinions to the decisions of foreign courts. Although this argument has seemed to occupy the foreground in political discussions about the role of foreign law, it turns out to prove relevant to only a small part of that role, and one that cannot but recede set against the examples discussed elsewhere in this book.

To understand the controversy, one must keep in mind the fact that the Supreme Court of the United States is a domestic court, not an international court. Its job is to interpret and apply the Constitution, federal statutes, and sometimes treaties. At one time that work might have had little to do with the law of other nations. But the world has shrunk considerably since the Founding, particularly during the past few decades. We have seen how that development, which reflects changes in technology, communications, and political organization, as well as the rise of problems that ignore national boundaries, has made it necessary for the Court ever more frequently to consider matters of international law and the laws of other nations. It has significantly affected the nature of the Court's work, making it ever more important for the justices to understand, and to take account of, foreign legal practices. But in doing so, the justices have sometimes evoked strongly adverse political reactions.

To take an example, in February 2002, the Court heard a case presenting a controversial question: Does the Constitution's Eighth Amendment, prohibiting the imposition of "cruel and unusual punishments," bar the execution (for murder) of a mentally retarded defendant?[1] A group of American diplomats filed a "friend of the Court" brief claiming that only the United States and Kyrgyzstan routinely continue this practice.[2] The news media reported the claim. When *The New York Times* referred to it in an editorial, an unhappy ambassador from Kyrgyzstan wrote a letter to the *Times* explaining that, although a few other nations may have maintained the death penalty, Kyrgyzstan had, since independence, abolished all executions in practice.[3]

But returning to the matter at hand, should it matter in respect to the Eighth Amendment's application whether many nations, a few (only Kyrgyzstan and the United States), or even the United States alone executes mentally retarded defendants? If so, just how does it matter, and why? What exactly was the relevance of the American diplomats' assertion, and why did they believe the absence of the death penalty abroad was particularly relevant? Was it that this made the punishment "unusual" (contrary to the Eighth Amendment)? Or was there something more to this objection? Before answering, let us look to a somewhat similar case that came before the Court in 2004.

In *Roper v. Simmons*, the Court held, by a vote of five to four, that the Eighth Amendment forbids the application of the death penalty to those who were under the age of eighteen when they committed a murder.[4] In his opinion for the Court, Justice Kennedy wrote that "the United States now stands alone in a world that has turned its face against the juvenile death penalty."[5] He added that it was "proper that we acknowledge the overwhelming weight of international opinion against the juvenile death penalty."[6]

Justice Kennedy had made a similar argument in *Lawrence v. Texas,* the landmark case in which the Court held that the Due Process Clause of the Constitution was at odds with Texas's laws against same-sex (consensual) sodomy. In that opinion, too, he drew on foreign law and practices to support the Court's holding.[7] Writing for the majority, he referred to similar determinations made by foreign legislatures and courts during the latter half of the twentieth century.[8] And in so doing he meant to show that Chief Justice Warren Burger had been wrong in an earlier case (*Bowers v. Hardwicke*) when he wrote, in a concurring opinion, that "Western civilization" had consistently condemned same-sex intimacy.[9] Thus that precedent was overturned.

Some members of the Court, dissenting in both the death penalty and the sodomy cases, objected strongly to the use of foreign law.[10] But more to the point of politics, the Court's references to foreign authorities in these opinions drew sharp criticism from elected officials. Seventy-four members of Congress sponsored legislation in 2004 stating "that judicial determinations regarding the meaning of the laws of the United States should not be based in whole or in part on judgments, laws, or pronouncements of foreign institutions unless such foreign judgments, laws, or pronouncements . . . inform an understanding of the original meaning of the laws of the United States."[11]

A sponsoring member of the House said that were the bill to become law, judges who deliberately violated it might "subject themselves to the ultimate remedy, which would be impeachment."[12] And the acceptability of referring to foreign court decisions has become the subject of considerable debate in political,[13] judicial,[14] and scholarly forums.[15]

Why have these references to foreign law generated so much reaction? One could argue that the death penalty cases present no general "foreign law" issue, for the relevant constitutional provision, the Eighth Amendment, refers to "unusual punishments" without specifying whether "unusual" matters only in relation to the United States, to countries that follow the common law, to European nations, or to some other subset of the world's nations. Nor does the sodomy case, *Lawrence,* raise a general issue about the use of foreign law, for Justice Kennedy had referred to it simply to rebut a claim about foreign law made in a prior case. He did not claim foreign practices independently added support to the Court's conclusion.[16]

It is, of course, possible that some version of the psychological phenomenon of displacement is at work: If you are upset about *A*, you may blame *B*.[17] The critics, upset about the Court's death penalty and sodomy conclusions, are quick at least in part to blame foreign law, here an innocent victim.

But there are better reasons for the political controversy. Jeremy Waldron has written at some length about them, analyzing the underlying problems in depth.[18] I shall draw upon what he has said.

It is possible that the critics of cross-referencing worry that the practice of citing foreign decisions will lead American judges to decide cases not through legal analysis but through "nose-counting"—that is, tallying up the number of countries on each side.[19] There is a further worry, not entirely unfounded, that foreign opinions are subject to misunderstanding, because American judges are unlikely to grasp the foreign contexts in which those decisions arise.[20] Moreover, even if the decisions of foreign courts do not bind American judges, they can influence them—indeed, that is the very aim of the cross-referencing practice. Finally, those who see judges throughout the world as belonging to the same social caste—one sharing generally "leftish" political views, and perhaps including state court judges, law professors, and lawyers generally—may not believe that this influence is salutary. Wielded by those whom Americans have virtually no voice in choosing, this influence, it is feared, could easily get out of hand, undermining basic American democratic values.[21]

There are replies to these claims, many of which Waldron discusses. Where, for example, references to foreign law or practices are not, strictly speaking, legally necessary to arrive at a ground of decision, those references can nonetheless help judges produce better decisions without constraining their decisional autonomy. Since the end of World War II, ever more nations have relied upon independent judiciaries with the power to invalidate legislation contrary to their constitutions (i.e., through the power of judicial review).[22] Foreign constitutions, in turn, have often been crafted and modified to resemble our own, including provisions that protect both democratic political systems and basic individual liberties.[23] As judges throughout the world undertake to fulfill their responsibilities of reviewing their countries' laws and regulations for constitutional validity, they have all found themselves facing somewhat similar problems. And if someone with a job roughly like my own, facing a legal problem roughly like the one confronting me, interpreting a document that resembles the one I look to, has written a legal opinion about a similar matter, why not read what that judge has said? I might learn from it, whether or not I end up agreeing with it.

Indeed, our own Court frequently learns something of value from the opinions of lower court judges, including, for example, the renowned judges Henry Friendly and Learned Hand;[24] still, we do not always reach the same conclusions. Opinions often note useful law review articles, books of history, statistical studies, and all sorts of other sources, and they should be transparent, embodying the judge's reasoning and supporting materials. So why not include foreign court decisions as well?

To learn from foreign opinions or to consider their reasoning is to find in them something of use in interpreting *American*, not foreign, law. It is not to treat law as an abstract "brooding omnipresence."[25] Foreign as well as domestic experience can be of help in understanding the commands of American sovereigns, whether federal or state, that have enacted the particular legal phrase in question.

Judicial decision making, particularly in the Supreme Court, is not a mechanical effort at applying clear legal rules to new factual situations. The task is more appropriately seen as a kind of problem solving, an effort at using text, history, tradition, precedent, statutory or constitutional purposes or values, and consequences to interpret law and arrive at a ground of decision.[26] The growing complexity of problems, taken together with the need to produce a judgment in a few weeks or months at most, adds value to the experience of other judges who have faced comparable problems. The wheel needn't be reinvented every time.

Let us, for example, consider a federal statute imposing a duty upon state officials to enforce federal gun registration laws. The Court was asked to decide whether it violated basic constitutional principles of federalism. A majority thought it did, by interfering with a state's basic right to control the work of its own officials.[27] But I disagreed, and I supported my argument, in part, by referring to the fact that other roughly analogous forms of political organization, such as the European Union, believed that analogously subordinate political units (such as member states) should enforce virtually all EU law through their own member-state civil service.[28] Avoiding the expansion of the larger federal civil service, it is believed by individual member states, only increases—it does not diminish—their autonomy.[29] The Swiss Federation rests upon somewhat similar principles.[30] Are such models beside the point when interpreting a Constitution that reflects James Madison's efforts to survey the world, ancient and contemporary, for examples of governmental arrangements that, among other things, would help to ensure state autonomy as well as individual freedom? Why should modern instances, even if they do not convince the majority, be unworthy even of consideration?

Finally, there is a well-established American legal tradition of learning from foreign sources, consisting predominately but not entirely of common law materials. Abraham Lincoln, after all, learned law by the light of the fire from Sir William Blackstone's treatise on English law, which in part reflected (often via Sir Edward Coke's judgments) commercial law as practiced on the European continent.[31] Supreme Court justices from John Marshall to Felix Frankfurter have filed opinions with reference to decisions by foreign courts.[32] References to the decisions and practices of common law courts outside the United States are legion, perhaps because America's law draws substance from that same common law tradition. But the Court has also referred (in much the same way that Justice Kennedy did) to practices of courts outside that tradition.

In 1977, for example, the Court held in *Coker v. Georgia* that the Eighth Amendment's prohibition of "cruel and unusual punishments" applied to, and forbade, an execution for rape of an adult woman.[33] Justice Byron White, writing for the majority, observed that the Court had previously "note[d] the climate of international opinion concerning the acceptability of a particular punishment," though in this case he found it "not irrelevant . . . that out of 60 major nations in the world surveyed in 1965, only 3 retained the death penalty for rape where death did not ensue."[34]

Similarly, in 1982 the Court held that the Eighth Amendment forbids applying the death penalty to a defendant who took part in a robbery where someone was killed, but did not himself participate in, or intend, the murder.[35] Justice White, again writing for the Court, found it "worth noting that the doctrine of felony murder has been abolished in England and India, severely restricted in Canada and a number of other

Commonwealth countries, and is unknown in continental Europe."[36] In both cases several justices dissented, but in neither did the dissenters object to the majority's references to foreign practice. Indeed, in the second case, the dissenters themselves drew support from the fact that felony murder had been "a fixture of English common law until 1957."[37]

Justice White's opinions are not historical anomalies. In 1937 the distinguished jurist Justice Benjamin Cardozo looked to "established procedure in the law of Continental Europe" to help determine whether the Fifth Amendment's protection against "double jeopardy" is a "fundamental" liberty.[38] And in 1908 the Court considered the "jurisprudence of civilized and free countries outside the domain of the common law" to help answer a similar question in respect to the Fifth Amendment's privilege against self-incrimination.[39] In both cases, the Court held that the right in question was not "fundamental," though both findings would later be overruled based on changes in the law.[40] But in neither case did dissenters complain, at the time or later, about the Court's referring to foreign law or to the practices of nations outside the common law tradition.

Finally, consider *Trop v. Dulles*,[41] a 1958 case that concerned a U.S. Army private who deserted in Morocco and was court-martialed, dishonorably discharged, and later told he had lost his American citizenship. The Court held five to four that stripping an individual of his citizenship for having committed such a crime violated the Eighth Amendment.[42] Chief Justice Earl Warren, in his plurality opinion for four members of the majority, wrote that the amendment's words "cruel and unusual" are of international origin. "The phrase in our Constitution," he wrote, "was taken directly from the English Declaration of Rights of 1688, and the principle it represents can be traced back to the Magna Carta."[43] The amendment, he added, "must draw its meaning from" a society's "evolving standards of decency," which are revealed in part by the fact that "[t]he civilized nations of the world are in virtual unanimity that statelessness is not to be imposed as punishment for crime. . . . The United Nations' survey of the nationality laws of 84 nations of the world reveals that only two countries, the Philippines and Turkey, impose denationalization as a penalty for desertion."[44]

Again, the four dissenters did not object to the plurality's having referred to foreign practices. Indeed, they did likewise, arguing that it showed that "many civilized nations impose loss of citizenship for indulgence in designated prohibited activities."[45]

The first criticism that I can find of the *practice* of referring to foreign law appears in 1988. In *Thompson v. Oklahoma*, the Court held five to three that the Eighth Amendment forbade imposing capital punishment on an offender under the age of sixteen (when he committed the crime).[46] Writing for four members of the majority, Justice Stevens found that many common law nations, Western European nations, and the Soviet Union would not impose the death penalty on such a juvenile.[47] In dissenting, however, Justice Scalia wrote that the "plurality's reliance" upon what "other countries" do "is totally inappropriate as a means of establishing the fundamental beliefs of this Nation."[48] And the practice since then has seemed controversial—at least where the Eighth Amendment is at issue.[49]

Foreign courts have long referred to American decisions, as well as cross-referenced one another's decisions—sometimes famously. In 1932, for example, confronted with the question of whether a manufacturer of ginger beer should be liable for allowing a mouse to creep into a bottle, Lord Atkin looked abroad to help find the answer. He wrote:

> It is always a satisfaction to an English lawyer to be able to test his application of fundamental principles of the common law by the development of the same doctrines by the lawyers of the Courts of the United States. . . . The mouse had emerged from the ginger-beer bottle in the United States before it appeared in Scotland.[50]

He then discussed at length Justice (then judge) Cardozo's opinion in *MacPherson v. Buick Motor Co.*, which interpreted New York State law as imposing liability upon manufacturers for injuries caused to ultimate consumers of their products.[51] Other nations' courts, including India, South Africa, Britain, and Canada, have also referred to our constitutional decisions, as well as to one another's decisions, with some regularity.[52]

Still, the criticisms that I have thus far recited do not get to the heart of the matter. The strength and the persistence of aversions to foreign law, as well as the detailed scholarly work on the subject, suggest a concern deeper than any I have yet mentioned. Congressman Bob Goodlatte well expressed that concern at a seminar I attended on this subject. It is a concern for American sovereignty. And I would set it forth as follows:

As James Madison long ago wrote, the American Constitution is a "charter of power granted by liberty," and not a "charter of liberty . . . granted by power."[53] By that he meant that here, a naturally free people sought to delegate limited powers to the federal government, while in Europe, a king of virtually unlimited "power" might delegate "liberty" to the people. The difference is that Americans see their ungoverned condition as one of liberty; they understand the judicial power in America to flow not only from the Constitution but from its source, the *People* themselves, who, if they do not elect their judges directly, elect representatives, who in turn appoint and confirm them.

Foreign judges have little or no such connection to the American electorate. We did not elect them. We did not elect anyone who appointed them. Why should persons so totally removed from our electoral process nonetheless possess the power to interpret our documents and thereby to tell us what to do?

With their concern about "sovereignty," the critics worry that as American judges rely ever more heavily upon the work of their foreign counterparts, our judiciary will come to substitute foreign legal concepts and values for those upon which Americans have long built their lives.[54] They fret that cross-referencing, by some insidious incrementalism, puts our future in the hands of jurists whose principles may differ considerably from those underlying our Constitution. In a word, they worry that an increased foreign say in interpreting our Constitution and statutes threatens to corrupt what has long been a great American treasure—a legal system that, over the course of two hundred years, has secured America's democracy and freedom, while steadfastly leading a diverse body of citizens to resolve important differences in the courts, not the streets, and under the rule of law.

As mentioned at the start, to put such anxieties in perspective is largely my reason for not addressing them earlier. My hope is that the cases I've now discussed suggest that the critics' concerns about judicial references to foreign law are beside the point. Their fears don't much resonate when one understands the way in which foreign law and practices are actually considered. They do not respond directly to the kinds of internationally related legal problems that American judges are now asked to dive into and resolve. It is not the cosmopolitanism of some jurists that seeks this kind of engagement but the nature of the world itself that demands it.

An argument, such as Waldron and others offer, in favor of considering foreign law, while relevant, should not be necessary. As we have seen, a great many recent cases—whether involving treaties, the foreign reach of American statutes, or questions of U.S. jurisdiction over activity taking place abroad—made it unavoidable that the Court analyze foreign or international legal rules, statutes, or practices to arrive at a reasoned decision. In such cases, doing so was not simply helpful but essential. At the same time, I find little evidence that it has led to any result not entirely consistent with American laws and practice. The objections of critics, though important in the abstract, do not reflect the reality of today's federal court dockets, including the Supreme Court's; nor do I find a direct relation between the underlying fears they express and corresponding changes in American jurisprudence.

If I am right, those who hold a negative view of cross-referencing at best overstate their concerns. There is little reason to think that the practice will, for better or for worse, lead to the emergence of a Kantian universal law—a single rule of law for the whole world. Irrespective of the arguments that might be made for (or against) such a system, nothing in the nature of our docket suggests that one is likely to emerge in the foreseeable future.

At most, cross-referencing will speed the development of "clusters" or "pockets" of legally like-minded nations whose judges learn things from one another, either as a general matter or in particular areas of law, such as security, commerce, or the environment.[55] But these groupings need not be formal, and their members can insist on the conformity of any legal rule with their own nation's basic legal values. As we have seen, despite holdings by the European Court of Justice that EU law trumps member-state law, many national courts have insisted on retaining the final word as to whether a rule of European law conforms to their own constitutional requirements. And if this is so among nations committed to a measure of political and economic union, how much less likely is foreign law to impinge upon the sovereignty of one not so encumbered?

In sum, one must consider the political objection to cross-referencing against the background of foreign-related cases that our Court's docket actually presents. To do so is to appreciate that the demands of the Court's work make impossible the sort of hermetically sealed legal system some might imagine America able to sustain, if indeed it ever existed. It is also to be able to see that if potential for influence exists in our engagement with the legal world beyond our shores, it is far likelier to be our influence on international law as yet unwritten than foreign influence on American law long enshrined. Were the Court to leave the world, the world would continue without our participation. By engaging the world and the borderless challenges it presents, we can promote adherence to and the adoption of those basic constitutional and legal values for which the Court and the Constitution stand, and which we have bequeathed to others. Cross-referencing is more likely to advance those values than to undermine them.

PART IV

The Judge as Diplomat

I have thus far described how particular cases have required American judges to take account of the world abroad—foreign legal regimes and practices—in order to resolve disputes over activities and between parties not confined to one nation's borders. But even outside the context of specific litigation, federal judges are increasingly thinking about and discussing foreign and international law. This is happening through encounters with members of foreign judiciaries, which are occurring ever more frequently out of a common wish to share professional experiences.

During my time on the Court, its members, like many other American judges, have increasingly conferred not only with judges but also with lawyers, legal scholars, and law students from foreign nations. That fact owes something to practical considerations, given how easy international travel and communication have become. But it is also the case that American and foreign jurists have found they have more in common than they used to. They confront similar problems. They perform the same kinds of judicial tasks following similar charters offering similar protections to democratic government and to individual human rights. American and foreign judges furthermore have the same desire—as well as the requisite experience—to advance the rule of law even as the world threatens to become more turbulent.

To some degree, the meeting process has become formalized. In 1993 the Judicial Conference of the United States, the central administrative group of federal trial court and appellate court judges, established a Committee on International Judicial Relations.[1] With the active help of the State Department, the committee has coordinated talks, conferences, and meetings both in the United States and abroad.[2] Since 2010, American judges have met with judges, prosecutors, and judicial administrators from, for example, Albania, Bangladesh, Brazil, Botswana, Bulgaria, Cambodia, China, Colombia, Ecuador, Ghana, Indonesia, Ireland, Liberia, Mauritania, Nambia, Qatar, Russia, Ukraine, Tunisia, and the United Arab Emirates.[3] They have discussed not only general subjects, such as the rule of law, the practice of judging in a democracy, and criminal law, but also specialized ones, such as intellectual property, electronic surveillance, global asset forfeiture, terrorism, customs disputes, mediation, and judicial case management.[4]

Most members of our Court also have participated in organized exchanges with members of supreme courts, or the equivalent, of many other jurisdictions, among them, the European Union, Britain, France, Germany, South Africa, and India. Justice Kennedy has spent time with Chinese jurists, Justice O'Connor with members of African courts, Justice Ruth Bader Ginsburg with judges in Egypt and North Africa, and other justices with members of other courts. These kinds of meetings have become increasingly substantive, sometimes involving the preparation of staff papers concerning aspects of criminal law, double jeopardy, federalism, free speech, alternative dispute resolution, and other topics. Individual members of other supreme courts regularly visit our Court, and the visits are typically reciprocated. At the same time, informal meetings, visits, and lectures with foreign judges, lawyers, and law students grow more frequent.

In terms of time, I should guess that individual justices, who may devote, on average, one evening, lunchtime, or dinner three or four times a month to meeting with American law students and legal professionals, have similar encounters with foreign colleagues about once every month or two. And these are more than mere exercises in public relations, though I could hardly have said as much just twenty years ago. Meeting at that time with a group of professors in New York, I enthusiastically observed that my attendance at a recent foreign judicial exchange had taught me much that would prove useful. But when a Finnish professor asked me to name one example, I was hard-pressed to reply. Today I would have no such difficulty.

The description that best fits these encounters is the one Michael Oakeshott attached to the "pursuit of learning." The "pursuit of learning," he said, is another way of saying "a conversation." It is not an argument; its "tone is neither tyrannous nor plangent"; it has "no predetermined course"; we do not "judge its excellence by its conclusion" for "it has no conclusion"; its interest "springs from the quality of the voices which speak, and its value lies in the relics it leaves behind in the minds of those who participate."[5]

I have participated in many such conversations—in China, in Africa, at the Court, and at universities—for example, at Yale Law School, which for many years has sponsored an annual seminar with its faculty and supreme court justices from abroad. Having no conclusion, the conversations are likely to continue as members of constitutional courts agree to meet regularly (e.g., at the World Conference on Constitutional Justice) and as courts increasingly provide English translations of their judgments, to facilitate broader circulation and comprehension of those writings. But the basic question remains: How do these discussions with and among foreign judges affect the law?

CHAPTER 11

Interchange and Substantive Progress

For the most part, when we meet with foreign judges, law professors, lawyers, or students, we learn something about the background of foreign systems. That can help us not only when we consider cases such as those I have discussed—ones like *Sosa* that cross borders—but also when we examine problems within our own legal system. From judges in continental Europe, for example, we learn about the mechanics of their criminal law system, which is an "inquisitorial" system. That has nothing to do with Torquemada; rather, it involves prosecutors who are trained as judges and investigators and wield a high degree of influence over the outcome of the trials in which they participate.[1] Learning this, one might immediately ask, "So do American prosecutors have less influence than their European counterparts?" Actually, though, in our "adversarial" system, fewer than 10 percent of all criminal cases go to trial—they are resolved through guilty pleas, which the American prosecutor can influence through his or her power to recommend sentencing.[2] In this way, the American prosecutor in fact has just as much, and likely more, power over the outcome than his European counterpart. In light of this, one might ask, "Should we be training our prosecutors to act as judges, as, say, the French do?" Such questions don't challenge any sacred American legal principle; they simply inquire about the relative strengths of alternative arrangements for the administration of the law.

Sometimes, however, discussions we've had can affect the way we understand our own solutions to legal problems entirely within our own system. Let me provide a few examples, beginning with one that presents the specter of what many critics of foreign law most fear: an American judge's approach to a particular legal problem being affected by the way foreign judges analyze a similar one. I believe that the discussions in question, far from harming, affirmatively helped my effort better to apply the Constitution in conformity with American values. But I leave it to the reader to make up his or her own mind.

EUROPEAN ANALYSIS

There is a legal concept often used by European and other foreign judges called proportionality. I have found it useful in describing and applying classical American rules of constitutional law. To explain how, I must first explain a few basic elements of First Amendment law, an area where proportionality can play an important role.

The First Amendment says that "Congress shall make no law . . . abridging the freedom of speech."[3] Aspiring to apply these words almost literally, Justice Black used to point to them and say, "'No law' means no law."[4] But even he had to agree that the words "abridging the freedom of speech" do not explain themselves. Justice Holmes observed that the amendment does not preclude laws that forbid patrons from shouting "fire" in a crowded theater,[5] or those barring an individual from directly inciting a riot, knowing in advance that it is likely to lead to the deaths of innocent people.[6] So what laws do the amendment's words prohibit? And how are judges to decide?

The Court has long recognized the impossibility of interpreting the amendment as treating all instances of speech alike. In fact, many varieties of speech are not free. We regulate speech when securities laws impose requirements upon what sales brochures can say; when health laws forbid tobacco advertising; when communications laws require cable systems to carry programs of stations that broadcast over the air; and when we limit the amount of money an individual can give to a politician's campaign. Since societies conduct virtually all their communal activities in speech, we could hardly carry on without some restrictions. But there has been variation in their severity. Too strong a version of the First Amendment could forbid laws regulating speech activities such as sales pitches related to pharmaceuticals or securities, calling to mind the days of *Lochner v. New York* (1905),[7] when the Court read the Constitution as forbidding much modern social legislation (in that case, a rule about work hours). But too weak a version of the First Amendment could permit government to regulate speech by forbidding unpopular political advertising, by censoring films or other works of art, by jailing antiwar protesters or others who favor unpopular causes, and so on. Assuming both those arrangements sound extreme, how do we distinguish among kinds of speech in applying the First Amendment?

The Court has developed three categories—a form of judge-made doctrine designed to facilitate the First Amendment's application. In the first, which is called "strict scrutiny," the Court places significant restrictions on laws that regulate political speech.[8] Since free political speech is critical to the "open marketplace" of ideas upon which democracy depends,[9] the Court has also said that it will scrutinize strictly any limits that distinguish among the "viewpoints" of different speakers[10] (for instance, a measure that would allow the speech of those who favor some legislative action while silencing their opponents). And it has said the same of all "content-based" limits—those based on the content of one's message, as against how it is expressed.[11] The Court has described "strict scrutiny" as forbidding a constraint on speech unless the government can show that it is *necessary* to *"promote a compelling Government interest"* and that *"less restrictive alternative[s]"* could not similarly promote that objective.[12] This test is hard to satisfy; hence to categorize a limitation as subject to "strict scrutiny" most often means that the Court will hold that it violates the First Amendment.[13]

The second category, called "intermediate scrutiny,"[14] includes restrictions on truthful commercial advertising.[15] The Court interprets the First Amendment as permitting this kind of regulation as long as "the State ... show[s] ... that the statute directly advances a substantial [as opposed to a "compelling"] governmental interest and that the measure is drawn to achieve that interest";[16] that is, the limitation "does not burden substantially more speech than necessary to further" that interest.[17]

The third category captures just about everything else, including government economic or social regulation. It would include, for instance, a law that, as part of a larger regulatory market scheme, requires a nectarine producer to contribute money to a fund used to advertise nectarines.[18] And it includes much traditional business regulation.[19] The Court has sometimes said that the First Amendment allows this kind of restriction as long as it rests upon a rational basis.[20] Hence its name "rational-basis scrutiny."

The three levels of "scrutiny," along with "content regulation" and "viewpoint regulation," are not the only categories that apply in free speech cases. The Court has written, for example, that "prior restraints on speech and publication [e.g., prohibiting in advance publication of *The Pentagon Papers*] are the most serious and the least tolerable infringement on First Amendment rights."[21] The Court has said it will review with "intermediate scrutiny" rules that simply limit the time, place, and manner in which a person or group can engage in expression[22] (such as might apply to sound trucks[23] adjacent to a school while classes are in session,[24] or in particular places at a fairground[25]). And it has said that certain forms of expression, such as child pornography, fall outside the First Amendment and enjoy no protection at all.[26]

Certainly this framework helps judges apply the First Amendment, reflecting its purposes and the values it means to protect. No one would argue for the categories' abandonment, but they are not, and cannot be, the whole story where the First Amendment is concerned. They are not so much ironclad precepts as judge-made rules of thumb, guiding the judge toward a conclusion without requiring him to adopt the one that the relevant category suggests. Rather, courts must supplement the guidance of categories with a form of balancing. And that is where proportionality comes in.

In the name of proportionality, foreign courts often practice a kind of balancing that is needed to decide cases in which general legislation comes into conflict with individual rights. Their analysis normally begins with questions very similar to those an American judge will ask when faced with a government law that restricts a basic right: (1) What kind of interest does the government's limitation seek to protect or to advance? How important is that interest? How legitimate? (2) What is the rational connection between the restriction and that objective? (3) Is there a less restrictive way to achieve that end?[27]

If answering those three questions does not resolve the case, the judge will ask a fourth: Does the limitation impose a restriction that is *disproportionate* to the legitimate interests the government seeks to achieve? To answer that one requires the judge explicitly to balance the harm to the protected interest (e.g., speech) against the need for the limitation to protect a critically important objective.[28]

The European Court of Justice, in a case involving economic interests and rights, put the matter this way:

> The Court has consistently held that the principle of proportionality is one of the general principles of [European] Community law. By virtue of that principle, the lawfulness of the prohibition of an economic activity is subject to the condition that the prohibitory measures are appropriate and necessary in order to achieve the objectives legitimately pursued by the legislation in question; when there is a choice between several appropriate measures recourse must be had to the least onerous, and the disadvantages caused must not be disproportionate to the aims pursued.[29]

In the case just cited, the ECJ was asked to determine whether a directive banning the use of certain hormones in livestock caused unwarranted injury to the economic rights of manufacturers, farmers, and others.[30] It applied proportionality analysis to conclude that the measure was valid; there was no way to achieve the law's objective "by means of less onerous measures," and "the importance of the objectives pursued is such as to justify even substantial negative financial consequences for certain traders."[31] The court relied not on the type of categorization often seen in American constitutional jurisprudence—particularly in the First Amendment area—but instead on balancing. And it made that balancing transparent and explicit.

Granted, the application of proportionality analysis may seem in part subjective; the judge inevitably considers countervailing effects, degrees of harm, and of importance. But even judges who explicitly write only in terms of categories are implicitly balancing harms and objectives. And where such is the case, I believe it is preferable to organize the balancing through a doctrine such as proportionality, thus making the calculus behind an opinion explicit so that it can be seen and criticized. By categories alone, we either pretend that the balancing does not exist amid our putatively objective criteria, or else we relegate it to the realm of unexpressed judicial impulse. I would favor adding the judge-made concept of proportionality as a guide in deciding First Amendment cases.

One must also realize that cases do not always fall neatly into categories. To take a recent example: a federal criminal statute forbade a person "falsely" to "represent[] himself or herself, verbally or in writing, to have been awarded any decoration or medal authorized by Congress for the Armed Forces of the United States."[32] An individual who had falsely claimed to have won the Congressional Medal of Honor was convicted of violating this statute.[33] Our Court then held (by a vote of six to three) that the statute violated the First Amendment.[34]

A plurality of four justices relied heavily upon categorization alone. It wrote that the First Amendment protects speech that is false as well as true; that the restriction, being "content-based," called for the "most exacting scrutiny," and that (by that measure) it violated the First Amendment.[35] In my view (expressed in a concurrence), less reliance upon category, and more upon balancing, would have produced a better analysis.[36] Can we simply say that the First Amendment protects false statements? Sometimes it does. Consider statements of religion, philosophy, history. "The earth is flat" would be protected irrespective of whether one believes it true or false. But sometimes it does not. Consider false commercial speech, fraud, perjury, false claims of terrorist attack, impersonation of police officials, trademark infringement, and other instances where protection would be unwarranted.[37] Looking at the matter through the lens of proportionality, I would have certainly considered the First Amendment interest harmed by the regulation to be significant: the statute focuses upon statements that are often made in a political context, and the statute might inhibit such expression. At the same time, it finds a strong offsetting justification in the need to preserve the integrity of the nation's highest awards for military valor. Still, less restrictive alternatives would seem to be available, perhaps a statute covering a narrower range of military decorations, requiring a showing of harm, and accompanied with a creation of a publicly available register of awards.[38] Although the result is the same, I believe such analysis goes more directly to the legal heart of the matter.

The use of proportionality can also help to avoid constitutional anomalies. Consider *Sorrell v. IMS Health Inc.*[39] Vermont enacted a statute forbidding pharmacies from selling records identifying doctors by the medicines they prescribed.[40] It did so fearing that the sale of this information to pharmaceutical companies would allow their sales forces to tailor pitches to individual doctors (in light of the drugs they normally used) with the aim of getting them to prescribe more high-priced branded drugs and fewer low-priced generics.[41] The drug companies complained that this law violated their First Amendment rights[42]—that is, their freedom to tailor their sales pitch as they wished.

Our Court decided the case by categorizing the statute as a "content-based" restraint, subject to "heightened scrutiny."[43] And the majority struck it down as insufficiently justified.[44] In dissent, I questioned whether the "content-based" category (warranting "heightened scrutiny") was right, suggesting rather that this expression should be assigned to the "economic regulation" category (warranting the more relaxed "rational basis" standard). After all, economic regulations routinely impose restrictions on the basis of content. Electricity regulators oversee the content of energy company proposals, the Federal Reserve Board oversees the content of banks' loan proposals, the Food and Drug Administration oversees the content of labels, and so forth.[45]

Rather than debate the category, if the Court had instead reasoned in terms of proportionality, it might have found that category did not make so much difference. Without rejecting the potential relevance of the "content-based" versus "economic regulation" restrictions, it could have considered the nature of the protected interest (a sales pitch); the harm caused due to a drug company's inability to obtain information (in my view, not much); and the justification for the regulation (lower prices). It would have then asked whether Vermont might have achieved that objective less restrictively. (No one showed that it could have done so.) And that would likely have been the end of the matter: little harm, reasonable justification, no obvious less restrictive alternative.

Of course, following that method, my view of the case would likely have prevailed. But even if not, the analysis would have required the Court to compare other instances of economic regulation, to spell out the nature of the harm more precisely, and to consider the state legislature's views of the matter more closely. The resulting opinion would have been written with reasoning more directly aimed at the purposes of the laws in question, both the First Amendment and the Vermont statute. As such, the opinion would have had greater explanatory and persuasive power.

Further, the use of "proportionality" would often lead the Court to examine more closely the details of how the statute was applied. That too, I believe, would produce results more consistent with the First

Amendment's purposes. Consider *Holder v. Humanitarian Law Project,*
a case decided a year before the Court decided the prescription drug
case *Sorrell.*[46] A federal law forbade individuals from "provid[ing] material support or resources to a foreign terrorist organization."[47] The statute defined *material support* as including "expert advice or assistance."[48]
A group of Americans (including a retired administrative law judge)
wished to help a Kurdish group that was on the State Department's
"terrorist" watch list with "expert advice or assistance" but could not
do so for fear of prosecution by the government. The intended advice
or assistance consisted of (1) training in the use of "humanitarian and
international law to peacefully resolve disputes," (2) "engag[ing] in political advocacy on behalf of Kurds who live in Turkey," and (3) explaining "how to petition various representative bodies such as the United
Nations for relief."[49]

Holding that the statute was constitutional, the Court majority
said it could be applied to the three peaceful activities just mentioned,[50]
arguing that the "interest in combating terrorism is an urgent objective
of the highest order."[51] It further concluded that, given the difficulty of
separating peaceful from nonpeaceful activities, the application of the
law to peaceful ends was justified in the effort to combat terrorism.[52]
The dissenters (of which I was one) pointed out that the law restricted
political speech (thus warranting "strict scrutiny"); we agreed that combating terrorism was a "compelling" countervailing interest; but we did
not believe the government had presented any evidence that the restriction (as applied, for example, to petitioning the United Nations) was
necessary to further that interest.[53] In a word, application of the restriction here *disproportionately* restricted speech.

Foreign courts that work with the concept of proportionality often
perform such close circumstance-specific analysis. Had our Court done
so here, I believe (as I said in the dissent) that it would not have upheld
a statute forbidding what is a form of political speech—namely, teaching a minority political group how to petition the United Nations for
redress.

At the least, to consider proportionality brings to the surface
and makes explicit the judicial balancing that is frequently called for
when there are important interests on both sides of a legal question—
sometimes even conflicting individual rights—say, free speech versus

personal privacy. Imagine a law that forbids recording private conversations applied to a recording made of labor leaders discussing a strike. Can the press (which did not participate in making the recording) print that conversation, in accordance with the First Amendment, or would the Amendment allow it to be suppressed? Whatever categories the Court uses to resolve this problem, it ultimately will have to balance "privacy" and "free speech" interests. In some form or other, the judge will have to ask: Does the statute as applied here impose a restriction on speech that is disproportionate to its benefits to privacy, taking into account the kind, the importance, and the extent of those benefits, as well as the need for the restrictions in order to secure them?

However useful, then, categories such as "strict scrutiny," "content regulation," and even "compelling interest" and "less restrictive means" cannot by themselves resolve many of the difficult constitutional questions that appear before us. Many cases involve significant and competing constitutional interests relating to one another in complex ways. The Court has often scrutinized a statute's impact on those interests, and it has balanced them.[54] That has entailed asking whether the statute necessarily burdens any one such interest in a manner that is disproportionate to the statute's salutary effects upon others. Indeed, proportionality analysis itself is neither foreign nor new. Many great American judges, including Learned Hand,[55] Felix Frankfurter,[56] and Louis D. Brandeis,[57] among others, have engaged in balancing. It has a long history in American constitutional law.

Compared to categorization, this kind of analysis is sometimes complex and difficult. But what is the alternative? Today's Court should not base its answers to the kinds of questions illustrated here by referring solely to the facts and circumstances of eighteenth-century society. Nor should a judge have to rely on his or her own unexamined intuitions about a proper balance. Far preferable to the pretense of objectivity afforded by blunt categories is an opinion that must spell out in some detail just how the balance, admittedly subjective, was achieved.

Foreign courts, as I say, routinely use the proportionality concept, and so through discussions with foreign judges, professors, and lawyers, Americans can better understand its strengths and weaknesses as well as its relevance in American legal contexts. These occasions have helped me clarify how the analysis works, the need for precision in using it, and even the possibility of avoiding the ultimate balancing question by properly answering the preceding questions about interests, harms, and alternatives.

It bears emphasizing that such discussions do not involve advocacy of or any sort of campaigning for the adoption of foreign ways; their value is in the thoughts they provoke, the questions asked, and the "relics" (to use Oakeshott's term) they leave in the minds of the participants. They have not led me to abandon categorization, which must also play an important role in constitutional analysis. Rather, they have helped me understand how to apply balancing in the American context. They have helped show how constitutional analysis can become more precise and transparent and thereby help to clarify American law.

AMERICAN ANALYSIS

The conversation among judges can also prove useful in the other direction—with tools from American judicial experience proving useful to foreign judges. One example is the way in which our Supreme Court has interpreted the American Constitution's Commerce Clause as compared with its European equivalent. The Commerce Clause grants to Congress the power to "regulate commerce with foreign nations, and among the several states."[58] One of its major objectives is the creation and maintenance of a national market. Consistent with this objective, the Court has interpreted the Clause as forbidding states to enact laws that unduly interfere with the operation of national or international markets.[59] The Court refers to this aspect of the clause as the "dormant Commerce Clause," for its prohibitions apply in the absence of congressional legislation.[60]

In applying the dormant Commerce Clause, the Court must decide just when a state law *unduly* interferes with interstate commerce. And that is often easier said than done. On the one hand, a state cannot discriminate against goods or services coming from out of state.[61] On the other hand, the clause does not forbid states "'from legislating on all subjects relating to the health, life, and safety of their citizens, though the legislation might indirectly affect'" commerce.[62] "Nondiscriminatory regulations" are valid as long as they "have only incidental effects on interstate commerce" and do not impose a burden on commerce that "is clearly excessive in relation to the putative local benefits."[63] So how does the Court decide which state laws are which?

The European Court of Justice faces somewhat similar problems. The treaties that have created the European Union forbid member nations to impose "[q]uantitative restrictions on imports and all measures having equivalent effect";[64] the agreements also establish the rights of free movement of workers,[65] services,[66] and capital[67] among those nations. At the same time, the treaties allow member nations to enact laws protecting, for example, health, safety, and the environment, provided that the law does not disproportionately discriminate against goods or services coming from other member nations.[68] How does the European Court of Justice tell the two kinds of member-nation laws apart?

There are no easy answers to this question, or to the similar one facing American courts. Although we often defer to legislative judgment when economic questions are involved, we cannot do so here. That is because the legislature, whether of an American state or a European nation, has no electoral motive for taking into account the interests of voters in other states against whose goods or services the local law may discriminate. To the contrary, those legislators may have a clear electoral interest in discriminating against producers from outside the state and thereby favoring their own producers. That is the very legislative tendency that the dormant Commerce Clause and the European treaty provisions seek to attack.

Nor can courts necessarily resolve the problem by looking for discrimination on the face of a statute. Consider a Swiss law uniformly forbidding the sale of milk produced by farmers (Swiss or non-Swiss) with cows pastured at altitudes lower than ten thousand feet. That law says it applies uniformly, but in fact it would discriminate against virtually all milk producers except the Swiss.

The laws that come before our courts can present the same sort of problem but far more subtly; often they are very technical, and their merits depend heavily upon facts. A law might prohibit bringing into a state peaches grown with the use of a certain pesticide. Or it might require the use of special steel for elevator cables, or prohibit interstate trucks from transporting dynamite during daytime. Are these laws designed primarily to protect the state's citizens from, respectively, dangerous pesticides, substandard elevators, or risks of an explosion? Or are they primarily designed to protect a state's producers from out-of-state competition?

The Court has examined these matters independently—that is, without deference to the state legislature's judgment. It has looked to the facts. And in a sense, it has weighed the evidence. But in doing so, it has recognized its comparative lack of expertise in fact-based technical matters. It has consequently provided an escape hatch. Congress remains free to overturn a court decision by enacting *federal* legislation. Indeed, Congress can authorize a state to reenact the very law that the Court has struck down. More than that, Congress can delegate this authority to an administrative agency. Thus the federal Department of Transportation might have the last word as to whether a state's dynamite transportation law unduly interferes with the national market. The department might authorize the state to keep the law. And if so, the courts would review the department's decision only for administrative error, determining, for example, whether the decision is "arbitrary, capricious, an abuse of discretion."[69]

This tripartite arrangement permits the Court to work cooperatively with both the legislative and the executive branches of government, taking advantage of their comparative expertise and thereby improving the application of a fundamental constitutional principle, that of American federalism.

The European Court of Justice has faced similar problems. Consider a recent, difficult case.[70] When Laval, a Latvian employer, wanted to bring Latvian workers to Sweden to work on a school, a Swedish trade union tried to negotiate a higher wage for them. When Laval refused to accept the proposed terms, the union went on strike (blocking Laval's construction sites).[71] And Swedish law authorizes that strike. But did the strike violate the European Union treaty provision that insists upon "freedom to provide services within the Community"?[72]

The court held that the strike did violate the treaty. That was because, as authorized, the action made it "less attractive, or more difficult" for businesses from outside Sweden "to carry out construction work in Sweden."[73] The court added that a restriction on the "freedom to provide services" is lawful "only if it pursues a legitimate objective compatible with the Treaty and is justified by overriding reasons of public interest."[74] Moreover, it "must be suitable for securing the attainment of the objective which it pursues and not go beyond what is necessary in order to attain it."[75] Because Laval had already paid its workers the EU's minimum wage, and because the union's proposed arrangement made it too difficult to determine what he would have to pay, the union's strike failed the test.[76]

The ECJ's test, though strict, is general, leaving decisions to turn on a case's particular facts. In this respect, the European legal problem is similar to the American "dormant Commerce Clause" problem. How can the courts know enough about particular, often technical areas, to reconcile general quasi-constitutional rules that favor free movement with laws of member nations designed to protect health, safety, the environment, and other important local interests? Perhaps in this area, European courts will find American experience helpful and look for ways to bring European legislative bodies into the process.

PROCEDURE

A third example of useful discussions pertains to interactions between American judges and their counterparts in India. During the last half century, both nations have seen the number of their court cases grow steadily. In the United States, the caseload of the federal trial courts alone grew from about 127,000 cases filed in 1970[77] to more than 375,000 in 2013.[78] During the same period, one federal appellate circuit saw its docket grow from around 1,500 cases per year[79] to more than 9,000.[80] Meanwhile, the Supreme Court of India saw its docket increase from about 7,000 cases filed annually to more than 37,000 over the same interval.[81] And the Indian judicial system as a whole had, by 2008, developed a backlog of close to 30 million undecided cases.[82]

Backlogs mean delay, expense, and injustice, so it is important to reduce them. And there are only three basic ways to do so. One can cut down on "intake" by reducing the kinds of cases that the judicial system will handle. One can widen the "pipeline" by appointing more judges. Or one can handle cases more efficiently. Each approach has its drawbacks. The first risks unfairly closing courthouse doors. The second risks the creation of too complex a judicial system. And the third runs up against limitations of time and fairness.

In the United States, we have tried all three approaches to some degree. The federal system has often emphasized the third, many federal courts having developed a system of judicial "case management." The judge, often with the help of a federal magistrate, tries early on to focus the parties upon the main issues in a case, to limit the use of discovery, to set firm trial dates, and to sanction the parties for unreasonable delays. Courts have also endorsed alternative dispute resolution (ADR). ADR can mean sending the disputing parties to experienced lawyers or retired judges, who will evaluate the claim, thus encouraging settlement. It can be done with arbitrators, who will produce a binding decision outside the courtroom, or mediators, who, without binding the parties, help them find a basis for settlement, perhaps a middle ground. Successful ADR will provide less expensive and speedier ways to resolve disputes.

Beginning in the 1980s, India and several other South Asian nations began to experiment with the use of ADR. In 1994 former chief justice A. M. Ahmadi of the Indian Supreme Court met with two members of our Court, Justices Scalia and Ginsburg, who discussed the use of ADR in the United States. Two years later Chief Justice Ahmadi organized a National Judicial Academy Study Group, which worked together with an American nonprofit, the Institute for the Study and Development of Legal Systems, to produce a study regarding possible reform of the civil justice system.[83] The group held conferences in Delhi, Mumbai, Calcutta, Chennai, and Hyderabad; it met with numerous Indian lawyers and judges; it spent several weeks in the United States learning about American systems of case management and ADR; and it produced papers, studies, and reports, eventually recommending the use of case management and voluntary ADR in India.[84]

The recommendation proved controversial. Many lawyers and judges favored the use of these systems, but others feared that their use would prove unfair, reducing attorney compensation and threatening to deprive many Indian citizens of lawyers. In 2001 Justice O'Connor and I, along with former Ninth Circuit chief judge Clifford Wallace, visited India. At that time ADR was under consideration, but it was not being implemented. We discussed ADR programs and issues with members of the Indian Supreme Court. We described the strengths and weaknesses of ADR in light of the American experience. And we listened as the justices talked about how America's systems might be modified to fit India as well as how the Supreme Court of India might monitor ADR's implementation.

The subsequent developments were impressive. In 2002 India finally put into effect a change to its procedural codes to allow ADR.[85] The Indian Supreme Court later held that change to be constitutional.[86] Private mediation programs were developed in Ahmedabad, Mumbai, Chennai, and Madurai,[87] and in 2005 pilot programs began in the Delhi trial courts.[88] As of 2014, the ADR program in one city, Delhi, had settled about 29,000 cases.[89] Other mediation centers had begun to resolve cases as well.[90]

Although the credit for these legal and programmatic developments goes to the Indian legal professionals involved, I believe that our meetings helped to build confidence in adopting a modified ADR system. The discussions at the least permitted members of India's court to demonstrate to the legal public the seriousness of the study they were making of the backlog problem. For instance, in 2003 Justice M. Jagannadha Rao presented a paper at the International Conference on ADR and Case Management, which was held in New Delhi. He observed that the United States, among other countries, had adopted systems of ADR despite initial resistance from the bar and from some judges. "[G]radually," he wrote, "once the systems were implemented, the Bar and the Bench found that litigants did benefit enormously in terms of time and money." In the United States, the settlement rate rose and "[c]onciliation or mediation became very popular." To Justice Rao, the success of ADR in America led to one obvious question: "Would [c]onciliation and [m]ediation succeed in [Indian] Courts?"[91] I believe that the judicial and other legal exchanges helped to bring India's judges and lawyers to the point where they could answer Justice Rao's question in the affirmative.

Returning to the larger subject, let us consider other procedural matters that we have discussed. Judges of foreign courts, for example, often want to know how we conduct our case screening, a process that (like those of the British[92] and French[93] supreme courts) reduces the number of potential cases to the handful that the Supreme Court fully considers each year. We explain that state law, not federal law, accounts overwhelmingly for the lion's share of laws in the United States. (Almost all domestic relations law, and most criminal law, business law, accident law, education law, and even environmental law is state law.) And our Court considers only matters of federal law, including the federal Constitution.

Even so, each year we receive about eight thousand petitions for full hearings,[94] but in each case the litigants have already obtained a decision from a district court and review by an appeals court. We see our function, in the words of Chief Justice William Howard Taft, as being "for the purpose of expounding and stabilizing principles of law for the benefit of the people of the country, passing upon constitutional questions and other important questions of law for the public benefit. [And] [i]t is to preserve uniformity of decision among the intermediate courts of appeal."[95]

Thus we divide the petitions for full hearing (about 150 per week) among thirty or so staff members (our law clerks), who each write memoranda summarizing about five petitions per week. We consequently receive a stack of about 150 memoranda per week; we go through the stack, examining with particular care those that appear to raise questions of law that have divided the lower courts; where necessary, we go back to the original documents; and at our weekly conference we discuss any case that any member of the Court wishes to be discussed. We hear any case that four or more justices vote to hear, and that will generally include any case in which a lower court held a federal statute unconstitutional.

How, we are often asked, do we square this screening system with the average citizen's belief that, at the end of the day, he or she can appeal to the Supreme Court? That question has no logical answer, but it does have a practical one. Appellate judges, in my experience, can themselves write no more than forty to fifty full opinions in a year. And to try to produce significantly more would entail opinions written by staff, or simple statements of conclusions, or the like. So what is the point of trying to decide hundreds of cases per year? It cannot be done, at least not with as much thought, analysis, and full expression of reasons that typify the best appellate court work. That being so, I would opt for not claiming to accomplish more than you actually can. To do otherwise breeds public cynicism, which ultimately erodes respect for the courts. That the American public generally accepts our findings provides some evidence for that point of view.

Some judges agree with this reasoning; others do not. And so the conversation continues.

Another procedural topic that judges from different countries often discuss with shared interest concerns the merits of writing dissenting opinions. Some dissents wind up persuading a majority, in which case they are transformed into opinions of the Court. But what about the others? By pointing out flaws in a majority draft opinion, a dissent can lead to revisions of that opinion, modifying the ways in which it states the law. A dissent can thereby lead to a better-reasoned holding, which strengthens the Court's standing, producing greater public acceptance for judicial work. A dissent may also ultimately lead Congress (in a statutory case) to enact a new measure changing the law; it can even help to bring about constitutional change at a later time.

On the other hand, as French judges often point out, a single opinion may lead the public to believe that a court's statement of the law reflects not simply the views of a few individual judges but the law itself. The need for a single opinion can also bring about a more reasonable or acceptable result by forcing members of a court to understand and see one another's points of view and ultimately to compromise. It avoids the distinctly American "cult of the individual judge," which sees an opinion as reflecting "the Constitution according to Justice X or Justice Y" rather than "the Constitution according to the Supreme Court of the United States." And in some instances, where a judge is subject to reappointment by a national government (as is true of the European Court of Justice), anonymity can free him or her from potential political pressures.

In my own view, the appearance of unanimity where it does not exist is not helpful, either to the law or to a court's standing. The public always suspects disagreement; it builds trust to acknowledge differences rather than to hide them. But this is just one view. Others disagree. And so the conversation continues.

Of procedural questions, there is no end of topics. British judges, for instance, like some American ones, do not use legislative history when interpreting statutes. Will that tendency continue, particularly as British courts increasingly find themselves interpreting statutes enacted by foreign legislatures with different drafting traditions? Will European judges start to put greater weight upon a statute's purposes, as they are more frequently called to interpret the laws of other nations with legislatures that do not use the same statutory drafting conventions as their own? I suspect so. . . . Should Supreme Court opinions be shorter? I think they should be, but that is easier said than done. . . . Should an opinion reveal its reasoning or just state the conclusion? As one might imagine, I vote for reasoning. . . . Should the opinion answer every argument the parties make? Though many courts, including the International Court of Justice, try to do so, I think it better not to try, for brevity's sake but also because silence too has its purposes. . . . Should oral arguments be longer or shorter? I find ours are too short, though in the United Kingdom they are perhaps too long—but that is just one judge's opinion. . . . Should the table at which the justices sit when they confer privately be round, as in Canada, or rectangular, as in the United States? I should prefer round, for I suspect, though cannot prove, that a round table would produce a better discussion.

My point here is not to address the merits of different procedures but to give the flavor of judicial discussions. As I said at the outset, they are no more than discussions: there is no debate; no winner and no loser; no effort to convince; and there is no vote. There is only an exchange of information and ideas, an open invitation for each judge to consider his or her own system in light of others. The result is a broadening of vision. I find those conversations valuable.

CHAPTER 12

Advancing the Rule of Law

The interchange among judges, lawyers, and law students can help build support for a more basic goal, furthering the rule of law itself. Ever since King John's barons forced him to sign the Magna Carta at Runnymede eight hundred years ago, that document has symbolized the importance of governments' acting only according to "the law of the land."[1] That rule of law prevents its opposite—namely the arbitrary, the capricious, the autocratic, the despotic, the unreasonable, the dictatorial, the illegal, the unjust, and the tyrannical. But judges and lawyers, law professors and law students, all understand this. So how does it help if they talk about it among themselves? Some examples:

Several members of our Court, including Justice Kennedy, Justice Scalia, Justice Ginsburg, and Justice O'Connor, have participated in conversations about law in China. In 2002 I traveled to China as part of a delegation, arranged by the Yale Law School's China Law Center, for the purpose of discussing administrative law and regulation. Our Chinese counterparts were well versed in the subject and, among other things, saw in administrative law a method of preventing arbitrary action by regional government authorities.

In 2012 I spoke about constitutional law to a group of law students and faculty at Tsinghua University's Law School in Beijing. The audience revealed considerable depth of knowledge about the United States' legal system. They understood perfectly well, and they ably discussed, the value of a constitution, of democratic forms of government, of protection of human rights, and of an independent judicial system. They wanted to know how such a legal system could be developed in China—but without risking anarchy or chaos along the way. Our discussion was interesting and encouraging but highly general.

In late November 2012 I spoke at a Brookings Institution seminar in Washington with He Weifang, a Chinese law professor and the author of a recent book on the rule of law in China.[2] In 2009 Professor He had signed a manifesto arguing for democracy, human rights, and a rule of law, resulting in his exile for two years to a small city in Xinjiang. On his return to Beijing, he wrote a letter criticizing the authority of Bo Xilai, the party secretary of Chongqing, and his chief of police, thereby risking retaliation and further punishment. But as the professor pointed out, by 2012 he was in Washington speaking freely, while the target of his criticism, the party secretary, was in a Chinese jail. China, he said, is perfectly capable of developing increased protection of human rights.

Jerome Cohen, a great American expert on China, made a similar point. He described the current Chinese practice of deciding important legal cases in advance, through meetings among the local prosecutor, the head of the court, and a high-ranking Communist Party official—namely, the chief of police. Their decisions typically become the decisions of the courts. Professor Cohen also pointed to the fact that acquittal in a criminal case did not always mean freedom for the defendant. The local police chief retained the power to send the acquitted defendant out of the city to a work camp in the countryside. Cohen noted that Taiwan had long followed the same kind of practice, but Taiwan had recently changed the system, abolishing the party's interference and the practice of police chiefs imposing countryside transfer penalties. Thus change was not impossible.

Professor He thought that legal reform in China would have to involve transferring power and authority from the party to members of the National People's Congress; permitting the party to nominate, but not to select, court presidents; eliminating party interference in individual cases; reducing the power of court presidents and of chief prosecutors; and establishing a new system of constitutional review, with a constitutional court.

What can a practicing judge add to this conversation among China experts? In this context, an American judge can speak to basic but more specific rules, procedures, and institutions that work well in the United States and might help China find the desired path. The fact that a few may seem technical in nature may make them less politically controversial, thereby helping to make them more useful to those in China who hope to move in the direction of a "rule of law."

We discussed a few, for example:

• A Magna Carta supplement well known to administrative lawyers: All laws must be public. If a law is not public, it is not a law. A government official cannot punish first and make up the legal rule afterward.

• No *ex parte* communications with a judge. With a few exceptions, this technical-sounding rule bars government officials (and others) from conferring with a judge about a case without the other side being present. Thus meaningful communications normally take place in public, and the public can be made aware of what is happening.

• Minimum guarantees of due process of law: a neutral decision maker, an opportunity to present proofs and arguments, and an opportunity to hear the proofs and arguments of the other side.

• Habeas corpus. This ancient British legal writ enables any imprisoned person who can get word to a judge to insist that the judge summon the jailer and demand to know the legal basis for imprisonment. For hundreds of years this writ has helped to prevent arbitrary imprisonment, thereby helping to sustain a rule of law.

• Independence of the press, of lawyers, and of judges. An independent press, despite potential for abuse, is a necessity, for without the press, the public is not informed, and only an informed public can guarantee a rule of law. An independent bar is one whose members will freely (but politely) say to the judge, "Judge, you are wrong," without fear of adverse consequences. Judicial independence is the contrary of what judges in Communist Russia used to call "telephone justice," whereby the party boss would call the judge and dictate the result of a particular case. "Why did we do it?," I once heard one Russian judge ask another. "You know perfectly well why" was the reply. "We needed an apartment to live in, food on the table, schools for our children. And the party controlled them."

Financial security and tenure, *ex parte* communications rules, and the like all help produce judicial independence, but they cannot guarantee the creation or the survival of that institution. Rather, as Justice Kennedy once said to a group of Russian judges, independence is a state of mind. Only the judge knows if he or she has dealt honestly with the facts of a case, ruled without regard to what the press (for instance) would say, worked through the details, and spent the time and effort necessary to reach a proper result. The challenge for China, as for every country, is to create an environment that can help produce that state of mind. Compensation, job security, a free bar, and a free press all can help, but they cannot guarantee the necessary independence of the institution.

I have tried to capture the flavor of what I consider a productive discussion. Such discussions cannot by themselves bring about change. But they can, for example, break down larger problems, such as how to establish the rule of law, into more manageable, technical components, like *ex parte* communications rules. Lawyers and judges are good at such breakdowns. And their input can help show countries such as China that the choice needn't be as stark as "repression" on the one hand or "full blown democracy with human rights guarantees" on the other. There are many ways to advance toward human rights, and discussing the different ways may increase the likelihood that the journey will be undertaken.

A second example consists of a conversation in January 2012 with professors, students, and constitutional authorities in Tunis. It took place via the Internet, with me at an American law school and the others in a Tunis classroom. Portions of the transcript (which I have edited) can help convey the gist of the questions and answers:

STUDENT (YOUNG WOMAN): Our constitution has always sounded fine, but our problem is whether the government will respect it. Do we need a supreme court here to be sure the government will respect the constitution?

SB: The Founders of our nation believed the Constitution would work better if an independent group of judges—not the President and not Congress—could decide whether the President's actions and the laws enacted by Congress were consistent with the Constitution.

It has taken a long time for us to get to the point where the American public has thought it natural to follow what the judges say in those circumstances. I believe a key moment was when, in 1957, President Eisenhower sent paratroopers to enforce the order of a judge that nine black children integrate an all-white school in Little Rock, Arkansas. A few years earlier the Supreme Court had said the Constitution requires treating black and white citizens alike and there can be no separation based on race. But not much happened until the President sent the troops to enforce the order. Even then it took many years to dismantle racial segregation in the South. And it took the participation of many Americans who were not lawyers or judges but were ordinary citizens. That is why I believe you must help the ordinary citizens of the country to understand the importance of a rule of law.

STUDENT (YOUNG WOMAN): You spoke of your Constitution being written at the right level of abstraction. What did you mean?

SB: On the one hand, the Constitution creates institutions for governing through a democratic system. Many of those provisions must be specific, for example, that the House of Representatives is based on representation by population, and that population is determined by a census that takes place every ten years. On the other hand, the Constitution embodies basic values that must endure over time, such as freedom of expression, equality, and a rule of law. The words embodying those values must be general, for even though the values do not change over time, the circumstances to which they apply change often. George Washington did not know about the Internet, but the value of "free speech" must apply to the Internet. That is what our great Chief Justice

John Marshall meant when he wrote, "It is a constitution we are expounding."

STUDENT (YOUNG MAN): What makes a judge independent?

SB: We have guarantees in our Constitution—that a federal judge cannot be removed from office (except for bad behavior) during his or her lifetime and that his pay cannot be diminished (though inflation reduces the value of this guarantee). These guarantees help. A federal judge, for example, does not normally expect to be promoted to a higher position (or demoted). But these guarantees are far from the whole story. The habits and customs, not just of judges but of the people of the country, help, too. They expect judges to decide independently; judges, then, when they become judges, try to live up to this expectation. That is why I say that ordinary people, not just jurists, must understand the value of a rule of law, which includes judicial independence. Lawyers and judges and law students too can help for they can speak to the press, to the public, about what they see as the value of a rule of law.

STUDENT (YOUNG WOMAN): What is your opinion of the problem of religion? Do you believe that some will put religious values into the Constitution? And will they then try to impose those values on others, depriving them of the benefits of other rights that are in the Constitution? Can the Constitution be threatened by [religious] conservatives who try to impose their religious values on others?

SB: (The light dawns! She is concerned that a new government might forbid her, for example, to become a lawyer. What should I say? Here is my effort.) I know that in Europe in the seventeenth century people fought terrible wars of religion. Eventually they reached a compromise. In England they decided to follow a principle: "You practice your religion (and teach it to your children), and I shall practice mine." This is the principle of freedom of religion. It was the font from which many other liberties, including free speech, sprang. Later, we in America adopted that constitutional principle and added to it a principle of separation of Church and State: the government cannot become too involved in religion. It is rather like the French principle of *laicism*.

Whether, or how, you in Tunisia decide to adopt similar principles, or reach other solutions, is, of course, up to you, for you cannot simply copy what we have done, but you can learn from us and adapt what you learn to your circumstances. I would add that we have more recently come to the conclusion that the Constitution protects equality among the sexes. The law must show equal respect to men and to women, treating them alike. I say this because I believe that the role of women will prove important in your country particularly in solving the problems to which you allude. That is to say, I understand your concerns, I have no pat answers, but you do have my sympathetic support. I believe that ultimately it must be up to you and to the others in your classroom today to help solve the problem that you raise.

STUDENT (YOUNG WOMAN): How can we prevent the judge from deciding arbitrarily, perhaps on political grounds?

SB: That is the kind of question I often receive from American students. My answer is that judges, at least some federal judges, have political experience and may personally favor one party or another. But once they put on the judge's robes, they are politically neutral. They do not favor one party or another. I have not seen judges try to act politically in the true sense of the word *politics*—Are you a Republican or a Democrat? Which party is more popular? Where are the votes?

But there is a different concept, often confused with the first: Do the judges act ideologically? Are they committed to a theory of, say, laissez-faire liberalism or socialism? Here the answer is still no. But it can sometimes happen. Still, if a judge thinks he is acting ideologically, he knows he is doing the wrong thing and will try to stop.

Then there is a third concept, which sometimes does explain why people think the judges act politically. Many great constitutional questions have unclear answers: the word *liberty* in the Fourteenth Amendment does not explain itself. Nor does the First Amendment phrase "the freedom of speech." In interpreting these open phrases, a judge may in part have to face the fact that he cannot jump out of his own skin, he cannot escape his own background, and he is guided by a highly general jurisprudential philosophy that he will likely have accepted over the course of many professional years. I went to public schools in San Francisco; I grew up during the 1950s; I am inevitably the lawyer I am. That means in respect to views about the nature of the Constitution or of law, their relation to the people of the United States, and the way in which law affects people, I cannot escape my own general views. Law is not computer science, and those views matter. That is why it is a good thing, in a country as diverse as ours, with well over three hundred million people, that different judges have different general jurisprudential views. I should add that judges serve long terms, but over time different presidents will appoint different judges with different highly general jurisprudential views. The Court can change its nature very slowly over time. And in a few cases it can reflect, in a highly abstract general sense, the nature of the country.

Obviously, this exchange does not provide solutions to the problems posed, which are complex and whose remedy in any context would take time, but its spirit does show how the support of professional jurists in our nation can encourage the advancement of the rule of law in another.

A third example is a conversation I had with the president of the Supreme Court of Ghana, who was visiting Washington. It elaborates on one of the answers I gave the Tunisian students and which I have given to many students in America. The president of the Ghana court had been working with others in Ghana trying to solidify a rule of law, along with democracy and the protection of human rights. "Why," she asked me, "do the people of the United States do what you say? Why do they follow the decisions of your Court, particularly when those decisions are highly unpopular?"

It was a question perhaps foreseen by Alexander Hamilton, who recognized more than two hundred years ago that the judiciary was weak, lacking the powers of the purse and of the sword.[3] That was one reason he thought it a safe place to lodge the power to review the constitutionality of democratically enacted laws (rather than leaving the job to the President, who would thereby become too powerful, or to Congress, which might refuse to follow the Constitution where doing so was unpopular).[4] But being weak, how can the judiciary enforce its decisions? How does it keep itself from seeming a source of mysterious bluster like Shakespeare's Owen Glendower, the Welsh general, who boasts to Hotspur, "I can call spirits from the vasty deep." "Why, so can I," responds Hotspur, a practical Englishman. "[S]o can any man. But will they come when you do call for them?"[5]

There is no "secret," no single miraculous reason why the rulings of our Court are followed. There is only the accretion of customs, habits, and understandings about the rule of law, built and maintained over the course of many years. The United States, which now has little need to think about the question, in fact has a history during which the answer was long in doubt. The best answer I could give to the president of Ghana's court was to describe for her a few relevant incidents from that history. (I have devoted a previous book to considering these examples in depth.)[6]

The first goes back to the 1830s. The Cherokee tribe owned land in northern Georgia. After gold was found in their territory, the Georgians seized the land. A challenge to the seizure eventually reached the Supreme Court, and the Court held that the land belonged to the Indians.[7] But Andrew Jackson, then President of the United States, supposedly said of John Marshall, then chief justice, "John Marshall has made his decision; now, let him enforce it."[8] And later in that decade Jackson sent federal troops to Georgia, not to enforce the decision of the Court but to evict the Indians. They were forced to travel thousands of miles to Oklahoma, where their descendants live to this day.[9]

Consider a second, happier instance. In 1954 the Court decided, in the case of *Brown v. Board of Education,* that the Constitution of the United States forbids racial segregation, such as existed in the South, where it had been authorized by law.[10] But the South resisted. When a federal judge ordered integration in Little Rock, the governor of Arkansas, Orville Faubus, refused. He called out the National Guard and gave them orders not to let the black schoolchildren enter the white school.[11]

This time, however, the President of the United States, Dwight Eisenhower, responded differently. He decided to send in parachutists from the 101st Airborne Division, the division noted for its heroism during the World War II invasion of Normandy.[12] The paratroopers took the brave young black schoolchildren into the white school—as the world watched through the eyes of the press and its photographers.[13] It took longer since that dramatic day than one might think, but eventually legal racial segregation was ended, and that was a great victory for the rule of law.

A third instance is more recent. Following the 2000 presidential election, the Court decided *Bush v. Gore,* a case that might have affected, or at least would have been thought to affect, the outcome.[14] The decision was important to millions of Americans; it was unpopular among roughly half of them.[15] Judges, being human, can err. I thought (and wrote) that the Court got that one wrong.[16] But that is not my point here.

The most interesting comment on the decision was made by the former Senate majority leader, Harry Reid, a Democrat and therefore a supporter of the litigant who lost the case. He pointed out that despite the controversial nature of the finding, its importance, and the fact that many Americans thought it seriously flawed, there were no riots in the streets, no gunshots, no deaths.[17] The public collectively accepted a decision many thought was wrong. And that fact is much to the credit of the American nation. It is testament to the long road Americans have traveled toward acceptance of a rule of law. It suggests that, despite a history that includes slavery, racial segregation, and a host of other horrors, more than 315 million people have learned to live together under law.

I offer these examples because I want my friend and colleague from Ghana to see what I see—namely, that it is not judges and jurists alone who must work for the acceptance of a rule of law. To establish that rule, and to maintain it, must be the work of ordinary citizens as well. It is not an easy task to enlist those in the villages, the towns, and the cities in such a cause; the time and effort of every human being is limited. Nor is it easy to explain to them the virtues of a system that requires them to accept judicial decisions that are sometimes hugely consequential, unpopular, and wrong, or that the alternatives are worse.

When judges from different countries discuss different substantive approaches to legal problems, compare procedures, and evaluate the efficacy of judicial practices, they are not only exchanging ideas about specific tools of the trade. There is more. The underlying, but often unspoken, theme of any such meeting is the sustained struggle against arbitrariness. If the objective is ambitious, it has been so since the time of Hammurabi. The enterprise is not without setbacks. Often, like Penelope's weaving, what we create during the day is undone at night. But the effort is worthwhile. Civilization has always depended upon it. It still does. And now, to an ever greater extent, jurists from many different countries engage in that effort together.

Epilogue

This book shows how and why the Supreme Court must increasingly consider the world beyond our national frontiers. In its growing interdependence, this world of laws offers new opportunities for the exchange of ideas, together with a host of new challenges that bear upon our job of interpreting statutes and treaties and even our Constitution. I do not pretend to offer any ultimate or even provisional solutions to those challenges. This book merely surveys what is for many an unfamiliar and still-changing legal landscape, in the hope of raising awareness and stimulating further discussion. That discussion, in turn, will help us to revise concepts, practices, and institutions as necessary.

Why is it so important that American courts meet these challenges? As I have suggested, the simplest answer is that they cannot be avoided. The increasingly international nature of so many routine transactions, from car and home rentals to major financial investments, along with instantaneous communications and the increased global flow of individuals—all these new realities give rise to legal questions affecting not just foreigners but Americans as well. There is no Supreme Court of the World to answer those questions for us. Yet to answer them ourselves, with sound legal judgments, requires information and understanding that often lie outside our borders. We no longer have the luxury, even if we once did, of operating solely within the confines of our own country, as if the only law that mattered were our own.

If that answer is too simplistic, perhaps a more satisfying one begins with the observation that the interdependent world of which we are part is characterized by, among other things, a fragile international economy, economic divisions between North and South, increased environmental risks, insecurity, and in some places anarchy, fanaticism, and terrorism. Little wonder that in many countries cynicism abounds about the efficacy and honesty of government and its institutions. If there is any hope of solving such complex problems, which belong to no one nation, the effort will have to be a collective one.

We Americans have an essential contribution to make to that effort. And it is a contribution strongly tied to who we are, in that who we are has much to do with the nature of our government. As a lawyer and judge, I see our government as a kind of experiment in which Americans have long engaged. At a time when democracy was to be found nowhere else in the world, Thomas Jefferson described the experimental hypothesis generally when he wrote that we Americans thought it "self-evident that all men are created equal," that "they are endowed by their Creator with certain inalienable rights," that "among these are life, liberty, and the pursuit of happiness," and that "to secure these rights governments are instituted among men deriving their just powers from the consent of the governed."

The Founders filled in the details when they created a constitutional system, which managed to maintain a democratic form of government, to protect basic human rights, to ensure a degree of equality, to divide power among numerous states and three federal branches, lest any single group of officials become too powerful, and to require that government action be taken only in accordance with law. The experiment continued.

Abraham Lincoln would reiterate its hypothesis at Gettysburg when he began, "Four score and seven years ago our fathers brought forth upon this continent a *new* nation, conceived in liberty and dedicated to the proposition that all men are created equal." But he spoke well aware that the Founders' experiment was still fragile and uncertain: "Now we are engaged in a great civil war, testing whether that nation, *or any nation* so conceived and so dedicated, can long endure."[1]

The Civil War proved that a nation "so conceived" could at least survive. And we Americans have continued to be identified as the people who persist at that experiment. Despite many ups and downs, it has survived. As I often explain to foreign judges, from Ghana to Romania to Burkina Faso, our constitutional system now holds together a diverse group of 315 million citizens committed to resolving their disputes through law. It has created a judiciary, including a Supreme Court, which over two centuries has made many unpopular and sometimes incorrect decisions that the public has nonetheless followed without resorting to violence. That history may not explain our system's success, but it should at least promote confidence that we can (though often with difficulty) handle problems of the kind discussed in this book without compromising our most basic values.

Other nations continue their long-standing association with our experiment or have joined it anew: England, which planted the seeds of our inviolable rights with the Magna Carta and effected substantial democratic reform in the early nineteenth century, in the wake of American independence; France, whose revolution, shortly after our own, toppled their monarchy; and ever more nations since the end of World War II. Nevertheless, there are open questions that remain critical to the experiment's success. Can Europe, for example, maintain a union committed to democracy, widespread prosperity, and the avoidance of war? Can fledgling democracies sustain themselves in the face of the new challenges I've mentioned?

One major reason I believe it vital that our Court meet these challenges is for the sake of our nation's defining experiment: to show that our system, far from being a hindrance, or worse, in the face of new realities, is perfectly well equipped to meet them. If in addition to sustaining a strong economy and a well-educated workforce, and holding together a highly diverse nation, our system can also address the world's common problems, our example will continue to be influential. Thus we can maintain our "soft power," or what used to be called the "prestige" that our legal system enjoys abroad, as matters of security, trade, the environment, and so on are resolved. But as I have said, the world will follow someone's example if not ours. Failing to lend our voice, we may find ourselves not so well served by, or happy with, the results.

This brings us to perhaps the most pertinent reason for attempting to address today's transnational problems through law: any success in that effort helps to advance the rule of law itself. The rule of law represents the polar opposite of the "arbitrary," which the dictionary equates with the unjust, the illegal, the unreasonable, the autocratic, the despotic, and the tyrannical. Like democracy and human rights, the rule of law is something more than an ideological commitment for Americans; it is a sine qua non for our system, and where it does not exist, our interests cannot be secure. At the time of 9/11, Justice Sandra Day O'Connor and I were in India, about to discuss the rule of law with Indian jurists.

Our reception there made clear to us that the important divisions in the world are not geographical, racial, or religious but between those who believe in a rule of law and those who do not. Jurists across the world help to weave this fabric in their day-to-day work, persisting in their labors even if, in the manner of Penelope's handiwork, what is woven by day sometimes unravels during the night. Yet we continue working, not as politicians but as technicians, hopeful but uncertain of success.

Our perseverance is not merely a matter of an inexhaustible hope but reflects the vulnerability of what we create. At the end of his book *The Plague*, the French writer Albert Camus offers a parable of the Nazi occupation of France. "[T]he germ of the plague," he writes, "never dies nor does it ever disappear. It waits patiently in our bedrooms, our cellars, our suitcases, our handkerchiefs, our file cabinets. And one day, perhaps, to the misfortune or for the education of men, the plague germ will reemerge, reawaken its rats, and send them forth to die in a once happy city."[2]

The rule of law is but one defense against the plague germ, but it requires constant use to prevent the arrival of that unhappy day Camus describes. It is vital to our struggle to build a humane, democratic, and just society. I have written this book in order to show how the interdependence of today's world, as it has become manifest in our Court's docket, poses considerable challenges for our judiciary. It is above all the need to maintain a rule of law that should spur us on, jurists and citizens, at home and abroad, to understand these challenges and to work at meeting them together.

Acknowledgments

This book reflects many years of attendance at a Yale Law School seminar, which once a year brings judges from around the world to meet and discuss with faculty and each other professional subjects and concerns. I am grateful to the school, to its deans, Harold Koh and Robert Post, and to the Gruber Foundation, for having supported the seminar, to Paul Gewirtz and Judith Resnik for having organized and managed the seminar, to the faculty for the materials they prepared, and to both academic and judicial participants for their valuable discussion. I also am grateful to Yale for having supported the research assistance of two of its students, Daniel Herz-Roiphe and Geoffrey Shaw, as well as for the support of Yale Research Fellow (and my former law clerk) Sara Solow.

I am particularly grateful to Sara Solow. Her tireless efforts, her research, her editing, her comments and suggestions, her thoughts and ideas, made this book possible. I also want to thank specially Richard Stewart for his help with the discussion of treaties, and I thank Sabino Cassese as well. I thank George Bermann for his help with the discussion of arbitration, Catherine Barnard for her help with European law, and Paul Gewirtz for his continued encouragement and for his help with nearly everything.

The discussion of current national security problems reflects the help of Michael Leiter and Jake Sullivan. The steel seizure discussion embodies materials that Charles Nesson and I prepared many years ago. The discussion of "cross-citation" reflects the writing of Jeremy Waldron. I also thank Josh Geltzer for his help with several parts of the book.

In addition, I express much appreciation to others who read, and commented upon, earlier versions of the manuscripts, including Robert Post, Strobe Talbot, Lisa Bressman, Bruce Ackerman, Cass Sunstein, and Elizabeth Drew.

I very much thank George Andreou for his fine editing, and I thank the many others at Knopf who helped with this book.

Finally, I thank my family—Joanna, my children, and my grandchildren, too, for their patience, help, and encouragement.

Notes

INTRODUCTION

1. *See* Kirtsaeng v. John Wiley & Sons, Inc., 133 S. Ct. 1351 (2013).
2. *See* Clapper v. Amnesty Int'l USA, 133 S. Ct. 1138 (2013).

PART I: THE PAST IS PROLOGUE

1. *Cf.* Terminiello v. City of Chicago, 337 U.S. 1, 37 (1949) (Jackson, J., dissenting) ("There is danger that, if the Court does not temper its doctrinaire logic with a little practical wisdom, it will convert the constitutional Bill of Rights into a suicide pact.").
2. U.S. CONST. art. 1, § 8.
3. *Id.* art. 2, § 2.
4. *Id.* amends. I, V.

CHAPTER 1

Silence: Cicero and His "Political Question" Counterpart

1. *See* WILLIAM H. REHNQUIST, ALL THE LAWS BUT ONE: CIVIL LIBERTIES IN WARTIME 11–25 (2d ed. 2001).
2. *Id.* at 6–7.
3. *Id.* at 18–25.
4. Jeffrey D. Jackson, *The Power to Suspend Habeas Corpus: An Answer from the Arguments Surrounding Ex Parte Merryman*, 34 U. BALT. L. REV. 11, 16 (2004).
5. REHNQUIST, *supra* note 1, at 26.
6. U.S. CONST. art. I, § 9, cl. 2.
7. REHNQUIST, *supra* note 1, at 33–34.
8. *See id.* at 38.
9. *Id.* at 44.
10. *Id.* at 38–39; Jackson, *supra* note 4, at 20–23.
11. REHNQUIST, *supra* note 1, at 45–50.
12. *Id.* at 49.
13. *Id.* at 173–81.

14. *See id.* at 191.

15. *See Ex parte* Milligan, 71 U.S. (4 Wall.) 2, 6–9 (1866).

16. *Id.* at 14.

17. *Id.* at 20 (emphasis added).

18. *Id.* at 136–39 (Chase, C.J., concurring).

19. *Id.* at 121–22 (majority opinion).

20. Marbury v. Madison, 5 U.S. (1 Cranch) 137, 165–66 (1803).

21. Martin v. Mott, 25 U.S. (12 Wheat.) 19, 20–23 (1827).

22. *Id.* at 28; U.S. CONST. art. I, § 8.

23. *Mott,* 25 U.S. (12 Wheat.) at 29.

24. *See id.* at 32 ("The argument is, that the power confided to the President is a limited power, and can be exercised only in the cases pointed out in the statute, and therefore it is necessary to aver the facts which bring the exercise within the purview of the statute.").

25. *Id.* at 29–30 (emphasis added).

26. Luther v. Borden, 48 U.S. (7 How.) 1 (1849).

27. *See* U.S. CONST. art. IV, § 4.

28. *Luther,* 48 U.S. (7 How.) at 43.

29. Chi. & S. Air Lines, Inc. v. Waterman S.S. Corp., 333 U.S. 103 (1948).

30. *Id.* at 111–12 (internal citations omitted).

31. *See, e.g.,* Holtzman v. Schlesinger, 484 F.2d 1307 (2d Cir. 1973) (holding that a challenge to the legality of bombing in Cambodia presented a nonjusticiable political question); DaCosta v. Laird, 471 F.2d 1146 (2d Cir. 1973) (holding that a challenge to the continuation of air and naval strikes in Vietnam presented a nonjusticiable political question); Luftig v. McNamara, 373 F.2d 664 (D.C. Cir. 1967) (holding that a suit by an army private seeking to enjoin the military from sending him to Vietnam presented a nonjusticiable political question).

32. *See, e.g.,* Holtzman v. Schlesinger, 414 U.S. 1304 (1973) (upholding the circuit court's stay of an injunction to cease bombing in Cambodia). The circuit court had noted that "[n]umerous courts have dismissed suits challenging American involvement on the ground that a 'political question' was involved" and that in virtually all of these cases the Supreme Court denied review. *Holtzman,* 484 F.2d at 1312 n.3.

33. Colegrove v. Green, 328 U.S. 549 (1946).

34. *Id.* at 556 (emphasis added).

35. Baker v. Carr, 369 U.S. 186 (1962).

36. *Id.* at 210–17 (describing situations in which the "political question" doctrine properly applies).

37. *Id.* at 217.

38. *See* Goldwater v. Carter, 444 U.S. 996 (1979).

39. *See id.* at 1002 (Rehnquist, J., concurring) ("I am of the view that the basic question presented by the petitioners in this case is 'political' and therefore nonjusticiable because it involves the authority of the President in the conduct of our country's

foreign relations and the extent to which the Senate or the Congress is authorized
to negate the action of the President.").

40. *See id.* at 1007 (Brennan, J., dissenting) ("The issue of decisionmaking authority
must be resolved as a matter of constitutional law, not political discretion; accordingly, it falls within the competence of the courts.").

41. *See id.* at 996 (Powell, J., concurring) ("I would dismiss the complaint as not ripe for
judicial review. . . . Prudential considerations persuade me that a dispute between
Congress and the President is not ready for judicial review unless and until each
branch has taken action asserting its constitutional authority.").

42. *See id.* at 996 (majority opinion).

43. *See* Zivotofsky v. Clinton, 132 S. Ct. 1421 (2012).

44. *See id.*

45. *See* Zivotofsky v. Sec'y of State, 571 F.3d 1227 (D.C. Cir. 2009); Zivotofsky v. Sec'y
of State, 511 F. Supp.2d 97 (D.D.C. 2007).

46. *Zivotofsky,* 132 S. Ct. at 1427.

47. *Id.* at 1426–27 ("The lower courts concluded that Zivotofsky's claim presents a
political question and therefore cannot be adjudicated. We disagree."); *see also id.*
at 1431 (Sotomayor, J., concurring) (finding "the inquiry required by the political
question doctrine to be more demanding than that suggested by the Court," though
ultimately agreeing with the majority's "conclusion that this case does not present a
political question").

48. *Id.* at 1431 (majority opinion).

49. *Id.* at 1439 (Breyer, J., dissenting).

50. Brief for Respondent at 38–39, Zivotofsky v. Clinton, 132 S. Ct. 1421 (2012)
(No. 10–699).

51. *Zivotofsky,* 132 S. Ct. at 1437–41 (Breyer, J., dissenting).

CHAPTER 2

A Second Approach: "The President Wins"

1. United States v. Curtiss-Wright Exp. Corp., 299 U.S. 304 (1936).

2. For historical background on the circumstances leading to *Curtiss-Wright,* see
H. Jefferson Powell, *The Story of Curtiss-Wright Export Corporation, in* PRESIDEN-
TIAL POWER STORIES 195 (Christopher H. Schroeder & Curtis A. Bradley eds.,
2009); and Charles A. Lofgren, United States v. Curtiss-Wright Export Corporation: *An Historical Reassessment,* 83 Yale L.J. 1 (1973).

3. *See* J. DAVID SINGER & MELVIN SMALL, THE WAGES OF WAR 1816–1965: A
STATISTICAL HANDBOOK 67 (1972) (estimating the death toll of the Chaco War at
130,000); *see also* BRUCE W. FARCAU, THE CHACO WAR: BOLIVIA AND PARAGUAY,
1932–1935 (1996) (providing historical background on the Chaco War); ALEJANDRO
QUESADO, THE CHACO WAR 1932–35: SOUTH AMERICA'S GREATEST MODERN
CONFLICT (2011) (same).

4. Franklin Delano Roosevelt, *First Inaugural Address* (Mar. 4, 1933) ("In the field of
world policy I would dedicate this Nation to the policy of the good neighbor—

the neighbor who resolutely respects himself and, because he does so, respects the rights of others—the neighbor who respects his obligations and respects the sanctity of his agreements in and with a world of neighbors.").

5. *See* Powell, *supra* note 2, at 200–01 ("A commitment to peace did not, in FDR's view, require the United States to ignore the difference between aggressors and their victims, and the president ought to have the authority to take peaceful steps to identify and punish aggression.").

6. *Id.* at 201.

7. *See Chaco Arms Ban Pressed in House; Hull Spurs Action: Roosevelt Resolution for an Embargo Is Reported Out by Committee,* N.Y. TIMES, May 23, 1934, at 1 (reprinting the text of a letter from Secretary of State Cordell Hull to Samuel McReynolds, chairman of the House Committee on Foreign Affairs, and Key Pittman, chairman of the Senate Committee on Foreign Relations, dated May 22, 1934). Secretary Hull wrote, "The United States should be willing to join other nations in assuming moral leadership to the end that their citizens may no longer, for the sake of profits, supply the belligerent nations with arms and munitions to carry on their useless and sanguinary conflict." *Id.*

8. *Id.; see also* Powell, *supra* note 2, at 202 ("The papers reported speculation that the real issue was over American investment in Bolivia.").

9. Lofgren, *supra* note 2, at 1–2 ("On May 24, 1934, six days after it had been introduced, Congress approved a Joint Resolution providing that 'if the President finds that the prohibition of the sale of arms and munitions of war in the United States to those countries engaged in conflict in the Chaco may contribute to the establishment of peace between those countries,' he might proclaim an embargo on American arms shipments to the belligerents. Violators would be fined, imprisoned, or both. Franklin D. Roosevelt signed the Joint Resolution and issued an embargo proclamation on May 28.").

10. Joint Resolution, Act of May 28, 1934, ch. 365, 48 Stat. 811.

11. Franklin Delano Roosevelt, Proclamation No. 2087, 48 Stat. 1744 (1934), http://www.presidency.ucsb.edu/ws/index.php?pid=14888#axzz1pVgJyPc.

12. *See* Powell, *supra* note 2, at 206 ("Curtiss-Wright Export had a practical monopoly on the sale of warplanes to Bolivia . . . maintained through a 5% kickback to the Bolivian comptroller general.").

13. *See id.* at 207 (explaining that Curtiss-Wright executives "and a clerk had . . . crated . . . embargoed guns with the fighters and then filed false export declarations about the contents of the crates").

14. *Id.* (describing how the Department of Justice "secured indictments for conspiracy to sell the machine guns to Bolivia against [Executives] Webster, Allard, Curtiss-Wright Export and a couple of subordinates at the end of January 1936").

15. United States v. Curtiss-Wright Exp. Corp., 14 F. Supp. 230, 231–33 (S.D.N.Y. 1936) ("The defendants have demurred to the conspiracy count because they object to facing a criminal charge for which they assert that there is no constitutional basis. . . . It is said that this constitutes an attempt to substitute Executive determination, as to the probable future efficacy of a given law, for legislative judgment on

the subject, and that the Constitution confides no such function to other than the law-making department of our government.").

16. United States v. Exp. Corp., 299 U.S. at 304 (1936).

17. *See* Robert A. Margo, *Employment and Unemployment in the 1930s*, 7 J. ECON. PERSPECTIVES 42, 43 (1993) (discussing various scholarly estimates of unemployment during the Great Depression).

18. For background on the Court-packing legislation, see JOSEPH ALSOP & TURNER CATLEDGE, THE 168 DAYS (1938); LEONARD BAKER, BACK TO BACK: THE DUEL BETWEEN FDR AND THE SUPREME COURT (1967); William E. Leuchtenburg, *FDR's Court-Packing Plan: A Second Life, A Second Death*, 1985 DUKE L.J. 673 (1985); William E. Leuchtenburg, *The Origins of Franklin D. Roosevelt's "Court-Packing" Plan*, 1966 SUP. CT. REV. 347.

19. *See Election of 1936*, AM. PRESIDENCY PROJECT, http://www.presidency.ucsb.edu /showelection.php?year=1936 (last visited Feb. 7, 2015).

20. *E.g.*, United States v. Butler, 297 U.S. 1 (1936) (striking down provisions of the Agricultural Adjustment Act); Louisville Joint Stock Land Bank v. Radford, 295 U.S. 555 (1935) (striking down the Frazier-Lemke Farm Bankruptcy Act); R.R. Ret. Bd. v. Alton R.R. Co., 295 U.S. 330 (1935) (striking down provisions of the Railroad Retirement Act).

21. A.L.A. Schechter Poultry Corp. v. United States, 295 U.S. 495 (1935).

22. *Id.* at 537–38 ("Congress cannot delegate legislative power to the President to exercise an unfettered discretion to make whatever laws he thinks may be needed or advisable for the rehabilitation and expansion of trade or industry.").

23. Panama Refining Co. v. Ryan, 293 U.S. 388 (1935).

24. *Id.* at 418.

25. *Id.* at 415.

26. *See* National Industrial Recovery Act, Pub. L. No. 73–67, 48 Stat. 195 (1933).

27. *Schechter*, 295 U.S. at 531 ("The act does not define 'fair competition.'").

28. *Id.* at 538.

29. *Id.* at 542 ("[T]he discretion of the President in approving or prescribing codes, and thus enacting laws for the government of trade and industry throughout the country, is virtually unfettered. We think that the code-making authority thus conferred is an unconstitutional delegation of legislative power.").

30. *Id.* at 553 (Cardozo, J., concurring) ("This is delegation running riot. No such plenitude of power is susceptible of transfer. The statute, however, aims at nothing less, as one can learn both from its terms and from the administrative practice under it. Nothing less is aimed at by the code now submitted to our scrutiny.").

31. *See* United States v. Curtiss-Wright Exp. Corp., 299 U.S. at 304, 312 (1936).

32. *Id.* at 318.

33. *Id.*

34. *Id.* at 319.

35. *Id.* at 319–20.

36. *Id.* at 320.

37. During World War II, Curtiss-Wright supplied "142,840 aircraft engines[,] 146,468

electric propellers[, and] 29,269 airplanes." *Company History,* CURTISS-WRIGHT, http://www.curtisswright.com/company/history (last visited Feb. 7, 2015).

38. Korematsu v. United States, 323 U.S. 214 (1944); *see also* GARY Y. OKIHIRO, THE COLUMBIA GUIDE TO ASIAN AMERICAN HISTORY 104 (2001) ("Of about 127,000 Japanese on the U.S. mainland, more than 112,000 lived in concentrated enclaves along the West Coast."); *Relocation and Incarceration of Japanese Americans During World War II,* JAPANESE AM. RELOCATION DIGITAL ARCHIVES, http://www.calisphere.universityofcalifornia.edu/jarda/historical-context.html (last visited Feb. 7, 2015) ("The majority of those interned—nearly 70,000, over 60%—were American citizens.").

39. *See* Jamal Greene, *The Anticanon,* 125 HARV. L. REV. 379 (2011) (presenting and analyzing the significance of such a list).

40. PETER IRONS, JUSTICE AT WAR: THE STORY OF THE JAPANESE-AMERICAN INTERNMENT CASES 6–7 (1983) (quoting press coverage).

41. *See id.* at 41–42, 58–59.

42. *Id.* at 41.

43. *See* EARL WARREN, THE MEMOIRS OF CHIEF JUSTICE EARL WARREN 149 (1977) ("Whenever I thought of the innocent little children who were torn from home, school friends, and congenial surroundings, I was conscience-stricken. It was wrong to react so impulsively, without positive evidence of disloyalty, even though we felt we had a good motive in the security of our state. It demonstrates the cruelty of war when fear, get-tough military psychology, propaganda, and racial antagonism combine with one's responsibility for public security to produce such acts.").

44. IRONS, *supra* note 40, at 27–29, 280–81.

45. Exec. Order No. 9066, 7 Fed. Reg. 1407 (Feb 19, 1942).

46. Act of Mar. 21, 1942, Pub. L. No. 77–503, 56 Stat. 173.

47. IRONS, *supra* note 40, at 69.

48. *Id.* at 70–74.

49. *Id.* at 93–94; Neil Gotanda, *The Story of* Korematsu*: The Japanese-American Cases,* in CONSTITUTIONAL LAW STORIES 249, 267–68 (Michael C. Dorf ed., 2004).

50. *See* IRONS, *supra* note 40, at 99.

51. *See id.* at 117 (discussing the beginning of Besig's representation of Korematsu). Although Besig had recruited Korematsu as a litigant, Besig's "duties as director of the San Francisco branch [of the ACLU] and his lack of California bar membership precluded any courtroom role in the case." *Id.* at 111. For Korematsu's formal representation, Besig "turned to Wayne M. Collins, a young San Francisco lawyer with a practice so marginal that he shared a secretary with the firm from which he rented a room." *Id.* "Collins continued to represent Korematsu throughout the Supreme Court proceedings . . . [and] took up some of the most difficult and controversial issues on behalf of Japanese Americans." Gotanda, *supra* note 49, at 268. The ACLU itself filed an amicus brief in the Supreme Court supporting Korematsu. *See* Brief for the American Civil Liberties Union, Amicus Curiae, Korematsu v. United States, 323 U.S. 214 (1944) (No. 22).

52. *See* Gotanda, *supra* note 49, at 268.

53. *Korematsu,* 323 U.S. at 215.

54. Hirabayashi v. United States, 320 U.S. 81 (1943).

55. *Id.* at 93.

56. *Id.*

57. *Id.* at 101.

58. *Id.* at 101–02.

59. Irons, *supra* note 40, at 278.

60. *Id.* at 279.

61. *Id.* at 279–80.

62. *Id.* at 280–84.

63. Brief of the United States at 12 n.2, Korematsu v. United States, 323 U.S. 214 (1944) (No. 22) ("The Final Report of General DeWitt (which is dated June 5, 1943, but which was not made public until January 1944) . . . is relied on in this brief for statistics and other details concerning the actual evacuation and the events that took place subsequent thereto. We have specifically recited in this brief the facts relating to the justification for the evacuation, of which we ask the Court to take judicial notice, and we rely upon the *Final Report* only to the extent that it relates to such facts."); *see also* Irons, *supra* note 40, at 286–87 (describing the inclusion of the footnote, which was intended to "wave a red flag before the Supreme Court" and "alert the Court to the Justice Department's disavowal of the DeWitt report").

64. Irons, *supra* note 40, at 315 ("Before he relinquished the podium, . . . Horsky fired a parting shot at General DeWitt and the veracity of the *Final Report* . . . call[ing] the Court's attention to the 'extraordinary footnote' in the Government's brief.").

65. *See id.* at 268–73.

66. Korematsu v. United States, 323 U.S. 214, 219 (1944) ("We uphold the exclusion order as of the time it was made and when the petitioner violated it.").

67. *Id.* at 217–18 ("In the light of the principles we announced in the Hirabayashi case, we are unable to conclude that it was beyond the war power of Congress and the Executive to exclude those of Japanese ancestry from the West Coast war area at the time they did.").

68. *Id.* at 223.

69. *Id.* at 224.

70. *Id.* at 225 (Frankfurter, J., concurring) ("To recognize that military orders are 'reasonably expedient military precautions' in time of war and yet to deny them constitutional legitimacy makes of the Constitution an instrument for dialectic subtleties not reasonably to be attributed to the hard-headed Framers, of whom a majority had had actual participation in war.").

71. *Id.* at 232 (Roberts, J., dissenting) ("This case cannot . . . be decided on any such narrow ground as the possible validity of a Temporary Exclusion Order under which the residents of an area are given an opportunity to leave and go elsewhere in their native land outside the boundaries of a military area. To make the case turn on any such assumption is to shut our eyes to reality.").

72. *Id.* at 233 (Murphy, J., dissenting) ("Such exclusion goes over 'the very brink of constitutional power' and falls into the ugly abyss of racism.").

73. *Id.* at 245 (Jackson, J., dissenting).

74. *Id.* at 247 ("I should hold that a civil court cannot be made to enforce an order which violates constitutional limitations even if it is a reasonable exercise of military authority. The courts can exercise only the judicial power, can apply only law, and must abide by the Constitution, or they cease to be civil courts and become instruments of military policy.").

75. *Id.* at 246.

76. Civil Liberties Act of 1988, Pub. L. No. 100–383, 102 Stat. 903 (enacted to "apologize on behalf of the people of the United States for the evacuation, relocation, and internment of such citizens and permanent resident aliens" and to provide some restitution to people who were interned).

77. *See* Carlos M. Vasquez, *"Not a Happy Precedent": The Story of* Ex parte Quirin, *in* FEDERAL COURTS STORIES 219, 221 (Vicki C. Jackson & Judith Resnik eds., 2010) (discussing the citizenship status of the saboteurs and stating that both Ernest Burger and Herbert Haupt were U.S. citizens). For background on *Ex parte Quirin,* see Morris D. Davis, *The Influence of* Ex Parte Quirin *and Courts-Martial on Military Commissions,* 103 Nw. U. L. Rev. COLLOQUY 121 (2008); Andrew Kent, *Judicial Review for Enemy Fighters: The Court's Fateful Turn in* Ex parte Quirin, *the Nazi Saboteur Case,* 66 VAND. L. REV. 153 (2013).

78. Davis, *supra* note 77, at 122.

79. Kent, *supra* note 77, at 161.

80. Davis, *supra* note 77, at 122.

81. *Id.*

82. *Id.* at 122–23.

83. *Id.* at 123.

84. *Id.* at 124.

85. *Id.*

86. *Id.*

87. Kent, *supra* note 77, at 164.

88. *Ex parte* Quirin, 47 F. Supp. 431, 431 (D.D.C. 1942).

89. *Id.* ("I do not consider that *Ex parte Milligan* . . . is controlling in the circumstances of this petitioner."); *see also* Davis, *supra* note 77, at 123 n.7 (observing that the judge's treatment of *Milligan* came "without explanation").

90. Kent, *supra* note 77, at 164.

91. *Ex parte* Quirin, 317 U.S. 1, 11 (1942) (per curiam).

92. *Id.*

93. For the Court's full opinion, see *id.* at 18–48.

94. *See* Kent, *supra* note 77, at 165–69 (discussing "The Court's Two Decisions").

95. *Id.* at 223 (reporting the contents of Justice Murphy's conference notes).

96. Proclamation No. 2561, 7 Fed. Reg. 5101 (July 7, 1942) (declaring that persons tried before the commissions "shall not be privileged to seek any remedy or maintain any proceeding directly or indirectly, or to have any such remedy or proceeding sought on their behalf, in the courts of the United States").

97. *Ex parte* Quirin, 47 F. Supp. 431, 431 (D.D.C. 1942).

98. *Quirin,* 317 U.S. at 19 (noting "the duty which rests on the courts, in time of war as well as in time of peace, to preserve unimpaired the constitutional safeguards of civil liberty").

99. Kent, *supra* note 77, at 179 (quoting 1 WILLIAM BLACKSTONE, COMMENTARIES *372–73).

100. *Id.* at 182 (quoting Sparenburgh v. Bannatyne (1797), 126 Eng. Rep. 837 (C.P.) 837–39).

101. *See* Kent, *supra* note 77, at 206 ("Like all previous wars, World War I came and went without a single known case arising in which an enemy prisoner of war sought habeas corpus or other judicial relief in a state or federal court in the United States."); Seymour W. Wurfel, *Military Habeas Corpus: II,* 49 MICH. L. REV. 669, 709 (1951) (counting only "324 military prisoners" of any kind, likely not alien enemies, who "had sought habeas corpus relief" in the five years after World War II).

102. Kent, *supra* note 77, at 234 ("[C]ourts had . . . generally held that alien enemies had a right to defend themselves if sued, even though they might lack the ability to affirmatively sue themselves."). In addition, "[h]abeas corpus has always been conceived of as an affirmative civil proceeding that was separate and distinct from the criminal trial or other process that resulted in detention." *Id.* at 235.

103. *Quirin,* 317 U.S. at 25 (emphasis added).

104. *Ex parte* Milligan, 71 U.S. (4 Wall.) 2 (1866).

105. *Quirin,* 317 U.S. at 29 ("It is unnecessary for present purposes to determine to what extent the President as Commander in Chief has constitutional power to create military commissions without the support of Congressional legislation. For here, Congress has authorized trial of offenses against the law of war before such commissions.").

106. *Id.* at 34.

107. *Id.* at 31.

108. *Id.* at 37.

109. *Id.* at 42.

110. *Id.* at 44.

111. *Id.* at 45.

112. *Id.*

113. *Id.*

114. *Id.*

CHAPTER 3

A Third Approach: "The President Goes Too Far"

1. Franklin Delano Roosevelt, *Fireside Chat* (Sept. 7, 1942), http://www.presidency.ucsb.edu/ws/?pid=16303.

2. *Id.*

3. *See* Hamdi v. Rumsfeld, 542 U.S. 507, 536 (2004) ("[A] state of war is not a blank check for the President when it comes to the rights of the Nation's citizens.").

4. *See* GRANT MCCONNELL, THE STEEL SEIZURE OF 1952 34–36 (1960) (describing the events of April 8, 1952).

5. Roosevelt, *supra* note 1.

6. Youngstown Sheet & Tube Co. v. Sawyer, 343 U.S. 579 (1952).

7. JON HALLIDAY & BRUCE CUMINGS, KOREA: THE UNKNOWN WAR 8–9 (1988) (establishing a timeline of the war).

8. 1 WAGE STABILIZATION BOARD, WAGE STABILIZATION PROGRAM 1950–1953 1, 4 (1953) (reporting that "[t]he Wholesale Price Index of the Bureau of Labor Statistics, which stood at 157.3 in June 1950 . . . shot up . . . to 180.1 in January 1951," a roughly 15 percent increase).

9. Defense Production Act of 1950, Pub. L. No. 81–774, 64 Stat. 798 (1950).

10. Patricia L. Bellia, *The Story of the* Steel Seizure *Case, in* PRESIDENTIAL POWER STORIES 233, 235 (Christopher H. Schroeder & Curtis A. Bradley eds., 2009).

11. *See* 1 U.S. LEADERSHIP IN WARTIME: CLASHES, CONTROVERSY, AND COMPROMISE 746 (Spencer Tucker ed., 2009) (explaining the nicknames).

12. *See* Exec. Order No. 10,233, 16 Fed. Reg. 3503 (Apr. 21, 1951) (establishing the structure of the Wage Stabilization Board).

13. *See id.* (establishing the board's powers); MAEVA MARCUS, TRUMAN AND THE STEEL SEIZURE CASE: THE LIMITS OF PRESIDENTIAL POWER 24 (1994) (describing the structure of the board); MCCONNELL, *supra* note 4, at 11 (describing the board).

14. *See, e.g.,* John T. Dunlop, *The Social Utility of Collective Bargaining, in* CHALLENGES TO COLLECTIVE BARGAINING, PROCEEDINGS OF THE THIRTEENTH AMERICAN ASSEMBLY 7–19 (Lloyd Ulman ed., 1967).

15. *See* ARCHIBALD COX & DEREK BOK, LABOR LAW 891–900 (5th ed. 1962) (discussing the government's possible roles in resolving labor disputes).

16. Charles E. Russell, *Compulsory Arbitration: The Next Battle Prize; Why It Failed in New Zealand, in* SELECTED ARTICLES ON THE COMPULSORY ARBITRATION AND COMPULSORY INVESTIGATION OF INDUSTRIAL DISPUTES 183, 187 (Lamar T. Beman ed., 1920) (reprinting Russell's article from the April 1920 edition of the short-lived magazine *Reconstruction: A Herald of the New Time*).

17. *Id.* at 188.

18. *Id.*

19. *See* THEODORE W. KHEEL, REPORT TO SPEAKER ANTHONY J. TRAVIA ON THE TAYLOR LAW: WITH A PROPOSED PLAN TO PREVENT STRIKES BY PUBLIC WORKERS 8–13 (1968).

20. COX & BOK, *supra* note 15, at 885–86.

21. *Id.*

22. *Id.* at 889–90.

23. Taft-Hartley Act of 1947, Pub. L. No. 80–101, 61 Stat. 136.

24. *See* Pub. L. No. 64–252, 39 Stat. 721 (1916).

25. *See* Pub. L. No. 88–108, 77 Stat. 132 (1963).

26. *See* Bellia, *supra* note 10, at 236 ("Under the administration's approach to such cases, the Director of Price Stabilization would grant a price increase only under its exist-

ing formula, which tied price increases to the industry's profit level over a period of years."); *id.* at 236 n.8 ("More specifically, under the 'industry earnings standard,' OPS would increase a price ceiling only when an industry could not absorb cost increases without reducing its earnings below 85 percent of the three best years of the 1946–49 period."); *see also* MARCUS, *supra* note 13, at 14 (describing the Industry Earnings Standard); James A. Durham, *The Present Status of Price Control Authority,* 52 COLUM. L. REV. 868 (1952) (discussing the imposition of mandatory price ceilings).

27. *See* MCCONNELL, *supra* note 4, at 2–3.

28. *See* Edward B. Shils, *Arthur Goldberg: Proof of the American Dream,* 120 MONTHLY LAB. REV. 55, 60 (1997) (noting that "the Steelworkers . . . had prospered" during and after World War II, "growing from 460,000 members in 1942 to about 1 million [by late 1944], if one counted the prospective military returnees").

29. *See* MCCONNELL, *supra* note 4, at 13.

30. *See id.* at 13–14; Bellia, *supra* note 10, at 235–36.

31. *See* MCCONNELL, *supra* note 4, at 13–14.

32. *Id.* at 14.

33. *See id.* at 14–16; Bellia, *supra* note 10, at 235.

34. MARCUS, *supra* note 13, at 65; MCCONNELL, *supra* note 4, at 24.

35. MCCONNELL, *supra* note 4, at 14.

36. *Id.* at 16.

37. *See id.* at 16–17.

38. 2 HARRY TRUMAN, YEARS OF TRIAL AND HOPE 466 (1956).

39. MCCONNELL, *supra* note 4, at 17.

40. *See id.* at 18.

41. *See* MARCUS, *supra* note 13, at 14 (describing how wage increases would be calculated); *General Wage Regulations 6–10 and Ceiling Price Regulations 2–7,* 72 MONTHLY LAB. REV. 409, 409–411 (1951) (publicizing General Wage Regulations allowing firms paying "satisfactory" wages in January 1950 to calculate their new wages based on inflation adjustments from the 1950 baseline).

42. *General Wage Regulations 13–15; Ceiling Price Regulations, 55–66,* 73 MONTHLY LAB. REV. 302 (1951) (publicizing General Wage Regulation 13, governing fringe benefits).

43. COLLECTED TEACHING MATERIALS: THE STEEL SEIZURE OF 1952, at 46–47 (unpublished manuscript) (on file with the author) [hereinafter STEEL SEIZURE MATERIALS].

44. *See id.* at 50.

45. *See id.* at 48–50 ("The Union's argument that January 1950 steel wages were too low rested on the claim that the Union had not freely bargained steel wages since April, 1947.").

46. *Id.* at 47 ("The Union argues . . . most of the 16 cent increase negotiated in October 1950 was meant to compensate the workers for pre-January 1950 inequities and not meant to compensate them for the increase in the cost of living in 1950.").

47. *Id.* at 50.

48. *See id.* at 81 (discussing productivity); *id.* at 65 (discussing comparisons with other industries); *id.* at 54–55 (discussing industry profits).

49. *Id.* at 64 ("The Companies claimed that the total cost of the Union's demands (wages and fringe benefits) would be about 56 cents per hour or $753.3 million per year. The Union argued that this figure was much too high and that 35 cents was a more accurate estimate.").

50. *See id.* at 82–83 (discussing fringe benefits).

51. *Id.* at 84 ("The companies responded that weekend steel operations must continue, for steel is a 'continuous' process industry and that very few such industries paid premiums for weekend work.").

52. *Id.* at 64.

53. *See* Marcus, *supra* note 13, at 64–65 ("The issues involved were so numerous and the testimony so detailed that the panel could not complete its report until March 13, 1952. . . . Finally, on March 20, the WSB recommendations, including the dissenting opinion of the Industry members, were made public."); *id.* at 64 n.32 ("The transcript of the testimony is over 3,100 pages long; more than 145 special exhibits were included as evidence.").

54. *See* Steel Seizure Materials, at 78 ("[T]he unions' arguments were based on comparisons with other industries, as revealed in a survey of 143 contracts covering 3,196,000 workers in 35 major industries.").

55. *See* Marcus, *supra* note 13, at 64–65; Bellia, *supra* note 10, at 236.

56. *See* Marcus, *supra* note 13, at 65; McConnell, *supra* note 4, at 24.

57. Steel Seizure Materials, at 93 (reporting the chairman's statement on fringe adjustments).

58. *Id.*

59. *Id.* at 95–96 (reporting on the dissenting opinion of industry members).

60. McConnell, *supra* note 4, at 24.

61. Bellia, *supra* note 10, at 236.

62. McConnell, *supra* note 4, at 24.

63. *Id.* at 26.

64. *Id.* at 27.

65. *See* Truman, *supra* note 38, at 468 (1956) ("Charles E. Wilson, Director of Defense Mobilization, reported to me on March 24 that the companies would flatly reject the recommended settlement. He said that there would be an industry refusal followed by a prolonged strike and that the only thing that would prevent a shutdown of the mills would be to grant the price increase requested by the companies.").

66. McConnell, *supra* note 4, at 28.

67. *Id.* at 29.

68. *See id.* at 24, 26.

69. *See id.* at 34–36; Bellia, *supra* note 10, at 236–37.

70. Truman, *supra* note 38, at 469.

71. *Id.*

72. *Id.* at 469–70.

73. *Id.* at 470.

74. *Id.*

75. *Id.*

76. *Id.*

77. *See* Irving Bernstein, The Lean Years: A History of the American Worker 391–95 (2010) (describing labor's hostility to such injunctions).

78. *See* Bellia, *supra* note 10, at 242 (describing the disadvantages of the Taft-Hartley Act as a solution).

79. *See* Marcus, *supra* note 13, at 62–65 (describing the position of the Office of Price Stabilization); McConnell, *supra* note 4, at 28 (describing the OPS's position).

80. *See* Marcus, *supra* note 13, at 28–29 (describing the Capehart amendment).

81. *See* Steel Seizure Materials, at 125–29 (describing the OPS's calculation of the impact of the recommendations on industry).

82. *See id.* at 127–32 (detailing the forecasted impact of the recommendations).

83. *Id.* at 135 (reporting on the statement of OPS director Arnall).

84. Marcus, *supra* note 13, at 74 ("[O]n April 3, . . . Arnall secretly offered the steel companies a price adjustment totaling $4.50 a ton: $2.75 allowed by the Capehart amendment plus $1.75."); *id.* at 74 n.82 (explaining that some scholars believe this figure "was devised by Arnall" and others believe it "originated with . . . the President").

85. *See* Note, *Wage-Price Guidelines: Informal Government Regulation of Labor and Industry,* 80 Harv. L. Rev. 623, 625–26 (1967) (describing President Kennedy's response to a 1962 steel crisis).

86. *See* Marcus, *supra* note 13, at 79–80 (describing last-minute negotiations).

87. *See id.* at 78–79 (explaining why the option of requesting "congressional legislation to authorize seizure of the steel mills, was quickly rejected by the White House staff").

88. *See* Harry S. Truman, *Special Message to the Congress Reporting on the Situation in the Steel Industry* (Apr. 9, 1952), https://www.trumanlibrary.org/publicpapers/index.php?pid=966 [hereinafter *Special Message to Congress*].

89. *See* Archibald Cox, *Seizure in Emergency Disputes, in* Emergency Disputes and National Policy 226–27, 230–32, 235–41 (Irving Bernstein et al. eds., 1955) (describing the costs and benefits of seizure).

90. In an appendix to his concurrence in *Youngstown,* Justice Frankfurter listed eighty-five total previous seizures. He counted fifty-nine seizures during the "World War II Period" and twelve more in the period "Between VJ Day and the Expiration of the War Labor Disputes Act Seizure Powers, Dec. 31 1946." Youngstown Sheet & Tube Co. v. Sawyer, 343 U.S. 579, 620–28 (1952) (Frankfurter, J., concurring); *see also* Marcus, *supra* note 13, at 154–58 (discussing historical precedents for seizure).

91. McConnell, *supra* note 4, at 34–35.

92. *Id.* at 35–36.

93. Harry S. Truman, *Radio and Television Address to the American People on the Need for Government Operation of the Steel Mills* (Apr. 8, 1952), http://trumanlibrary.org/publicpapers/index.php?pid=965.

94. Exec. Order No. 10,340, 17 Fed. Reg. 3139 (Apr. 8, 1952).

95. *Special Message to Congress, supra* note 88.

96. Letter from Phillip Murray, President, Congress of Indus. Orgs., to Charles Sawyer, Sec'y of Commerce (Apr. 9, 1952) (reporting that he had told union members "to continue at work").

97. Clarence B. Randall, President, Inland Steel Co., *Address: These Are the Facts, Mr. President* (Apr. 9, 1952).

98. *See* McCONNELL, *supra* note 4, at 37–38.

99. Youngstown Sheet & Tube Co. v. Sawyer, 103 F. Supp. 978, 979–80 (D.D.C. 1952).

100. *Id.* at 981.

101. *Id.* ("[T]he plaintiffs have an adequate remedy in suits for damages. . . . [I]f the seizure is illegal, an action for damages lies against the United States under the Federal Tort Claims Act.").

102. 98 CONG. REC. 4131 (1952) (emphasis added).

103. McCONNELL, *supra* note 4, at 38.

104. Bellia, *supra* note 10, at 245.

105. Youngstown Sheet & Tube Co. v. Sawyer, 103 F. Supp. at 569, 572. (D.D.C. 1952).

106. Transcript of Record at 371–72, Youngstown Sheet & Tube Co. v. Sawyer, 343 U.S. at 579 (1952) (Nos. 744, 745).

107. *Youngstown,* 103 F. Supp. at 573–77.

108. Transcript of Record, *supra* note 106, at 313.

109. *See* Bellia, *supra* note 10, at 252–53.

110. *Youngstown,* 343 U.S. at 589.

111. *Id.* at 585.

112. *Id.* at 587.

113. *Id.* at 589 (Frankfurter, J., concurring).

114. *Id.* at 631–32 (Douglas, J., concurring).

115. *Id.* at 635 (Jackson, J., concurring).

116. *Id.* at 637.

117. *Id.* at 637–38.

118. *Id.* at 648.

119. *Id.* at 639.

120. *Id.* at 595 (Frankfurter, J., concurring).

121. *See id.* at 598–602.

122. *Id.* at 613, 620–28.

123. *Id.* at 660 (Burton, J., concurring) (emphasis added).

124. *Id.* at 662–63 (Clark, J., concurring in the judgment).

125. *Id.* at 702–03 (Vinson, C.J., dissenting).

126. *See id.* at 704.

127. *See id.* at 600 n.3 (Frankfurter, J., concurring).

128. Selective Service Act of 1948, Pub. L. No. 80–759, 62 Stat. 604.

129. Defense Production Act of 1950, Pub. L. No. 81–774, 64 Stat. 798.

130. McCONNELL, *supra* note 4, at 31–32.

131. *See Youngstown,* 343 U.S. at 702–03 (Vinson, C.J., dissenting).

132. Exec. Order No. 10,340, 17 Fed. Reg. 3139 (Apr. 8, 1952).

133. *Id.*
134. *See Youngstown,* 343 U.S. at 678–80.
135. *Id.* at 683–700.
136. *Id.* at 677.
137. 4 THE WORKS OF ALEXANDER HAMILTON 432 (Henry Cabot Lodge ed., 1904).
138. 6 THE WRITINGS OF JAMES MADISON 138 (Gaillard Hunt ed., 1906).
139. THEODORE ROOSEVELT, AN AUTOBIOGRAPHY 356–57 (Charles Scribner's Sons, 1922).
140. WILLIAM HOWARD TAFT, OUR CHIEF MAGISTRATE AND HIS POWERS 140 (1916).
141. Roosevelt, *supra* note 1.
142. *See* Bellia, *supra* note 10, at 256.
143. Youngstown Sheet & Tube Co. v. Sawyer, 343 U.S. 579, 651 (1952) (Jackson, J., concurring).
144. *Id.* at 652.
145. *Id.* at 654 (quoting WOODROW WILSON, CONSTITUTIONAL GOVERNMENT IN THE UNITED STATES 68–69 (1908)).
146. *Id.*
147. *Id.* at 655.
148. *Id.* at 652.
149. *See* Bellia, *supra* note 10, at 259.
150. *Youngstown,* 343 U.S. at 634–35.
151. *See* McCONNELL, *supra* note 4, at 47–48.
152. *Id.* at 48–49.
153. *Id.* at 50–52.
154. Irving Bernstein, *The Economic Impact of Strikes, in* EMERGENCY DISPUTES AND NATIONAL POLICY 38–42 (Irving Bernstein et al. eds., 1955).
155. McCONNELL, *supra* note 4, at 47–48.
156. Bernstein, *supra* note 154, at 38–42.
157. OFFICE OF LABOR, NAT'L PROD. AUTH., THE IMPACT OF THE 1952 STEEL STRIKE 9–10 (1953).

CHAPTER 4

"No Blank Check": Guantanamo

1. *See* New York Times Co. v. United States, 403 U.S. 713 (1971).
2. *See* Miranda v. Arizona, 384 U.S. 436 (1966) (rights of arrested persons); New York Times Co. v. Sullivan, 376 U.S. 254 (1964) (protections for the press); Gideon v. Wainwright, 372 U.S. 335 (1963) (right to counsel).
3. *List of Parties to the Geneva Convention,* INT'L COMM. OF THE RED CROSS, https://www.icrc.org/applic/ihl/ihl.nsf/States.xsp?xp_viewStates=XPages _NORMStatesParties&xp_treatySelected=375 (last visited Feb. 7, 2015).
4. *The Universal Declaration of Human Rights: History,* UNITED NATIONS, http://www .un.org/en/documents/udhr/history.shtml (last visited Nov. 12, 2014).
5. *The Court in Brief,* EUROPEAN COURT OF HUMAN RIGHTS, http://www.echr.coe .int/Documents/Court_in_brief_ENG.pdf (last visited Nov. 12, 2014).

6. *See* Convention on the Rights of the Child, Nov. 20, 1989, 1577 U.N.T.S. 3; Convention Against Torture and Other Cruel, Inhuman or Degrading Treatment or Punishment, Dec. 10, 1984, 1465 U.N.T.S. 85; Convention on the Prevention and Punishment of the Crime of Genocide, Dec. 9, 1948, 78 U.N.T.S. 277.

7. *See* INTER-AMERICAN COURT OF HUMAN RIGHTS, http://www.corteidh.or.cr/index.php/en (last visited Nov. 11, 2014); AFRICAN COURT ON HUMAN AND PEOPLES' RIGHTS, http://www.african-court.org/en (last visited Nov. 11, 2014).

8. *See generally* VICKI C. JACKSON & MARK TUSHNET, COMPARATIVE CONSTITUTIONAL LAW 297–409, 748–60, 1780–90 (2014).

9. Authorization for Use of Military Force, Pub. L. No. 107–40, 115 Stat. 224 (2001).

10. *See The Guantánamo Docket,* N.Y. TIMES, http://projects.nytimes.com/guantanamo (last visited May 1, 2015) (offering a comprehensive database of all detainee arrivals and transfers).

11. ALBERT T. CHURCH, U.S. DEP'T OF DEFENSE, REVIEW OF DEPARTMENT OF DEFENSE DETENTION OPERATIONS AND DETAINEE INTERROGATION TECHNIQUES 99 (2005).

12. *See, e.g.,* Rasul v. Bush, 215 F. Supp.2d 55, 57–58 (D.D.C. 2002).

13. *See, e.g., id.* at 72–73.

14. Rasul v. Bush, 542 U.S. 466, 470–73 (2004).

15. 28 U.S.C. § 2241(a) (2012) (emphasis added).

16. *See Rasul,* 542 U.S. at 475–76.

17. Hamdi v. Rumsfeld, 542 U.S. 507, 510–13 (2004).

18. *Id.* at 525–26.

19. *Rasul,* 542 U.S. at 478–84.

20. *Id.* at 474 (quoting Shaughnessy v. United States *ex rel.* Mezei, 345 U.S. 206, 218–19 (1953) (Jackson, J., dissenting).

21. *Id.* at 474–75 (citing *Ex parte* Quirin, 317 U.S. 1 (1942)).

22. *Id.* at 484–85 (quoting Disconto Gesellschaft v. Umbreit, 208 U.S. 570, 578 (1908)).

23. *Id.* at 482 (quoting *Ex parte* Mweyna, [1960] 1 Q.B. 241, 303 (C.A.) (Lord Evershed, M.R.)).

24. *Id.* at 467–68.

25. *See id.* at 475.

26. *Id.* at 475–76 (quoting Johnson v. Eisentrager, 339 U.S. 763, 777 (1950)).

27. *Id.* at 476 ("Petitioners in these cases differ from the *Eisentrager* detainees in important respects: They are not nationals of countries at war with the United States, and they deny that they have engaged in or plotted acts of aggression against the United States; they have never been afforded access to any tribunal, much less charged with and convicted of wrongdoing; and for more than two years they have been imprisoned in territory over which the United States exercises exclusive jurisdiction and control.").

28. *Id.* at 485.

29. *Id.* at 487 (Kennedy, J., concurring).

30. *Id.* at 487–88.

31. *Id.* at 488.

32. *Id.* at 504–05 (Scalia, J., dissenting).

33. *Id.* at 493.

34. *Id.* at 498–99.

35. Hamdi v. Rumsfeld, 542 U.S. 507 (2004).

36. *Id.* at 510.

37. *Ex parte* Quirin, 317 U.S. 1 (1942).

38. *Hamdi*, 542 U.S. at 520 ("It is a clearly established principle of the law of war that detention may last no longer than active hostilities.").

39. *See id.* at 541 (Souter, J., concurring) ("The Government has failed to demonstrate that the Force Resolution authorizes the detention complained of here even on the facts the Government claims. If the Government raises nothing further than the record now shows, the Non-Detention Act entitles Hamdi to be released.")

40. *See id.* at 554 (Scalia, J., dissenting).

41. *Id.* at 554 ("Absent suspension [of habeas corpus] . . . the Executive's assertion of military exigency has not been thought sufficient to permit detention without charge.").

42. *Id.* at 524 (plurality opinion).

43. *Id.* at 527 (quoting Brief for Respondents at 26, *Hamdi*, 542 U.S. 507 (No. 03–6696)).

44. *Id.* ("At most, the Government argues, courts should review its determination that a citizen is an enemy combatant under a very deferential 'some evidence' standard.").

45. *See id.* at 540–41 (Souter, J., concurring).

46. *Id.* at 531 (opinion of O'Connor, J.).

47. *Id.* at 531–32.

48. *Id.* at 531.

49. *Id.*

50. *Id.* at 533.

51. *Id.*

52. *Id.*

53. *Id.*

54. *Id.* at 536.

55. *Id.* (emphasis added).

56. Hamdan v. Rumsfeld, 548 U.S. 557 (2006).

57. *Id.* at 566.

58. *Id.* at 570.

59. *See id.* at 572.

60. *See id.* at 613–15 ("The accused and his civilian counsel may be excluded from, and precluded from ever learning what evidence was presented during, any part of the proceeding that either the Appointing Authority or the presiding officer decides to 'close.'").

61. *Id.* at 592 (quoting *Ex parte* Milligan, 71 U.S. (4 Wall.) 2, 140 (1866)).

62. *Id.* at 593 (quoting 10 U.S.C. § 821 (2006)).

63. *Id.* at 600 ("[T]he offense alleged must have been committed both in a theater of war and *during,* not before, the relevant conflict.").

64. *Id.* at 620 (quoting 10 U.S.C. § 836(b) (2006)).

65. *Id.* at 622 ("[W]e conclude that the 'practicability' determination the President has made is insufficient to justify variances from the procedures governing courts-martial.").

66. *Id.* at 629 (quoting Geneva Convention (III) Relative to the Treatment of Prisoners of War, Aug. 12, 1949, [1955] 6 U.S.T. 3316, 3318).

67. *Id.* at 630 (quoting Geneva Convention (III), *supra* note 66, 6 U.S.T. at 3320).

68. *Id.* at 634 (internal quotation omitted).

69. *See id.* at 637 (Kennedy, J., concurring) ("[D]omestic statutes control this case.").

70. Boumediene v. Bush, 553 U.S. 723 (2008).

71. *See id.* at 735 ("Subsection (e) of § 1005 of the DTA [Detainee Treatment Act] amended 28 U.S.C. § 2241 to provide that 'no court, justice, or judge shall have jurisdiction to hear or consider . . . an application for a writ of habeas corpus filed by or on behalf of an alien detained by the Department of Defense at Guantanamo Bay, Cuba.'" (quoting Detainee Treatment Act of 2005, Pub. L. No. 109-148, 119 Stat. 2739, 2742)); *id.* at 732 ("Petitioners present a question not resolved by our earlier cases relating to the detention of aliens at Guantanamo: whether they have the constitutional privilege of habeas corpus, a privilege not to be withdrawn except in conformance with the Suspension Clause.").

72. Detainee Treatment Act of 2005, Pub. L. No. 109-148, 119 Stat. 2739, 2742.

73. Boumediene v. Bush, 476 F.3d 981 (D.C. Cir. 2007) (dismissing the habeas petitions after Congress passed the Detainee Treatment Act of 2005).

74. U.S. CONST. art. I, § 9, cl. 2 (emphasis added).

75. Rasul v. Bush, 542 U.S. 466, 484 (2004) ("We therefore hold that § 2241 confers on the District Court jurisdiction to hear petitioners' habeas corpus challenges to the legality of their detention at the Guantanamo Bay Naval Base."); *see also id.* at 489 (Scalia, J., dissenting) ("The petitioners do not argue that the Constitution independently requires jurisdiction here.").

76. *See Boumediene,* 553 U.S. at 739–45.

77. *Id.* at 740 (internal quotation omitted).

78. 1 WILLIAM BLACKSTONE, COMMENTARIES 137 (referring to habeas corpus as "that second magna carta and stable bulwark of our liberties.").

79. THE FEDERALIST No. 84, at 418 (Alexander Hamilton) (Terence Ball ed., 2003) (also referring to Blackstone).

80. *See Boumediene,* 553 U.S. at 746–47 ("The Government argues the common-law writ ran only to those territories over which the Crown was sovereign. Petitioners argue that jurisdiction followed the King's officers. Diligent search by all parties reveals no certain conclusions. In none of the cases cited do we find that a common-law court would or would not have granted, or refused to hear for lack of jurisdiction, a petition for a writ of habeas corpus brought by a prisoner deemed an enemy combatant, under a standard like the one the Department of Defense has used in these cases, and when held in a territory, like Guantanamo, over which the Government has total military and civil control." (internal citation omitted)).

81. *Id.* at 753 (internal quotation omitted).

82. *Id.* at 751.

83. *Id.* at 762–64 (discussing *Eisentrager*).

84. *Id.* at 766.

85. *Id.* at 771 ("We hold that Art. I, § 9, cl. 2, of the Constitution has full effect at Guantanamo Bay. If the privilege of habeas corpus is to be denied to the detainees now before us, Congress must act in accordance with the requirements of the Suspension Clause.").

86. *Id.* at 827 (Scalia, J., dissenting) ("The writ of habeas corpus does not, and never has, run in favor of aliens abroad; the Suspension Clause thus has no application, and the Court's intervention in this military matter is entirely *ultra vires.*").

87. *Id.* at 802 (Roberts, C.J., dissenting).

88. *See id.* at 777–78 (majority opinion).

89. *Id.* at 794.

90. *Id.* (emphasis added).

91. *Id.* at 795.

92. *Id.* at 794.

93. *Id.* at 798.

94. *See, e.g.,* Rasul v. Bush, 542 U.S. 466, 475–479 (2004) (discussing *Eisentrager*).

95. *See, e.g.,* Hamdi v. Rumsfeld, 542 U.S. 507, 519 (2004) ("There is no bar to this Nation's holding one of its own citizens as an enemy combatant.").

96. *Rasul,* 542 U.S. at 484 ("We therefore hold that § 2241 confers on the District Court jurisdiction to hear petitioners' habeas corpus challenges to the legality of their detention at the Guantanamo Bay Naval Base.").

97. *Hamdi,* 542 U.S. at 533 ("We therefore hold that a citizen-detainee seeking to challenge his classification as an enemy combatant must receive notice of the factual basis for his classification, and a fair opportunity to rebut the Government's factual assertions before a neutral decisionmaker.").

98. Hamdan v. Rumsfeld, 548 U.S. 557, 567 (2006) ("We conclude that the military commission convened to try Hamdan lacks power to proceed because its structure and procedures violate both the UCMJ and the Geneva Conventions.").

99. Boumediene v. Bush, 553 U.S. 723, 771 (2008) ("We hold that Art. I, § 9, cl. 2, of the Constitution has full effect at Guantanamo Bay. If the privilege of habeas corpus is to be denied to the detainees now before us, Congress must act in accordance with the requirements of the Suspension Clause.").

100. Liversidge v. Anderson, [1942] A.C. 206 (H.L.) 244.

101. *See* Andrew Kent, *Judicial Review for Enemy Fighters: The Court's Fateful Turn in* Ex parte Quirin, *the Nazi Saboteur Case,* 66 VAND. L. REV. 153, 182 (2013) (quoting Sparenburgh v. Bannatyne (1797) 126 Eng. Rep. 837 (C.P.) 837–39).

102. *See* WILLIAM H. REHNQUIST, ALL THE LAWS BUT ONE: CIVIL LIBERTIES IN WARTIME 191 (2d ed. 2001).

103. Korematsu v. United States, 323 U.S. 214, 245 (1944); *id.* at 246 ("A military commander may overstep the bounds of constitutionality, and it is an incident. But if we review and approve, that passing incident becomes the doctrine of the Constitu-

tion. There it has a generative power of its own, and all that it creates will be in its own image. Nothing better illustrates this danger than does the Court's opinion in this case.").

104. *See* Rehnquist, *supra* note 102, at 28.

105. *Boumediene,* 553 U.S. at 766.

106. Al Maqaleh v. Hagel, 738 F.3d 312, 337 (D.C. Cir. 2013).

107. *See* Hamdi v. Rumsfeld, 542 U.S. 507, 533–35 (2004).

108. *See Boumediene,* 553 U.S. at 827 (Scalia, J., dissenting).

109. *See Hamdi,* 542 U.S. at 577 (Scalia, J., dissenting).

110. *See generally* Kent Roach, The 9/11 Effect: Comparative CounterTerrorism (2011) (discussing various international and national approaches to aspects of counterterrorism law and policy).

111. *Hamdi,* 542 U.S. at 598 (Thomas, J., dissenting).

112. *See* U.K. House of Commons, Constitutional Affairs—Seventh Report ¶¶ 44–66 (2005); David Jenkins, *There and Back Again: The Strange Journey of Special Advocates and Comparative Law Methodology,* 42 Colum. Hum. Rts. L. Rev. 279 (2011).

113. Sec'y of State for the Home Dep't v. AF, [2010] 2 A.C. 269 (H.L.) 354.

114. *See* Christopher Forsyth, *Principle or Pragmatism: Closed Material Procedure in the Supreme Court,* U.K. Const. L. Ass'n. (July 29, 2013), http://ukconstitutionallaw .org/2013/07/29/christopher-forsyth-principle-or-pragmatism-closed-material -procedure-in-the-supreme-court.

115. *See* Brief of Amici Curiae Specialists in Israeli Military Law and Constitutional Law in Support of Petitioners at 23–25, Boumediene v. Bush, 553 U.S. 723 (2008) (Nos. 06–1195, 06–1196).

116. Human Rights Watch, Concerns and Recommendations on Spain 5 (2014), http://www.hrw.org/sites/default/files/related_material/20140731%20HRW %20HRCttee%20submission_Spain.pdf.

117. Some, for example, have considered whether the United States could borrow something from the British model. *See* Robert S. Litt & Wells C. Bennett, Brookings Inst., Better Rules for Terrorism Trials 3 (2009) (discussing the creation of a "National Security Bar" of security-cleared lawyers for terrorism trials).

118. Clapper v. Amnesty Int'l USA, 132 S. Ct. 2341 (2013).

119. Brief of the Canadian Civil Liberties Association, et al., in Support of Respondents at 8, *Clapper,* 132 S. Ct. 1341 (No. 11–1025).

120. *See* Abdel Bari Atwan, After Bin Laden: Al Qaeda, the Next Generation 13–39 (2d ed. 2013); Brian Michael Jenkins, RAND Corporation, Al Qaeda in Its Third Decade: Irreversible Decline or Imminent Victory 25 (2012) (describing various views of Al Qaeda and outlining various potential threats).

121. *See* The Evolution of the Global Terrorist Threat: From 9/11 to Osama bin Laden's Death (Bruce Hoffman & Fernando Reinares eds., 2014) (examining

major terror plots related to Al Qaeda since 9/11 and their relative independence
from or reliance on centralized planning and organization).

122. *See* ALLY PREGULMAN & EMILY BURKE, CTR. FOR STRATEGIC & INT'L STUDIES,
HOMEGROWN TERRORISM 1–2 (2012).

123. *See* PETER BERGEN ET AL., BIPARTISAN POL'Y CTR., 2014: JIHADIST TERROR-
ISM & OTHER UNCONVENTIONAL THREATS 5 (2014) (noting that Al Qaeda has not
conducted a successful attack in the United States since 9/11, that Al Qaeda has
not conducted a successful attack in the West since the 2005 London subway
bombings, and that Al Qaeda–inspired terrorists have killed only twenty-one
people in the United States since 9/11).

124. *See* Peter Finn, *Al-Awlaki Directed Christmas "Underwear Bomber" Plot, Justice
Department Memo Says,* WASH. POST, Feb. 10, 2012.

125. *See* LIBERTY AND SECURITY IN A CHANGING WORLD: REPORT AND RECOMMEN-
DATIONS OF THE PRESIDENT'S REVIEW GROUP ON INTELLIGENCE AND COMMU-
NICATIONS TECHNOLOGIES 10–13 (Dec. 12, 2013), http://www.whitehouse.gov/sites
/default/files/docs/2013–12–12_rg_final_report.pdf.

126. *See* Tony Romm, *President Obama's Surveillance Board Packed with Insiders,* POLIT-
ICO (Aug. 28, 2013), http://www.politico.com/story/2013/08/obama-surveillance
-board-insiders-96003.html.

127. *Technologists' Comment to the Director of National Intelligence Review Group on
Intelligence and Communications Technology,* CENTER FOR DEMOCRACY & TECH.,
at 1 (Oct. 4, 2013), https://www.cdt.org/files/pdfs/nsa-review-panel-tech-comment
.pdf.

128. *Cf.* LITT & BENNETT, *supra* note 117, at 3 (discussing the creation of a "National
Security Bar").

129. *See generally About the Court,* U.S. FOREIGN INTELLIGENCE SURVEILLANCE CT.,
http://www.fisc.uscourts.gov/about-foreign-intelligence-surveillance-court (last
visited Feb. 8, 2015).

130. MARY MADDEN, PEW RESEARCH CTR., PUBLIC PERCEPTIONS OF PRIVACY AND
SECURITY IN THE POST-SNOWDEN ERA 3 (Nov. 2014), http://www.pewinternet.org
/files/2014/11/PI_PublicPerceptionsofPrivacy_111214.pdf.

131. *Id.*

PART II: AT HOME ABROAD

CHAPTER 5

Regulating International Commerce

1. *See* Joel R. Paul, *The Transformation of International Comity,* 71 LAW & CONTEMP.
PROBS. 19, 20–22 (2008).

2. *See id.* at 22–23.

3. *See* Dan E. Stigall, *International Law and Limitations on the Exercise of Extrater-*

ritorial *Jurisdiction in U.S. Domestic Law*, 35 HASTINGS INT'L & COMP. L. REV. 323, 335–39 (2012).

4. *World DataBank: World Development Indicators*, WORLD BANK, http://databank .worldbank.org (last accessed Oct. 1, 2014).

5. *Id.*

6. Galina Hale & Bart Hobijn, *The U.S. Content of "Made in China"* 2 (Fed. Reserve Bank of S.F. Economic Letter No. 2011–25, Aug. 8, 2011), http://www.frbsf.org /economic-research/publications/economic-letter/2011/august/us-made-in-china /el2011–25.pdf.

7. *U.S. Travel to International Destinations Increased Two Percent in 2013*, INT'L TRADE ADMIN., DEP'T OF COMMERCE (July 21, 2014), http://travel.trade.gov /outreachpages/download_data_table/2013_Outbound_Analysis.pdf.

8. Multinational companies account for about 25 percent of U.S. private sector employment and constitute more than 40 percent of businesses with over 10,000 employees. *See* KEVIN B. BAREFOOT & RAYMOND J. MATALONI, JR., BUREAU OF ECON. ANALYSIS, OPERATIONS OF U.S. MULTINATIONAL COMPANIES IN THE UNITED STATES AND ABROAD: PRELIMINARY RESULTS FROM THE 2009 BENCH-MARK SURVEY 30 (Nov. 2011), http://www.bea.gov/scb/pdf/2011/11%20November /1111_mnc.pdf; Press Release, Bureau of Econ. Analysis, Summary Estimates for Multinational Companies: Employment, Sales, and Capital Expenditures for 2010 (Apr. 18, 2012), http://www.bea.gov/newsreleases/international/mnc/2012/mnc2010 .htm.

9. Sherman Antitrust Act of 1890, 26 Stat. 209 (codified as amended at 15 U.S.C. § 1 (2012)).

10. 15 U.S.C. §§ 1–2 (2012).

11. *Id.* § 15(a) ("[A]ny person who shall be injured in his business or property by reason of anything forbidden in the antitrust laws may sue therefor . . . and shall recover threefold the damages by him sustained, and the cost of suit, including a reasonable attorney's fee.").

12. United States v. Sisal Sales Corp., 274 U.S. 268 (1927).

13. United States v. Aluminum Co. of America (*Alcoa*), 148 F.2d 416 (2d Cir. 1945).

14. United States v. Watchmakers of Switz. Info. Ctr. Inc., 133 F. Supp. 40 (S.D.N.Y. 1955).

15. United States v. General Elec. Co., 115 F. Supp. 835 (D.N.J. 1953).

16. *See* United States v. N.V. Nederlandsche Combinatie Voor Chemische Industrie, No. 70 Civ. 2079, 1970 WL 505 (S.D.N.Y. July 8, 1970).

17. American Banana Co. v. United Fruit Co., 213 U.S. 347, 357 (1909).

18. *Alcoa*, 148 F.2d at 443–45 (holding that the agreements at issue "were unlawful, though made abroad, if they were intended to affect imports and did affect them").

19. *See* Ford v. United States, 273 U.S. 593, 623 (1927) ("[A] man who outside of a country willfully puts in motion a force to take effect in it is answerable at the place where the evil is done."); *see also* CHARLES DOYLE, CONG. RESEARCH SERV. R94–166, EXTRATERRITORIAL APPLICATION OF AMERICAN CRIMINAL LAW (2012) (detailing the extraterritorial reach of American criminal law). Within the

United States, courts have also applied an effects test to assert jurisdiction over out-of-state criminal defendants. *See* Strassheim v. Daily, 221 U.S. 280, 285 (1911) ("Acts done outside a jurisdiction, but intended to produce and producing detrimental effects within it, justify a state in punishing the cause of the harm as if he had been present at the effect if the state should succeed in getting him within its power."); U.S. *ex rel.* Pascarella v. Radakovich, 548 F. Supp. 125, 126–27 (N.D. Ill. 1982) ("It has long been established that a state may constitutionally attach criminal consequences to an act occurring outside the state that has an effect within the state."); People v. Blume, 505 N.W.2d 843, 845–46 (Mich. 1993) (finding "authority to exercise jurisdiction over acts that occur outside the state's physical borders" when those acts "are intended to have, and that actually do have, a detrimental effect within the state"); Innis v. State, 69 P.3d 413, 417 (Wyo. 2003) (finding "broad jurisdiction to punish a defendant . . . for an act committed outside this state, but which has an effect in this state"). Some private civil cases have adopted a similar framework. *See* Helicopteros Nacionales de Colombia, S.A. v. Hall, 466 U.S. 408 (1984); Int'l Shoe Co. v. Washington, 326 U.S. 310 (1945).

20. *See Alcoa,* 148 F.2d at 443–45.

21. Extraterritorial application of U.S. antitrust law also presented diplomatic difficulties. *See* Joseph P. Griffin, *Extraterritoriality in U.S. and EU Antitrust Enforcement,* 67 ANTITRUST L.J. 159, 160–61 (1999) (describing the "considerable backlash from foreign governments," as well as "diplomatic protests" and "counter actions by foreign courts," that took place in the 1950s, 1960s, and 1970s, as American courts began to assert broader extraterritorial jurisdiction in antitrust cases).

22. Timberlane Lumber Co. v. Bank of Am. (*Timberlane II*), 749 F.2d 1378 (9th Cir. 1984); Timberlane Lumber Co. v. Bank of Am. (*Timberlane I*), 549 F.2d 597 (9th Cir. 1976).

23. *Timberlane I,* 549 F.2d at 613.

24. *Id.* at 608.

25. *Id.* at 609.

26. *Id.*

27. *Id.* at 613.

28. *Id.* at 614.

29. Timberlane Lumber Co. v. Bank of Am. (*Timberlane II*), 749 F.2d 1378, 1384 (9th Cir. 1984).

30. *Id.* at 1384–85.

31. *Id.* at 1386.

32. *Id.*

33. *See, e.g.,* A. V. Lowe, *Blocking Extraterritorial Jurisdiction: The British Protection of Trading Interests Act, 1980,* 75 AM. J. INT'L L. 257, 268–69 (1981) ("[T]he main defect of the *Timberlane* approach is that it proceeds, after the event, on a case-by-case basis. Because foreign businesses could not know the exact circumstances in which a case might be brought against them—a problem greatly exacerbated by the right of private individuals to institute antitrust actions—and therefore could not predict either the nature or the 'weight' of the factors to be balanced by the American

court, they would still be obliged to conduct their activities in accordance with American regulations where there was a mere possibility that they might be found to be subject to American jurisdiction."); Edward L. Rholl, *Inconsistent Application of the Extraterritorial Provisions of the Sherman Act: A Judicial Response Based Upon the Much Maligned "Effects" Test*, 73 MARQ. L. REV. 435, 469 (1990) (arguing that a "weakness of the 'balancing' approach is its lack of precision. . . . [T]hese tests are susceptible to disparate application. In the first instance, courts are given no instruction as to how much weight to give each factor. Similarly, they are not given guidance as to how to balance the interests. . . . The result of this lack of precision is the uncertain application of the tests. The *Timberlane* court noted as much and in fact favored this result. However, because protection is an important factor in the application of United States antitrust law, both victims and potential violators need some certainty in order to understand where their actions stand under the law."); John Byron Sandage, *Forum Non Conveniens and the Extraterritorial Application of United States Antitrust Law*, 94 YALE L.J. 1693, 1706 (1985) ("[T]he fact that there is no way to standardize the relative importance of interest factors would undermine the predictable application of United States law. Only if the factors that prompt an American court to decline extraterritorial jurisdiction are relatively unambiguous and easily applied can economic actors predictably structure transactions. The largely standardless balancing required by *Timberlane* cannot yield such results."); John H. Shenefield, *Thoughts on Extraterritorial Application of the United States Antitrust Laws*, 52 FORDHAM L. REV. 350, 369 (1983) (observing that the *Timberlane* approach is not "necessarily predictable for litigants or those who must counsel clients"); *see also* MARK R. JOELSON, AN INTERNATIONAL ANTITRUST PRIMER: A GUIDE TO THE OPERATION OF UNITED STATES, EUROPEAN UNION, AND OTHER KEY COMPETITION LAWS IN THE GLOBAL ECONOMY 46 (2006) ("[S]ome commentators labeled the *Timberlane* doctrine and its ilk as being 'uncounselable law,' i.e., they questioned whether a lawyer striving to counsel a business person on legal compliance under the jurisdictional rule of reason could fairly anticipate what conclusion a court would subsequently reach in applying the complicated, many-factored jurisdictional test in a given case."); Steven A. Kadish, *Comity and the International Application of the Sherman Act: Encouraging Courts to Enter the Political Arena*, 4 Nw. J. INT'L L. & BUS. 130 (1982) (arguing "that the *Timberlane* analysis should be rejected, or at least limited . . . because there may be insurmountable practical difficulties in applying the analysis, and because the analysis encourages courts to enter the political arena"). For a judicial critique of *Timberlane* interest balancing, *see* Laker Airways Ltd. v. Sabena, Belgian World Airlines, 731 F.2d 909, 948 (D.C. Cir. 1984) ("Interest balancing in this context is hobbled by two primary problems: (1) there are substantial limitations on the court's ability to conduct a neutral balancing of the competing interests, and (2) the adoption of interest balancing is unlikely to achieve its goal of promoting international comity.").

34. Several other courts of appeals, in deciding whether the Sherman Act applies abroad, adopted balancing tests similar to the Ninth Circuit's test in *Timberlane I*. *See* Industrial Inv. Dev. Corp. v. Mitsui & Co., 671 F.2d 876, 885 (5th Cir. 1982) (dis-

cussing the *Timberlane I* test and its application); Montreal Trading Ltd. v. Amax, Inc., 661 F.2d 864, 869–70 (10th Cir. 1981) ("We believe that the analysis set forth in [*Timberlane*] contains the proper elements for consideration."); Mannington Mills, Inc. v. Congoleum Corp., 595 F.2d 1287, 1297–98 (3rd Cir. 1979) (expressing "substantial agreement" with the *Timberlane* "approach").

35. Foreign Trade Antitrust Improvements Act of 1982, Pub. L. No. 97–290, 96 Stat. 1246 (codified at 15 U.S.C. § 6(a) (2012)).

36. *Id.* (emphasis added).

37. *Id.*

38. *Id.*

39. For activity affecting U.S. import commerce, however, an arguably lower standard applies. The Department of Justice assumes that there only need be some effect on U.S. markets, even if not foreseeable. *See* U.S. Dep't of Justice & Fed. Trade Comm'n, Antitrust Enforcement Guidelines for International Operations § 3.11 (1995), http://www.justice.gov/atr/public/guidelines/internat.htm.

40. In fact, the House of Representatives Report on the legislation made this point explicit. *See* H.R. Rep. No. 97–686, at 10 (1982) ("[T]he bill is intended neither to prevent nor to encourage additional judicial recognition of the special international characteristics of transactions. If a court determines that the requirements for the subject matter jurisdiction are met, this bill would have no effect on the courts' ability to employ notions of comity . . . or otherwise to take account of the international character of the transaction."); *see also* Griffin, *supra* note 21, at 162 ("Congress took a neutral stance towards the Ninth Circuit's 'jurisdictional rule of reason' analysis, indicating that the Act simply stated the requirements for jurisdiction and was not intended to prevent or encourage balancing tests that might limit exercise of that jurisdiction.").

41. F. Hoffmann-La Roche Ltd. v. Empagran, S.A., 542 U.S. 155, 159 (2004).

42. Brief of the United States as Amicus Curiae at 1–3, *Empagran*, 542 U.S. 155 (No. 03–724).

43. *Empagran*, 542 U.S. at 159–60.

44. *Id.* at 160.

45. *Id.*

46. *Id.* at 164–68.

47. *See* William S. Dodge, *Understanding the Presumption Against Extraterritoriality*, 16 Berkeley J. Int'l L. 85 (1998).

48. 15 U.S.C. § 6a (2012).

49. *Empagran*, 542 U.S. at 164.

50. *See* Hartford Fire Ins. Co. v. California, 509 U.S. 764, 817 (1993) (Scalia, J., dissenting) ("The 'comity' [*Timberlane* and related cases] refer to is not the comity of courts, whereby judges decline to exercise jurisdiction over matters more appropriately adjudged elsewhere, but rather what might be termed 'prescriptive comity': the respect sovereign nations afford each other by limiting the reach of their laws."); *see also Empagran*, 542 U.S. at 164.

51. *Empagran*, 542 U.S. at 165 (emphasis omitted).

52. *Id.*
53. Paul, *supra* note 1, at 21–22.
54. *Id.* at 23–24.
55. Stigall, *supra* note 3, at 335–36.
56. *Id.* at 335 (quoting CEDRIC RYNGAERT, JURISDICTION IN INTERNATIONAL LAW 136–137 (2008)).
57. *See* RESTATEMENT (THIRD) OF FOREIGN RELATIONS LAW OF THE UNITED STATES § 403(1) (1987) ("Even when one of the bases for jurisdiction under § 402 is present, a state may not exercise jurisdiction to prescribe law with respect to a person or activity having connections with another state when the exercise of such jurisdiction is unreasonable.").
58. *Id.* § 403(2).
59. F. Hoffmann-La Roche Ltd. v. Empagran, S.A., 542 U.S. 155, 165–66 (2004) (emphasis omitted).
60. *Id.* at 165.
61. *See, e.g.*, Brief of the Governments of the Federal Republic of Germany and Belgium as Amici Curiae in Support of Petitioners at 1–3, *Empagran*, 542 U.S. 155 (No. 03–724) (discussing the strength of German and Belgian antitrust laws); Brief Amicus Curiae of European Banks in Support of Petitioners at 12, *Empagran*, 542 U.S. 155 (No. 03–724) ("The European Union and its Member States (among other foreign jurisdictions) have been aggressively prosecuting illegal cartels and levying large fines for violations of their own antitrust laws.").
62. *See, e.g.*, Brief for Amici Curiae Committee to Support the Antitrust Laws and National Association of Securities and Consumer Attorneys in Support of Respondents at 15–16, *Empagran*, 542 U.S. 155 (No. 03–724) (arguing for the application of U.S. law in addition to counterpart laws in foreign jurisdictions). Amici also argued that the international nature of cartels made it necessary to apply U.S. antitrust law to foreign price-fixing in order to generate a sufficient global deterrent. *See, e.g.*, Brief of Amici Curiae Economists Joseph E. Stiglitz and Peter R. Orszag in Support of Respondents at 2–12, *Empagran*, 542 U.S. 155 (No. 03–724) ("Failing to penalize global cartels for the harm they impose and profits they reap abroad thus would undermine one of the most fundamental objectives of the U.S. antitrust laws—using deterrence to discourage cartel formation in the United States.").
63. Brief of the United Kingdom of Great Britain and Northern Ireland, Ireland and the Kingdom of the Netherlands as Amici Curiae in Support of Petitioners at 9–10, *Empagran*, 542 U.S. 155 (No. 03–724).
64. *Id.* at 12.
65. *Id.*
66. Brief of the Government of Japan as Amicus Curiae in Support of Petitioners at 10, *Empagran*, 542 U.S. 155 (No. 03–724).
67. *Id.*
68. *Id.* at 11.
69. *Id.*
70. *Id.*

71. Brief for the United States as Amicus Curiae Supporting Petitioners at 20, *Empagran*, 542 U.S. 155 (No. 03–724).

72. Organization for Economic Cooperation and Development [OECD], *Revised Recommendation of the OECD Council Concerning Cooperation Between Member Countries on Restrictive Business Practices Affecting International Trade*, OECD Doc. No. C(86)44 (Final) (May 21, 1986), reprinted in 25 I.L.M. 1629 (1986).

73. *See* Griffin, *supra* note 21, at 373–78 (summarizing and analyzing the agreement).

74. Brief for the United States as Amicus Curiae Supporting Petitioners, *supra* note 71, at 22.

75. *Empagran*, 542 U.S. at 167.

76. *Id.*

77. *Id.* at 168–69.

78. *Id.* at 164–65.

79. Intel Corp. v. Advanced Micro Devices, Inc., 542 U.S. 241 (2004).

80. *Id.* at 250–51.

81. *Id.* at 251–52.

82. 28 U.S.C. § 1782(a) (2012) (emphasis added).

83. *See Intel*, 542 U.S. at 251 & n.5.

84. Advanced Micro Devices Inc. v. Intel Corp., No. C–01–7033, 2002 WL 1339088, at 1 (N.D. Cal. Jan. 7, 2002) (finding that the European Competition Directorate "lack[s] the qualities that make a proceeding adjudicative" (internal quotation omitted)).

85. Advanced Micro Devices, Inc. v. Intel Corp., 292 F.3d 664 (9th Cir. 2002).

86. *Id.* at 667 ("The Directorate makes its recommendations to the EC—a body authorized to enforce the EC Treaty with written, binding decisions, enforceable through fines and penalties. EC decisions are appealable to the Court of First Instance and then to the Court of Justice. Thus, the proceeding for which discovery is sought is, at minimum, one leading to quasi-judicial proceedings.").

87. *Id.* at 668–69 ("We find nothing . . . to require a threshold showing on the party seeking discovery that what is sought be discoverable in the foreign proceeding.").

88. Intel Corp. v. Advanced Micro Devices, Inc., 542 U.S. 255, 253–54 (2004).

89. *Id.* at 247 & n.1.

90. *Id.* at 248 (quoting Act of Sept. 2, Pub. L. No. 85–906, § 2, 72 Stat. 1743 (1965)).

91. *Id.* at 248–49.

92. Brief of Amicus Curiae the Commission of the European Communities Supporting Reversal, *Intel*, 542 U.S. 255 (No. 02–572).

93. *Id.* at 2.

94. *Id.*

95. *Id.* at 12.

96. *Id.* at 14.

97. *Id.* at 16, 18.

98. Brief for the United States as Amicus Curiae Supporting Affirmance, *Intel*, 542 U.S. 255 (No. 02–572).

99. *Id.* at 3–7, 26–28.

100. Brief of Amicus Curiae the Commission of the European Communities Supporting Reversal, *supra* note 92, at 4–9.

101. *Id.* at 14.

102. *Id.* at 14–15.

103. *Id.* at 15–16.

104. *Id.* at 11–12 (explaining that the narrower reading of § 1782 "in no way impairs the Commission's ability to carry out its investigative functions").

105. *See* S. Rep. No. 88–1580, at 7–8 (1964) ("The word 'tribunal' is used to make it clear that assistance is not confined to proceedings before conventional courts. For example, it is intended that the court have discretion to grant assistance when proceedings are pending before investigating magistrates in foreign countries. In view of the constant growth of administrative and quasi-judicial proceedings all over the world, the necessity for obtaining evidence in the United States may be as impelling in proceedings before a foreign administrative tribunal or quasi-judicial agency as in proceedings before a conventional foreign court. Subsection (a) therefore provides the possibility of U.S. judicial assistance in connection with all such proceedings.").

106. *See Intel,* 542 U.S. at 247–49.

107. *See id.* at 266 ("Nor do we know whether the European Commission's views on § 1782(a)'s utility are widely shared in the international community by entities with similarly blended adjudicative and prosecutorial functions.").

108. Brief of Amicus Curiae the Commission of the European Communities Supporting Reversal, *supra* note 92, at 9.

109. *Intel,* 542 U.S. at 271–72 (Breyer, J., dissenting).

110. *Id.* at 257–58 (majority opinion).

111. *Id.* at 256.

112. Hans Smit, *International Litigation Under the United States Code,* 65 Colum. L. Rev. 1015, 1027 (1965).

113. *Intel,* 542 U.S. at 256–57.

114. *Id.* at 248–49.

115. *Id.* at 259.

116. *Id.*

117. *Id.* at 268–70 (Breyer, J., dissenting).

118. Brief for the United States as Amicus Curiae Supporting Affirmance, *supra* note 98, at 26–28.

119. *Intel,* 542 U.S. at 264 (majority opinion).

120. *Id.*

121. *Id.* at 264–65.

122. Brief of Amicus Curiae the Commission of the European Communities Supporting Reversal, *supra* note 92, at 17.

123. *Id.*

124. *See id.* at 4.

125. *Id.* at 17.

126. *Id.*

127. Brief for the United States as Amicus Curiae Supporting Affirmance, *supra* note 98, at 29.

128. *See Intel,* 542 U.S. at 266.

129. Morrison v. Nat'l Austl. Bank Ltd., 561 U.S. 247 (2010).

130. Securities and Exchange Act of 1934, Pub. L. No. 73–291, 48 Stat. 881 (codified as amended at 15 U.S.C. §§ 78a–78pp (2012)).

131. Securities and Exchange Commission (SEC) Rule 10b–5, 17 C.F.R. § 240.10b–5 (2013).

132. IIT v. Cornfeld, 619 F.2d 909 (2d Cir. 1980).

133. *Id.* at 913.

134. *Id.* at 914.

135. *Id.*

136. *Id.* at 918.

137. *Id.*

138. *Id.* at 919–21.

139. *Id.* at 919–20.

140. *Id.* at 919.

141. *Id.* at 920.

142. *Id.* at 918 (emphasis added).

143. *Id.*

144. *Id.*

145. *Id.* at 920.

146. *Id.* (quoting IIT v. Vencap, Ltd., 519 F.2d 1001, 1017 (2d Cir. 1975)).

147. *Id.* at 918 (citing Leasco Data Processing Equip. Corp. v. Maxwell, 468 F.2d 1326 (2d Cir. 1982)).

148. *Id.* at 920.

149. *Id.* at 921.

150. *See, e.g.,* Zoelsch v. Arthur Andersen & Co., 824 F.2d 27, 35–36 (D.C. Cir. 1987) (adopting the Second Circuit's test and rejecting jurisdiction because not only were the purchasers and sellers foreign, but all the key activity had occurred abroad); Psimenos v. E.F. Hutton & Co., 722 F.2d 1041, 1047 (2d Cir. 1983) (noting that both factors that conferred jurisdiction in *Cornfeld* were present in the case); Grunenthal GmbH v. Hotz, 712 F.2d 421, 425–26 (9th Cir. 1983) (adopting a more liberal version of the Second Circuit test and concluding jurisdiction was present, even though the plaintiff and defendants were all foreign and the securities were not traded on a U.S. exchange, because much of the fraudulent conduct occurred in the United States); Continental Grain (Australia) Pty. Ltd. v. Pac. Oilseeds, Inc., 592 F.2d 409, 420–22 (8th Cir. 1979) ("[T]he absence of a domestic plaintiff, domestic securities, or the use of a national securities exchange . . . will not necessarily preclude a finding of subject matter jurisdiction. Instead, we examine the relationship between defendants' conduct in the United States and the alleged fraudulent schemes.").

151. *E.g.,* Kun Young Chang, *Multinational Enforcement of U.S. Securities Laws: The Need for Clear and Restrained Scope of Extraterritorial Subject-Matter Jurisdiction,* 9 FORDHAM J. CORP. & FIN. L. 89, 108–09 (2003) ("The problem here is that the

antifraud provisions are applied by the courts on an ad hoc judicial decision-making basis, not by clear rules that the legislative or executive branches have formulated. . . . [E]ach court has had to struggle with the difficult issue of the extraterritoriality of securities laws without congressional guidance, expanding or limiting its jurisdictional coverage according to its individual whims, instead of questioning the indeterminate and unrestrained reach of the tests. This lack of clear guidance has resulted not only in the tendency of U.S. courts to give the antifraud rules too broad a scope, but also in inconsistent standards for the determination of subject-matter jurisdiction. As a result, parties involved in transnational transactions cannot reasonably predict the jurisdictional consequences of their actions."); Stephen J. Choi & Linda J. Silberman, *Transnational Litigation and Global Securities Class-Action Lawsuits*, 2009 Wis. L. Rev. 465, 467–68 (2009) ("Unfortunately, much uncertainty surrounds the consideration of extraterritorial issues within securities class-action lawsuits. The individual doctrines applied within the courts—such as the conduct and effects tests—are often ambiguous and difficult to predict. . . . Not all courts approach the extraterritoriality issue in the same manner; often, whether foreign investors will ultimately have a remedy within a federal court turns on that court's selection of a specific doctrinal framework in which to consider extraterritoriality.").

152. Morrison v. Nat'l Austl. Bank Ltd., 561 U.S. 247 (2010).

153. *Id.* at 250–53.

154. *Id.* at 252.

155. *Id.* at 252–53.

156. Morrison v. Nat'l Austl. Bank Ltd., 547 F.3d 167, 176 (2d Cir. 2008) (finding no jurisdiction because "[t]he actions taken and the actions not taken by NAB in Australia were, in our view, significantly more central to the fraud and more directly responsible for the harm to investors than the manipulation of the numbers in Florida").

157. *Morrison*, 561 U.S. at 273.

158. *Id.* at 282 (Stevens, J., concurring in the judgment) (internal quotation marks omitted).

159. *Id.* at 278.

160. *Id.* at 281 (internal quotation marks omitted).

161. *See id.* at 281–82.

162. *Id.* at 281–86.

163. *Id.* at 273 (majority opinion) (emphasis added).

164. *Id.*

165. *Id.* at 257 (quoting Bersch v. Drexel Firestone, Inc., 519 F.2d 974, 985 (2d Cir. 1975)).

166. *Id.* at 255 (quoting EEOC v. Arabian Am. Oil Co. (*Aramco*), 499 U.S. 244, 248 (1991) (internal quotation marks omitted)).

167. *Id.* at 265.

168. *Id.* at 266.

169. *Id.* at 267–68.

170. *Id.* at 269 (quoting *Aramco*, 499 U.S. at 256).

171. *Id.*
172. *Id.* (emphasis added).
173. IIT v. Cornfeld, 619 F.2d 909, 921 (2d Cir. 1980).
174. *Id.* at 270.
175. Brief of the International Chamber of Commerce, et al. as Amici Curiae in Support of Respondents at 24, *Morrison,* 561 U.S. 247 (No. 08–1191).
176. *Id.* at 29.
177. *See, e.g., id.* at 4 ("The nations from which *amici* hail have enacted robust anti-securities fraud regimes that reflect thoughtful policy choices about how best to achieve investor protection. Applying U.S. law to deceptive devices or contrivances that occur abroad, effectively trumping non-U.S. policy choices, significantly undermines comity.").
178. Kirtsaeng v. John Wiley & Sons, Inc., 133 S. Ct. 1351, 1356 (2013).
179. *Id.*
180. *Id.*
181. *Id.* at 1357.
182. *Id.* at 1356.
183. *Id.*
184. *Id.* at 1357.
185. *Id.*
186. 17 U.S.C. § 106(3) (2012).
187. *Id.* § 109(a) (emphasis added).
188. *Kirtsaeng,* 133 S. Ct. at 1356.
189. *Id.*
190. 17 U.S.C. § 109(a) (2012) (emphasis added).
191. *Id.* § 602(a) (1) ("Importation into the United States, without the authority of the owner of copyright under this title, of copies . . . of a work that have been acquired outside the United States is an infringement of the exclusive right to distribute copies.").
192. *See Kirtsaeng,* 133 S. Ct. at 1357–58.
193. *See id.* at 1358 (discussing these two alternative readings of the phrase).
194. 17 U.S.C. § 104(a) (2012) ("The works . . . , while unpublished, are subject to protection under this title without regard to the nationality or domicile of the author.").
195. *Id.* § 104(b)(2) ("The works . . . are subject to protection under this title if . . . the work is first published in the United States or in a foreign nation that, on the date of first publication, is a treaty party.").
196. *Kirtsaeng,* 133 S. Ct. at 1359–60.
197. *Id.* at 1363 (quoting 2 EDWARD COKE, THE FIRST PART OF THE INSTITUTES OF THE LAWS OF ENGLAND § 360 (Francis Hargrave & Charles Butler eds., Robert H. Small 1853)).
198. *Id.*
199. *Id.* at 1361.
200. *See* Brief of Amici Curiae the American Library Association et al. in Support of Petitioner, *Kirtsaeng,* 133 S. Ct. 1351 (No. 11–697).

201. *See* 17 U.S.C. § 302 (providing that works created on or after January 1, 1978, now are protected for a term of the author's life, plus up to seventy years after the author's death).

202. *See Kirtsaeng,* 133 S. Ct. at 1364 (discussing considerations raised by the American Library Association).

203. Brief of Amici Curiae Public Knowledge et al. in Support of Petitioner at 10, *Kirtsaeng,* 133 S. Ct. 1351 (No. 11–697).

204. *Kirtsaeng,* 133 S. Ct. at 1365.

205. *See id.*

206. *Id.* at 1364–65.

207. *Id.* at 1365.

208. *Id.* at 1373, 1386–90 (Ginsburg, J., dissenting) ("The Court's parade of horribles . . . is largely imaginary.").

209. *Id.* at 1389–90.

210. *Id.* at 1385.

211. *Id.* at 1383–85.

212. Brief for the United States as Amicus Curiae Supporting Respondent, *Kirtsaeng,* 133 S. Ct. 1351 (No. 11–697).

213. *See* S. REP. No. 106–71, at 23. For example, 124 regulatory authorities have joined the International Organization of Securities Commissions (IOSCO). *See* IOSCO, Annual Report 2013 64–67, https://www.iosco.org/annual_reports/2013/pdf /annualReport2013.pdf. And American antitrust regulators work closely with foreign counterparts through informal agreements in order to develop coordinated enforcement strategies. As an illustrative example, in the 2012 merger of United Technologies and Goodrich—the largest in the history of the airline industry— American, Canadian, and European antitrust enforcers agreed to impose consistent conditions across their jurisdictions to facilitate a settlement. *See* Leslie C. Overton, Deputy Assistant Att'y Gen., U.S. Dep't. of Justice, Remarks at the Fifth Annual Chicago Forum on International Antitrust Issues: International Antitrust Engagement: Benefits and Opportunities 4–5 (June 12, 2014), http://www.justice.gov/atr /public/speeches/306510.pdf.

CHAPTER 6

Opening the Courthouse Doors: The Alien Tort Statute and Human Rights

1. *See* Filartiga v. Pena-Irala, 630 F.2d 876, 878 (2d Cir. 1980).

2. Dolly Filartiga, *American Courts, Global Justice,* N.Y. TIMES, Mar. 30, 2004, http:// www.nytimes.com/2004/03/30/opinion/american-courts-global-justice.html.

3. *See* JEFFREY DAVIS, JUSTICE ACROSS BORDERS: THE STRUGGLE FOR HUMAN RIGHTS IN U.S. COURTS 17–18 (2008).

4. *Filartiga,* 630 F.2d at 878–79.

5. 28 U.S.C. § 1350 (2012).

6. *Filartiga,* 630 F.2d at 879.

7. Respublica v. De Longchamps, 1 U.S. (1 Dall.) 111, 111–14 (O.T. Phila. 1784).

8. *See* Kiobel v. Royal Dutch Petroleum Co., 133 S. Ct. 1659, 1666 (2013); Sosa v. Alvarez-Machain, 542 U.S. 692, 716–18 & n.11 (2004).

9. *Kiobel,* 133 S. Ct. at 1666–67.

10. Curtis A. Bradley, *The Alien Tort Statute and Article III,* 42 Va. J. Int'l L. 587, 641–42 (2002) (quoting 3 Dep't of State, The Diplomatic Correspondence of the United States of America 447 (1837)).

11. Breach of Neutrality, 1 Op. Att'y Gen. 57 (1795).

12. *Id.* at 58–59.

13. *See, e.g.,* United States v. Smith, 18 U.S. (5 Wheat.) 153, 162 (1820) (referring to "the general practice of all nations in punishing all persons, whether natives or foreigners, who have committed [piracy] against any persons whatsoever, with whom they are in amity").

14. Peter Henner, Human Rights and the Alien Tort Statute: Law, History, and Analysis, 37–43 (2009). Henner notes that plaintiffs asserted jurisdiction under the Alien Tort Statute in twenty-one cases prior to the decision in *Filartiga,* but that jurisdiction was sustained in only two cases, one from 1795 and one from 1961. *Id.* at 43.

15. IIT v. Vencap, Ltd., 519 F.2d 1001, 1015 (2d Cir. 1975).

16. *Id.*

17. *Id.*

18. *Id.*

19. *Id.*

20. Filartiga v. Pena-Irala, 630 F.2d 876, 880 (2d Cir. 1980) (describing the lower court's rulings).

21. *Id.*

22. *Id.* (quoting United States v. Smith, 18 U.S. (5 Wheat.) 153, 160–61 (1820)).

23. *Id.* at 880–81 (quoting The Paquete Habana, 175 U.S 677, 694, 700 (1900)).

24. *Id.* at 881 n.8 (citing the Statute of the International Court of Justice arts. 38, 59, June 26, 1945, 59 Stat. 1055, 1060).

25. *Id.* at 884.

26. U.N. Charter arts. 55–56.

27. Egon Schwelb, Human Rights and the International Community: The Roots and Growth of the Universal Declaration of Human Rights, 1948–1963, at 70 (1964).

28. Universal Declaration of Human Rights, G.A. Res. 217 (III) (A), art. 5, U.N. Doc. A/RES/217(III) (Dec. 10, 1948).

29. G.A. Res. 2625 (XXV), U.N. Doc. A/Res/25/2625 (Oct. 24, 1970).

30. Memorandum of the United States as Amicus Curiae at 16 n.34, *Filartiga,* 630 F.2d 876 (No. 79–6090).

31. *Filartiga,* 630 F.2d at 881 (emphasis added).

32. *Id.* at 888.

33. *Id.* at 884.

34. *Id.* at 887.

35. *Id.* at 890.

36. *Id.*

37. Filartiga v. Pena-Irala, 577 F. Supp. 860, 867 (E.D.N.Y. 1984).

38. Beth Stephens, Filartiga v. Pena-Irala, *From Family Tragedy to Human Rights Accountability,* 37 Rutgers L.J. 623, 626 (2006) (quoting Dolly Filártiga).

39. Brief of the Am. Bar Assoc. as Amicus Curiae in Support of Petitioners at app. B, Kiobel v. Royal Dutch Petroleum Co., 133 S. Ct. 1659 (2013) (No. 10–1491); Jonathan Drimmer, *Resurrection Ecology and the Evolution of the Corporate Alien Tort Movement,* 43 Geo. J. Int'l L. 989, 996 (2012).

40. *In re* Estate of Ferdinand E. Marcos Human Rights Litig., 978 F.2d 492, 495–96 (9th Cir. 1992).

41. Ralph G. Steinhardt, *Fulfilling the Promise of* Filartiga: *Litigating Human Rights Claims Against the Estate of Ferdinand Marcos,* 20 Yale J. Int'l L. 65, 66 (1995).

42. *In re* Estate of Ferdinand Marcos Human Rights Litig., 25 F.3d 1467, 1475–76 (9th Cir. 1994); *see also* In re *Marcos,* 978 F.2d at 499–503 (upholding an earlier judgment).

43. In re *Marcos,* 25 F.3d at 1475 (emphasis added) (citing Filartiga v. Pena-Irala, 630 F.2d 876, 881 (2d Cir. 1980).

44. *Id.* (quoting *Filartiga,* 630 F.2d at 885–87).

45. Forti v. Suarez-Mason, 694 F. Supp. 707 (N.D. Cal. 1988).

46. Abebe-Jira v. Negewo, 72 F.3d 844 (11th Cir. 1996).

47. Xuncax v. Gramajo, 886 F. Supp. 162 (D. Mass. 1995).

48. Doe v. Qi, 349 F. Supp.2d 1258 (N.D. Cal. 2004). For more on ATS litigation, see Beth Stephens et al., International Human Rights Litigation in U.S. Courts 12–16 (2d ed. 2008).

49. Kenneth Anderson, Kiobel v. Royal Dutch Petroleum: *The Alien Tort Statute's Jurisdictional Universalism in Retreat,* 2012–2013, Cato Sup. Ct. Rev. 149, 163.

50. *See* Stephens et al., *supra* note 48, at 140 (explaining that torture "is one of the most widely recognized violations of international law, prohibited by the Convention Against Torture . . . as well as by the Universal Declaration of Human Rights (UDHR) and the Geneva Conventions" and that "every [U. S.] court to consider the issue has found that torture fits within [the ATS's] reach").

51. Universal Declaration of Human Rights, *supra* note 28, arts. 9, 12–13, 16, 18–19, 22–23.

52. Kadic v. Karadzic, 70 F.3d 232, 238–44 (2d Cir. 1995).

53. Doe v. Saravia, 348 F. Supp.2d 1112, 1157 (E.D. Cal. 2004) ("The assassination of Archbishop Romero meets the elements for establishing a crime against humanity. The Romero assassination occurred in an environment of state-sanctioned violence that was both widespread throughout El Salvador and constituted systematic, inhumane attacks on the civilian population by the ruling military. The death squad which perpetrated the murder . . . acted as part of a calculated strategy by the military to terrorize the civilian population into submission. The decision to kill

Romero was implemented to silence his criticism of the state security forces and state implemented repression. . . . Saravia knew that he was involved in an operation to commit the murder of one of the most important civilians in El Salvador, its revered Archbishop. Given that this particular act took place within the context of other widespread and systematic attacks against the civilian population . . . [it] meets the . . . criteria for establishing it as a crime against humanity.").

54. For examples of cases alleging environmental damage under the ATS that were dismissed, see Flores v. S Peru Copper Corp., 414 F.3d 233, 255–66 (2d Cir. 2003); and Beanal v. Freeport-McMoran, Inc., 197 F.3d 161, 166–67 (5th Cir. 1999). The district court case that was not dismissed on jurisdictional grounds, although it was subsequently dismissed on forum non conveniens grounds, was Aguinda v. Texaco, Inc., No. 93 Civ. 7527, 1994 WL 142006 (S.D.N.Y. Apr. 11, 1994), *dismissed sub nom* Jota v. Texaco, Inc., 157 F.3d 153 (2d Cir. 1998).

55. *See, e.g.,* Carmichael v. United Techs. Corp., 835 F.2d 109, 113–14 (5th Cir. 1988) (assuming that only acts of "official torture" fall within the purview of the ATS); Tel-Oren v. Libyan Arab Republic, 726 F.2d 774, 791–95 (D.C. Cir. 1984) (Edwards, J., concurring) (finding, in the context of claims against the nonstate Palestinian Liberation Organization, that "the consensus on non-official torture" did not "warrant[] an extension of *Filartiga* . . . to read section 1350 to cover torture by non-state actors").

56. *Karadzic,* 70 F.3d at 245; *see also* Tachiona v. Mugabe, 169 F. Supp.2d 259, 315–16 (S.D.N.Y. 2001) (finding the state action requirement satisfied in the case of a paramilitary group).

57. *Karadzic,* 70 F.3d at 239–43 (holding that prohibitions against slavery, piracy, genocide, and war crimes were all applicable to private individuals, on the basis of both contemporary international treaties, such as the Geneva Conventions, as well as historical materials); *accord, e.g., In re* Agent Orange Prod. Liab. Litig., 373 F. Supp.2d 7, 52–54 (E.D.N.Y. 2005); Iwanowa v. Ford Motor Co., 67 F. Supp.2d 424, 445 (D.N.J. 1999).

58. *See* STEPHENS ET AL., *supra* note 48, at 256–57.

59. *See, e.g.,* Cabello v. Fernandez-Larios, 402 F.3d 1148, 1157–58 (11th Cir. 2005); Doe v. Saravia, 348 F. Supp.2d 1112, 1148–49 (E.D. Cal. 2004); Eastman Kodak Co. v. Kavlin, 978 F. Supp. 1078, 1091 (S.D. Fla. 1997). This view finds support in Attorney General Bradford's opinion from 1795, which stated that "committing, *aiding, or abetting*" violations of the laws of nations gave rise to liability under the Alien Tort Statute. Breach of Neutrality, 1 Op. Att'y Gen. 57, 59 (1795) (emphasis added).

60. Doe I v. Unocal Corp., 110 F. Supp.2d 1294 (C.D. Cal. 2000); Doe I v. Unocal Corp., 963 F. Supp. 880 (C.D. Cal. 1997).

61. Doe I v. Unocal Corp., 395 F.3d 932, 947 (9th Cir. 2002).

62. Although the Ninth Circuit panel held the case could proceed, and that decision was granted rehearing en banc, the parties reached a confidential settlement and the case was voluntarily dismissed. *See* Doe I v. Unocal Corp., n 403 F.3d 708 (9th Cir. 2005) (en banc).

63. Drimmer, *supra* note 39, at 996.
64. *Id.* at 998.
65. Beth Stephens, *Upsetting Checks and Balances: The Bush Administration's Efforts to Limit Human Rights Litigation*, 17 HARV. HUM. RTS. J. 169, 179 (2004).
66. Anderson, *supra* note 49, at 169–71; Drimmer, *supra* note 39, at 996.
67. *See* Iwanowa v. Ford Motor Co., 67 F. Supp.2d 424, 446 (D.N.J. 1999) (concluding that a plaintiff who challenged Ford for actions taken under the Nazis stated a viable claim under the ATS).
68. Daimler AG v. Bauman, 134 S. Ct. 746, 761 n.19 (2014).
69. U.S. CONST. pmbl.
70. *See* JAMES H. READ, POWER VERSUS LIBERTY: MADISON, HAMILTON, WILSON, AND JEFFERSON 29 (2000) (quoting James Madison writing in the *National Gazette* in 1792).
71. *See* Filartiga v. Pena-Irala, 630 F.2d 876, 881 n.8 (2d Cir. 1980).
72. *See* Anderson, *supra* note 49, at 154–55.
73. *E.g.,* Sarei v. Rio Tinto, PLC, 671 F.3d 736, 756–57 (9th Cir. 2011) (observing that the State Department had originally submitted a Statement of Interest contending adjudication of the claims would "risk a potentially serious adverse impact on the peace process, and hence on the conduct of our foreign relations" with Papua New Guinea, but had since reversed its position); Corrie v. Caterpillar, Inc., 503 F.3d 974, 978 n.3 (9th Cir. 2007) (noting that the State Department filed an amicus brief urging dismissal due to the "political question" doctrine).
74. *See* John B. Bellinger III, *Enforcing Human Rights in U.S. Courts and Abroad: The Alien Tort Statute and Other Approaches*, 42 VAND. J. TRANSNAT'L L. 1, 10–12 (2009).
75. *See* Sosa v. Alvarez-Machain, 542 U.S. 692, 733 n.21 (2004) (discussing South Africa's opposition to district court actions in the United States); Khulumani v. Barclay Nat'l Bank Ltd., 504 F.3d 254, 295–311 (2d Cir. 2007) (Korman, J., concurring in part and dissenting in part) (documenting the objections of South African officials as well as of the State Department legal adviser's office to the apartheid litigation, which involved three ATS class actions on behalf of persons in South Africa between 1948 and the present date, brought against American, Canadian, and European corporations operating in South Africa during apartheid). Note, however, that after the Second Circuit declined to dismiss the apartheid ATS case, there was a change in administration in South Africa, and the litigation was narrowed due to the dismissal of certain claims. By 2009, South Africa's position was that it formally supported the litigation. *See* Ingrid Wuerth, *The Alien Tort Statute and Federal Common Law: A New Approach*, 85 NOTRE DAME L. REV. 1931, 1959 (2010).
76. *See* Doe v. Exxon Mobil Corp., 654 F.3d 11, 77–78 (D.C. Cir. 2011) (Kavanaugh, J., dissenting) (citing cases and primary sources); *Developments in the Law: Extraterritoriality*, 124 HARV. L. REV. 1226, 1283 (2011).
77. Anderson, *supra* note 49, at 170.
78. *See id.* at 170–71.
79. *See* Gabriel Bottini, *Universal Jurisdiction After the Creation of the International*

Criminal Court, 36 N.Y.U. J. Int'l L. & Pol. 503, 557–60 (2004) (listing criminal prosecutions brought against Augusto Pinochet in the United Kingdom, against the former dictator of Chad in Senegal, and against forty-six Argentinian persons in Spain, as well as criminal proceedings initiated against President George W. Bush and Ariel Sharon in Belgium, and the declaration of intent by three foreign judges to question Henry Kissinger).

80. Sosa v. Alvarez-Machain, 542 U.S. 692, 715 (2004) (citing 4 William Blackstone, Commentaries *68).

81. *See* Filartiga v. Pena-Irala, 630 F.2d 876, 890 (2d Cir. 1980) ("[F]or purposes of civil liability, the torturer has become—like the pirate and slave trader before him—*hostis humani generis,* an enemy of all mankind."); *In re* Estate of Ferdinand Marcos, Human Rights Litig., 25 F.3d 1467, 1475 (9th Cir. 1994) ("Actionable violations of international law must be of a norm that is specific, universal, and obligatory."); *see also* Kiobel v. Royal Dutch Petroleum Co., 133 S. Ct. 1659, 1675 (2014) (Breyer, J., concurring) (referring to both cases with approval); *Sosa,* 542 U.S. at 731–32 (also referring to both cases with approval).

82. Torture Victim Protection Act of 1991, Pub. L. No. 102–256, 106 Stat. 73.

83. Henner, *supra* note 14, at 67.

84. Rome Statute of the International Criminal Court art. 5, July 17, 1998, 2187 U.N.T.S. 90.

85. *Id.* art. 75.

86. *See* Dagmar Stroh, *State Cooperation with the International Criminal Tribunals for the Former Yugoslavia and for Rwanda,* 5 Max Planck Y.B. United Nations L. 249 (2001).

87. *See* David Davenport, *International Criminal Court: 12 Years, $1 Billion, 2 Convictions,* Forbes, Mar. 12, 2014.

88. *See* Brief for the United States as Amicus Curiae Supporting Petitioners at 29–30, *Kiobel,* 133 S. Ct. 1659 (No. 10–1491).

89. Sosa v. Alvarez-Machain, 542 U.S. 692, 697–98 (2004).

90. Alvarez-Machain v. United States, No. CV 93–4072SVW(SHX), 1999 WL 34976473, at 17 (C.D. Cal. Mar. 18, 1999).

91. Alvarez-Machain v. United States, 266 F.3d 1045, 1051–53 (9th Cir. 2001) (finding that under international customary legal norms, forcible transborder abduction and arbitrary detention were both forbidden).

92. Alvarez-Machain v. United States, 331 F.3d 604, 641 (9th Cir. 2003) (en banc).

93. 28 U.S.C. § 1350 (2012).

94. The argument that the ATS is purely jurisdictional, and that ATS claims require not just an alleged violation of international law but also a congressional law creating a cause of action, had been advanced by several judges on the D.C. Circuit in the years leading up to *Sosa. See* Al Odah v. United States, 321 F.3d 1134, 1146 (D.C. Cir. 2003) (Randolph, J., concurring); Tel-Oren v. Libyan Arab Republic, 726 F.2d 774, 801 (D.C. Cir. 1984) (Bork, J., concurring).

95. Sosa v. Alvarez-Machain, 542 U.S. 692, 719 (2004).

96. *Id.* at 712.

97. *Id.* at 713.
98. *Id.*
99. *Id.* at 714.
100. *Id.* at 715.
101. *Id.* at 720, 724, 730–32.
102. *Id.* at 725.
103. *Id.* at 732.
104. *Id.* (quoting Filartiga v. Pena-Irala, 630 F.2d 876, 890 (2d Cir. 1980)).
105. *Id.* at 728.
106. *Id.* at 725.
107. *Id.* at 727.
108. *Id.* at 727–28.
109. *Id.* at 728.
110. *Id.* at 729, 731.
111. *Id.* at 731–738.
112. *Id.* at 737 (quoting Restatement (Third) of Foreign Relations Law of the United States § 702 (1986)).
113. *Id.* at 761 (Breyer, J., concurring).
114. *Id.* (internal quotation omitted).
115. *Id.* at 762.
116. *Id.* at 762–63.
117. *Id.* at 763.
118. The case did not seem to inhibit the filing of Alien Tort Statute cases against corporations. The year *Sosa* was decided, six suits were filed against corporations; in the year after *Sosa*, twelve were filed. In 2009 that number jumped to twenty; and fifteen, then seventeen, suits were filed in the two years after that. *See* Drimmer, *supra* note 39, at 996.
119. Doe v. Exxon Mobil Corp., 654 F.3d 11 (D.C. Cir. 2011). Exxon had conceded that "extrajudicial killing, torture, and prolonged arbitrary detention [were] clearly established norms of international law." *Id.* at 17. Accordingly, the court of appeals did not question this concession, saying it was "reliev[ed] . . . from the task . . . of identifying the universe of international norms capable of giving rise to çauses of action in ATS lawsuits." *Id.* at 17 n.3. The question in the case was whether "aiding and abetting liability is [a]vailable under the ATS." *Id.* The court of appeals resolved that question in the affirmative. *Id.* at 15.
120. Sarei v. Rio Tinto, PLC, 487 F.3d 1193 (9th Cir. 2007).
121. Khulumani v. Barlcay Nat'l Bank Ltd., 504 F.3d 254 (2d Cir. 2007).
122. *Id.* at 258–59.
123. *Id.* at 260–64.
124. *In re* S. African Apartheid Litig., 617 F. Supp.2d 228, 296–97 (S.D.N.Y. 2009).
125. Kiobel v. Royal Dutch Petroleum Co., 621 F.3d 111, 123 (2d Cir. 2010).
126. *Khulumani*, 504 F.3d at 260.
127. *E.g.*, Presbyterian Church of Sudan v. Talisman Energy, Inc., 582 F.3d 244, 254–59 (2d Cir. 2009).

128. *Kiobel,* 621 F.3d at 120.

129. *Id.*

130. *Id.*

131. *Id.* at 151–54 (Leval, J., concurring in the judgment).

132. *Id.* at 152.

133. *Id.*

134. *Id.* at 188.

135. Kiobel v. Royal Dutch Petroleum Co., 133 S. Ct. 1659, 1663 (2013).

136. *Id.* at 1664.

137. *Id.* (quoting Morrison v. Nat'l Austl. Bank Ltd., 561 U.S. 247, 255 (2010)).

138. *Id.* (quoting EEOC v. Arabian Am. Oil Co., 499 U.S. 244, 248 (1991)).

139. *Id.* (quoting Sosa v. Alvarez-Machain, 542 U.S. 692, 727 (2004)).

140. *Id.* at 1665.

141. *Id.* at 1668. The Court then cited a writing of Joseph Story in 1822 observing that "'No nation has ever yet pretended to be the custos morum of the whole world.'" *Id.* (quoting United States v. The La Jeune Eugenie, 26 F. Cas. 832, 847 (C.C. Mass. 1822)).

142. *Id.*

143. *Id.* at 1669.

144. *Id.* at 1665.

145. *Id.* at 1668.

146. *Id.* at 1669.

147. *Id.*

148. *Id.* at 1672 (Breyer, J., concurring in the judgment) (quoting 28 U.S.C. § 1350 (2012)).

149. *Id.* (quoting Sosa v. Alvarez-Machain, 542 U.S. 692, 715 (2004)).

150. *Id.* (internal citation omitted).

151. *Id.* at 1673–74.

152. *Id.* at 1674. Namely, international law has "long included a duty not to permit a nation to become a safe harbor for pirates"; several treaties obligate signatory states to find and punish perpetrators of crimes committed by foreigners abroad; and other nations have created domestic mechanisms for plaintiffs to seek civil damages from foreign defendants for foreign-based conduct, by participating in criminal proceedings. *Id.* at 1674–76.

153. *Id.* at 1677–78.

154. *Id.* at 1678.

155. *Id.* at 1669 (Alito, J., concurring); *id.* (Kennedy, J., concurring).

156. *Id.* at 1669–70 (Alito, J., concurring).

157. *Id.* at 1669 (Kennedy, J., concurring).

158. *Id.*

159. *Id.* at 1671 (Breyer, J., concurring).

160. *Id.* at 1669 (Kennedy, J., concurring).

161. *Id.* (majority opinion).

162. Sosa v. Alvarez-Machain, 542 U.S. 692, 725 (2004) (internal quotation marks omitted).

163. Supplemental Brief for the United States as Amicus Curiae in Partial Support of Affirmance at 24–27, *Kiobel,* 133 S. Ct. 1659 (No. 10–1491).

164. *See* Philip Alston & Ryan Goodman, International Human Rights 1152 (2012).

165. *See* Antonio Cassese et al., Cassese's International Criminal Law 278 (2013) (noting "a trend towards considering that universal jurisdiction is allowed for the prosecution of international crimes"); Amnesty International, Universal Jurisdiction: A Preliminary Survey of Legislation Around the World—2012 Update 2, 13 (2012) (finding that more than 75 percent of U.N. member states provide for universal jurisdiction for at least some international crimes, though only about 48 percent specifically recognize universal jurisdiction for torture).

166. *See, e.g.,* Ashraf Ahmed El Hojouj, 400882/HA ZA 11–2252, 21 March 2012 (decision in Dutch); BBC News, *Dutch Court Compensates Palestinian for Libya Jail,* Mar. 28, 2012, http://www.bbc.com/news/world-middle-east-17537597.www.bbc .com/news/world-middle-east-17537597.

167. Rome Statute of the International Criminal Court, *supra* note 84, art. 75; *see also* Conor McCarthy, *Reparations Under the Rome Statute of the International Criminal Court and Reparative Justice Theory,* 3 Int'l J. Transitional Justice 250 (2009) (discussing the ICC reparations provision).

168. *See Kiobel,* 133 S. Ct. at 1675–76 (noting briefs from the European Commission, Netherlands, and United Kingdom); *Sosa,* 542 U.S. at 733 n.21 (discussing a brief from the European Commission).

PART III: BEYOND OUR SHORES

1. U.S. Const. art. II, § 2.

2. S. Rep. No. 106–71, at 21–26 (2001) (detailing the significant growth in congressional-executive agreements); Oona A. Hathaway, *Treaties' End: The Past, Present, and Future of International Lawmaking in the United States,* 117 Yale. L.J. 1236, 1286–301 (2008) (analyzing the growth of congressional-executive agreements).

3. *See* S. Rep. No. 106–71, at 23 (2001). For example, 124 regulatory authorities have joined the International Organization of Securities Commissions (IOSCO). *See* IOSCO, Annual Report, at 2013 64–67, https://www.iosco.org/annual_reports /2013/pdf/annualReport2013.pdf. And American antitrust regulators work closely with foreign counterparts through informal agreements in order to develop coordinated enforcement strategies. As an illustrative example, in the 2012 merger of United Technologies and Goodrich—the largest in the history of the airline industry—American, Canadian, and European antitrust enforcers agreed to impose consistent conditions across their jurisdictions to facilitate a settlement. *See* Leslie C. Overton, Deputy Assistant Att'y Gen., U.S. Dep't. of Justice, Remarks at the Fifth Annual Chicago Forum on International Antitrust Issues: International Antitrust Engagement: Benefits and Opportunities 4–5 (June 12, 2014), http://www .justice.gov/atr/public/speeches/306510.pdf.

4. *See id.* at 39 tbl.II–1 (counting sixty treaties concluded between 1789 and 1839, for an average of just over one per year, and 702 treaties concluded between 1939 and 1989, for an average of about fourteen per year). The number of executive agreements has increased more dramatically. *See id.* (counting twenty-seven executive agreements between 1789 and 1839 and 11,698 executive agreements between 1939 and 1989); *see also* Hathaway, *supra* note 2, at 1288 fig.1 (presenting data from the 1930s through 2006 showing that the number of executive agreements signed each year has increased dramatically while the number of treaties per year has fluctuated within a narrow band).

5. Following World War II, the international community ratified the U.N. Charter and the Statute of the International Court of Justice, the four Geneva Conventions, and a variety of other instruments such as the Convention on the Prevention and Punishment of the Crime of Genocide, Dec. 9, 1948, 78 U.N.T.S. 277; the Convention on the Prevention and Punishment of Crimes Against Internationally Protected Persons, Dec. 14, 1973, 1035 U.N.T.S. 167; the International Covenant on Civil and Political Rights, Dec. 16, 1966, 999 U.N.T.S. 171; and the Vienna Convention on Consular Relations, Apr. 24, 1963, 596 U.N.T.S. 261.

6. *See, e.g.,* United Nations Convention on International Bills of Exchange and International Promissory Notes, Dec. 9, 1988, U.N. Doc. A/43/820, 28 I.L.M. 170 (1989); Unidroit Convention on International Factoring, May 28, 1988, Unidraft Conf. 7/C.1/W.P.27, 27 I.L.M. 922 (1988); Unidroit Convention on International Lease Financing, May 28, 1988, Unidraft Conf. 7/C.1/W.P.27, 27 I.L.M. 922 (1988); Final Act of the United Nations Conference on Contracts for the International Sale of Goods, Apr. 11, 1980, U.N. Doc. A/CONF.97/18, 19 I.L.M. 668 (1980). For examples of new treaties concerning trade and intellectual property rights, see General Agreement on Trade in Services, Apr. 15, 1994, 1869 U.N.T.S. 183 (1994); Agreement on Trade-Related Aspects of Intellectual Property Rights, Apr. 15, 1994, 1869 U.N.T.S. 299, 33 I.L.M. 1197 (1994); General Agreement on Tariffs and Trade, Apr. 15, 1994, 1867 U.N.T.S. 187, 33 I.L.M. 1153 (1994); and General Agreement on Tariffs and Trade, Oct. 30, 1947, 61 Stat. pt. 5, T.I.A.S. No. 1700, 55 U.N.T.S. 194 (1947).

7. The major multilateral agreement on international arbitration is the United Nations Convention on the Recognition and Enforcement of Foreign Arbitral Awards, June 10, 1958, 21 U.S.T. 2517, 330 U.N.T.S. 3. The United States became a party in 1970. The United States also has dozens of BITs, which deal with arbitration. *See, e.g.,* Agreement for the Promotion and Protection of Investments, U.S.-Arg., Dec. 11, 1990, 1765 U.N.T.S. 38.

8. In the past several decades, the Hague Conference on Private International Law has overseen the writing and ratification of four treaties that facilitate international cooperation in cases involving children. These treaties are known as the Hague Children's Conventions. *See* Hague Convention on the Civil Aspects of International Child Abduction, Oct. 25, 1980, 1343 U.N.T.S. 49, 19 I.L.M. 1501–05 (1980) [hereinafter Hague Abduction Convention]; Hague Convention on the Protection of Children and Co-operation in Respect of Intercountry Adoption, May 29, 1993, 1870 U.N.T.S. 182, 32 I.L.M. 1134–46 (1993); Hague Convention on the Interna-

tional Recovery of Child Support and Other Forms of Family Maintenance, Nov. 23, 2007, 47 I.L.M. 257 (2008); Hague Convention on Jurisdiction, Applicable Law, Recognition, Enforcement, and Co-operation in Respect of Parental Responsibility and Measures for the Protection of Children, Oct. 19, 1996, 2204 U.N.T.S. 95, 35 I.L.M. 1391 (1996).

9. *See generally* Jose E. Alvarez, *The New Treaty Makers,* 25 B.C. Int'l & Comp. L. Rev. 213, 216–19 (2002) (documenting the proliferation of treaties in recent years, both as a general matter and those to which the United States is a party, and the broadened scope of their subject matter).

10. *See* S. Rep. No. 106–71, at 42–43 (2001) (detailing the expansion of multilateral treaties, both in general and to which the United States is a party, since 1945); Alvarez, *supra* note 9, at 216–17 (noting that "[f]rom 1970 through 1997, the number of international treaties more than tripled" and "of some 1,500 multilateral treaties in existence [as of 1995], nearly half were attributable to U.N. system organizations, and the rate of production of new treaties undertaken within the auspices of international organizations appears to be steadily increasing").

11. *See* S. Rep. No. 106–71, at 42 (2001) ("Some of these [treaties with international organizations] concern routine matters such as reimbursement of taxes of employees of these organizations, but others concern subjects of broader significance, such as the application of international atomic energy safeguards in the United States.").

CHAPTER 7

Treaty Interpretation: Child Custody

1. *See, e.g.,* Abbott v. Abbott, 560 U.S. 1, 16 (2012) ("In interpreting any treaty, '[t]he opinions of our sister signatories . . . are entitled to considerable weight'" (quoting El Al Isr. Airlines, Ltd. v. Tsui Yuan Tseng, 525 U.S. 155, 176 (1999)). For examples of the Court referencing foreign opinions to aid in its interpretation of a treaty, see, for example, *id.* at 16–17 (reviewing "the international case law," including decisions by the High Courts of Austria, South Africa, and Germany, to "confir[m] broad acceptance of the rule that *ne exeat* rights are rights of custody" under the child abduction treaty at issue); Lozano v. Alvarez, 134 S. Ct. 1224, 1235 (2014) (citing decisions of foreign tribunals to support the Court's holding that the child abduction treaty at issue did not include a rule of equitable tolling as to its one-year state of limitation).

2. *See* Sumitomo Shoji Am., Inc. v. Avagliano, 457 U.S. 176, 184–85 (1982) ("Although not conclusive, the meaning attributed to treaty provisions by the Government agencies charged with their negotiation and enforcement is entitled to great weight."); Kolovrat v. Oregon, 366 U.S. 187, 194 (1961) ("While courts interpret treaties for themselves, the meaning given them by the departments of government particularly charged with their negotiation and enforcement is given great weight.").

3. Vienna Convention on the Law of Treaties art. 31(1), May 23, 1969, 1155 U.N.T.S. 331.

4. *Id.* art. 31(3)(b).
5. *Id.* art. 32.
6. *Id.* art. 32(a)–(b).
7. The three cases are Lozano v. Alvarez, 134 S. Ct. 1224 (2014); Chafin v. Chafin, 133 S. Ct. 1017 (2013); and Abbott v. Abbott, 560 U.S. 1 (2010). The technical case that I will not discuss, *Chafin,* concerned when a case becomes moot under the treaty.
8. Hague Convention on the Civil Aspects of International Child Abduction Oct. 25, 1980, 1343 U.N.T.S. 49 [hereinafter Hague Abduction Convention]. *See* Susan L. Barone, *International Parent Child Abduction: A Global Dilemma with Limited Relief—Can Something More Be Done?,* 8 N.Y. INT'L L. REV. 95, 98–99 (1995) (discussing the growth in international child abductions, as a result of the growth in international marriages); Ann Laquer Estin, *Families Across Borders: The Hague Children's Conventions and the Case for International Family Law in the United States,* 62 FLA. L. REV. 47, 98–99 (2010) (discussing the transnational nature of modern family arrangements and explaining that such developments call for a body of international family law, exemplified by documents such as the Hague Abduction Convention); G. M. Filisko, *When Global Families Fail: As Family Law Takes on Global Dimensions, International Treaties May Hold the Key to Resolving Disputes,* 96 A.B.A. J. 56 (2010) (documenting how, "[a]s more domestic relations cases become international in nature, treaty law is playing a more important role in governing how they are resolved," particularly the Hague Abduction Convention).
9. *See* Tai Vivatvaraphol, Note, *Back to Basics: Determining a Child's Habitual Residence in International Child Abduction Cases Under the Hague Convention,* 77 FORDHAM L. REV. 3325, 3332–33 (2009) (discussing the unpredictable and varying results in international child abduction cases prior to the convention, and explaining how the need for more uniformity and predictability across jurisdictions motivated the treaty).
10. Brief for Respondent at 6–8, Abbott v. Abbott, 560 U.S. 1 (2010) (No. 08–645).
11. *See Abbott,* 560 U.S. at 5–6.
12. *Id.* at 5.
13. *See id.* at 6.
14. Hague Abduction Convention, *supra* note 8, art. 3(a).
15. *Id.* art. 12.
16. *See Abbott,* 560 U.S. at 7.
17. Hague Abduction Convention, *supra* note 8, art. 12.
18. *Id.* art. 3(a).
19. *Id.* art. 5(a).
20. *See Abbott,* 560 U.S. at 10 (discussing the Chilean law).
21. *Id.* at 11.
22. *Id.* at 11–13.
23. *Id.* at 20.
24. *Id.* at 19.
25. *Id.* at 15.
26. *Id.* at 16–17.

27. *Id.* at 18.
28. *Id.* at 26–27 (Stevens, J., dissenting).
29. Hague Abduction Convention, *supra* note 8, art. 5(a) (emphasis added).
30. *See Abbott,* 560 U.S. at 24.
31. Hague Abduction Convention, *supra* note 8, art. 5(b).
32. *See Abbott,* 560 U.S. at 35 (explaining the Chilean law).
33. *Id.* at 39–40 (emphasis removed).
34. *Id.* at 43–44.
35. *Id.* at 43 ("[T]he Department offers us little more than its own reading of the treaty's text. Its view is informed by no unique vantage it has, whether as the entity responsible for enforcing the Convention in this country or as a participating drafter. The Court's perfunctory, one-paragraph treatment of the Department's judgment of this matter only underscores this point.").
36. *Id.* at 42–43.
37. William Shakespeare, The Life of King Henry the Fifth act 1, sc. 2.
38. *See* Plantagenet Family Tree, http://www.skidmore.edu/~lopitz/KRII/pla_tree .gif (last visited Feb. 10, 2015) (showing the relation between Henry IV (Henry V's father) and Isabella of France (the daughter of King Philip IV of France)).
39. Shakespeare, *supra* note 37, act 1, sc. 2.
40. *Id.*
41. *Id.*
42. *Id.*
43. *Id.*
44. *See* Abbott v. Abbott, 560 U.S. 1, 8 (2010).
45. *Id.* at 23 (Stevens J., dissenting) ("Timothy Abbott . . . has no authority to decide whether his son undergoes a particular medical procedure; whether his son attends a school field trip; whether and in what manner his son has a religious upbringing; or whether his son can play a videogame before he completes his homework. These are all rights and responsibilities of . . . respondent Jacquelyn Abbott. It is she who received sole custody, or 'daily care and control,' of [the child] when the expatriate couple divorced while living in Chile in 2004. Mr. Abbott possesses only visitation rights." (Internal citation omitted)).
46. *Id.* at 11 (majority opinion).
47. Lozano v. Alvarez, 134 S. Ct. 1224 (2014).
48. *Id.* at 1227–30.
49. Hague Abduction Convention, *supra* note 8, art. 12.
50. *Id.* (emphasis added).
51. *Lozano,* 134 S. Ct. at 1230–31.
52. *See* Brief for the National Center for Missing and Exploited Children as Amicus Curiae in Support of Petitioner at 26–31, *Lozano,* 134 S. Ct. 1224 (No. 12–820).
53. *See* Brief for the Domestic Violence Legal Empowerment & Appeals Project (DV LEAP) et al. as Amici Curiae in Support of Respondent at 26–37, *Lozano,* 134 S. Ct. 1224 (No. 12–820).
54. *Lozano,* 134 S. Ct. at 1231.

55. *Id.* at 1235.
56. *Id.* at 1233.
57. *Id.* at 1235.
58. *See* Convention on the International Recovery of Child Support and Other Forms of Family Maintenance, Nov. 23, 2007, 47 I.L.M. 257; Convention on Protection of Children and Co-operation in Respect of Intercountry Adoption, May 29, 1993, 1870 U.N.T.S. 167.
59. *See* Convention on the Rights of the Child, Nov. 20, 1989, 1577 U.N.T.S. 3.

CHAPTER 8

Investment Treaties: Arbitration

1. *See, e.g.,* Learned Hand, *Historical and Practical Considerations Regarding Expert Testimony,* 15 HARV. L. REV. 40, 55–58 (1901) (arguing for a "tribunal of experts" to assist courts in cases where "specialized experience such as the ordinary man does not possess" is necessary).
2. At least that is what occurs in the usual case. Parties may also agree to arbitrate a dispute after it has already arisen, pursuant to what are often called "submission agreements."
3. Federal Arbitration Act of 1925, Pub. L. No 68–401, 43 Stat. 883 (codified at 9 U.S.C. §§ 1–16 (2012)); *see also* Gilmer v. Interstate/Johnson Lane Corp., 500 U.S. 20, 25 (1991) (finding that the FAA manifests "a liberal federal policy favoring arbitration agreements"); Charles L. Knapp, *Taking Contracts Private: The Quiet Revolution in Contract Law,* 71 FORDHAM L. REV. 761, 772 (2002) ("In 1925, Congress passed the Federal Arbitration Act, designed to overcome whatever pockets of judicial resistance might remain, and to provide a clear path to arbitration for those who had agreed to settle their disputes by that means.").
4. For an overview of the FAA, see STEPHEN K. HUBER & MAUREEN A. WESTON, ARBITRATION: CASES AND MATERIALS 9–11 (3d ed. 2011).
5. THOMAS E. CARBONNEAU, THE LAW AND PRACTICE OF ARBITRATION, at xiii (5th ed. 2014).
6. *Id.* at 94.
7. *Statistics: Judicial Business 2013,* U.S. COURTS, http://www.uscourts.gov/Statistics /JudicialBusiness/2013/us-district-courts.aspx (last visited Oct. 3, 2014).
8. *See* Press Release, Am. Arbitration Ass'n, Press Release, Am. Arbitration Ass'n, Commercial Section, Ass'n for Conflict Resolution, Neutral Elected to Second Term as Co-Chair, (Dec. 2, 2013), https://www.adr.org/aaa/ShowPDF ;jsessionid=7fbmTH1Qcdb1khr4GhtbH61v5cymLhkM41vC2z8jQL3JrVgGbYJH !102604678?doc=ADRSTAGE2017820 (noting that at the end of 2013, the AAA had "administered approximately 3.9 million alternative dispute resolution (ADR) cases since its founding 87 years ago").
9. Linda J. Demaine & Deborah R. Hensler, *"Volunteering" to Arbitrate Through Pre-dispute Arbitration Clauses: The Average Consumer's Experience,* 67 LAW & CONTEMP. PROBS. 55, 62 (2004).

10. *See Caseload Statistics 2014,* Admin. Office of U.S. Courts, http://www.uscourts
.gov/Statistics/FederalJudicialCaseloadStatistics/caseload-statistics-2014/caseload
-analysis.aspx (reporting that civil filings in federal district court have declined by
2.4 percent and civil appeals by 15 percent since 2005); *see also* Marc Galanter, *The
Vanishing Trial: An Examination of Trials and Related Matters in Federal and State
Courts,* 1 J. Empirical Legal Stud. 459, 462–63 (2004) (providing statistics about
the sharp decline of civil trials from 1962 to 2002).

11. *See, e.g.,* Thomas J. Stipanowich, *Arbitration: The "New Litigation,"* 2010 U. Ill. L.
Rev. 1, 8–24 (2010) (explaining that arbitration has become "formal, costly, [and]
time-consuming").

12. *See id.* at 24 (describing "expert decision making" as a "conventionally perceived
benefit" of arbitration).

13. *See* W. Mark C. Weidemaier, *Toward a Theory of Precedent in Arbitration,* 51 Wm. &
Mary L. Rev. 1895 (2010) (discussing and evaluating this line of thinking).

14. Kelley Brooke Snyder, *Note, Denial of Enforcement of Chinese Arbitral Awards on
Public Policy Grounds: The View from Hong Kong,* 42 Va. J. Int'l L. 339, 340 (2001).

15. *See* Valentina Vadi, *Critical Comparisons: The Role of Comparative Law in Investment Treaty Arbitration,* 39 Denv. J. Int'l L. & Pol'y 67, 73–76 (2010) (detailing the
expansion of investment treaties and of investment treaty-related arbitration, given
that so many such treaties include dispute resolution provisions, binding nation-
states and investors to the results of private arbitration).

16. Convention on the Recognition and Enforcement of Foreign Arbitral Awards
art. 5, June. 10, 1958, 330 U.N.T.S. 3.

17. *See* National Labor Relations of 1935, Pub. L. No. 74–198, §§3, 10, 49 Stat. 451
(codified at 29 U.S.C. §§ 153, 159–60 (2012)) (creating the National Labor Relations
Board).

18. *See* Dennis R. Nolan & Roger I. Abrams, *American Arbitration: The Early Years,* 35
U. Fla. L. Rev. 373, 418–21 (1983) (describing the growth in collective bargaining
agreements in the 1930s and 1940s that included binding arbitration provisions, but
also arguing that well before this period, "labor and management were largely convinced that grievance arbitration could be mutually advantageous" and had included
arbitration clauses in many contracts).

19. *See* Labor Relations Management Act of 1947, Pub. L. No. 80–101, §301, 61 Stat. 136
(codified at 29 U.S.C. § 401 et seq. (2012)); Nolan & Abrams, *supra* note 18, at 418
(explaining that "the biggest disincentive to labor arbitration agreements" prior to
this period had been "the lack of enforceability of collective bargaining agreements
and the arbitration clauses contained in them," in part due to "a continuing judicial
hostility to arbitration").

20. *See, e.g.,* Textile Workers Union of America v. Lincoln Mills, 353 U.S. 448, 455 (1957)
("Plainly the agreement to arbitrate grievance disputes is the quid pro quo for an
agreement not to strike.").

21. The Steelworkers' Trilogy refers to United Steelworkers v. American Manufacturing Co., 363 U.S. 564 (1960); United Steelworkers v. Warrior & Gulf Navigation

Co., 363 U.S. 574 (1960); and United Steelworkers v. Enterprise Wheel & Car Corp., 363 U.S. 593 (1960).

22. *See* William B. Gould IV, *Judicial Review of Labor Arbitration Awards—Thirty Years of the* Steelworkers' Trilogy: *The Aftermath of* AT&T *and* Misco, 64 Notre Dame L. Rev. 464, 465–66 (1989) (*"Steelworkers Trilogy* established the proposition that substantial deference was to be given to arbitration awards—deference more considerable than that enjoyed by the Labor Board and by the trial courts themselves.").

23. *Warrior & Gulf Navigation Co.*, 363 U.S. at 582–83.

24. U.S. Postal Serv. v. Nat'l Ass'n of Letter Carriers, 839 F.2d 146 (3d Cir. 1988).

25. *Enter. Wheel*, 363 U.S. at 597; *see also* United Paperworkers Int'l Union v. Misco, Inc., 484 U.S. 29, 36 (1987) ("As long as the arbitrator's award 'draws its essence from the collective bargaining agreement,' and is not merely 'his own brand of industrial justice' the award is legitimate. The function of the court is very limited when the parties have agreed to submit all questions of contract interpretation to the arbitrator. It is confined to ascertaining whether the party seeking arbitration is making a claim which on its face is governed by the contract." (quoting *Enter. Wheel*, 363 U.S. at 597)); Pinkerton's NY Racing Sec. Serv., Inc. v. Local 32E Serv. Emps. Int'l Union, 805 F.2d 470, 472–73 (2nd Cir. 1986) (upholding an arbitral award because "[i]t surely cannot be said that the substantive decision does not draw its essence from the parties' agreement or that the arbitrator did not provide a barely colorable justification for his holding" (internal quotation omitted)).

26. *See* Hall Street Assoc., L.L.C. v. Mattel, Inc., 552 U.S. 576, 588 (2008) (explaining that the Federal Arbitration Act should be understood as "substantiating a national policy favoring arbitration with just the limited review needed to maintain arbitration's essential virtue of resolving disputes straightaway. Any other reading opens the door to the full-bore legal and evidentiary appeals that can rende[r] informal arbitration merely a prelude to a more cumbersome and time-consuming judicial review process and bring arbitration theory to grief in post arbitration process" (internal quotation and citations omitted)).

27. AT&T Techs., Inc. v. Commc'ns Workers of Am., 475 U.S. 643 (1986).

28. *Id.* at 645.

29. *Id.* at 646–47.

30. *Id.* at 648–49 ("The first principle gleaned from the [*Steelworkers'*] Trilogy is that arbitration is a matter of contract and a party cannot be required to submit to arbitration any dispute which he has not agreed so to submit. This axiom recognizes the fact that arbitrators derive their authority to resolve disputes only because the parties have agreed in advance to submit such grievances to arbitration." (internal quotation omitted)).

31. *Id.* at 649.

32. *Id.*

33. *See* George Bermann, *The "Gateway" Problem in International Commercial Arbitration*, 37 Yale J. Int'l L. 1, 10–11 (2012) (describing competing meanings of *arbitra-*

bility). Note that Berman and others advise against using the term *arbitrability* in American legal doctrine, because in every other country, the term *arbitrability* has a narrower meaning—it refers to whether the claim being advanced is legally capable of being arbitrated, under that country's laws. Berman prefers a different terminology; he thinks "substantive arbitrability" issues should be described as questions of whether the arbitral tribunal has *jurisdiction,* and "procedural arbitrability" issues should be described as questions of whether a claim is *admissible* in the arbitral tribunal. This is consistent with how foreign countries distinguish between gateway arbitration questions.

34. *See id.* at 11–12.
35. *AT&T,* 475 U.S. at 651.
36. *See* Howsam v. Dean Witter Reynolds, Inc., 537 U.S. 79, 84 (2002); *see also, e.g.,* First Options of Chi., Inc. v. Kaplan, 514 U.S. 938 (1995) (holding that a court should decide whether an arbitration clause applied to a party who "had not personally signed" the document containing it).
37. *Howsam,* 537 U.S. at 85–86 (finding that an issue fell "within the class of gateway procedural disputes that do not present what our cases have called 'questions of arbitrability'" in which "the strong pro-court presumption as to the parties' likely intent does not apply"); *see also* Moses H. Cone Mem'l Hosp. v. Mercury Constr. Corp., 460 U.S. 1, 24–25 (1983) ("The Arbitration Act establishes that, as a matter of federal law, any doubts concerning the scope of arbitrable issues should be resolved in favor of arbitration, whether the problem at hand is the construction of the contract language itself or an allegation of waiver, delay, or a like defense to arbitrability.").
38. W.R. Grace & Co. v. Local Union 759, 461 U.S. 757, 766 (1983).
39. *Id.* (quoting Muschany v. United States, 324 U.S. 49, 66 (1945)).
40. United Paperworkers Int'l Union v. Misco, Inc., 484 U.S. 29, 43–44 (1987) ("[T]he formulation of public policy set out by the Court of Appeals did not comply with the statement [in *Grace*] that such a policy must be 'ascertained by reference to the laws and legal precedents, and not from general considerations of supposed public interests.' . . . The Court of Appeals made no attempt to review existing laws and legal precedents in order to demonstrate that they establish a 'well-defined and dominant' policy against the operation of dangerous machinery while under the influence of drugs. Although certainly such a judgment is firmly rooted in common sense . . . a formulation of public policy based only on 'general considerations of supposed public interests' is not the sort that permits courts to set aside an arbitration award." (quoting *W.R. Grace,* 461 U.S. at 766)).
41. *See, e.g., id.* at 38 ("Courts thus do not sit to hear claims of factual or legal error by an arbitrator as an appellate court does in reviewing decisions of lower courts.").
42. BG Group, PLC v. Republic of Argentina, 134 S. Ct. 1198, 1204 (2013).
43. *Id.*
44. Agreement for the Promotion and Protection of Investments art. 8(2)(a)–(b), U.S.-Arg., Dec. 11, 1990, 1765 U.N.T.S. 38.
45. *BG Group,* 134 S. Ct. at 1204–05.

46. *See* Republic of Argentina v. BG Group PLC, 715 F. Supp.2d 108 (D.D.C. 2010) (denying Argentina's petition to vacate or modify the arbitral decision); Republic of Argentina v. BG Group PLC, 764 F. Supp.2d 21 (D.D.C. 2011) (confirming the arbitral award).
47. Republic of Argentina v. BG Group PLC, 665 F.3d 1363 (D.C. Cir. 2012).
48. *BG Group,* 134 S. Ct. at 1205–07.
49. *Id.* at 1207–08.
50. *Id.* at 1212–13.
51. Brief for the United States as Amicus Curiae in Support of Vacatur and Remand at 15, BG Group PLC v. Republic of Argentina, 134 S. Ct. 1198 (2013) (No. 12–138) ("Applying *First Options* and *Howsam* wholesale to investment treaties, however, would be inconsistent with principles of treaty interpretation and the treaties' structure. Rather, the judicial standard of review should turn on the nature of the objection under the applicable treaty. Courts should review de novo arbitral rulings concerning objections based on the asserted lack of a valid agreement to arbitrate, even if the absence of an agreement is caused by a failure to comply with a requirement that resembles what might be viewed as a 'procedural' matter or a mere 'precondition' to arbitration in a private commercial dispute. Rulings on other objections should be reviewed deferentially, unless the treaty provides that the arbitral tribunal's authority to rule on such matters is more limited.").
52. *Id.* at 15–16 ("A crucial distinction between investor-state and private commercial arbitration, however, is that in the investor-state context, the relevant agreement concerning the arbitral tribunal's authority is contained in the investment treaty itself and reflects the *treaty* parties' agreement. . . . As a result, questions concerning the treaty parties' agreement—and therefore the existence and substance of a contracting State's agreement to arbitrate with an individual investor—are matters of treaty interpretation, and are not governed by any nation's domestic contract law.").
53. *Id.* at 18–19.
54. *BG Group,* 134 S. Ct. at 1208–09.
55. *Id.* at 1209.
56. *Id.* at 1210.
57. *Id.* at 1208–09 ("We do not accept the Solicitor General's view as applied to the treaty before us. . . . While we leave the matter open for future argument, we do not now see why the presence of the term 'consent' in a treaty warrants abandoning, or increasing the complexity of, our ordinary intent-determining framework.").
58. Bermann, *supra* note 33, at 13–14 & n.44. German law, similar to American law, allows parties to obtain de novo judicial review of "arbitrability" determinations— that is, as to whether an arbitration agreement exists or as to whether it covers the dispute at hand—through filing interlocutory motions with courts. *Id.* at 20.
59. *Id.* at 15–16.
60. *Id.* at 16–17 (emphasis added). This doctrine, termed "separability," functions "to enable an arbitral tribunal to declare a contract invalid or unenforceable on the merits, without thereby necessarily destroying the basis of its authority to make that very ruling." *Id.* at 22.

61. Yahoo!, Inc. v. La Ligue Contre Le Racisme et L'Antisemitisme, 169 F. Supp.2d 1181 (N.D. Cal. 2001). French users could access the materials on the auction site either through Yahoo.com directly, or through a link on Yahoo's French affiliate website, Yahoo.fr. *Id.* at 1184.

62. *Id.* at 1184.

63. *Id.* at 1184–85.

64. *Id.* at 1185.

65. *Id.* at 1194 ("Even assuming for purposes of the present motion that Yahoo! does possess such technology, compliance still would involve an impermissible restriction on speech.").

66. Yahoo!, Inc. v. La Ligue Contre Le Racisme et L'Antisemitisme, 433 F.3d 1199, 1213–14 (9th Cir. 2006) (en banc) (quoting RESTATEMENT (THIRD) OF FOREIGN RELATIONS LAW OF THE UNITED STATES § 482(2)(d) (1987)).

67. Convention on the Recognition and Enforcement of Foreign Arbitral Awards, *supra* note 16, art. 3.

68. *Id.* art. 5(2)(b).

69. *See, e.g.*, Banco de Seguros del Estado v. Mut. Marine Office, Inc., 344 F.3d 255, 264 (2d Cir. 2003) (drawing on the labor arbitration cases to hold that the "public policy" exception under the New York Convention is to be applied narrowly, and only for a very explicit and well-defined public policy); Rive v. Briggs of Cancun, Inc., 82 F. App'x 359, 364 (5th Cir. 2003)("[C]ourts construe this public policy defense narrowly and only apply it when enforcement of the foreign arbitration award would violate the forum state's most basic notions of morality and justice."); Karen Maritime Ltd. v. Omar Int'l Inc., 322 F. Supp.2d 224, 226–27 (E.D.N.Y. 2004)(reviewing cases in which federal and appellate courts have enforced foreign arbitral awards over public policy objections, and observing that to apply the exception in the current case could mark the first time "any American jurisdiction" has done so).

CHAPTER 9

The Treaty Power: Structure

1. U.S. CONST. art. VI, cl. 2.

2. This was the central question in *Missouri v. Holland,* 252 U.S. 416 (1920). Congress had enacted a migratory bird statute in 1918 pursuant to "a treaty between the United States and Great Britain [that] was proclaimed by the President." *Id.* at 431. Earlier Supreme Court precedent had suggested that Congress lacked the authority under the Constitution to directly enact legislation dealing with migratory birds, and so the question in the case was whether Congress could exceed its delegated legislative powers, if acting pursuant to a treaty that called upon signatory nations to pass appropriate legislation. *Id.* at 432–33. The Court held in the affirmative. *Id.* at 435.

3. *See, e.g.,* Reid v. Covert, 354 U.S. 1, 16 (1957) ("[N]o agreement with a foreign nation can confer power on the Congress, or on any other branch of Government, which is free from the restraints of the Constitution.").

4. See UNION OF INT'L ASS'NS, HISTORICAL OVERVIEW OF NUMBER OF INTERNA-
   TIONAL ORGANIZATIONS BY TYPE (2013), http://www.uia.org/sites/uia.org/files
   /misc_pdfs/stats/Historical_overview_of_number_of_international_organizations
   _by_type_1909–2013.pdf. These figures include intergovernmental organizations
   listed as types "A" through "G" in the UIA's data.
5. *See* S. REP. NO. 106–71, at 39 (2001).
6. *See* U.S. Dep't of State, UNITED STATES CONTRIBUTIONS TO INTERNATIONAL
   ORGANIZATIONS: SIXTY-FIRST ANNUAL REPORT TO CONGRESS FOR FISCAL YEAR
   2012 (2013), http://www.state.gov/documents/organization/213206.pdf. The CIA
   World Factbook provides a list of approximately sixty-five international organizations of which the United States is a member. *See* CIA, *International Organization
   Participation, in* THE WORLD FACTBOOK (2013), https://www.cia.gov/library
   /publications/the-world-factbook/fields/2107.html#us (last visited Oct. 4, 2014).
   For a listing of all bilateral and multilateral treaties and agreements to which the
   United States is a party, *see* U.S. DEP'T OF STATE, TREATIES IN FORCE: A LIST
   OF TREATIES AND OTHER INTERNATIONAL AGREEMENTS OF THE UNITED
   STATES IN FORCE ON JANUARY 1, 2013 (2013), http://www.state.gov/documents
   /organization/218912.pdf.
7. 5 YEARBOOK OF INTERNATIONAL ORGANIZATIONS 2012–2013, at 54 fig.3.3 (49th ed.
   2013).
8. *Id.* at 46 fig.3.1 (adding the numbers given for Groups A–G).
9. *Id.* at 54 fig.3.3.
10. *Id.* at 25 fig.2.1.
11. *Id.* at 25 fig.2.1.
12. *Id.* at 29 fig.2.5.
13. *Id.* at 20.
14. SABINO CASSESE, THE GLOBAL POLITY: GLOBAL DIMENSIONS OF DEMOCRACY
    AND THE RULE OF LAW 109 (2012).
15. Which of these international organizations has the capacity to bind its members
    legally is a complicated question. While "some constituent treaties expressly confer
    on organizations the power to issue decisions binding on their members," many
    others offer a less clear delegation of authority. Dapo Akande, *International Organi-
    zations, in* INTERNATIONAL LAW 248, 261 (Malcolm Evans ed., 4th ed. 2014). How-
    ever, even when international organizations do not have authority to issue decisions
    that are binding on members, "the non-binding nature of [their] decisions does not
    mean that a particular decision is devoid of legal effect for its members." *Id.* Some
    organizations, such as the International Labour Organization, may require member
    states to consider their decisions in good faith or issue nonbinding decisions that
    "contain rules of law which are or become binding through other processes of inter-
    national law." *Id.* at 262.
16. CASSESE, *supra* note 14, at 53; *see also* Suzannah Linton & Firew Kebede Tiba, *The
    International Judge in an Age of Multiple International Courts and Tribunals,* 9 CHI. J.
    INT'L L. 407, 409 (2009) ("Until the 1990s, there were only six permanent interna-
    tional judicial bodies: the International Court of Justice ('ICJ'), the Court of Justice

of the European Communities ('ECJ'), the Court of Justice of the Andean Community, the Court of Justice of the Benelux Economic Union, the European Court of Human Rights ('ECtHR'), and the Inter-American Court of Human Rights ('IACtHR').").

17. CASSESE, *supra* note 14, at 53–54. The Project on International Courts and Tribunals emphasizes the diversity and evolving nature of the "international judiciary" and in 2004 identified sixteen currently functioning "international judicial bodies" and eighty-two "quasi judicial bodies." *The International Judiciary in Context,* PROJECT ON INT'L CTS. & TRIBUNALS (2004), http://www.pict-pcti.org/publications /synoptic_chart/synop_c4.pdf. In this taxonomy, "international judicial bodies . . . (a) are permanent institutions; (b) are composed of independent judges; (c) adjudicate disputes between two or more entities, at least one of which is either a State or an International Organization; (d) work on the basis of predetermined rules of procedure; and (e) render decisions that are binding." *Id.* By contrast, quasi-judicial "bodies and mechanisms which, while not meeting several or all of the above mentioned standards, also play a role in the enforcement, interpretation and implementation of international law." *Id; see also* Jonathan I. Charney, *The Impact on the International Legal System of the Growth of International Courts and Tribunals,* 31 N.Y.U. J. INT'L L. & POL. 697, 699 (1999) (analyzing the consequences of the growth of international judicial bodies); Benedict Kingsbury, *Foreword: Is the Proliferation of International Courts and Tribunals A Systemic Problem?*, 31 N.Y.U. J. INT'L L. & POL. 679, 680 (1999) (discussing the proliferation of international courts and tribunals); Cesare P.R. Romano, *The Proliferation of International Judicial Bodies: The Pieces of the Puzzle,* 31 N.Y.U. J. INT'L L. & POL. 709, 709–10 (1999) ("When future international legal scholars look back at international law and organizations at the end of the twentieth century, they probably will refer to the enormous expansion and transformation of the international judiciary as the single most important development of the post–Cold War age. Since 1989, almost a dozen international judicial bodies have become active or have been extensively reformed, compared to only about six or seven previously populating the international scene.").

18. The United States signed the Rome Statute, but the Senate has not ratified the treaty. For a summary of the history of the United States' position on the Rome Statute and the ICC, see Stephen Eliot Smith, *Definitely Maybe: The Outlook for U.S. Relations with the International Criminal Court During the Obama Administration,* 22 FLA. J. INT'L L. 155, 160–66 (2010); and Diane F. Orentlicher, *Unilateral Multilateralism: United States Policy Toward the International Criminal Court,* 36 CORNELL INT'L L.J. 415 (2004).

19. *See* Understanding on Rules and Procedures Governing the Settlement of Disputes, Apr. 15, 1994, 1869 U.N.T.S. 401.

20. *See* North American Free Trade Agreement ch. 19, U.S.-Can.-Mex., Dec. 17, 1992, 107 Stat. 2057, 32 I.L.M. 289 (1993).

21. See ICSID, Convention on the Settlement of Investment Disputes Between States and Nationals of Other States, *in* ICSID CONVENTION, REGULATIONS AND RULES 7 (2006).

22. *See United States Affirms Support for ICTY, Denies Karadzic Amnesty Deal*, 103 Am. J. Int'l L. 591, 591 (2009) ("As part of an ongoing commitment to assist the work of the ICTY, the United States regularly provides information to both prosecution and defense counsel.").

23. *See* U.S. Dep't of State, United States Contributions to International Organizations (2010), http://www.state.gov/documents/organization/199431.pdf (listing the financial contributions to international organizations, including ICTR and ICTY).

24. *See* Padraic J. Glaspy, *Justice Delayed? Recent Developments at the Extraordinary Chambers in the Courts of Cambodia*, 21 Harv. Hum. Rts. J. 143, 146 (2008) ("After the U.N. pulled out of the process in 2002 . . . , it was only the intervention of interested countries led by Japan, France, Australia, and the United States that ultimately salvaged the tribunal.").

25. Statute of the International Court of Justice, June 26, 1945, 59 Stat. 1055 [hereinafter ICJ Statute].

26. U.N. Charter art. 94.

27. ICJ Statute, *supra* note 25, art. 34(1).

28. *Id.* art. 36.

29. *Id.* art. 36(1)–(2).

30. *Id.* art. 59.

31. Vienna Convention on Consular Relations, Apr. 24, 1963, 596 U.N.T.S. 261.

32. *Id.* art. 36(1)(b).

33. *Id.*

34. *Id.* art. 36(2).

35. Optional Protocol Concerning the Compulsory Settlement of Disputes, Apr. 24, 1963, 596 U.N.T.S. 487.

36. *Id.* art. I.

37. *See* Letter from Condoleezza Rice, Secretary, to Kofi A. Annan, Secretary-General of the United Nations (Mar. 7, 2005), http://www.state.gov/documents/organization/87288.pdf.

38. *See* LaGrand Case (Ger. v. U.S.), Application Instituting Proceedings, ¶¶ 4–8 (Mar. 2, 1999), http://www.icj-cij.org/docket/files/104/7153.pdf.

39. LaGrand Case (Ger. v. U.S.), Request for the Indication of Provisional Measures, 1999 I.C.J. 9, ¶ 5 (Mar. 3).

40. *Id.* ¶ 29.

41. LaGrand Case (Ger. v. U.S.), 2001 I.C.J. 466, ¶ 34 (June 27).

42. *Id.* ¶¶ 17–21.

43. *Id.* ¶¶ 22–24.

44. *Id.* ¶ 82.

45. *Id.* ¶ 74.

46. *Id.* ¶ 90

47. *Id.*

48. *Id.* ¶ 91.

49. *Id.* ¶ 123.

50. *Id.*
51. *Id.* ¶ 125.
52. *Id.* ¶ 126.
53. Avena and Other Mexican Nationals (Mex. v. U.S.), 2004 I.C.J. 12 (Mar. 31).
54. *Id.* ¶ 15.
55. *Id.* ¶ 90 ("The Court accordingly concludes that, with respect to each of the individuals [except one] . . . , the United States has violated its obligation under Article 36, paragraph 1(*b*) of the Vienna Convention to provide information to the arrested person."). The Court found that Mexico had "failed to prove the violation of the United States . . . in the case of" the one exceptional defendant, Ramon Salcido Bojorquez. *Id.* ¶ 74. The United States was able to establish that this defendant had claimed American citizenship at the time of his arrest. *Id.* ¶ 66.
56. *Id.* ¶ 88. The Court suggested that the obligation to notify commences "as soon as it is realized that the person is a foreign national, or once there are grounds to think that the person is probably a foreign national." *Id.*
57. *Id.* ¶ 89.
58. Vienna Convention on Consular Relations, *supra* note 31, art. 36(2).
59. *Avena,* 2004 I.C.J. 12, ¶ 112 (quoting *LaGrand,* 2001 I.C.J. 466, ¶ 90).
60. *Id.* ¶ 113.
61. *Id.* (quoting Vienna Convention on Consular Relations, *supra* note 31, art. 36(2)).
62. *Id.*
63. *Id.* ¶ 114.
64. *Id.* ¶ 153(9).
65. *Id.* ¶ 121.
66. In 2013, the U.S. courts of appeals handled more than 15,000 prisoner petitions. *See Judicial Business 2013: U.S. Courts of Appeals,* ADMIN. OFFICE OF U.S. COURTS, http://www.uscourts.gov/Statistics/JudicialBusiness/2013/us-courts-of-appeals .aspx#table2 (last visited Feb. 2, 2015).
67. Sanchez-Llamas v. Oregon, 548 U.S. 331 (2006). The case also addressed the appeal of Moises Sanchez-Llamas, a Mexican national who asserted that he was not informed of his Vienna Convention right to contact the Mexican consulate after being arrested for shooting a police officer in the leg. *Id.* at 339–40.
68. *Id.* at 340–41; *see also* Brief for Petitioner Mario A. Bustillo at 4–5, *Sanchez-Llamas,* 548 U.S. 331 (Nos. 04–10566, 05–51).
69. *Sanchez-Llamas,* 458 U.S. at 341.
70. *Id.*
71. *Id.*
72. *Id.* It appears that Bustillo's trial counsel may have been aware of the Vienna Convention, however, and simply chose not to contact the consul. *See* Transcript of Oral Argument at 58–59, *Sanchez-Llamas,* 548 U.S. 331 (Nos. 04–10566, 05–51).
73. *See* Brief for Petitioner Mario A. Bustillo, *supra* note 68, at 8–9.
74. *See* Brief for Amici Curiae Republic of Honduras and Other Foreign Sovereigns at 24–25, *Sanchez-Llamas,* 548 U.S. 331 (Nos. 04–10566, 05–51).
75. *Sanchez-Llamas,* 548 U.S. at 341.

76. *Id.*
77. *Id.*
78. *Id.* at 342.
79. *See id.* at 351.
80. *Id.* at 342.
81. *See* Brief for Petitioner Mario A. Bustillo, *supra* note 68, at 2.
82. *Id.*
83. Vienna Convention on Consular Relations, *supra* note 31, art. 36(2).
84. *Id.*
85. *See Avena,* 2004 I.C.J. 12, ¶ 112–13.
86. *Id.* ¶ 113.
87. *Sanchez-Llamas,* 548 U.S. at 353. *See also* Brief of International Court of Justice Experts as Amici Curiae, *Sanchez-Llamas,* 548 U.S. 331 (Nos. 04–10566, 05–51) ("The Optional Protocol serves as a forum selection clause, with the effect that parties that have selected the ICJ as the forum to decide their disputes are bound to carry out its decisions. Thus, once having given consent to both the Vienna Convention and the designated forum for dispute settlement, the United States is obligated to comply with the Convention, as interpreted by the ICJ."). The chief justice pointed out, however, that "shortly after *Avena,* the United States withdrew from the Optional Protocol concerning Vienna Convention disputes. Whatever the effect of *Avena* and *LaGrand* before this withdrawal, it is doubtful that our courts should give decisive weight to the interpretation of a tribunal whose jurisdiction in this area is no longer recognized by the United States." *Sanchez-Llamas,* 548 U.S. at 355.
88. *Sanchez-Llamas,* 548 U.S. at 353.
89. *Id.* at 354.
90. *Id.* (quoting ICJ Statute, *supra* note 25, art. 59).
91. U.N. Charter art. 94, para 1 (emphasis added); *see Sanchez-Llamas,* 548 U.S. at 355.
92. *Sanchez-Llamas,* 548 U.S. at 355.
93. *Id.* (quoting Breard v. Greene, 523 U.S. 371, 375 (1998)).
94. *See id.* at 382–83 (Breyer, J., dissenting).
95. *See id.* at 383.
96. *See* Counter-Memorial of the United States at 61 n.128, *Avena,* 2004 I.C.J. 12 (Nov. 3, 2003) (noting that "it is well-settled" that an ICJ decision "may serve as authority beyond a particular case").
97. *See Sanchez-Llamas,* 548 U.S. at 384–85 (listing examples of such cases).
98. Human Rights Act, 1998, c.42, § 3(1) (U.K.) ("So far as it is possible to do so, primary legislation and subordinate legislation must be read and given effect in a way which is compatible with the Convention rights.").
99. *Id.* § 2(1) ("A court or tribunal determining a question which has arisen in connection with a Convention right must take into account any . . . judgment, decision, declaration or advisory opinion of the European Court of Human Rights.").
100. *See* Robert Stevens, The English Judges: Their Role in the Changing Constitution 124 & n.15 (2002).

101. Lord Irvine of Lairg, *Address at University College London: A British Interpretation of Convention Rights* 1 (Dec. 14, 2011), http://www.laws.ucl.ac.uk/wp-content /uploads/2014/11/Lord_Irvine_Convention_Rights.pdf.

102. *Sanchez-Llamas,* 548 U.S. at 355 (majority opinion).

103. *Id.* at 353 (quoting LaGrand Case (Ger. v. U.S.), 2001 I.C.J. 466, ¶ 91 (June 27)).

104. *Id.* at 357 ("If the state's failure to inform the defendant of his Article 36 rights generally excuses the defendant's failure to comply with relevant procedural rules, then presumably rules such as statutes of limitations and prohibitions against filing successive habeas petitions must also yield in the face of Article 36 claims.").

105. *Id.* (quoting Vienna Convention on Consular Relations, *supra* note 31, art. 36(2)).

106. *See Sanchez-Llamas,* 548 U.S. at 386–87 (Breyer, J., dissenting).

107. *Avena,* 2004 I.C.J. 12, ¶ 113.

108. *See Sanchez-Llamas,* 548 U.S. at 387–88 (Breyer, J., dissenting).

109. *Avena,* 2004 I.C.J. 112, ¶ 153(9); *see also LaGrand,* 2001 I.C.J. 466, ¶ 125.

110. *See Avena,* 2004 I.C.J. 112, ¶ 153(9).

111. Medellin v. Texas, 552 U.S. 491, 501 (2008).

112. *Id.* at 500.

113. *Id.* at 501.

114. *Id.*

115. *Id.* ("Medellín first raised his Vienna Convention claim in his first application for state postconviction relief.")

116. *Id.* at 501–2 (internal quotation and brackets omitted); *see also id.* ("The state trial court held that the claim was procedurally defaulted because Medellín had failed to raise it at trial or on direct review. The trial court also rejected the Vienna Convention claim on the merits . . . , finding that Medellín had 'fail[ed] to show that any non-notification of the Mexican authorities impacted on the validity of his conviction or punishment.' The Texas Court of Criminal Appeals affirmed.").

117. *Id.* at 502 ("Medellín then filed a habeas petition in Federal District Court. The District Court denied relief, holding that Medellín's Vienna Convention claim was procedurally defaulted and that Medellín had failed to show prejudice arising from the Vienna Convention violation.").

118. *Avena,* 2004 I.C.J. 12, at ¶16 (listing *Medellin*).

119. *Id.* at ¶ 153(9).

120. *Id.* at ¶ 121 ("It follows that the remedy to make good these violations should consist in an obligation on the United States to permit review and reconsideration of these nationals' cases by the United States courts, as the Court will explain further in paragraphs 128 to 134 below, with a view to ascertaining whether in each case the violation of Article 36 committed by the competent authorities caused actual prejudice to the defendant in the process of administration of criminal justice.").

121. *See Medellin,* 552 U.S. at 563 (Breyer, J., dissenting) ("While Texas has already considered that matter, it did not consider fully, for example, whether appointed counsel's coterminous six-month suspension from the practice of the law caused actual prejudice to the defendant—prejudice that would not have existed had Medellín

known he could contact his consul and thereby find a different lawyer." (internal quotation omitted)).

122. *Id.* at 503 (majority opinion).

123. *Id.* The Court granted certiorari, but then dismissed the case as improvidently granted after Medellín began pursuing new claims in lower courts that the President's Memorandum entitled him to relief. The Supreme Court granted certiorari again once those proceedings had concluded. *See id.* at 503–4.

124. *Id.* at 503.

125. *Id.*

126. *Id.* at 504.

127. U.S. Const. art. VI, cl. 2.

128. Vienna Convention on Consular Relations, *supra* note 31, art. 36(2).

129. Optional Protocol Concerning the Compulsory Settlement of Disputes to the Vienna Convention art. I, Apr. 24, 1963, 21 U.S.T. 325, 326.

130. U.N. Charter art. 94(1).

131. ICJ Statute, *supra* note 25, art. 59.

132. Case Concerning Avena and Other Mexican Nationals (Mex. v. U.S.), 2004 I.C.J. 12, ¶ 153 (Judgment of Mar. 31, 2004).

133. Medellin v. Texas, 552 U.S. 491, 503 (2008).

134. *Id.* at 499.

135. *Id.* at 505 ("In sum, while treaties 'may comprise international commitments . . . they are not domestic law unless Congress has either enacted implementing statutes or the treaty itself conveys an intention that it be 'self-executing' and is ratified on these terms.'" (quoting Iguarta-De La Rosa v. United States, 417 F.3d 145, 150 (1st Cir. 2005))).

136. U.S. Const. art. VI, cl. 2.

137. *See* Ware v. Hylton, 3 U.S. (3 Dall.) 199 (1796).

138. *Id.* at 204.

139. *Id.* at 272 (opinion of Iredell, J.) ("The fourth article in question, I consider to be a provision, the purpose of which could only be effected by the Legislative authority; because when a nation promises to do a thing, it is to be understood, that this promise is to be carried into execution, in the manner which the Constitution of that nation prescribes.").

140. *See id.* at 272–80.

141. Foster v. Neilson, 27 U.S. (2 Pet.) 253, 314 (1829) ("Our constitution declares a treaty to be the law of the land. It is, consequently, to be regarded in courts of justice as equivalent to an act of the legislature, whenever it operates of itself without the aid of any legislative provision. But when the terms of the stipulation import a contract, when either of the parties engages to perform a particular act, the treaty addresses itself to the political, not the judicial department; and the legislature must execute the contract before it can become a rule for the Court.").

142. *See* Medellin v. Texas, 552 U.S. 491, 568–69 (2008) (Breyer, J., dissenting) (providing a list of Supreme Court cases finding treaty provisions self-executing).

143. *See, e.g., Medellin,* 552 U.S. at 506.

144. U.N. Charter, art. 94(1) (emphasis added).

145. *Medellin,* 552 U.S. at 508. ("The Executive Branch contends that the phrase 'undertakes to comply' is not 'an acknowledgement that an ICJ decision will have immediate legal effect in the courts of U.N. members,' but rather 'a *commitment* on the part of U.N. members to take *future* action through their political branches to comply with an ICJ decision.' We agree with this construction of Article 94." (internal citation omitted)).

146. *Id.* at 511 ("Medellín's view that ICJ decisions are automatically enforceable as domestic law is fatally undermined by the enforcement structure established by Article 94.").

147. *Id.* at 516.

148. *Id.* at 517 (emphasis added).

149. *Id.* at 551 (Breyer, J., dissenting) ("Enforcement of a court's judgment that has 'binding force' involves quintessential judicial activity.").

150. *See id.* at 568 (listing "[e]xamples of Supreme Court decisions considering a treaty provision to be self-executing").

151. *Id.* at 546–49.

152. *Id.* at 549–51.

153. *Id.* at 556 ("[L]ogic suggests that a treaty provision providing for 'final' and 'binding' judgments that 'settl[e]' treaty-based disputes is self-executing insofar as the judgment in question concerns the meaning of an underlying treaty provision that is itself self-executing.").

154. *Id.* at 519 (majority opinion).

155. *Id.* at 521.

156. *Id.*

157. *Id.* at 522.

158. *See* Oona A. Hathaway, Sabria McElroy & Sara Aronchick Solow, *International Law at Home: Enforcing Treaties in U.S. Courts,* 37 YALE J. INT'L L. 51, 91–95 (2010) (proposing that Congress enact legislation making subsets of treaties automatically self-executing).

159. *See, e.g.,* 22 U.S.C. § 1650a(a) (2012) ("An award of an arbitral tribunal rendered pursuant to chapter IV of the [Convention on the Settlement of Investment Disputes] shall create a right arising under a treaty of the United States. The pecuniary obligations imposed by such an award shall be enforced and shall be given the same full faith and credit as if the award were a final judgment of a court of general jurisdiction of one of the several States."); 9 U.S.C. §§ 201–208 (2012) ("The [U.N.] Convention on the Recognition and Enforcement of Foreign Arbitral Awards of June 10, 1958, shall be enforced in United States courts in accordance with this chapter."); *see also Medellin,* 552 U.S. at 519–20 ("Our holding does not call into question the ordinary enforcement of foreign judgments or international arbitral agreements.").

160. *See Medellin,* 552 U.S. at 547–48 (Breyer, J., dissenting) ("[D]omestic status-determining law differs markedly from one nation to another. . . . Britain, for

example, taking the view that the British Crown makes treaties but Parliament makes domestic law, virtually always requires parliamentary legislation. On the other hand, the United States, with its Supremacy Clause, does not take Britain's view. And the law of other nations, the Netherlands for example, directly incorporates many treaties concluded by the executive into its domestic law even without explicit parliamentary approval of the treaty." (internal citations omitted)); *see also* NATIONAL TREATY LAW AND PRACTICE (Duncan B. Hollis, Merritt R. Blakeslee & L. Benjamin Ederington eds., 2005) (examining treaty law, including in the Netherlands and the United Kingdom).

161. *Medellin,* 552 U.S. at 567 (quoting Book Review, *Mr. Root Discusses International Problems,* N.Y. TIMES, July 9, 1916, at 26).

162. Convention on the Prohibition of the Development, Production, Stockpiling and Use of Chemical Weapons and on Their Destruction, Jan. 13, 1993, 1974 U.N.T.S. 45.

163. *Id.* art. I(1).

164. *Id.* art. II(1)(a).

165. *Id.* art. II(2).

166. *Id.* art. II(9)(a).

167. Chemical Weapons Convention Implementation Act of 1998, Pub. L. No. 105–277, 112 Stat. 2681 (codified at 18 U.S.C. § 229 *et seq.;* 22 U.S.C. § 6701 *et seq.*).

168. 18 U.S.C. § 229(a).

169. *Id.* § 229A(a).

170. Bond v. United States, 134 S. Ct. 2077, 2085–86 (2014).

171. *Id.*

172. *Id.* at 2086. This was actually the second time Bond had appeared before the Third Circuit and before the Supreme Court. In an earlier phase of the litigation, both courts considered the question of whether Bond had standing to challenge her conviction under the Tenth Amendment, and held that she did. *Id.*

173. Missouri v. Holland, 252 U.S. 416 (1920).

174. *Id.* at 431–33.

175. *Id.* at 431–32.

176. *Id.* at 432.

177. *Id.* at 433 (quoting Andrews v. Andrews, 188 U.S. 14, 33 (1903)).

178. *Id.* at 435.

179. Neely v. Henkel, 180 U.S. 109 (1901).

180. *Id.* at 121.

181. Prigg v. Pennsylvania, 41 U.S. (16 Pet.) 539, 619 (1842).

182. STEPHEN E. AMBROSE, EISENHOWER: THE PRESIDENT 68 (1984).

183. DUANE TANANBAUM, THE BRICKER AMENDMENT CONTROVERSY: A TEST OF EISENHOWER'S POLITICAL LEADERSHIP 91–92 (1988).

184. Letter from President Dwight D. Eisenhower to William F. Knowland, Majority Leader, U.S. Senate (Jan. 25, 1954), *in* 9 CONGRESSIONAL QUARTERLY ALMANAC 236 (1953).

185. Memorandum by L. Arthur Minnich, Assistant White House Staff Secretary

(Jan. 11, 1954), *in* 1 FOREIGN RELATIONS OF THE UNITED STATES, 1952–1954, at 1832 (William Z. Slany et al. eds., 1983).

186. *Treaties and Executive Agreements: Hearing Before the S. Comm. on the Judiciary, 84th Cong.* 986–92 (1955).

187. *See* TANANBAUM, *supra* note 183, at 169–81.

188. Bond v. United States, 134 S. Ct. 2077, 2089 (2014) (quoting BFP v. Resolution Trust Corp., 511 U.S. 531, 544 (1994)).

189. *Id.* at 2090.

190. *Id.* at 2091.

191. *Id.* (internal quotation marks and citations omitted).

192. *Id.* at 2093–94.

193. *Id.*

194. *Id.* at 2098 (Scalia, J., concurring) (emphasis added).

195. *Id.* at 2098–99.

196. *Id.* at 2099.

197. *Id.*

198. *Id.* at 2100 (quoting Curtis A. Bradley & Jack L. Goldsmith, *Treaties, Human Rights, and Conditional Consent,* 149 U. PA. L. REV. 399, 400 (2000)).

199. *Id.* at 2103 (Thomas, J., concurring).

200. *Id.* at 2105 (quoting THE FEDERALIST NO. 42 (James Madison)).

201. *Id.* at 2108.

202. *Id.* at 2110.

203. *Id.* at 2110–11 (internal citation omitted).

204. *Id.* at 2111 (Alito, J., concurring).

205. *See* Gonzales v. Raich, 545 U.S. 1 (2005) (marijuana); Wickard v. Filburn, 317 U.S. 111 (1942) (wheat).

206. United States v. Lopez, 514 U.S. 549 (1995).

207. Reid v. Covert, 354 U.S. 1, 17 (1957).

208. *See* Bundesverfassungsgericht [BVerfG] [Federal Constitutional Court] May 29, 1974, [1974] 2 C.M.L.R. 540, 545, 557 (Ger.).

209. Bundesverfassungsgericht [BVerfG] [Federal Constitutional Court] Sept. 12, 2012, [2013] C.M.L.R. 3 (Ger.).

210. *See* David Jolly & Jack Ewing, *French Court Clears Adoption of European Fiscal Treaty,* N.Y. TIMES, Aug. 10, 2012.

211. Bundesverfassungsgericht [BVerfG] [Federal Constitutional Court] June 30, 2009, [2010] C.M.L.R. 13 (Ger.).

212. [1974] 2 C.M.L.R. at 558.

213. [2013] C.M.L.R. at 103–04.

214. Yale Global Constitutionalism Seminar, Supplemental Distribution: Europe's Challenges 24 (Aug. 20, 2012) (unpublished manuscript) (on file with author).

215. [2010] C.M.L.R. 3, ¶ 351; *accord* ¶¶ 363–66 (interpreting the treaty's provisions on criminal law in a "correspondingly limiting fashion" so as to preserve each member nation's authority to define and enforce its domestic criminal laws).

216. Richard B. Stewart, *Remedying Disregard in Global Regulatory Governance: Accountability, Participation, and Responsiveness*, 108 AM. J. INT'L L. 211, 216–17 (2014).

217. Sabino Cassese, *Administrative Law Without the State? The Challenge of Global Regulation*, 37 INT'L L. & POL. 663, 678 (2005).

218. *Id.* at 664–66.

219. CASSESE, *supra* note 14, at 120.

220. Curtis A. Bradley, *International Delegations, the Structural Constitution, and Non-Self-Execution*, 55 STAN. L. REV. 1557, 1575 (2003).

221. CASSESE, *supra* note 14, at 120–21.

222. Stewart, *supra* note 216, at 222; *see also* S.C. Res. 1333, para. 8(c), U.N. Doc. S/RES/1333 (Dec. 19, 2000) (obliging member states to "freeze without delay funds and other financial assets of . . . individuals and entities associated" with Osama Bin Laden and Al Qaeda, as determined by the Security Council's sanctions committee).

223. Richard B. Stewart, *U.S. Administrative Law: A Model for Global Administrative Law?*, 68 LAW & CONTEMP. PROBS. 63, 76 (2005).

224. CASSESE, *supra* note 14, at 46 n.77.

225. Bradley, *supra* note 220, at 1578.

226. Kimberly Ann Elliot, *The ILO and Enforcement of Core Labor Standards*, INT'L ECON. POL'Y BRIEFS, July 2000, at 1, http://www.iie.com/publications/pb/pb00-6.pdf.

227. *See* CASSESE, *supra* note 14, at 22–28 (cataloging the divergences between the governance of the "global polity" and national governance); Stewart, *supra* note 216, at 216–20 (discussing the proliferation of private and public-private international organizations); *id.* at 244–55 (considering the problems of accountability that such organizations pose and proposing solutions).

228. Dep't of Transp. v. Pub. Citizen, 541 U.S. 752 (2004).

229. *Id.* at 759–60.

230. *Id.* at 762.

231. *Id.* at 761–62.

232. *Id.* at 769–70 ("[T]he legally relevant cause of the entry of the Mexican trucks is *not* FMCSA's action, but instead the actions of the President in lifting the moratorium and those of Congress in granting the President this authority while simultaneously limiting FMCSA's discretion.").

233. Natural Res. Def. Council v. Envtl. Prot. Agency (*NRDC*), 464 F.3d 1 (D.C. Cir. 2006).

234. *Id.* at 4–5.

235. *Id.* at 5.

236. *Id.* (internal quotation omitted).

237. *Id.*

238. 42 U.S.C. § 7671c(6) (2012).

239. *NRDC*, 464 F.3d at 8.

240. *Id.*

241. *Id.*

242. *Id.* (citing Comm. of U.S. Citizens Living in Nicaragua v. Reagan, 859 F.2d 929 (D.C. Cir. 1988)).

243. Medellin v. Texas, 552 U.S. 491 (2008).

244. *See* HM Treasury v. Ahmed & Others, [2010] UKSC 2, para. 18 (opinion of Lord Hope).

245. *Id.* para. 40 (opinion of Lord Hope).

246. *See id.* paras. 83–84; *id.* paras. 155–57 (opinion of Lord Phillips) (agreeing with Lord Hope's conclusion that the Treasury orders were illegal under British law); *id.* paras. 174–77, 185–87 (opinion of Lord Rodger) (same).

247. *Id.* para. 50 (opinion of Lord Hope).

248. *Id.* paras. 66–68 (citing Joined Cases C–402/05P & C–415/05P, Kadi v. Council, 2008 E.C.R. I–06351).

249. *Id.* para. 81; *accord id.* paras. 82–84.

250. Stewart, *supra* note 216, at 77.

251. David Zaring, *Sovereignty Mismatch and the New Administrative Law* 91 WASH. U. L. REV. 59, 110 (2013). For a similar proposal, see Jean Galbraith, *Prospective Advice and Consent,* 37 YALE J. INT'L L. 247 (2012) (recommending that the Senate prospectively consent to treaties negotiated by the executive branch by passing a resolution approving a zone of acceptable agreements).

252. Stewart, *supra* note 216, at 239–41, 243, 253–54.

253. *Id.* at 249–50 (describing how "a growing number of specialized tribunals have been established within global regulatory regimes that provide review as a matter of course" and that "[r]eview may be direct, by a tribunal . . . that is part of the same regime complex as the decisional body, or indirect, through review by a domestic court of a domestic agency's implementation of global rules and decisions"); *id.* at 266 & n.207 (citing examples of international regulatory organizations which have established "regime-specific reviewing bodies that afford review as a right").

254. Stewart, *supra* note 216, at 99–103 (detailing how several international regulatory bodies are adopting new operational procedures, borrowed from domestic administrative law structures, which promote greater transparency, more participation by affected persons during the rule-making process, and possibilities for appellate and judicial review of decision making).

255. In English: "Who will watch the watchmen?"

256. Crowell v. Benson, 285 U.S. 22 (1932).

257. *See* 5 U.S.C. §§ 500 *et. seq.*

CHAPTER 10

Postscript / Home Alone: A Political Discussion

1. Atkins v. Virginia, 536 U.S. 304 (2002).

2. Brief of Amici Curiae Diplomats Morton Abramowitz et al. in Support of Petitioner at 6–7, McCarver v. North Carolina, 533 U.S. 975 (2001) (No. 00–8727). Though originally produced for the related case of *McCarver v. North Carolina,*

the brief was later refiled in *Atkins*. *See* Joint Motion of All Amici in McCarver v. North Carolina, No. 00–8727, to Have Their McCarver Amicus Briefs Considered in This Case in Support of Petitioner, *Atkins*, 536 U.S. 304 (No. 00–8452).

3. Baktybek Abdrisaev, Letter to the Editor, *Penalties in Kyrgyzstan*, N.Y. TIMES, June 30, 2001, at A14.

4. Roper v. Simmons, 543 U.S. 551 (2005).

5. *Id.* at 577.

6. *Id.* at 578.

7. Lawrence v. Texas, 539 U.S. 558 (2003).

8. *Id.* at 572–73, 576 (noting that laws banning homosexual sodomy had been repealed in Britain, that the European Court of Human Rights had held antisodomy laws invalid under the European Convention on Human Rights, affecting all members of the Council of Europe (forty-five countries at the time *Lawrence* was decided), and that other nations had "taken action consistent with an affirmation of the protected right of homosexual adults to engage in intimate, consensual conduct").

9. *Id.* at 571–76 (referring to Chief Justice Burger's opinion in Bowers v. Hardwick, 478 U.S. 186, 196 (1986) (Burger, C.J., concurring), which observed that "state intervention" to prevent homosexual sexual conduct had been practiced "throughout the history of Western civilization").

10. *See Roper*, 543 U.S. at 608 (Scalia, J., dissenting) ("I do not believe that the meaning of our Eighth Amendment . . . should be determined by the subjective views of five Members of this Court and like-minded foreigners."); *Lawrence*, 539 U.S. at 598 (Scalia, J., dissenting) ("The court's discussion of these foreign views . . . is therefore meaningless [and dangerous] dicta.").

11. H.R. Res. 568, 108th Cong. (2004); *see also* Constitution Restoration Act of 2004, H.R. 3799, 108th Cong. (similar proposed legislation that attracted 37 sponsors); H.R. Res. 372, 110th Cong. (2007) (another similar bill introduced in the House in 2007, now with forty-nine co-sponsors).

12. *Appropriate Role of Foreign Judgments in the Interpretation of American Law: Hearing on H. Res. 568 Before the H. Comm. on the Judiciary*, 108th Cong. (2004) (statement of Rep. Nadler) (quoting Rep. Feeney).

13. *See, e.g., id.* (congressional hearing on the appropriateness of citing foreign law).

14. *See, e.g.,* Justices Antonin Scalia, Assoc. Justice, U.S. Supreme Court., & Stephen Breyer, Assoc. Justice, U.S. Supreme Court., Discussion at the American University Washington College of Law: Constitutional Relevance of Foreign Court Decisions (Jan. 13, 2005), http://domino.american.edu/AU/media/mediarel.nsf/1D265343BDC 2189785256B810071F238/1F2F7DC4757FD01E85256F890068E6E0?OpenDocument (Justices Scalia and Breyer debating the merits of citing foreign law, with Justice Breyer arguing in favor and Justice Scalia arguing against).

15. *See, e.g.,* Steven G. Calabresi, *"A Shining City on a Hill": American Exceptionalism and the Supreme Court's Practice of Relying on Foreign Law*, 86 B.U. L. REV. 1335, 1337 (2006) (arguing that unlike the "elites" at the Supreme Court, "[m]ost Americans think instead that the United States is an exceptional country that differs sharply from the rest of the world and that must therefore have its own laws and Constitu-

tion"); Daniel A. Farber, *The Supreme Court, the Law of Nations, and Citations of Foreign Law: The Lessons of History*, 95 Calif. L. Rev. 1335, 1336 (2007) (claiming that "foreign law has deeply permeated our legal system from the very beginning, not only in private law but also in constitutional discourse and adjudication"); Mark Tushnet, *When Is Knowing Less Better Than Knowing More? Unpacking the Controversy over Supreme Court Reference to Non-U.S. Law*, 90 Minn. L. Rev. 1275, 1277 (2006) (arguing that criticisms of citing foreign law "are either irrelevant, not distinctive to the use of non-U.S. law, or seriously overstated"); Jeremy Waldron, *Foreign Law and the Modern* Jus Gentium, 119 Harv. L. Rev. 129, 132 (2005) (suggesting that "the citation of foreign law can rest on the idea of the law of nations").

16. *See* Lawrence v. Texas, 539 U.S. at 558, 572–73, 576–77 (2003).

17. *See* Salman Akhtar, Comprehensive Dictionary of Psychoanalysis 82 (2009).

18. *See* Jeremy Waldron, "Partly Laws Common to All Mankind": Foreign Law in American Courts (2012).

19. *See, e.g.*, Ernest A. Young, *Foreign Law and the Denominator Problem*, 119 Harv. L. Rev. 148, 150–51 (2005) (discussing how citation of foreign law could turn into "counting noses, with little regard to the reasons that led to the adoption or rejection of a practice in any particular jurisdiction").

20. *See, e.g.*, Roger P. Alford, *Misusing International Sources to Interpret the Constitution* 98 Am. J. Int'l L. 57, 58 (2004) (expressing doubt that citation of international sources "could be (and would be) done in a rigorously empirical, rather than a haphazard, manner").

21. *See, e.g., id.* ("[A] robust use of international sources could have the unintended consequence of undermining rather than promoting numerous constitutional guarantees.").

22. *See* Tom Ginsburg, *The Global Spread of Constitutional Review, in* The Oxford Handbook of Law and Politics 81, 81 (Keith E. Whittington et al. eds., 2008) (finding that in the wake of World War II, only a "handful" of constitutions allowed for judicial review, whereas in 2008, 158 out of 191 constitutional systems did).

23. *See* David S. Law & Mila Versteeg, *The Declining Influence of the United States Constitution*, 87 N.Y.U. L. Rev. 762 (2012) (documenting the considerable influence the U.S. Constitution has had on global constitution formation but also arguing that this influence is beginning to decline).

24. *See, e.g.*, Rosemond v. United States, 134 S. Ct. 1240, 1248 (2014) (citing Judge Learned Hand's "canonical formulation" of the state of mind required for aiding and abetting liability); Blueford v. Arkansas, 132 S. Ct. 2044, 2057 (2012) (citing Judge Friendly's statements on acquittal-first jury instructions in *United States v. Tsanas*, 572 F.2d 340, 346 (2d Cir. 1978)).

25. *See* S. Pac. Co. v. Jensen, 244 U.S. 205, 222 (1917) (Holmes, J., dissenting) ("The common law is not a brooding omnipresence in the sky, but the articulate voice of some sovereign or quasi sovereign that can be identified.").

26. *See generally* Philip Bobbitt, Constitutional Fate (1982) (discussing different modalities of constitutional interpretation).

27. Printz v. United States, 521 U.S. 898, 935 (1997).

28. *Id.* at 976 (Breyer, J., dissenting) ("[T]he United States is not the only nation that seeks to reconcile the practical need for a central authority with the democratic virtues of more local control. . . . The federal systems of Switzerland, Germany, and the European Union, for example, all provide that constituent states, not federal bureaucracies, will themselves implement many of the laws, rules, regulations, or decrees enacted by the central 'federal' body.").

29. *Id.* ("They do so in part because they believe that such a system interferes less, not more, with the independent authority of the 'state,' member nation, or other subsidiary government.").

30. *Id.* at 976–77.

31. *See* Mark E. Steiner, *Abraham Lincoln and the Rule of Law Books*, 93 MARQ. L. REV. 1283, 1302–09 (2010) (describing Lincoln's study of Blackstone).

32. *See* Steven G. Calabresi & Stephanie Dotson Zimdahl, *The Supreme Court and Foreign Sources of Law: Two Hundred Years of Practice and the Juvenile Death Penalty Decision*, 47 WM. & MARY L. REV. 743, 763–80 (2005) (chronicling Chief Justice Marshall's citations to foreign law); *id.* at 840–46 (doing the same for Justice Frankfurter).

33. Coker v. Georgia, 433 U.S. 584 (1977).

34. *Id.* at 596 n.10.

35. Enmund v. Florida, 458 U.S. 782 (1982).

36. *Id.* at 796 n.22.

37. *Id.* at 816 (O'Connor, J., dissenting).

38. Palko v. Connecticut, 302 U.S. 319, 326 n.3 (1937).

39. Twining v. New Jersey, 211 U.S. 78, 113 (1908).

40. *See* Benton v. Maryland, 395 U.S. 784 (1969) (overruling *Palko*); Malloy v. Hogan, 378 U.S. 1 (1964) (partly overruling *Twining*).

41. Trop v. Dulles, 356 U.S. 86 (1958).

42. *Id.* at 101.

43. *Id.* at 100.

44. *Id.* at 101, 102–03.

45. *Id.* at 126 (Frankfurter, J., dissenting).

46. Thompson v. Oklahoma, 487 U.S. 815, 838 (1988).

47. *Id.* at 830–31.

48. *Id.* at 868 n.4 (Scalia, J., dissenting). *But see* Hartford Fire Ins. Co. v. California, 509 U.S. 764, 817 (1993) (Scalia, J., dissenting) ("The 'comity' [*Timberlane* and related antitrust cases] refer to is not the comity of courts, whereby judges decline to exercise jurisdiction over matters more appropriately adjudged elsewhere, but rather what might be termed 'prescriptive comity': the respect sovereign nations afford each other by limiting the reach of their laws.").

49. *See, e.g.*, Atkins v. Virginia, 536 U.S. 304, 347–48 (2002) (Scalia, J., dissenting) (criticizing the majority for appealing to the views "of the so-called 'world community'" on the question of whether execution of the mentally retarded is cruel and unusual); Stanford v. Kentucky, 492 U.S. 361, 389–90 (1989) (Brennan, J., dissenting)

(criticizing the majority for failing to appreciate the fact that "[w]ithin the world community, the imposition of the death penalty for juvenile crimes appears to be overwhelmingly disapproved").

50. Donoghue v. Stevenson, [1932] A.C. 562 (H.L.) 598 (appeal taken from Scot.).

51. *See id.* at 598–99 (discussing MacPherson v. Buick Motor Co., 217 N.Y. 382 (1916)).

52. *See, e.g.,* R. v. Tessling, [2004] 3 S.C.R. 432 (Can.) (discussing U.S. privacy law precedents in resolving when law enforcement may use thermal imaging devices); Naz Found. v. Gov't of NCT of Delhi, (2009) WP(C)7455/2001, 150 DLT 277 (India) (making extensive use of American case law to support the conclusion that a prohibition of sodomy violated the fundamental rights protected in India's constitution); HCJ 316/03 Bakri v. Israel Film Council 58(1) PD 249 [2003] (Isr.) (citing a dozen American cases as part of the court's free speech analysis); Taunoa v. Attorney-General [2008] 1 NZLR 429 (SC) (citing twenty-two American cases in a discussion of how the New Zealand Bill of Rights Act applies to prisoners); S v. Makwanyane 1995 (3) SA 391 (CC)(S. Afr.) (consulting the laws of Canada, Germany, Hungary, India, Tanzania, the United Kingdom, the United States, and Zimbabwe to help determine whether the death penalty was cruel and degrading); *see also* JEREMY WALDRON, TORTURE, TERROR, AND TRADE-OFFS: PHILOSOPHY FOR THE WHITE HOUSE 286 n.46 (2010) (discussing the New Zealand Supreme Court's use of foreign law in *Taunoa*). For analysis and empirical data on the volume of citations to American and foreign law in constitutional courts around the world, see generally THE USE OF FOREIGN PRECEDENTS BY CONSTITUTIONAL JUDGES (Tania Groppi & Marie-Claire Ponthoreau eds., 2013).

53. *See* JAMES H. READ, POWER VERSUS LIBERTY: MADISON, HAMILTON, WILSON, AND JEFFERSON 29 (2000) (quoting James Madison writing in the *National Gazette* in 1792).

54. *See, e.g.,* Calabresi, *supra* note 15, at 1337.

55. *See* Waldron, *supra* note 18, at 202–10 (discussing the growth of legal "clusters"); *cf.* STROBE TALBOTT, THE GREAT EXPERIMENT: THE STORY OF ANCIENT EMPIRES, MODERN STATES, AND THE QUEST FOR A GLOBAL NATION (2008) (calling for a move toward global governance).

PART IV: THE JUDGE AS DIPLOMAT

1. Hon. Cynthia H. Hall & Hon. Michael M. Mihm, *The History of the Committee on International Relations of the United States Judicial Conference*, 42 ST. LOUIS U. L.J. 1163, 1165 (1998).

2. *Id.* at 1165–80; U.S. JUDICIAL CONFERENCE, COMM. ON INT'L JUDICIAL RELATIONS, A RESOURCE FOR THE JUDICIARIES OF OTHER NATIONS (2002), http://www.fjc.gov/public/pdf.nsf/lookup/IJR00012.pdf/$file/IJR00012.pdf.

3. U.S. JUDICIAL CONFERENCE, COMM. ON INT'L JUDICIAL RELATIONS, SUMMARY OF THE REPORT OF THE JUDICIAL CONFERENCE COMMITTEE ON INTERNATIONAL JUDICIAL RELATIONS (2015) (on file with the CIJR). U.S. JUDICIAL CONFERENCE, COMM. ON INT'L JUDICIAL RELATIONS, REPORT OF THE JUDICIAL

CONFERENCE COMMITTEE ON INTERNATIONAL JUDICIAL RELATIONS (2013) (on file with the Committee on International Judicial Relations (CIJR)); U.S. JUDICIAL CONFERENCE, COMM. ON INT'L JUDICIAL RELATIONS, REPORT OF THE JUDICIAL CONFERENCE COMMITTEE ON INTERNATIONAL JUDICIAL RELATIONS (2012) (on file with the CIJR); U.S. Judicial Conference, Comm. on Int'l Judicial Relations, *Report of the Judicial Conference Committee on International Judicial Relations* (Mar. 2012) (on file with the CIJR); U.S. JUDICIAL CONFERENCE, COMM. ON INT'L JUDICIAL RELATIONS, REPORT OF THE JUDICIAL CONFERENCE COMMITTEE ON INTERNATIONAL JUDICIAL RELATIONS (2011) (on file with the CIJR).

4. *See* sources cited *supra* note 3.
5. MICHAEL OAKESHOTT, THE VOICE OF LIBERAL LEARNING 109–10 (1989).

CHAPTER 11

Interchange and Substantive Progress

1. For a more thorough discussion of the role of European prosecutors and a comparison with prosecutors in the United States, see THE PROSECUTOR IN TRANSNATIONAL PERSPECTIVE (Erik Luna & Marianne L. Wade eds., 2012).
2. Richard A. Oppel, Jr., *Sentencing Shift Gives New Clout to Prosecutors,* N.Y. TIMES, Sept. 26, 2011, at A1. In 2010, less than 3 percent of criminal cases in the federal district courts made it to trial. *Id.* And according to data from nine states, in 2009 only 2.3 percent of felony cases in those states made it to trial. *Id.*
3. U.S. CONST. amend. I.
4. *See, e.g., Justice Black and First Amendment "Absolutes": A Public Interview* 37 N.Y.U. L. REV. 549, 553 (1962).
5. A unanimous Supreme Court in 1919 declared that "[t]he most stringent protection of free speech would not protect a man in falsely shouting fire in a theatre and causing a panic." Schenck v. United States, 249 U.S. 47, 52 (1919).
6. *See* Brandenburg v. Ohio, 395 U.S. 444, 447 (1969) ("[T]he constitutional guarantees of free speech and free press do not permit a State to forbid or proscribe advocacy of the use of force or of law violation except where such advocacy is directed to inciting or producing imminent lawless action and is likely to incite or produce such action.").
7. Lochner v. New York, 198 U.S. 45 (1905).
8. *See, e.g.,* McIntyre v. Ohio Elections Comm'n, 514 U.S. 334, 346–47 & n.10 (1995).
9. *See* N.Y. State Bd. of Elections v. Lopez Torres, 552 U.S. 196, 208 (2008) ("The First Amendment creates an open marketplace where ideas, most especially political ideas, may compete without government interference."); *see also McIntyre,* 514 U.S. at 346 ("Discussion of public issues and debate on the qualifications of candidates are integral to the operation of the system of government established by our Constitution. The First Amendment affords the broadest protection to such political expression in order to assure [the] unfettered interchange of ideas for the bringing about of political and social changes desired by the people . . . [T]here is practically universal agreement that a major purpose of th[e First] Amendment was to protect

the free discussion of governmental affairs, . . . of course includ[ing] discussions of candidates. This no more than reflects our profound national commitment to the principle that debate on public issues should be uninhibited, robust, and wide-open." (citations and internal quotation marks omitted)).

10. *See* McCullen v. Coakley, 134 S. Ct. 2518, 2530 (2014) (holding that if an act "favors one viewpoint about abortion over the other . . . then the [a]ct must satisfy strict scrutiny").

11. *See, e.g.,* Turner Broad. Sys., Inc. v. FCC, 512 U.S. 622, 641–42 (1994); Sable Commc'ns of Cal., Inc. v. FCC, 492 U.S. 115, 126 (1989).

12. United States v. Playboy Ent'mt Grp., Inc., 529 U.S. 803, 813 (2000) (emphasis added).

13. Recently, the Court observed that "[i]n the ordinary case it is all but dispositive to conclude that a law is content-based and, in practice, viewpoint-discriminatory." Sorrell v. IMS Health Inc., 131 S. Ct. 2653, 2667 (2011).

14. *See, e.g.,* Fl. Bar v. Went For It, Inc., 515 U.S. 618, 623 (1995) ("[W]e engage in 'inter-mediate' scrutiny of restrictions on commercial speech.").

15. See *id.* at 622–24.

16. *Sorrell,* 131 S. Ct. at 2667–68.

17. Turner Broad. Sys., Inc. v. FCC, 520 U.S. 180, 189 (1997).

18. *See* Glickman v. Wileman Bros. & Elliot, Inc., 521 U. S. 457 (1997).

19. *See, e.g.,* Giboney v. Empire Storage & Ice Co., 336 U.S. 490, 502 (1949).

20. *See Glickman,* 521 U.S. at 477 ("In sum, what we are reviewing is a species of eco-nomic regulation that should enjoy the same strong presumption of validity that we accord to other policy judgments made by Congress.").

21. Neb. Press Ass'n v. Stuart, 427 U.S. 539, 559 (1976).

22. *See* Ward v. Rock Against Racism, 491 U.S. 781, 791 (1989).

23. *See* Kovacs v. Cooper, 336 U.S. 77, 86–87 (1949).

24. *See* Grayned v. City of Rockford, 408 U.S. 104, 114–21 (1972).

25. *See* Heffron v. Int'l Soc'y for Krishna Consciousness, Inc., 452 U.S. 640, 643, 647–56 (1981).

26. *See* New York v. Ferber, 458 U.S. 747, 764 (1982) ("[C]hild pornography . . . is unpro-tected by the First Amendment.").

27. Alec Stone Sweet & Jud Mathews, *Proportionality Balancing and Global Constitu-tionalism,* 47 Colum. J. Transnat'l L. 72, 75 (2008). Stone Sweet and Mathews trace the spread of proportionality analysis from Germany across Europe and beyond. *Id.* at 96–152.

28. *Id.* at 75–76.

29. Case C–331/88 R v. Minister of Agric., Fisheries & Food *ex parte* Fedesa, 1990 E.C.R. I–4063, para. 13.

30. *Id.* at I–4027, 4031–32.

31. *Id.* at I–4063–64.

32. 18 U.S.C. § 704(b) (2012), *invalidated by* United States v. Alvarez, 132 S. Ct 2537 (2012).

33. *Alvarez,* 132 S. Ct at 2542.

34. *Id.* at 2551.

35. *Id.* at 2544–51.

36. *Id.* at 2551–52 (Breyer, J., concurring).

37. *Id.* at 2553–55.

38. *Id.* at 2555–56.

39. Sorrell v. IMS Health Inc., 131 S. Ct. 2653 (2011).

40. *Id.* at 2659–60.

41. *Id.* at 2661.

42. *Id.*

43. *Id.* at 2663–64.

44. *Id.* at 2667–72.

45. *Id.* at 2673–79 (Breyer, J., dissenting).

46. Holder v. Humanitarian Law Project, 561 U.S. 1 (2010).

47. 18 U.S.C. § 2339B(a)(1) (2012).

48. *Id.* § 2339A(b)(1).

49. *Humanitarian Law Project,* 561 U.S. at 10, 14–15.

50. *Id.* at 39.

51. *Id.* at 28.

52. *Id.* at 29–38.

53. *Id.* at 42–55 (Breyer, J., dissenting).

54. *See, e.g.,* Burson v. Freeman, 504 U.S. 191, 198–211 (1992); Buckley v. Valeo, 424 U.S. 1, 25–29 (1976); Storer v. Brown, 415 U.S. 724, 736 (1974).

55. *See, e.g.,* United States v. Dennis, 183 F.2d 201, 212 (2d Cir. 1950) ("In each case [courts] must ask whether the gravity of the 'evil,' discounted by its improbability, justifies such invasion of free speech as is necessary to avoid the danger.").

56. *See, e.g.,* Communist Party of U.S. v. Subversive Activities Control Bd., 367 U.S. 1, 91 (1961) ("Against the impediments which particular governmental regulation causes to entire freedom of individual action, there must be weighed the value to the public of the ends which the regulation may achieve."); Dennis v. United States, 341 U.S. 494, 542–43 (1951) (Frankfurter, J., concurring) ("A survey of the relevant decisions indicates that the results which we have reached are on the whole those that would ensue from careful weighing of conflicting interests. . . . 'No matter how rapidly we utter the phrase "clear and present danger," or how closely we hyphenate the words, they are not a substitute for the weighing of values. They tend to convey a delusion of certitude when what is most certain is the complexity of the strands in the web of freedoms which the judge must disentangle.'" (quoting Paul A. Freund, On Understanding the Supreme Court 27–28 (1950))).

57. *See, e.g.,* Whitney v. California, 274 U.S. 357, 377 (1927) (Brandeis, J., concurring) ("[E]ven imminent danger cannot justify resort to prohibition of [free speech and assembly], unless the evil apprehended is relatively serious. Prohibition of free speech and assembly is a measure so stringent that it would be inappropriate as the means for averting a relatively trivial harm to society.").

58. U.S. Const. art. I, § 8, cl. 3.

59. *See, e.g.,* Camps Newfound/Owatonna, Inc. v. Town of Harrison, Me., 520 U.S. 564 (1997).

60. The word *dormant,* as used in the phrase "dormant Commerce Clause," originated in an opinion by Chief Justice Marshall in the 1820s. He wrote that the power to regulate commerce "must be placed in the hands of agents, or lie dormant." Gibbons v. Ogden, 22 U.S. (9 Wheat.) 1, 189 (1824). The Supreme Court has explained that dormant Commerce Clause cases "involv[e] situations where the silence of Congress or the dormancy of its power has been taken judicially . . . as forbidding state action." Prudential Ins. Co. v. Benjamin, 328 U.S. 408, 423–24 (1946). But Congress is not bound by the implied prohibition; instead, it may "later disclaim the prohibition or undertake to nullify it." *Id.* at 424.

61. *See* Brown-Forman Distillers Corp. v. N.Y. State Liquor Auth., 476 U.S. 573, 579 (1986) ("When a state statute directly regulates or discriminates against interstate commerce, or when its effect is to favor in-state economic interests over out-of-state interests, we have generally struck down the statute without further inquiry.").

62. Huron Portland Cement Co. v. City of Detroit, 362 U.S. 440, 443 (1960) (quoting Sherlock v. Alling, 93 U.S. 99, 103 (1876)).

63. Or. Waste Sys., Inc. v. Dep't of Envtl. Equal., 511 U.S. 93, 99 (1994) (internal quotation marks omitted).

64. Treaty Establishing the European Community (Nice consolidated version) art. 28 (2002), http://eur-lex.europa.eu/legal-content/EN/TXT/HTML/ ?uri=CELEX:12002E/TXT&from=EN.

65. *See id.* art. 39 (requiring "[f]reedom of movement for workers . . . within the Community").

66. *See id.* art. 49 (prohibiting "restrictions on freedom to provide services within the Community . . . in respect of nationals of Member States who are established in a State of the Community other than that of the person for whom the services are intended").

67. *See id.* art. 56 (prohibiting, within the framework set out by the Treaty, "all restrictions on the movement of capital between Member States").

68. *See, e.g.,* Case C–76/90 Manfred Sager v. Dennemeyer & Co. Ltd, 1991 E.C.R. I–4221, para. 15 ("Having regard to the particular characteristics of certain provisions of services, specific requirements imposed on the provider, which result from the application of rules governing those types of activities, cannot be regarded as incompatible with the Treaty. However, as a fundamental principle of the Treaty, the freedom to provide services may be limited only by rules which are justified by imperative reasons relating to the public interest and which apply to all persons or undertakings pursuing an activity in the State of destination, in so far as that interest is not protected by the rules to which the person providing the services is subject in the . . . Member State in which he is established. In particular, those requirements must be objectively necessary in order to ensure compliance with professional rules and to guarantee the protection of the recipient of services and they must not exceed what is necessary to attain those objectives.").

69. *See* 5 U.S.C. § 706 (2012).

70. *See* Case C–341/05, Laval un Partneri Ltd v. Svenska Byggnadsarbetareförbundet, 2007 E.C.R. I–11767.

71. *Id.* at I–11864–67.

72. Treaty Establishing the European Community, *supra* note 64, art. 49.

73. *Laval,* 2007 E.C.R. at I–11886.

74. *Id.* at I–11887.

75. *Id.*

76. *Id.* at I–11889–90.

77. ADMIN. OFFICE OF THE U.S. COURTS, ANNUAL REPORT OF THE DIRECTOR, 1970, at 106 (1971) [hereinafter 1970 COURT REPORT] (reporting 127,280 cases filed in the federal district courts in the 1970 fiscal year).

78. ADMIN. OFFICE OF THE U.S. COURTS, ANNUAL REPORT OF THE DIRECTOR, 2013 (2014), http://www.uscourts.gov/Statistics/JudicialBusiness/2013.aspx.

79. 1970 COURT REPORT, *supra* note 77, at 212 (reporting 1,585 cases).

80. ADMIN. OFFICE OF THE U.S. COURTS, ANNUAL REPORT OF THE DIRECTOR, 2000, at 82 (reporting 9,147 cases were filed in the Ninth Circuit in the twelve-month period ending on September 30, 2000).

81. SUPREME COURT OF INDIA, ANNUAL REPORT 2008–09, at 65–66; *see also* Nick Robinson, *A Quantitative Analysis of the Indian Supreme Court's Workload,* 10 J. EMPIRICAL LEGAL STUD. 570 (2013) (analyzing the Indian Supreme Court's docket from 1993 to 2011).

82. Neeta Lal, *Huge Case Backlog Clogs India's Courts,* ASIA TIMES ONLINE (June 28, 2008), http://atimes.com/atimes/South_Asia/JF28Df02.html.

83. Hiram E. Chodosh et al., *Indian Civil Justice System Reform: Limitation and Preservation of the Adversarial Process* 30 N.Y.U. J. INT'L L. & POL. 1, 12–13 (1998).

84. *Id.* at 14–17.

85. *See* India Code Civ. Proc. § 89.

86. *See* Salem Advocates Bar Ass'n v. Union of India (2005) 6 S.C.C. 344.

87. Janet Martinez et al., *Dispute System Design: A Comparative Study of India, Israel and California,* 14 CARDOZO J. CONFLICT RESOL. 807, 809 (2013); Gregg F. Relyea, *Mediation and Case Management: Legal Reforms Promise to Transform Legal Landscape in India,* DISP. RESOL. MAG., Summer 2003, at 15.

88. *History,* DELHI MEDIATION CENTRE, http://delhimediationcentre.gov.in/history .htm (last visited Dec. 30, 2014).

89. *General Statistical Report,* DELHI MEDIATION CENTRE, http:// delhimediationcentre.gov.in/statistical.htm (last visited Dec. 30, 2014).

90. In 2007 the Bangalore Mediation Centre was opened. As of August 2014, it has helped parties to settle more than 20,000 cases. *General Statistical Report,* BANGALORE MEDIATION CENTRE, http://www.bangaloremediationcentre.kar.nic.in /statistics.html (last visited Dec. 30, 2014).

91. Justice M. Jagannadha Rao, Would Conciliation & Mediation Succeed in Our Courts?, Presentation at the International Conference on ADR and Case Management (May 3–4, 2003), http://lawcommissionofindia.nic.in/adr_conf/mediation %20succed%20Rao%202.pdf.

92. In England, the British Supreme Court generally hears only cases in respect to which it or a court of appeal has granted "leave to appeal." Constitutional Reform Act, 2005, § 40 (U.K.). The act provides that "[a]n appeal lies to the Court from any order or judgment of the Court of Appeal in England and Wales in civil proceedings" but that such appeals "lie[] only with the permission of the Court of Appeal or the Supreme Court." *Id.* § 40(2), (6). With respect to appeals from courts in Scotland, "[a]n appeal lies . . . if an appeal lay from that court to the House of Lords at or immediately before the commencement of" the legislation creating a Supreme Court. *Id.* § 40(3).

93. The French constitutional court screens cases, taking those certified by the appellate courts to present a significant constitutional question. 1958 Const. art. 61–1 (Fr.), http://www2.assemblee-nationale.fr/langues/welcome-to-the-english-website-of-the-french-national-assembly#Title7. The Constitutional Court also reviews certain acts before their promulgation. *Id.* art. 61. *See also* Olivier Dutheillet de Lamothe, Sherrill Lecture: The Transformation of Judicial Review in France: From Corneille to Racine (Feb. 17, 2014), http://vimeo.com/114560226.

94. John Roberts, 2013 Year-End Report on the Federal Judiciary (2013), http://www.supremecourt.gov/publicinfo/year-end/2013year-endreport.pdf. The Chief Justice stated that in the Court's last reporting period, the 2012 term, it received 7,509 case filings, a decrease from 7,713 in the 2011 term. *Id.* at 12.

95. *Jurisdiction of Circuit Courts of Appeals and the United States Supreme Court: Hearing on H.R. 10479 Before the House Comm. on the Judiciary,* 67th Cong. 2 (1922) (statement of Chief Justice William Howard Taft).

CHAPTER 12

Advancing the Rule of Law

1. *See* Magna Carta, ch. 39 ("No free man shall be taken, imprisoned, disseised, outlawed, banished, or in any way destroyed, nor will We proceed against or prosecute him, except by the lawful judgment of his peers and by the law of the land."). For a helpful discussion of the significance of the Magna Carta in American law, see generally A. E. Dick Howard, The Road from Runnymede: Magna Carta and Constitutionalism in America (1968).

2. A video and uncorrected transcript of the event are available at *Events,* Brookings Inst., http://www.brookings.edu/events/2012/11/28-china-law (last visited Feb. 9, 2015).

3. *See* The Federalist No. 78, at 378 (Alexander Hamilton) (Terence Ball ed., 2003) ("The judiciary . . . has no influence over either the sword or the purse; nor direction either of the strength or the wealth of the society; and can take no active resolution whatsoever.").

4. *See id.*

5. William Shakespeare, Henry IV, Part I act 3, sc. 1.

6. Stephen Breyer, Making Our Democracy Work: A Judge's View (2010).

7. *See* Worcester v. Georgia, 31 U.S. (6 Pet.) 515 (1832).

8. 2 Charles Warren, The Supreme Court in United States History 219 (1922). Warren points out that no historian appears to have quoted Jackson's alleged statement until 1864; he characterizes it as "a matter of extreme doubt . . . whether Jackson ever uttered the[] words." *Id.* at 219 & n.1.

9. For a lengthier treatment of the forcible eviction of Cherokees and the events leading up to it, see Grace Steele Woodward, The Cherokees 192–218 (1963).

10. Brown v. Bd. of Educ., 347 U.S. 483 (1954).

11. Tony A. Freyer, Little Rock on Trial: *Cooper v. Aaron* and School Desegregation 112–13 (2007).

12. David A. Nichols, A Matter of Justice: Eisenhower and the Beginning of the Civil Rights Revolution 195 (2007).

13. Freyer, *supra* note 11, at 115–16.

14. Bush v. Gore, 531 U.S. 98 (2000).

15. *See* Jeffrey L. Yates and Andrew B. Whitford, *The Presidency and the Supreme Court After* Bush v. Gore: *Implications for Institutional Legitimacy and Effectiveness,* 13 Stan. L. & Pol'y Rev. 101 (2002) (reporting the results of a series of polls related to the results of the 2000 election and the decision in *Bush v. Gore*).

16. *See* Bush v. Gore, 531 U.S. at 144–58 (Breyer, J., dissenting).

17. The author was present to hear Senator Reid's remarks.

EPILOGUE

1. Abraham Lincoln, *The Gettysburg Address* (Nov. 19, 1863).

2. Albert Camus, La Peste 312–313 (1947) (translated by the author), available at http://www.ebooksgratuits.com/pdf/camus_la_peste.pdf.

Index

ACTIVE LIBERTY
Interpreting Our Democratic Constitution

For Justice Stephen Breyer, the Constitution's primary role is to preserve and encourage what he calls "active liberty": citizen participation in shaping government and its laws. As this book argues, promoting active liberty requires judicial modesty and deference to Congress; it also means recognizing the changing needs and demands of the populace. Indeed, the Constitution's lasting brilliance is that its principles may be adapted to cope with unanticipated situations, and Breyer makes a powerful case against treating it as a static guide intended for a world that is dead and gone.

Law

MAKING OUR DEMOCRACY WORK
A Judge's View

Charged with the responsibility of interpreting the Constitution, the Supreme Court has the awesome power to strike down laws enacted by our elected representatives. Why does the public accept the Court's decisions as legitimate and follow them, even when those decisions are highly unpopular? What must the Court do to maintain the public's faith? How can it help make our democracy work? In this groundbreaking book, Justice Stephen Breyer tackles these questions and more, offering an original approach to interpreting the Constitution that judges, lawyers, and scholars will look to for many years to come.

Law